Testing to the Limits

Dedicated to all pilots who have flown for Britain's aircraft manufacturers, especially those who have ventured into the unknown in a prototype

For Pam

Testing to the Limits
British Test Pilots Since 1910
1: Addicott to Huxley

Ken Ellis

www.crecy.co.uk

Crécy Publishing Ltd

Published by Crécy Publishing Ltd 2015

A CIP record for this book is available from the British Library

ISBN 9780859791847

Printed In Malta by Melita Press

Crécy Publishing Limited
1a Ringway Trading Estate, Shadowmoss Road, Manchester M22 5LH

www.crecy.co.uk

Front cover: Despite the passage of half a century, the TSR.2 remains the subject of much debate. Roland Beamont took the only example to fly, XR219, for its maiden flight

Rear cover main image: A fully-instrumented and telemetry-laden dummy blasting through the cockpit of an Aermacchi/EMBRAER AMX in a MBA Mk.10L seat, circa 1982. *Martin-Baker Aircraft*

Rear cover clockwise from top right:
Sir Alan Cobham seated in a Tiger Moth, 1932. *KEC*
The prototype HP.42 G-AAGX *Hannibal,* flown by Tom Harry England and Jim Cordes on its maiden flight. *Handley Page*
Jimmy Dell wearing state-of-the-air g-suit, Warton, 1960. *English Electric via Graham Pitchfork*
Ronnie Ellison getting airborne in a Beaufighter TF.X for a test flight from Weston-super-Mare. *Bristol Aeroplane*

Front flap top: A jubilant Neville Duke in the cockpit of all red Hunter Mk.3 WB188. *via Graham Pitchfork*

Front flap bottom: Avro 707A WD280, first flown by 'Roly' Falk on 14th June 1951. *Avro*

Rear flap top: Steve Fletcher – Key Publishing www.flypast.com

Table of Contents

Foreword

When I opened the draft of Ken's book for the first time and began to read I was metaphorically and happily transported back to my childhood in the early post World War Two years when the British aircraft industry was in robust health with new types and research projects being commissioned at a frequency unimaginable from the perspective of the 21st Century. Given the lengthy gestation period of modern aircraft, it seems almost incomprehensible that the Farnborough Airshow was then an annual event for British aviation where every aircraft entered was either new or had a significant modification.

The senior test pilots of that era were household names and had a celebrity status akin to modern-day footballers. For a young boy with a burning ambition to fly they were my heroes and role models. As I grew older I came to realise that, as in other walks of life, for every 'star' test pilot there were many others who, day in and day out, flew missions ranging from the frequently mundane to the difficult and dangerous and who thus contributed to the progressive development of every new or modified aircraft and piece of equipment. The development of an aircraft has always been a careful and progressive process, usually by a small group of test pilots supporting the design team, building from the first flight to a final product, or cancellation.

As I read further and explored the professional lives of the pilots presented therein, my journey moved back and forward happily and smoothly through the history of manned flight in the UK. I read of test pilots, some famous and many more now largely forgotten, who in their own way made a crucial and valuable contribution either to aeronautical research or the development of aircraft from the drawing board to practical machines. I also had the pleasure of being reminded of friends and colleagues, now mostly retired, whose careers are recorded in meticulous and fascinating detail.

Of the featured test pilots both familiar and forgotten, this book answers three linked questions, how did they rise to this position, what did they do and what did they do next? The answers are varied, always interesting and frequently surprising.

These detailed biographies capture the essence of 'test flying'. Far from the shallow myths and tales of derring-do so often found in the popular media, this book captures the reality of day-to-day testing and development where risks are recognised, mitigated and accepted. Proper test flying has no place for thoughtless acts of bravado and self aggrandisement. It is essential to overcome problems and return the aircraft intact and armed with cold, hard facts delivered to the design team in an objective way that allows them to understand what was right, what needed correction and how to move the programme forward. All these test pilots intrinsically either knew or came to learn this reality.

Even as aviation moves towards a future of ever more automated aircraft and remotely piloted vehicles it is essential to remember that while there are manned aircraft in development, test pilots with experience and training will need to fly it and help develop it. Test pilots can answer the twin questions, does it perform its design missions successfully and can an 'average' pilot fly it safely and effectively when he is tired, systems have failed, the weather is bad and events are conspiring against him? It is these fundamental issues that link a test pilot in the 21st Century with all those who throughout the history of manned aviation, climbed into a prototype aircraft and with varying degrees of confidence and stoicism first took it into the air.

Chris Yeo

Chris Yeo first flew the pioneering ACT Jaguar, on 21st October 1981, and the UK prototype Eurofighter Typhoon DA.2 (illustrated) on 6th April 1994. *BAE Systems via Chris Yeo*

Introduction

The story goes like this: As the test pilot climbs out of the wreck of an experimental aircraft, having torn off the wings and tail in the crash landing, the emergency services arrive. A rescuer sees the bloodied aviator and asks, "What happened?" Stoically, the pilot replies: "'I don't know. I've only just got here myself!" Gags like that, and the exceptional test pilot sketch, from the 'steam' typewriter of Ray Galton and Alan Simpson, delivered to perfection by Tony Hancock and Kenneth Williams in *Hancock's Half Hour* on BBC radio in 1959, sum up the black humour associated with test piloting. (For a taste of the latter, see the back of the book.)

Roland Beamont provided a typically low-key and wry assessment of the nature of the work, in Constance Babington Smith's *Testing Time – A Study of Man and Machine in the Test Flying Era*: "I'm afraid I'm just not that sort of test pilot – the sort who wears white overalls and loves telling about the screamingly funny time when the wing came off. I'm the sort of test pilot who catches the 8.15 to work."

To bring things into the 21st century, I unwittingly played straight man to a Lockheed Martin test pilot that I met at a Museum of Flight function in Seattle, Washington State, in 2002. He announced that he'd driven up the coast from California after: "having carried out the most dangerous manoeuvre a test pilot can do in an advanced combat aircraft". I earnestly leapt in, asking if it was an extreme high-alpha profile, a double re-light, or a flat, inverted, spin. He grinned:

Taxying at the 1950 Farnborough airshow, the real 'star' of the 1952 film *The Sound Barrier*, Swift prototype VV119 which played the part of the Ridgeway Prometheus. *KEC*

"Nope, I needed to press CTRL, ALT, DELETE!" (To retaliate, he said I was not to name the type he flew. I'll keep to my word, but as a clue try an anagram of parrot!)

The comedic side is but a fraction of how test pilots have been portrayed in the UK press, books and films. The lasting image has been of a clean-cut pioneer taking risks for Great Britain, a hero of the modern age. This was especially so in the 1950s when they were household names. By the end of the 1960s the 'cult of personality' had moved on from test pilots. Spacemen, sorry astronauts, took up the cudgel but that soon waned. Aerospace companies were keen not to 'hype' individuals and to emphasize the team effort. In an era of increasing complexity, multi-national programmes and the advent of pilot-less systems this was inevitable. Most of us would struggle to name *any* present-day test pilot.

Books and film

Books were a vital part of my life from an early age, and I thank my parents for encouraging a son who often became reclusive while consuming tomes on British aviation and 19th and 20th century history in conveyor-belt fashion. The first I recall devouring on test flying was Mike Lithgow's *Mach One*. He led the way to de Havilland, Duke, Penrose, Quill, Twiss, Waterton – each taking me to other discoveries.

Not quite 'on message' but wholly absorbing was Nevil Shute's *No Highway*, a fictional insight into the world of the 'boffins' at Farnborough. Theodore Honey was an astonishing reluctant hero and the flawed Rutland Reindeer airliner reflected the perils of 'pushing the envelope' while striving for profits. I caught up with the Henry Koster 1951 movie on the 'telly' in the early 1970s, and thought the incredible James Stewart did Mr Honey proud. *No Highway* led to *all* of Shute's novels and his autobiography *Slide Rule* engendered a love of the 'underdog' aircraft manufacturer, Airspeed. I digress, but only partially...

Films have always been a passion, but lagging behind the compulsion of words-on-paper. Despite its four-star rating and Spencer Tracy, when I caught up with Victor Fleming's 1938 *Test Pilot* I was nonplussed, but then my aviation interest was always *very* GB-based. It will come as no surprise then that David Lean's 1952 *Sound Barrier* is for me a work of art, dripping in impeccable character-building, oozing tension with healthy portions of derring-do. With great respect to Ralph Richardson, Ann Todd, Nigel Patrick, Denholm Elliott and the rest of the band, the star was decidedly metallic in the form of the Prometheus. As it flashed across the screen the serial number VV119 screamed out and it took no time at all to pin that down to the Supermarine Type 535 Swift prototype. I was delighted to discover it had been 'first flighted' by 'my' Mike Lithgow in its original 'tail-dragger' guise in March 1950 and in its 'trike' form six months later. During my researches for this book, I added two more names to the film's 'cast' list, Les Colquhoun and David Morgan piloted VV119 for aerial unit director Anthony Squire.

Autobiographies and biographies have continued to appear over the decades and a couple of publishers, Crécy abd Grub Street in particular, were determined to keep some of the 'classic' titles in print, to be enjoyed by new generations. Among these came two shining beacons that I still regard as ground-breaking. In 1982 Don Middleton wrote a book on Airspeed (told you earlier I wasn't *completely* digressing!) and I got a genial reply to a couple of questions. Don let it be known that he was busy writing a book on test pilots. He could relax; he'd made *at least* one sale! Don's *Test Pilots* appeared in 1985; it is an era-by-era examination of the subject, mostly from the British perspective, made all the more appealing by the author's engaging prose and personal acquaintance with many of the leading lights. By this time I'd morphed from Liverpudlian teacher to Rutland-based editor of Key Publishing's flagship magazine, *FlyPast*.

For the other shot in the arm I had to wait until 2010. James-Hamilton-Paterson's *Empire of the Clouds – When Britain's Aircraft Ruled the World* was consumed in one session – when it comes to non-fiction that is unheard of in the Ellis household. It painted a picture of the UK industry as I had grasped it – warts and all. *Empire of the Clouds* helps to explain the painful evolution the industry went through to those of us who lived through it and for those since who have wondered where all those famous 'names', like Avro, de Havilland, Shorts, went.

Germ of an idea

All that I had read was building my knowledge and passion for the subject, but there were plenty of gaps and lots of seeming dead ends. Northampton-based Don Middleton was just down the road from the *FlyPast* offices in Stamford and we struck up a friendship. Don was more than pleased to take up my offer to write for *FlyPast* on test pilots and I came up

with the strapline 'Tests of Character' for the series. It was Don that pointed me to a couple of gems that had passed me by: 'Sandy' Powell's *Test Flight* of 1956 and *Men with Wings* of the following year and Constance Babington Smith's *Testing Time* published in 1961. Don was busy with his own follow-up to *Test Pilots* and was delighted when I suggested he call it *Tests of Character*. Sadly, a short illness meant that Don's book was published posthumously in 1995. The baton had been passed on to me and the germ of an idea that I'd tackle *all* of the names, famous and unsung, began to take form. Whenever I could find the time, of course. Decades later, I hope this tome serves as a reminder of Don, a very gifted writer.

Long before I got to know Don, I had been encouraged and mentored by Peter Green since 1972 when he also replied to an enquiring letter. We became firm friends. His knowledge of British aviation was unrivalled – seldom were we stuck for conversation! Peter was also 'taken' by test pilots and prototypes and he whole-heartedly supported me when I announced that it was my ambition to produce a comprehensive study of 'first flighting' men. He sifted through his legendary archive and took to commenting on the first drafts of this volume with his usual gusto and authority. Peter was so looking forward to seeing this in print, but chronology overtook him and he died in December 2014. He is much missed, but I take great solace from his having made his mark on every page of *Testing to the Limits*.

Don and Peter were the spurs that transformed this from a whimsical notion into a full-blown project. Until the mid-1980s the *inspiration* for the book remained aloof, reachable only in the pages of autobiographies, in magazine articles and in TV documentaries. The editorship of *FlyPast* was the stuff of dreams and it offered the prospect of meeting some of my heroes. It is not my intention to 'drop names' but I hope you will allow one. On a visit to the Tangmere Military Aviation Museum in 1985 my knees went when my guide asked if I would like to meet the collection's honorary president, Neville Duke, as he was popping in. I was flustered by random paragraphs from his book *Test Pilot* rolling through my head as I shook his hand. This was a wholly redundant reaction as you could not hope to meet a more unassuming and charming character; he put me at my ease and conversation flowed. I have gone on to meet many more and, with very few exceptions, all have been engaging, encouraging, keen to help and constantly amazed that people such as myself put them on a pedestal.

There is someone else who deserves not just my thanks, but those of the test pilot fraternity and everyone who appreciates our heritage. That is Dick Richardson, the former manager of the wonderful Popham aerodrome which is owned by the incredibly supportive Susie Church. Dick was keen to honour test pilots of all sorts and, with the help of Susie and all at Popham's Spitfire Flying Club and the support of organisations such as Rolls-Royce, the first test pilots reunion was held at the Hampshire aerodrome in 1996. The event blossomed and was eagerly anticipated, but the 2013 gathering was the last. In its time the reunion brought together many old comrades, allowed memories to flow, wine to pour and a tribute was paid to an incredible fraternity. Thanks for bringing the memories alive, Dick!

A selection of formative biographies from the author's shelves. Some first editions, others later; some pristine, others have seen many a battle!

 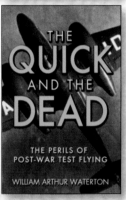

Acknowledgements

Over the time that this book has been a-brewing many people have helped in one way or another within its two-decade creation. Test pilots and members of the UK's aviation industry, past and present, will recognise their input within these pages and my thanks go out to them all. Sources referred to are acknowledged in the Bibliography. Every effort has been made to secure permissions for quotes from books that appear in the text, but in the over-riding majority of cases there has been a 'nil' return. My thanks go to: Tony Buttler author of *British Experimental Combat Aircraft of World War Two*, John Davis of Grub Street, James Hamilton-Paterson author of *Empire of the Clouds*, Nigel Walpole author of *Swift Justice* and, of course Crécy Publishing. Likewise, attributions to the origin of illustrations have been made where-ever possible.

The following all threw themselves into helping answer specific questions, or other needs, and I thank them all: Roy Bonser for his exceptional archive; Tony Buttler who helped source images and pin down elusive stats; Brian Cocks purveyor of 'extinct' books; Miles Davis for perfect background; Howard Heeley of the Newark Air Museum; Steve Jones, ace computer 'whisperer'; Rebecca and Jerry Lockspeiser for images of David; Graham Pitchfork for backgrounds on biographies and a source of images; Nigel Price Editor of *FlyPast* for his patience and encouragement; Hugh Trevor for imagery; Tom Singfield, Percival specialist; Graham Skillen, Short problem-solver; Julian Temple of the Brooklands Museum; Guy Warner for imagery; Les Whitehouse of the Boulton Paul Association.

Alan Curry, Andrew McClymont and Dean Wright checked, revised, added to and above all enriched the manuscript. That said, all errors and omissions are to be laid firmly at my door.

Eric Bucklow guided me through the unsung world of production testing and tackled my enquiries with forbearance and and humour. John Farley and Chris Yeo not only patiently answered my questions, but both honoured me by agreeing to write the forewords – Chris in this volume, John in Volume Two. Not content with that, they also commented on the manuscript and reassured me when morale flagged. I am indebted to them both.

The incredible staff at Crécy Publishing didn't flinch when this hare-brained scheme was floated in their general direction! Jeremy Pratt whole-heartedly made suggestions, all of which enhanced the book. Gill Richardson guided, cajoled and managed this mostly errant author with serenity and Rob Taylor took pixels and turned them into the finished, polished, product. Finally, and especially, Pam and feline Rex provided their unique brands of support and encouragement during the creation of this mammoth project.

Unknown unknowns

Chapter One explains the aims, intentions and the 'rules of engagement' of *Testing to the Limits* and further notes can be found at the beginning of Chapter Seven. In trying to chart the life and times of *all* test pilots who have taken a prototype into the air for the first time there has been a bewildering variety of sources to plunder, ranging from the men themselves – in person or via their writings – to snippets in magazines and newspapers. The manufacturers that they flew for are all largely defunct, merged or 'globalised' and accessible, organised, archives are few and far between.

All of this has meant that compiling the available material has been a constant revelation and full of tangents that just *had* to be travelled down. There have been many problems of inconsistency of sources and several that appeared at first to be reliable proved to be ill-founded, or worse. I have not shirked from emphasizing where I think things are not how they have been 'accepted' in the past. The book is about *people* and their *endeavours* and far less about the nitty-gritty of aviation nomenclature. Well-known types are given scant background on the basis that the reader will be familiar with them while more obscure ones are explained, but briefly. No attempt has been made to supply blow-by-blow development histories, or production totals. Registrations, serials numbers and other means of identity are presented to allow those who know these things far better than the writer to get a 'handle' on what is being discussed.

I find myself compelled to quote from that accidental intellectual giant, former US Secretary of Defense Donald Henry Rumsfeld. In early 2002 he was doing his best to explain the lack of evidence relating to Iraqi weapons of mass destruction. He said: "there are things we know we know. We also know there are known unknowns... But there are also unknown unknowns ...it is the latter category that tend to be the difficult ones." In compiling this tribute to exceptional pilots of the last hundred years, I've discovered that Donald Henry was spot on! I have managed to turn quite a few 'unknown unknowns' into 'known unknowns' and some *at least* into 'known knowns'. *Testing to the Limits* makes no claims to be comprehensive, but it *is* the most extensive work to date on this fascinating subject. I hope that readers will help set me on the road to upgrading still more of the 'unknown unknowns' of test piloting heritage.

This book is dedicated to all of the pilots that have flown for Britain's aircraft manufacturers, especially those who have ventured into the skies in a prototype. In particular, I hope it highlights the unsung personalities and reminds us that their contribution was just as vital as that of those who became 'household names'. Each and every one has helped to spearhead a world renowned industry.

Don't forget, this is a two-pronged assault – details of Volume Two can be found at the back!

Ken Ellis
People's Republic of Rutland
April, 2015

Myddle Cottage,
13 Mill Lane,
Barrowden,
Oakham LE15 8EH
sillenek@gmail.com

CHAPTER ONE

What is a Test Pilot?

We need to iron out just *what* a test pilot is. At its widest, it is anyone who takes (or attempts to take) an aircraft into the sky with the aim of seeing if it will fly, or how a new engine makes it perform, or if the new leading edge slots improve the slow speed envelope, or check it out for renewal of its certificate of airworthiness, or how it reacts when a missile is fired from it, or if the veterans who flew it in 1944 were correct about a newly-rebuilt warbird's characteristics on landing. In the most extreme of cases, to discover why a previous example ended in a steaming crater following a deep stall. You get the picture. *Anyone* trying something new with an aeroplane can be considered a test pilot.

For *Testing to the Limits* the defining word is: manufacturer. A pilot who assesses the products of a British aircraft company, be that a small enterprise or a multi-national giant. At first, I decided to feature only pilots who carried out the maiden flight on a brand new design, or of a significantly different new variant. This brings to mind all the famous

names that put the throttle forward – or twisted the collective in helicopters – to take a prototype into the air while the designer and the chairman paced up and down, wondering if they had a winner, or a turkey, on their hands.

But the more I read and enquired, I realised that there were plenty of wonderful stories about deputy chief test pilots, or more humble aviators in the flight office, and that they also deserved a mention, in one form or another. After all, if the Chief had been unavailable, then the next in line might well have been the one in the limelight. They also took risks and sometimes paid the ultimate price. Chapter Three pays tribute to the individuals who made sure every aircraft built beyond the prototypes is fit for purpose and *some* of them are outlined in Chapter Seven.

Pilots born overseas who have test flown UK-built types are included. Occasionally a pilot undertaking a first flight of an foreign type as part of his UK-based employment is covered. An example is 'Pat' Fillingham and the de Havilland Canada Chipmunk. This logic is extended to the British pilots who have taken Airbus designs on maiden flights – see Peter Chandler for the A350 and Ed Strongman in Volume Two for the A400M.

Alliot Verdon Roe made the first powered flight in the UK in an all-British aircraft on 13th July 1909, and went on to create an aviation industry dynasty. *British Aerospace*

While these ventures took place in France and Spain respectively, by value to 'UK plc' the production of wings, engines, systems for the entire Airbus range has eclipsed many UK-flown programmes. British-born aviators working full-time for overseas manufacturers, other than the partially UK-owned Airbus are not included. There have been quite a number of these, spearheading other aircraft industries. For example, Sqn Ldr Robert 'Bob' A Moore, previously with Rolls-Royce, became chief test pilot (CTP) for Sweden's SAAB and flew the prototype J29 'Flying Barrel' on 1st September 1948.

Other than those who trial aircraft for manufacturers, there are plenty of other individuals who rightly and proudly call themselves test pilots. This category includes a lot of 'trades' and the introductory chapters outline their background, roles and pays brief tribute to them. These are: Chapter Four, *The Sum of the Parts*, which outlines those who test fly for engine, or propeller, radar and avionics companies and, in a special case, literally by the seat of the pants. Such aviators work in a very similar manner to the test pilots as defined above and a greater study of their endeavours is long overdue. Chapter Five, *Trials and Tribulations,* considers pilots at establishments like Boscombe Down, Farnborough, Felixstowe and Maintenance Units who face a 'new' aircraft or situation on a day-to-day basis. All of these daily place their skills on the line to make flying safer for someone. Further examples are highlighted in Volume Two.

Testing Time – A Study of Man and Machine in the Test Flying Era written by Constance Babington Smith (CBS) and published in 1961 is packed with anecdotes and insights into many famous names, but it also examines the nature and the definition of just *what* test piloting is. Her name should ring a bell, 'Babs' was an RAF photo-interpreter based at Medmenham and on 13th November 1943 while poring over countless air-to-ground images, spotted a little aircraft on Karlshagen airfield, near Peenemünde on Germany's Baltic coast. She had discovered the V-1 'doodle-bug' and very soon was to link it with the mysterious 'ski ramps' to be found nearby. After the war, she became a very gifted writer and anyone with a copy of *Testing Time* is a fortunate reader. While some readers may bemoan that service test pilots are not included in depth in this book, CBS could not have put it better for me: "I have purposely focused attention upon 'creative' test flying by which I mean the work of the most experienced pilots employed by the aircraft companies, as distinct from those service test pilots whose role is essentially that of critic."

If that sounds harsh, Hawker test pilot Philip Lucas, previously of Boscombe Down, summed up the difference as quoted from E Lanchberry's *Against the Sun* (Cassell, 1955) by CBS: "The service is more interested in you, the pilot, than it is in your aircraft. We are not. We are interested first and last in the aircraft. If you run into serious trouble in the air, your duty as a fighter pilot is to bale out and get down in one piece, ready to go up again in another aircraft. A test pilot's duty is to stay with the aircraft and try to get it back in one piece, particularly if it is an experimental prototype. As a test pilot you should never think of baling out whilst there is the smallest chance of saving the aircraft and bringing back intact the evidence of whatever it is that has failed." He should know; he was awarded the George Medal for bringing back one of the Typhoon prototypes in May 1940.

That's pretty much defined the personalities dealt with in *Testing to the Limits*, now we should spend some time examining what sorts of aircraft are included. The best way to do that is to explain what is *excluded*. Home-designed and built one-offs, plans-built, kit-based, partial-build and all other combinations of light and sport aviation – while frequently pushing the boundaries of format, construction and performance – are beyond the realms of this book. Staying with light and sport aviation, in general microlights, gyrocopters and all lighter-than-air types are not covered. Sailplanes and gliders equally are not included except for assault gliders and those that formed part of an experimental programme, supporting powered projects. This is not to belittle all those that take such creations into the skies for the first time, because they are, in every sense, test pilots. Several 'names' have carried out such work; for example, take a look at the later exploits of Roland Beamont.

Increasingly, aircraft programmes are evolving *without* a pilot on board. Sometimes the pilot, sitting at a console, can be in a different continent from the runway or the launch pad. These come under an ever-widening series of acronyms – UCAS for unmanned combat air system and UAV for unmanned aerial vehicle being the most prevalent as these words are typed. The word 'drone' is frowned upon, but universally used by the 'media'. As might be guessed, the likes of UCASs, UAVs and all other forms of that lexicon are not part of the remit of this book. That said take a look at Chapter Six, *A 'Desk' Job?*

SAAB's swept-wing J29 'Flying Barrel' had its maiden flight in the hands of a 'Brit', Sqn Ldr Robert 'Bob' A Moore on 1st September 1948. *SAAB*

Who was first?

The first person to fly in a heavier-than-air device in Great Britain is reputed to be Sir George Cayley's coachman in the grounds of Brompton Hall, near Scarborough, in 1853. The man was put inside the 'fuselage' of his master's glider, which was then towed by a horse, released and sailed across a valley for about 500 yards, ending in a heavy landing… The hapless employee is believed to have said: "Please Sir George, I wish to give notice, I was hired to drive, not to fly!" In *Testing Times* CBS dismisses the coachman as 'Britain's first test pilot' with typical gusto: "Cayley's coachman was not, of course, any more a test pilot than a dog in a Sputnik…"

As his biplane stuttered its way across Farnborough Common on 16th October 1908, propelled by an Antoinette engine, Samuel Franklin Cody became the first person to achieve powered, controlled and sustained flight in the UK. Did that also make him the first test pilot in Britain? (Note the 'in Britain', not *British*, as at that time Cody was an American citizen.) He was certainly *testing* his aeroplane, but to my mind he was *not* a test pilot. While Cody built several aircraft, it would be difficult to call him a manufacturer. Cody was the UK's prototype designer-pilot and as such, he is featured in Chapter Two *Giving an Idea Wings*.

On 13th July 1909 Alliot Verdon Roe made the first powered flight in the UK in an all-British aircraft. Roe went on to create an aviation industry dynasty. By my definition he also was not a test pilot, but he set in train a process that created demand for a large number of the breed. Another famous name that went on to build a world-renowned manufacturing giant was Geoffrey de Havilland. Now he *was* a test pilot. What? Not when he was a designer-pilot at Crux Easton in April 1910, but when he joined the Balloon Factory later that year. At Farnborough, his job description included the word 'pilot' as well as 'designer'. This was also the case when he worked for George Holt Thomas's Aircraft Manufacturing Company (Airco) at Hendon. Having created a company carrying his name, Geoffrey continued to conduct maiden flights of prototypes, but then he was part of a large team, all helping to earn a living for one another. De Havilland was very much a family concern; Geoffrey having to bear the tragedy of losing two of his sons to the dangers of flight test. Another example was David Lockspeiser, when he was testing his innovative LDA-01 in 1971. David was a test pilot who became a designer-pilot and test flew his creation – see also Chapter Two *and* Volume Two.

There is a writer that has guided me for decades through aviation history. Former Westland test pilot Harald Penrose turned to writing in his retirement, penning wholly absorbing books laced with the authority of someone who had 'been there'. Crowning his works is the five-part *British Aviation* series which takes the story of all aspects of flying in the UK from 1903 to 1939. It remains unsurpassed as *the* chronicle of this incredible era.

In the first of the quintet, *The Pioneer Years 1903-1914*, Harald calls his seventh chapter, which covers 1909, *The Beginning of an Industry*. Here we find the pioneer British manufacturers, headed by the Short brothers, Oswald, Horace and Eustace, who had signed the equivalent of a licence agreement with another set of siblings, Orville and Wilbur Wright. As the

ink dried on the document, the three Englishmen set about 'Shorts' becoming the world's first series aircraft manufacturer. It will be no surprise then that it was with this set-up, that Harald attributed the first British test pilot – Irish-American Cecil Grace. Cecil was what would have then been called a man 'of independent means', so it is unlikely he was looking for a wage, more that he was seduced by the new-found flying 'bug'. In 1909, he was one of the original customers for the batch of Short-Wright biplanes and for this privilege he shelled out £1,000 – a cool £110,000 in present-day purchasing values.

Chapter Seven deals with Cecil in more depth but in April 1910, he was granted Aviators' Certificate No.4 on a Short-Wright at Eastchurch. By this time he was already lobbying Horace Short that the French Farman layout was a far more practical aeroplane. He switched his order to what became known as the S.27 and he flew this for the first time in June 1910 and began instructing Royal Navy would-be pilots on the type. Cecil's vision went further; he was also advocating the 'tractor' biplane as the ultimate flying machine – both the Wrights and the Farmans being 'pushers'. By July, orders and ideas were rolling in and Cecil was demonstrating the S.27 with considerable skill and regarded as the company test pilot. Tragically, it was all over too soon. On 22nd December 1910 he was flying from Calais to Dover and was never seen again. To quote Penrose: "The first test pilot to be employed by a British constructor had made his brief appearance and taken his curtain". Don Middleton – see the Introduction – agrees with Harald's assessment of Grace's place in British test piloting history and who am I to doubt these worthies?

Cecil Grace's rating as No.1 was a close-run thing. While the Short brothers were pioneering on the Isle of Sheppey in Kent, across in Bristol, Sir George White, founder the British and Colonial Aeroplane Company, was also making headway with the Farman format. Sir George turned to French 'mercenaries' for his flight testing needs. Maurice Edmond was flying the first Boxkite at Lanark in the last days of July 1910. Others skilled in the foibles of the Farman hired by Sir George were Messrs Duray, Jullerot, Tétard and Versepuy. All of these had re-crossed the Channel by the autumn of 1910. After that, as Chapter Seven and Volume Two reveal, the numbers of test pilots sky-rocketed.

A replica Short S.27 on display at the Fleet Air Arm Museum, Yeovilton. Cecil Grace trained the first Naval pilots on an S.27 at Eastchurch in 1910. *Ken Ellis*

Origins of a profession

As more and more manufacturers became established, so the demand for test pilots blossomed. The need for careful study, good critique and exceptional flying skills meant that good candidates were few and far between as Great Britain lumbered towards the Great War. Freelancers were the preferred method for many organisations but, as they became more and more in demand, it was prudent to retain personnel to ensure they were available when needed.

Designer-pilot Lt John William Dunne, once with the Balloon Factory at Farnborough and latterly ploughing his own furrow staged an incredible exhibition at Eastchurch in 1910. Dunne had invented the tail-less, swept wing aeroplane as the solution to the problem of stability. His D.5 was built by Shorts at Leysdown and he was flying it from neighbouring Eastchurch by April 1910. On 22nd December he decided to demonstrate the D.5's flying characteristics to Orville Wright, who was visiting Eastchurch along with his agent, Griffith Brewer. Orville was amazed at the biplane's arrow-like format, but quizzical of the designer's claim that the configuration conveyed 'automatic stability'. Dunne proposed what he called the 'writer's test' and showed them an empty notebook, then took off and proceeded to circle. He came back with what might well have been the first airborne written test pilot observations: "Engine revs 1400, levers normal, strong wind in face, turning now, straight again".

Test piloting expanded and matured at an ever-quickening rate. Mervyn O'Gorman, Superintendent of Farnborough's Royal Aircraft Factory, wrote a paper, *Testing Aeroplanes*, in May 1914. This rapidly became accepted as the 'word' on the new craft.

It is time to mention another book for the serious student of test piloting. In retirement, Wg Cdr H P 'Sandy' Powell wrote *Test Flight* in 1956 and followed this up with *Men With Wings*. Sandy was Commanding Officer of 'C' Flight of the Aeroplane & Armament Experimental Establishment (A&AEE) at Boscombe Down, then Assistant Commandant of the Empire Test Pilots' School and CTP for Percival. Another case of 'been there, done that'. *Test Flight* takes the reader, in an open and chatty style from just what a prototype is, to the physiology and psychology of test pilots and much more. It is a great 'primer' charting how 'mercenaries' became an industry in their own right.

Sandy provides a snapshot of the diversity of roles for a CTP in the heady mid-1950s: "The flight development of new prototypes until they are accepted by the services or airlines. The development of new equipment and proving the modifications of existing aircraft – for example, flight trials with a new engine. Production test flying of aircraft from the production line and those that have been modified or repaired. Demonstrations to the services, military missions, airlines and overseas customers. Occasional long range demonstration flights, record attempts etc." Deliveries might also be carried out by the CTP, especially if for an important customer and the first example to be handed over, or if the destination were suitably exotic!

Sandy also added that planning each day's flying schedule/programme for other pilots on the staff was also an important role. For larger, or more complex, aircraft the CTP would have a staff of flight test observers, engineers or navigators – the latter long since gone, yet vital in long delivery flights before the age of navigation aids and GPS. For larger companies, there may well have been deputies, or assistants, to take over the work of the CTP – these mostly being known as Development, or Experimental, Test Pilots. With large productions runs, a Chief of Production Test Pilots may well have administered pilots shaking down new aircraft before hand-over or ferry to customers. The role of the PTP is examined in Chapter Three, *Testing the Production Line.*

Along for the Ride – in Praise of FTOs

Before we go any further it is vitally important to remind readers that many an inaugural flight, and even more developmental sorties, did not just involve a pilot or two. Always to be borne in mind while reading through this book are what became known as Flight Test Observers (FTOs – later called Flight Test Engineers), navigators and others. Depending on the complexity, and/or size of the aircraft, FTOs etc served to reduce pilot workload and bring their own specialist skills and disciplines to analysing a prototype. A scan through Chapter Seven will reveal 'back-seaters' who lost their lives in accidents; occasionally when the pilot or pilots got out courtesy of an easier egress route or via an ejector seat.

An example of the perils faced by FTOs is well illustrated by the Canberra PR.9 development programme. The high-altitude, high-performance PR.9 'spy plane' was developed and built under contract from English Electric (EE) by Shorts at Sydenham, Belfast. A PR.7, WH793, was given lengthened outer wings to act as an interim prototype by Napier at Luton, and tested there by Mike Randrup. The definitive PR.9 prototype, XH129, was completed at Sydenham and Peter Hillwood from EE carried out the maiden flight on 27th July 1958. He then handed over to Alex Roberts of Shorts for a 25-hour shake down before it was due to be ferried to EE's headquarters at Warton for assessment by Don Knight, the PR.9 project pilot. Secreted in the nose of XH129 during this period was Shorts FTO Maurice Rose-Meyer. On 11th September Alex and Maurice flew XH129 to Warton. With Don Knight at the controls and EE FTO P H Durrant in the nose, XH129 took off on a low-level test sortie on 9th October, 1958. Off Blackpool's 'Golden Mile', Don pulled hard for a high-'g' turn and one of the wings broke off outboard of the engine nacelle. Don had just enough time to eject, his FTO stood no chance; Durrant's body was discovered still strapped in his seat in the wreckage.

Alex and Maurice were faced with taking up the next PR.9 to investigate what had gone wrong. The wing leading edge attachment was believed to be at fault and strain-gauges and a lot of high-stress (both for the airframe and the aircrew!) manoeuvres were needed to confirm the cause and bring about a 'fix'. This accident brought about a major redesign of the PR.9's nose section, giving the navigator an ejection seat that fired out through a frangible panel above his head – in front of the pilot's tear-drop canopy. A new, swing-open, nose provided access to the nav's 'office'.

The Ulster Aviation Society publishes an exceptional house journal, *Air Mail*, and in its October 2012 edition Maurice Rose-Meyer provided another example of the FTO's prowess.

He was again flying with Alex in a PR.9, taking drag measurements at 20,000ft. All was well until Maurice: "noticed that the speed was far from steady. When I heard Alex burst into song and the aircraft manoeuvring to his tune, I realised he was lacking oxygen. He initially paid no attention to the suggestion that he descend to a lower altitude, until I changed the next test point to 5,000ft even though it was [supposed] to be at 40,000ft. Once back at 5,000ft we mutually decided to head back and have his oxygen equipment replaced."

On 16th March 1959 Armstrong Whitworth CTP Eric Franklin put the throttles forward on G-APRL, the second prototype Argosy four-turboprop freighter at Bitteswell. Alongside him was a second pilot and within the capacious fuselage two FTOs watching a barrage of dials and telemetry terminals. As well as *Romeo-Lima* and the prototype, G-AOZZ, a third aircraft, G-APRM, was also involved in the test programme and all three were heavily instrumented for specific trials. *Romeo-Lima* was kitted out for Rolls-Royce Dart and propeller vibration trails, engineering systems evaluation and, later, tropical trials in the Sudan and Kenya and autoland development. The illustrations give a vivid glimpse of what a large transport aircraft carried in terms of instrumentation and other test gear in the late 1950s and early 1960s.

As time has gone on, telemetry and other forms of 'real-time' data transmission have reduced the need for FTOs, but even in the 21st century, they have their place, even if the job titles have changed. Accompanying 'Brit' Peter Chandler on the maiden flight of the prototype Airbus A350 twin-jet from Toulouse, France, on 14th June 2013 were as follows: Guy Magrin, Project Test Pilot; Pascal Verneau, Project Test Flight Engineer; Patrick du Che, Head of Development Flight Tests; Emanuele Costanzo, Flight Test Engineer and Fernando Alonso, Head of Flight Operations. Throughout this work the emphasis is on pilots but please bear in mind the vital role of the FTO and all other aircrew who monitor the health of a prototype.

Back to School – Learn to Test, Test to Learn

World War Two brought about a massive increase in production of aircraft and also in the need to test new weapons, systems and types. Within the RAF and the Fleet Air Arm there were increasing worries relating to the safety of pilots functioning within the A&AEE, the Royal Aircraft Establishment (RAE), other trials and research bodies and maintenance units. Service pilots were seconded, or 'rested' with these organisations and with the manufacturers. There was a pressing need for some form of standardisation to train pilots for what was a radically different flying discipline from that of operations.

One of the catalysts for this was the large number of US-built types destined for the RAF and Fleet Air Arm, either purchased directly or under Lend-Lease. In 1941 Hawker CTP 'George' Bulman was temporarily seconded, with the rank of Group Captain, as the Head of the Test Branch, British Air Commission, Washington DC, USA. He led a delegation of Ministry of Aircraft Production aircrew liaising with US manufacturers regarding testing and acceptance standards, which differed alarmingly from one company to another. Alongside Bulman was Sqn Ldr John Francis Xavier 'Sam' McKenna AFC of A&AEE. From this initial visit, a permanent office was established at Washington, the British Joint Services Mission (BJSM).

At Boscombe Down, former Schneider Trophy pilot Wg Cdr D'Arcy Grieg DFC AFC, commanding officer of A&AEE, was asked in late 1942 to start a school for test pilots. He turned to Sqn Ldr 'Sammy' Wroath, in charge of 'A' Flight, promoted him to Wing Commander and told him to get cracking. Between Wroath and academic G MacLaren Humphreys a syllabus was written with the emphasis on standardisation and continuity. The first course started in April 1943, and the personnel who attended are detailed in the table. The Test Pilot School (TPS) was officially recognised on 21st

Shorts FTO Maurice Rose-Meyer in his 'office' in the nose of a Canberra PR.9 at Sydenham; test pilot Alex Roberts is at the foot of the ladder. After the crash of the prototype PR.9, the nose section was redesigned to give the navigator an ejection seat. It fired through the frangible panel in front of the pilot's windscreen. *Alex Roberts via Guy Warner*

The interior of the second prototype Argosy G-APRL, looking to the rear. *Armstrong Whitworth*

An Armstrong Whitworth FTO at his rearward-facing desk inside Argosy G-APRL, 1959. *Armstrong Whitworth*

June 1943 as a sub-unit of A&AEE and on 15th January 1944 it became an independent 'lodger' unit at Boscombe Down. Sammy Wroath was detailed to lead the BJSM in 1944 and so, in March 1944 he handed control of TPS to 'Sam' McKenna.

On 28th July 1944 the organisation took up its current name, the Empire Test Pilots' School – ETPS. It was open to all-comers, including civilians from the aviation industry and an increasingly wide sweep of nationalities; not just 'colonials' as the title might imply. The risks of the business were hammered home on 19th January 1945 when Sam McKenna carried out a familiarisation flight in North American Mustang IV KH648. At high speed, an ammunition box cover detached and the fighter lost a wing; it crashed near Old Sarum, killing the ETPS 'boss'. Sam is commemorated with an annual trophy in his name for the most outstanding pupil.

Boscombe was becoming far too busy to have a unit like ETPS within its midst and in October 1945 it moved to Cranfield. At the same time, the College of Aeronautics was being set up at Cranfield and the two bodies complemented one another. In March 1946, ETPS had an impressive fleet: Avro Anson I (2), DH Dominie I (1), Fairey Firefly FR.I (4), Avro Lancaster I (3), Avro Lincoln II (1), Gloster Meteor I and III (4), Airspeed Oxford I (2), Supermarine Seafire F.46 (1), Supermarine Spitfire IX and F.21 (4), Hawker Tempest II (2), DH Tiger Moth II (1), DH Vampire I (2), a former Luftwaffe DFS Grunau Baby glider and a several US types: Douglas Boston III (1), Douglas Dakota III (1), Lockheed Hudson I (1) and North American Harvard II (3).

While Cranfield had many advantages, it was considered more ideal to have ETPS return to its 'customer' base, and from 12th July 1947 its new home was Farnborough under the aegis of the RAE – a major employer of the school's output. In 1949 ETPS was granted its own badge and adopted the descriptive motto 'Learn to Test, Test to Learn'. The school returned to Boscombe Down on 29th January 1968 and was initially attached to A&AEE. The lexicon was thrown into turmoil in the late 1980s and beyond, with A&AEE being subsumed into: DGTE in 1992, DTEO in 1995 and, later still DERA – their full-out names need not concern us here! The

latter was privatised in June 2001 and from this came the Defence Science and Technology Laboratory (DSTL). Alongside DSTL is its commercial arm, QinetiQ (a play on kinetic force – note *both* capitals) which offers a wide range of services within aerospace, maritime, defence, robotics and security. (See also Chapter Five for more on the evolution of Boscombe Down.)

Within QinetiQ is ETPS which basks in a varied and capable fleet and simulators. Since the Cranfield days, the school has offered exchanges with other air arms and overseas test establishments and hires in exotic types to be evaluated by students. The ETPS fleet in late 2014 stood at: Agusta A109E Power (2 – ZE416 and QQ100), BAe RJ70 and RJ100 (QQ101 and QQ102), Beech King Air 200 (from Cranwell-based 45 Squadron when needed), Dornier-Breguet Alpha Jet (up to 7), HS Hawk T.1 (up to 4), HS Hawk ASTRA Advanced Stability Training and Research Aircraft – XX341), North American Harvard T.2B KF183, Piper Navajo (ZF622), Short Tucano T.1 (2), Sud Gazelle (up to 6), Westland Sea King (HC.4 ZA314, HU.5 XV651). Of these, the ASTRA Hawk has a variable-stability system, allowing the adoption of different flight characteristics. (Beagle Basset CC.1 XS743, now retired, also had a variable-stability system.) Since 1999 ETPS has had an arrangement with SAAB at Linköping in Sweden for the use of a two-seat Gripen B, and from 2014 this was changed to a D-model. Under QinetiQ, ETPS is actively seeking more clients within civil aerospace while maintaining its cherished status as *the* centre for test piloting excellence.

To test, trial and evaluate

In an age of computer-profiling, simulators, telemetry, data-streams and aircraft with no pilot and increasing autonomy, it may seem that the test pilot is rapidly becoming a thing of the past. There are far fewer, but the role looks set to be a permanent one. In 1916, a scientist, Lt Henry Thomas Tizard, made a remarkably far-sighted analysis of those who test, trial and evaluate. Tizard, later Sir Henry, was chairman of the Aeronautical Research Committee in the 1930s and became a champion of radar, among many other accolades. He had trained as a pilot and by 1916 was

The men of No.1 course, Test Pilots' School, plus hosts and staff, during a visit to Bristol at Filton, 1943. Back row, left to right: Flt Lt K J Sewell, Wg Cdr G V Fryer, Eric Swiss (Bristol – host), Sqn Ldr M W Hartford, Sqn Ldr D W Weightman. Middle row, left to right: I Llewellyn Owen (Bristol – host), Sqn Ldr A K Cook, Sqn Ldr J C Nelson, Flt Lt R V Muspratt, Flt Lt J C S Turner. Front row, left to right: Lt G P L Shea-Simmonds, Wg Cdr P H A Simmons, Wg Cdr S Wroath (Commandant ETPS), Bill Pegg (Bristol – host), Lt Cdr G R Callingham, G MacLaren Humphreys (Chief Technical Instructor ETPS), Hedley Hazelden. See also the table. *MoD – A&AEE*

involved in bombs, weapon release mechanisms and ballistics. He refused to sit at a desk, surrounded by theories, he was determined to fly and try things out for himself.

Harald Penrose in *British Aviation – The Great War and Armistice 1915-1919*, quoted him and the words remain a wonderful testament of why test pilots – champions of direct action – will always be in demand: "There are some who lay considerable emphasis on every last instrument being self-recording, but I place much more reliance on direct observation, as the results are there, and no time is lost through failure of a recording instrument to record; but whether recording or direct reading instruments are used, it is the flyer on whom accuracy of the test depends. I feel too great stress cannot be laid on this; he is the man who does the experiments, and like all experimenters in every branch of the science, he requires training and a great deal of practice. Although methods themselves may become greatly changed, this much can perhaps be claimed – that the general principles on which they are founded are sound, and will only be altered in detail."

The Blue Sky Belongs to Them

Just a short distance from where Cody first took to the skies, is the Farnborough Air Sciences Trust Museum. There, on 1st May 2013 legendary service test pilot Eric 'Winkle' Brown unveiled a plaque marking the presence within the building of the Test Flying Memorial. Along with Winkle at the moving ceremony was Harrier test pilot John Farley – see Chapter Seven. The legend on the plaque includes a very apt quote from the 18th century poet and philosopher Samuel Taylor

Gp Capt 'Sam' McKenna, second commandant of ETPS. *MoD – A&AEE*

No.1 Course Test Pilots' School, 1943

Name	Brief Notes
Lt Cdr G R Callingham RN	Became Officer Commanding 'C' Squadron, A&AEE and, by 1958 was Commander (Air) at RNAS Lossiemouth.
Sqn Ldr A K Cook DFC	Joined A&AEE, seconded as PTP to Avro at Woodford – see Chapter Seven.
Wg Cdr G V Fryer AFC	Became Commanding Officer of the Handling Squadron, Hullavington, February 1944 to July 1946.
Sqn Ldr M W Hartford DFC	Prior to the course, with A&AEE he had been involved in testing Avro Lancaster III ED825 with 'Provisioning' mods (in this case a 12,000lb steel ball) prior to the 'Dam Buster' raid, Manston April 1943. Loaned to Handley Page for the first flight of the prototype Hastings – see Chapter Seven.
Sqn Ldr Hedley Hazelden DFC	Seconded as PTP with Avro at Woodford on Lancasters. After the course carried out large aircraft testing at A&AEE 1944-1947. Became CTP Handley Page, 1947 – see Chapter Seven.
Flt Lt R V Muspratt DFC	Previously PTP for Hawker at Langley on Hurricanes and Typhoons. Moved to Australia 1948 for a non-aviation career, returning to the UK in the 1960s. Richard Vivian Muspratt died in 2009, aged 92 – the last survivor of No.1 Course.
Sqn Ldr J C Nelson AFC	Became PTP with Vickers late 1943. 1944-1945 with the Jet Development Flight at RAE Farnborough. Worked for F G Miles 1945-1948. By 1948 was a PTP with Avro at Woodford on Lincolns, later flew Athenas and the 707A. See Volume Two.
Flt Lt K J 'Pop' Sewell AFC DFM	Returned to ETPS 1946-1947 as a tutor and again 1954-1955 as CFI. Killed, along with two others, in ETPS-operated Percival Pembroke C.1 WV698 on 11th March 1955 after starboard engine failed and then caught fire – he was 44
Lt G P L Shea-Simmonds MBE RNVR	Became PTP for Westland on Seafires, then PTP for Supermarine on late series Spitfires, Seafires, Spitefuls and Seafangs. Owned Hawker Tomtit G-AFTA, once owned by Alex Henshaw, in 1946 – later flown by Neville Duke.
Wg Cdr P H A Simmons DFC	Killed, with his radio operator, while test flying DH Mosquito VI NS829 on 13th May 1947 after refurbishment by Fairey at Ringway, for supply to Turkey. After a ten-minute sortie, NS829 returned, making a high speed, low level run and rolled to starboard. While attempting a second roll, the aircraft struck the ground and exploded. Simmons *may* have been working for the ferry contractor British Aviation Services.
Flt Lt J C S Turner	While on loan to De Havilland on 12th September 1945, he was flying Vampire F.1 TG279 on a familiarisation sortie. Aircraft failed to come out of a dive and impacted on Greenham Common airfield, Turner was killed.
Wg Cdr P F Webster DSO DFC	(Absent from the visit to Filton illustration.) Joined 'A' Squadron A&AEE at Boscombe Down. On 19th October 1943, he was assigned to establish the rate of roll on Fairey Firefly I Z1839. During a series of fast rolls, the starboard wing failed and the aircraft impacted near Goodworth Clatford, Hampshire. Webster was killed.
Sqn Ldr D W Weightman DFC	As a PTP for Bristol at Filton, he was testing Brigand B.1 RH824 on 14th October 1948. Port engine failed and propeller blades separated, some impacting the nose section and starboard engine; all of the latter falling off. Over a populated area, he struggled with the controls and force-landed at Northwick; Weightman killed when RH824 impacted with trees. Douglas Weightman Safety Award initiated in his memory.

Coleridge: "and everywhere the blue sky belongs to them and is their appointed rest and their native country."

The remainder of the wording explains the nature of the memorial: "During the first century of British aviation, from 1908 to 2008, some 500 flight test aircrew – pilots, test observers, technicians and tradesmen – lost their lives in the line of duty. To mark their sacrifice, a Test Flying Memorial Roll of Honour was created in 2008 in order to provide a permanent record. That Roll of Honour is now preserved near this spot, within the Farnborough Air Sciences Trust Museum. It is available to be inspected, and reflected upon, by all who admire and respect the memory of these brave men and women."

CHAPTER TWO

Giving an Idea Wings

"Cody made no claim to be a high-flown theorist; to his mind the proof of the aeroplane was in the flying thereof, and all through the years there have been many who have agreed with him." In a chapter designed to highlight the role of the designer-pilot, the prototype of them all, Samuel Franklin Cody must be the prime example. The quote comes from Constance Babington Smith (CBS) in her exceptional 1961 work *Testing Time – A Study of Man and Machine in the Test Flying Era*. In Chapter One of this book the 'rules of engagement' were laid down and the notion of the designer-pilot was introduced. As far as *this* author is aware, CBS originally coined that term. As will be seen shortly, this is not restricted to the pioneering years of British aviation, 1909 to 1914. Hopefully, the 21st century may also have its share of designer-pilots.

American-born Cody came to the UK while touring with his 'Wild West' show; though he is not to be confused with William Frederick 'Buffalo Bill' Cody of greater fame in that form of entertainment. Samuel developed skills in building and

flying large kites, initially as another 'spectacular' for his shows. Eventually, these could lift a man aloft and the British Army became interested as a cheaper and more practical means of observation than gas balloons. Cody was appointed Chief Kiting Instructor in April 1906 at the Balloon Factory, precursor of the Royal Aircraft Factory, at Farnborough. He was quickly involved in more than kites, taking a major hand in the creation of the 'car' that hung under the airship *Nulli Secundus* (Second to None) of 1907. (A replica of this flying machine is on show at the RAF Museum Hendon.)

Lessons in propulsion garnered from the airship gave him a command of engines and propellers. In 1907 Cody decided to 'power up' one of his man-lifting kites. He fitted a 15hp French-made Buchet engine, added biplane-configured 'foreplanes', horizontal and vertical tail surfaces at the rear, and a wheeled undercarriage. This machine was destined never to take a man aloft, but it did engage in *pilot-less* flights of up to four minutes over Farnborough Common. Also engaged by the 'Factory' was Lt John William Dunne, but his notion of aerodynamics was taking him in a *very* different direction – see Chapter One.

Samuel Franklin Cody making history of Farnborough Common in British Army Aircraft No.1A, 16th October 1908. *Courtesy FAST*

For Cody, the next step was a much larger machine but essentially adopting the layout of the powered kite. He had the airframe ready long before a suitable powerplant was identified and in the end he utilised the 50hp Antoinette engine from *Nulli Secundus*. Cody named his creation British Army Aircraft No.1. On 16th October 1908 all was ready and he made several 'hops', getting up to around 150ft up in straight runs. Then, from a starting point near the Swan Inn on the eastern edge of the Common he made the first powered, controlled and sustained flight in the UK. The statistics were: distance 1,390ft, height of around 30ft, flight time 27 seconds, average speed around 27mph. He was the first pilot in Britain and the prototype designer-pilot.

Cody and Dunne parted company with the Balloon Factory by April 1909; both were allowed to keep their aeroplanes, less engines, despite having been financed, at least in part, by the State. Cody persuaded the authorities to let him to stay at Farnborough, developing his flying machines in a ramshackle hangar on Laffan's Plain. That October he became a British citizen. A series of large biplanes followed, each new creation consuming elements of its predecessor. These machines proved their practicality and robustness and Cody's exploits made him a household name.

As the War Office sought to standardise on a future type for the military, trials were to be held at Larkhill on Salisbury Plain during August 1912. The winning aircraft, and another example, would be purchased for the newly-formed Royal Flying Corps (RFC). The competition offered potentially rich pickings, with the prospect of large orders, as military aviation expanded. Cody came up with a monoplane but this was wrecked in July 1912 at Farnborough. With typical adaptability, he used as much of his previous biplane as possible and this became competitor No.31 in the hotly-contested trials. On 27th August 1912 Cody was declared the winner and in late November the Military Trials Biplane was handed over to the War Office at Farnborough. Given the RFC serial number 301, it was issued to 4 Squadron, which had formed at Farnborough on 16th September. In late December Cody set about building

a second, similar, machine and, as 304, this was taken on charge by 4 Squadron on 20th February 1913. Four days later, Lt L C Rogers-Harrison was killed when 301 broke up in the air. On the last day of March, 304 was damaged in an accident and by 3rd April was in store in Cody's sheds.

By July 1912 Cody had created another machine of large proportions equipped with floats and called the Hydro-Biplane. During tests in landplane guise on 7th August 1913 it broke up in the air. Both 51-year-old Cody and his passenger, W H B Evans, were thrown clear, but died of their injuries. News of Cody's death went around the world and in Britain a national hero was mourned. Samuel Franklin Cody became the first civilian to be buried at Aldershot Military Cemetery and the great aviator was given full military honours. A crowd, estimated at 100,000, lined the route that the cortège took and there were hundreds of wreaths left at the grave.

During the summer of 1913 Cody was close to floating a company, Cody and Sons Aerial Navigation Ltd. He had created eight powered aeroplanes, if the kite of 1907 is included. The death of Cody, and that of Rogers-Harrison in February, almost certainly convinced the War Office to dispose of 304 and today it graces the Science Museum in London. At the time of the Military Aeroplane Trials, the Royal Aircraft Factory's exceptional BE.2, designed by Geoffrey de Havilland (GDH), was ineligible for judging. Despite the Cody 'winning' it was BE.2 that was ordered in increasingly large numbers, setting the format for military aircraft for much of the 1914-1918 war. Apart from the abortive monoplane, Cody stuck doggedly to the large, pusher biplane format. As Chapter Seven shows, GDH's designs had evolved considerably from his twin-prop, pusher biplane of April 1910 – just 28 months later his BE.2 was a mature military aeroplane.

A very fine replica of British Army Aircraft No.1 was unveiled on the centenary of that first-ever flight at the Farnborough Air Sciences Trust (FAST) just a matter of feet from where Cody set off for the historic flight of 16th October 1908. Eric 'Winkle' Brown did the honours by unveiling a statue of Cody at FAST, commemorating the centenary of his death, on 7th August 2013.

Samuel Franklin Cody at the helm of the much-modified British Army Aircraft, 1909.
Peter Green Collection

Part of the crowd, estimated at 100,000, that lined the route for Cody's funeral, August 1912. *Peter Green Collection*

Unveiling the replica British Army Aircraft No.1 at the Farnborough Air Sciences Trust, 16th October 2008. *Ken Ellis*

Flying Land Rover

For another example of the designer-pilot, I have chosen a very different person and aircraft. David Lockspeiser's RAF career as a fast jet pilot (1949-1955) and his test piloting for Hawker (1955 to 1968), Lancashire Aircraft ('on loan' during 1959), British Aircraft Corporation (BAC – 1968 to 1976) and Lockheed Aircraft Services in Singapore (1977-1980) are not the centre of attention here – all of that can be found in Volume Two. My interview with David was one of the last for this book, staged at his Farnborough home in October 2012. David was very pleased that I not only knew of the prototype he designed, built and piloted, but I had seen him fly it several times. Sadly, he never got to read these words, he died on 23rd March 2014, aged 85.

David studied aircraft design at the Miles Aeronautical Technical School at Woodley from 1945 to 1947. Here he met the Miles brothers (Fred and George), and the former's gifted wife, 'Blossom', describing them as a: "wonderful family, very innovative". (See Volume Two for details of Fred and George Miles.) Woodley had a major impact on him, declaring he was: "so glad I did the design course". Miles Aircraft collapsed in 1947 and David moved to Armstrong Whitworth Aircraft (AWA) at Coventry, spending a lot of time in the drawing office. AWA was examining ways of entering the civil marketplace and David helped on the design of an aircraft merely referred to as the 'Agricultural Aircraft' by the factory. David said its configuration as "Vampire-like" – twin-boom with a podded fuselage. Power came from a Lycoming O-235 'flat-four' engine in the nose; the undercarriage was a fixed, tricycle arrangement. The 'pod' could be re-configured for other roles, removing the crop-dusting tank and dispersal gear left space for freight, or up to four passengers. Nothing came of this, but by 1957 AWA had dusted it off and released a three-view drawing of the type, and *perhaps* a brochure, to see if there was any interest. The Argosy transport project, see Chapter One and Eric Franklin in Chapter Seven, taking precedence.

The 'Agricultural Aircraft' struck a chord with David and he spent years: "mulling over the best layout for a simple utility aeroplane". While test piloting with Hawker from Dunsfold, he crystallised his thoughts, coming up with a radical single-engined pusher, with a rear-mounted main wing and a canard foreplane. All-up weight would be around 4,000lb and the rear wing was 39ft 6in in span. The tandem-wing layout provided for the maximum possible centre of gravity range. This format worked best with a pusher engine, providing the longest possible fuselage for the size of the aircraft and giving the pilot an exceptional view, particularly important when crop dusting or spraying.

The fuselage came in two configurations, a freighter/passenger/ambulance version with side-loading double doors, or a fuselage that could take a variety of special role packs. The packs, or pallets, could take light freight, or a tank with crop-spraying booms, or a crop-dusting hopper and spreader chute, or a retardant dispenser for fire-fighting, or in a military role, forward-firing guns or light missiles. The pack had been inspired by David's favourite aircraft, the Hunter. The four ADEN cannons in its nose were part of an integral, slot-in, drop-out, pack that included the ammunition.

To aid quick role change, a four-wheel undercarriage layout was proposed, as David said: "allowing the pilot to taxi over the pack, ready for it to be hoisted up on to the lower fuselage. The 'special pack' fuselage also had a hatch in the top to allow for the straight-in loading of fertiliser or spray liquid, or to help in the loading of bulky freight. Construction was kept very simple, for ease of maintenance in the field and with an eye on licence manufacture in 'Third World' countries. This was, as David put it, "a sort of flying Land Rover". The wings and the foreplane were interchangeable, as were the fins and rudders. Another innovative feature was what David called "the luggage rack" – attachment points under the fuselage to allow the carriage of large items, which could include a replacement wing.

David called his concept the Land Development Aircraft (LDA), but he liked the name 'Boxer' and mostly referred to it as such. When it was realised there was possible military interest, David used what he called "alphabetic juggling' to come up with an alternative meaning of LDA – Light Defence Aircraft. Lockspeiser Aircraft Ltd was founded and David decided to embark upon the construction of a 70% scale version to prove the concept. In 1967 it was registered as G-AVOR with the designation LDA-01 and was built under the permit to fly scheme administered by the Popular Flying Association. The rear wing had a span of 29ft and the all-up weight was 1,400lb. A tricycle undercarriage was adopted.

"Hawker allowed me to use a Nissen hut as a workshop" at Dunsfold from 1966, said David. The powerplant was initially to be an 85hp Continental C85, which David said was "a gift from the Lebanese Air Force as a 'thank you' for delivering two-seaters [Hunter T.66Cs] and training them up on them." (David carried out training in the famous demonstrator T.66A G-APUX – see 'Bill' Bedford in Chapter Seven.) In 1968 David joined BAC and its 'boss' Sir George Edwards was very co-operative regarding the project. On 24th August 1971, designer and builder David reverted to his full-time occupation as test pilot and flew *Oscar-Romeo* from the BAC airfield at Wisley. "It was airborne in just 300ft and flew much as I expected." A 160hp Lycoming O-320-D1A was later fitted, greatly improving what was already a spritely performance. In June 1975 David took G-AVOR to the Paris Salon at Le Bourget and in July the following year displayed it at the PFA Rally at Sywell, where the author was transfixed by it! Two months later it was at the SBAC display at Farnborough.

Despite a lot of interest in the LDA, nothing concrete came about and David was unable to finance further development. In 1986 fortunes seemed to change and there was the possibility of investment from Malaysia and perhaps licence construction of the full-scale version, which David referred to as the "Boxer 1000", in the Far East. *Oscar-Romeo* was re-registered as G-UTIL and moved to Old Sarum. Tragically, there was a hangar fire and among the aircraft consumed on 16th January 1987 was the LDA. David was deeply annoyed at the loss, especially after having his hopes raised that all of his endeavours might well finally be rewarded.

Chapter Seven and Volume Two includes examples of other test pilots that contributed significantly to a design, or took a major or even lead role in creating a new type. I can only think of David who conceived, designed, financed, built, test flew and demonstrated his own creation; offering incredible practicality from such a radical layout.

David Lockspeiser, designer-test pilot. *Courtesy Rebecca and Jerry Lockspeiser*

The LDA-01 in the static at the Paris Salon, Le Bourget, June 1975. *KEC*

David Lockspeiser flying the LDA-01 at the PFA Rally, Sywell, July 1976. G-AVOR was instantly recognisable from any angle, but this view emphasizes the canard, tandem wing format. *Ken Ellis*

CHAPTER THREE

Testing the Production Line

Chief production test pilot Ronnie Ellison getting airborne in Beaufighter TF.X LZ114 from Weston-super-Mare on 7th August 1943. Ronnie was about to give a spirited demonstration to a delegation from MAP, hence the Mk.XV torpedo slung under the centre-section. *Bristol Aeroplane Company*

Except when commissioned to create an exotic one-off for experimental purposes, the aim of an inaugural flight is to go from prototype to a long and lucrative production run. Once test and development flying is complete, the customer – armed forces, airlines, private operators – becomes the next focus and the factory starts ramping up. Each aircraft coming out of the flight sheds needs testing, shaking down and signing off ready for acceptance by the end-user or so that company pilots can deliver it. Technically, this exercise – 'first flighting' – is low-risk, yet pilots have come to grief frequently. Once a design is proven, this form of flying is the 'bread and butter' of test piloting.

When other developmental commitments are pressing, the Chief Test Pilot and his deputies will not embark on production test work. This is the domain of the production test pilot – PTP. For major programmes, there could be a small army of PTPs to clear the output of a busy factory, particularly in wartime.

Two pilots have been selected to illustrate the role of the PTP, one from World War Two and one who takes the story up to the swing-wing Tornado.

As mentioned in Chapter One, initially the intention was not to cover PTPs, but that would be gross omission of a vital element of test piloting. A chapter in Volume Two bravely tries to cover the many PTPs that have worked in the industry. This has proved to be a nigh on impossible task and it will have holes in it, but at least it will start the ball rolling. Inevitably, a lot of World War One, Two and 'Cold War' surge PTPs – many of them short-term postings – have slipped the net.

Harnessing the powerhouses of industry

From the moment the UK was plunged into war in 1939 it was clear that aircraft would provide the major means of defence of the British Isles and the principal method of taking the fight to Germany. Purchases in Canada and the USA could provide only *some* of the surge needed and so a massive increase in production was required from UK factories. Deficiencies in the existing British industry had been highlighted during the re-armament scramble from 1936. For example, the ability of Supermarine to mass produce Spitfires was brought into doubt. Fuselages and 'tail feathers' were stacked awaiting the arrival of the beautiful, but complex and difficult to make wings. Consideration was even given to switching production at Woolston to the Hurricane.

The decision was taken to establish a government body to oversee the situation and the Ministry of Aircraft Production (MAP) came into being in May 1940. Churchill turned to the Anglo-Canadian newspaper magnate Lord Beaverbrook to head MAP in an all-encompassing role that today might well be called 'Tsar'. This made sense as the massive investment needed could only come from government, as would planning permissions, requisitions, recruitment and myriad other elements – all required with great urgency.

The concept of 'shadow factories' had already been established by the Air Ministry. These were expansion sites, mostly run by existing aircraft and aero engine manufacturers, sub-contractors and specialist suppliers. MAP embraced this, but expanded the scope and the scale incredibly. As with World War One, engineering companies and vehicle manufacturers – experienced in mass production – were also recruited. When discussing MAP, one site in particular comes to mind, the incredible Castle Bromwich Aircraft Factory (CBAF) in the Midlands. Synonymous with the huge plant is perhaps the most famous PTP ever, exceptional racing and long-distance pilot Alex Henshaw. His tenure at CBAF is a study in itself and he will appear in Volume Two.

Master of the Beaufighter

Bristol's plant at Filton could only be expanded so much and, nestled near the city from which it took its name, was very vulnerable to Luftwaffe raids. Weston-super-Mare aerodrome was identified as suitable for a shadow factory, with the Beaufighter as its main priority. A massive factory was built at Elborough, immediately south of the non-airfield RAF Station at Locking. This was usually referred to as Banwell, from the larger settlement to the west. South of Weston-super-Mare was the town's grass aerodrome and huge production line and flight shed buildings were erected on the northern and southwest boundaries. The latter site was close to the village of Oldmixon and this name became the 'generic' title for the multi-site plant. As well as creating the factories, MAP was busy improving or diverting roads, creating railway sidings off the adjacent Bristol to Exeter line. Concrete runways were built by 1943.

With construction work going on all around, on 1st January 1941, Ronald C W Ellison was appointed as the chief test pilot for the MAP plant at Oldmixon. As production got into swing, 33-year-old Ronnie appointed Flt Lt George Reston as his assistant on 9th September with Hugh Statham joining on 1st June 1943. Ronnie took the first Oldmixon Beaufighter, Mk.If X7540, for its maiden flight on 20th February 1941. The plan was to produce one every day by the end of the year. Ronnie's path to Beaufighters started by joining the RAF in April 1929 and in the following year got his hands on a Bristol product, Bulldog IIs with 17 Squadron at Upavon. An instructor course at Central Flying School at Wittering and then instructing at the RAF College Cranwell followed. His final posting was with 501 (City of Bristol) Squadron Auxiliary Air Force at Filton on Westland Wapiti IIs and Wallace Is and IIs. It was during this period that he became known to the Bristol Aeroplane Company and he took the post of instructor with the firm's flying school in 1934 as well as some development test flying for the aero engine branch. From there, he moved to Weston-super-Mare.

Being the 'boss', Ronnie made sure that he flew the 'milestones' as production ramped up at Oldmixon – he was at the helm of 1,000th, the 2,000th and the 3,000th Beaufighter when they were ready for air test. On 21st September 1945 he presided over the end of an era when he took TF.X SR919 into the air. It was the 5,562nd and last Beaufighter built, and Oldmixon's 3,336th. Since February 1941 when Ronnie had flown X7540, the men and women of Banwell and Oldmixon had averaged just over two 'Beaus' a day. Ronnie also flew some Beauforts, very likely helping out at Filton. The 'Weston' plants also built 50 Tempest IIs for Hawker. Ronnie took the first, MW374, on its

The last Beaufighter built, TF.X SR919, was first flown at Weston-super-Mare by Ronnie Ellison on 21st September 1945. *Bristol Aeroplane Company*

'Bea' Beamont presenting Eric Bucklow with a silver Jaguar model after he had completed his 100th production first flight, on Omani SO.10, at Warton 31st March 1978. *British Aerospace via Eric Bucklow*

maiden flight on 4th October 1944. The bulk of these saw no service with the RAF, going to India in 1947 and 1948.

Ronnie and Hugh Statham went to Filton with the end of Beaufighter production. As detailed in Volume Two, Hugh was tragically killed, along with 14 others, in Britannia 311 G-ANCA on approach to Filton on 6th November 1957. Ronnie carried out further development work for Bristol's aero engine division – as he did in the late 1930s – and also flew as PTP for Type 170 Freighters, Buckinghams, Buckmasters and Brigands. He was appointed Assistant CTP, to 'Bill' Pegg in 1949, his work including pilot conversion training, deliveries and demonstrations. With around 7,000 hours under his belt, Ronnie Ellison retired in 1952 from flying with Bristol.

Ronnie was back in harness at Weston-super-Mare the following year, test flying the first Bristol 170 to be assembled by Western Airways under sub-contract to Bristol. This was Mk.31 G-AMRY which he flew on 29th September 1953, ending the flight at Filton. In all, 36 Type 170s were assembled at Weston, including the last examples of the breed, completed in 1957. Ronnie Ellison died in 1996, aged 88.

Destined for Canberras

W E Johns and his books on James 'Biggles' Bigglesworth had a primal effect on countless pilots, including Eric Bucklow. Born in 1937 at Harrow, Middlesex, after discovering Captain Johns' aviator-adventurer, young Eric was soon thinking: "I'm going to be Biggles." Eric describes himself as "a bit of a

swot" at school and that he did not take the standard route of a plane-mad youth – the Air Training Corps, or even the Scouts. He preferred to "plough my own furrow". Early flying included a gliding course at Dunstable and a couple of trips in an Auster out of Elstree. In one of the latter, he well remembers an encounter with the prototype Handley Page Victor on a sortie out of nearby, Radlett, circa 1953-1954.

He studied aeronautical engineering at the University of London and joined the University of London Air Squadron (ULAS) in 1956. This was based at Kenley when Eric started his training, but it relocated to Biggin Hill in April 1957. Just prior to the move, Eric became the first of his course to go solo, on a DHC Chipmunk T.10. He enjoyed his two years with ULAS, knowing full well that it was a "passport to the RAF". The following year, he got his first taste of jets with a sortie in a Gloster Meteor T.7. It was during this time that it gelled with Eric that what he *most* wanted to do was be a test pilot. Part of his degree course included visits to industry; at Wisley a meeting with 'Jock' Bryce in January 1958 reinforced his vision of the future. Jock was very encouraging, telling Eric to join the RAF for five years, that attendance at the Empire Test Pilots' School was not essential, and to "come and see us again".

Eric – 'Buckers' to his colleagues – started his RAF flying training in the autumn of 1958 on Percival Provost T.1s at 6 Flying Training School, Tern Hill, Shropshire, before jet conversion at 5 FTS, Oakington on DH Vampire T.11s. From April 1960 he was at Little Rissington on an instructor course at the Central Flying School before flying Gloster Meteor T.7s and F.8s at the RAF Flying College, Manby. All the while Eric was hoping to be streamed for fighters. This was not to be and EE Canberras were deemed to be his future, starting with 231 Operational Conversion Unit at Bassingbourn in November 1960, followed by 58 Squadron at Wyton in May 1961, equipped with photo-recce PR.7s. Eric had started a flying life with Canberras that was to last 23 years.

Airliner interlude

After completing his five years in the RAF in September 1963, there was a gap before Vickers was ready for Fg Off Eric Bucklow to "come and see us again". Never one to twiddle his thumbs, Eric busied himself with a gliding course, an Airline Transport Pilots Licence and he married Ann. Remembering the date when he was told to attend an interview was easy, that evening Eric told Ann: "Kennedy's been shot and I've got an interview" – 22nd November 1963. By this time Vickers had become a part of the British Aircraft Corporation (BAC), along with English Electric and Bristol and the Chief Test Pilot was Brian Trubshaw. Air Marshal Sir Geoffrey Tuttle, Vice-Chairman in charge of flying programmes, also attended the meeting.

Eric had given some thought to what he was looking for in terms of a salary. As a Flying Officer he was on about £900 a year (about £18,000 in present-day values); so he felt it important to "push things" and see if they'd take something around £1,200. The interview went well and Sir Geoffrey enquired what Eric thought would be a reasonable salary. Before he could come up with a figure, Sir Geoffrey suggested £2,000 – a great welcome! Subsequently, Eric was to realise that it was Vickers that had got the bargain, Trubshaw was on *five times* that – but he was very experienced and running the flight test department. As the Concorde programme got closer to fruition, management at Vickers discovered how the Continentals rated their test pilots Major André Turcat of Sud Aviation 'aced' Trubshaw by a factor of three!

Eric was taken on as test pilot under training on the Vickers VC-10 with additional duties flying the company DH Dove, Heron, Percival President and, later, HS.125 'taxis'. When Eric joined the team at Wisley, they were still coming to terms with the loss of Mike Lithgow and his crew when the prototype BAC One-Eleven crashed on 22nd October 1963. Eric thought the VC-10 was a "gorgeous aeroplane" but was less enamoured by the One-Eleven, which became his next task. During 1964 and 1965, Eric was 'seconded' to Hunting at Luton to help Reg Stock and 'Dizzy' Addicott with production testing of Jet Provosts, including the delivery of a T.52 to Iraq in April 1965. (Hunting had been absorbed into BAC in September 1960.)

By the end of 1966, Eric was still in the right-hand seat (a second pilot, or P2), and looked set to be so for a considerable time. As he put it: "the prospect was that of waiting for Concorde, but there were others further up the queue, and it was likely I'd still be a P2". A fairly regular passenger in the Dove or Heron 'shuttle' was 'Bea' Beamont, who headed flight test at Warton. Eric had got to know him well as they both had the Canberra in their blood. Bea offered Eric work on Canberras and in late 1966 he took the plunge.

Canberras to Tornados

Arriving at Warton in February 1967, Eric was put to work shaking down Canberra T.17 electronic countermeasures trainers for the RAF and TT.18 target-tugs for the RAF and the Royal Navy, all converted from 'first generation' B.2 airframes. Eric was heavily involved in testing the last UK variant, the T.22 target facilities version for the Royal Navy, converted from PR.7 airframes; carrying out the maiden flight of the prototype, WT510, on 28th June 1973 from Samlesbury. Additionally, there was a still a market for refurbished examples for overseas customers and in March 1967 he carried out the first of several ferry flights to Venezuela. As well as this, Eric shared development and production test flying with Reg Stock on the Jet Provost T.5 and Strikemaster programmes, including delivering Strikemaster Mk.80s to Saudi Arabia. On a visit to Warton in March 1965, Eric got his first taste of a Lightning, co-piloting T.5 XS421. Ruefully noting that, when it came to Lightnings, there were "never enough to go round" Eric acted as P2 on air tests of several T.55s bound for Saudi Arabia in 1967 and 1969.

The year 1969 had been a momentous one for BAC and Anglo-French co-operation. Brian Trubshaw – Eric's former 'boss' – had piloted the first British-built Concorde on its maiden voyage at Filton on 9th April. Up at Warton on 12th October, 'Jimmy' Dell had put the throttles forward on SEPECAT Jaguar S.06, the first British example. While the supersonic airliner took all the headlines, it was the Jaguar that was to become bread-and-butter for BAC (and Breguet in France), production running all the way to 1984 and India taking on licence manufacture. Eric spent seven years on development and production testing Jaguars, a type for which he clearly has great affection.

I asked Eric how he achieved the step from Canberras and 'JPs' to the Jaguar. He explained that he took a couple of trips in the rear seat of the first UK two-seater, B.08 XW566, with Dave Eagles in late 1972. "The thinking was that if you could land it from the back, you'll probably be alright." His first solo was in GR.1 XX113 on 8th June 1973 which he described as "perfectly fine other that the usual reheat [fire] warning" that necessitated a shut-down and a single-engined landing. Eric noted that there were a lot of issues with the Rolls-Royce/Turboméca Adour turbofans at the time. Eric's Jaguar work included delivery flying, including the challenging, multi-stage route to Ecuador.

I asked Eric to describe a production test flight on the Jaguar and he chose the first two-seater for Oman, BO.1, on 4th November 1976. Vic Malings was his 'back-seater' for the trip and most of the day was spent in the crew room waiting for the aircraft to be signed off. As a rule, a flight could take place no later than an hour before sunset; otherwise it was to be re-scheduled for the following day. In the nick of time BO.1 was declared good to go. First off was "a nip to 5,000ft followed by turning it upside-down". This was to establish that nothing was loose in the cockpit and that the Adours functioned in all attitudes. Getting the Jaguar back to wings level, Eric checked the controls and discovered that he could not get the stick back beyond the neutral position. He did some quick calculations about his landing speed if he could not bring the nose up for a flare – a sizzling 250 knots – and ruled out Warton's runway. The long stretch of concrete at Boscombe Down was always designated as an alternative in these circumstances. The flaps functioned, but with jammed controls, they would probably exacerbate the situation. Then the port Adour ran true to form and a fire warning came on. Eric shut the offending turbofan down and reconsidered his options. He decided to go back to basics and repeat the original manoeuvre. He inverted the aircraft while applying more than a little "wiggle". This worked but it did not stop Eric being 'greeted' back at Warton by the airfield fire crews and men from the Lancashire force; none of whom were needed. When BO.1 was examined, a rivet was found in a control box – this 'rogue' had caused the seizure.

As with the Jaguar, so it was to be with the looming Panavia Tornado programme. Eric flew the 'chase' Canberra during test flights of the British prototypes, including the first flight of P.02 XX946 on 30th October 1974 with Paul Millet at the controls. Lessons from the cancelled TSR.2 and the expanding knowledge base generated by Jaguar culminated in the exceptional Anglo-German-Italian swing-wing strike aircraft. Production, from three sites and including the Warton-originated air defence variant, ended in 1990 with substantial upgrade programmes continuing throughout the type's service life.

In 1977 Eric was appointed as Senior Production Test Pilot and in 1980, Chief PTP. He attended many meetings as the tri-national Panavia organisation formulated the test flying. Eric drew up a schedule and devised cards that provided a check-list of trials to be carried out prior to sign-off. If all went well, two flights of 60-90 minutes each would suffice. The first session concentrated on airframe and engine handling, including supersonic flight. The second dealt with the avionics, weapon aiming, navigation and put the Tornado's terrain-following radar through its paces with a low-level run through the Lake District or Scotland. Eric first flew in a Tornado, British prototype P.03, XX947, in October 1977. His debut as a front-seater was in GR.1 ZA320 on 1st March 1980 with Dave Eagles in the back. Beyond this he went on to first fly over 100 GR.1s, F.2 development interceptors and the definitive F.3s. (Both XX947 and ZA320 are extant, the former with an Ipswich-based dealer, the latter as an instructional airframe at the Defence School of Aeronautical Engineering, RAF Cosford.) Sadly, Eric's lack of a formal test piloting qualification caught up with him, Panavia decreeing that he be permitted only to carry out production testing and no development flying.

Deliveries, Displays and Other Duties

Some of Eric's extensive delivery flights have already been mentioned. During his Wisley days, he was offered the "plum task" of taking a BAC One-Eleven to Mohawk Airlines in the USA. Eric realised just *why* it had come his way when told that the departure date was 22nd December 1965 – nobody else wanted to be away over Christmas! He did a dozen trips taking Canberras to Venezuela, delivered one to Peru and another to Ethiopia – for which he was given a gold medal. In addition to Ecuador, Jaguar ferries included Nigeria. As well as Strikemasters for Saudi Arabia, he delivered four Tornados to that country. Warton had four or five navigators on the flight staff to carry out the planning, liaison and diplomatic

Eric Bucklow at the controls, with Les Hurst in the rear seat, during the maiden flight of the first production Tornado F.2 ZD899 at Warton 12th April 1984. *British Aerospace via Eric Bucklow*

clearances, as well as accompanying the pilot on two-seaters, for what could very challenging flying.

For the September 1970 Farnborough airshow, Eric alternated displaying Argentine Canberra B.62 G-AYHP (civil registered for the event) with colleague Tim Ferguson. Both pilots developed slightly different routines and worked these up at altitude in Lancashire airspace, until coming down to display height at Warton. Then both would display in front of 'Bea' Beamont to give the 'OK' and the blessing of the flying control committee at Farnborough was the final hurdle. An unusual sortie on 16th February 1983 involved only local flying, but the 'interception' of an Avro Vulcan! The Manchester Vulcan Bomber Society had purchased Vulcan B.2 XL391 from the Ministry of Defence and had arranged for it to be kept at Blackpool's Squires Gate airport. For '391's last-ever flight, it was decided that it would be appropriate to have the V-bomber escorted and Eric was delegated, flying Canberra T.22 WH797. This Canberra had originally been flight tested, by Eric, in 1973 but was back at Samlesbury for radio trials and was ideal to greet the mighty delta. As it touched down Eric carried out a fly-by to salute the new arrival. (Gradually decaying, XL391 was scrapped in 2006.)

The main section of this book deals with those test pilots who have applied the throttle (or the collective) to take a brand new type on its maiden flight. That honour was bestowed upon Eric, but not as part of his 'day job'. A spare time team led by Roger Hardy of the Advanced Projects Office at Warton had set to creating a man-powered aircraft from the late 1970s. When working for Scottish Aviation at Prestwick, Roger had previously conceived the Dragonfly, which was unsuccessful. Dragonfly 2 was designed to be as light as possible and initially, it had an incredible empty weight of 35lb. As might be imagined, it was *very* fragile and flight could only be attempted in the calmest of conditions. An outing in August 1981 resulted in a structural failure of the wing at the moment of take-off. Rethought and repaired, it was moved to Squires Gate and on 18th October, with Eric as test pilot *and* powerplant, it made a series of 'hops'. (Early in their endeavours Cody, Roe and others would have been envious of the height and distance achieved and they had some

A line-up of Warton test pilots in front of Tornado F.2 A.03 ZA283 after its first flight at Warton, 18th November 1980. Left to right: Peter Orme, Peter Gordon-Johnson, Don Thomas, Jerry Lee, Dave Eagles, Paul Millett, Eric Bucklow, Chris Yeo, Keith Hartley, Sandy Aitken, Reg Stock. *British Aerospace via Eric Bucklow*

mechanical horsepower to rely on!) Eric then had to 'talk through' sports cyclist Duncan Lawrie about how to fly. Eric inspired Duncan to climb to about 6ft before Dragonfly 2 collapsed on to the runway in a heap. It was not repaired.

Warton test pilots retired at 50 in those days, it later became 55. In November 1987 Eric stopped fast jet checking,

moving office at Warton to run the company's 'mini-airline' which included a Cessna 421 twin, two BAe Jetstream 31 twin turboprops, three HS.125 executive jets and, later, a HS.146 regional jet. After 15 years of this work, and having clocked up over 15,700 flying hours, Eric retired and now lives close to Warton.

Piloting Canberra T.22 WH797, Eric over-flying Vulcan B.2 XL391 at Blackpool airport as the latter makes its last-ever touchdown, 16th February 1983. *via Eric Bucklow*

CHAPTER FOUR

The Sum of the Parts

Without a powerplant, propellers (if appropriate) or undercarriage, or radar and many other elements, an airframe can go nowhere. That is why every time a prototype soars into the air, the adage 'The whole is greater than the sum of the parts' is very appropriate. These days, organisations supplying powerplants, systems, sub-systems and other major elements of a programme are known as OEMs – original equipment manufacturers. As time has gone on, static test-beds, computer analysis and increasing digitisation has meant that the need to flight test such items has diminished dramatically, with 'shake-downs' taking place within the development schedule of the prototypes.

D Napier and Sons diversified into aero engines during World War One, producing the famous 12-cylinder Lion from 1917. From 1952 to 1961 a massive effort was put into developing the Eland turboprop for commercial applications. All three company-funded test-beds took off from Luton to create this 1956 formation, from the rear: second prototype Varsity VX835 (first flew with Elands in 1954), Ambassador G-ALFR (converted 1955) and Convair 340 G-ANVP (converted February 1956). The final powerplant from Napier was the Gazelle turboshaft – as tested by Malcolm Muir – which became a Rolls-Royce product when the company was absorbed in 1962. *D Napier and Sons*

When thinking of major suppliers, it is of course the engine manufacturers that spring to mind. Most of the major British producers, Alvis, Armstrong Siddeley, Bristol, de Havilland, Napier and Rolls-Royce, all operated fleets of test-beds. As well as engine builders, propeller manufacturers such as de Havilland and Dowty have also had test pilots and flying test-beds. De Havilland Propellers morphed into Hawker Siddeley Dynamics, by which time the products were missiles; munitions development being another area requiring test and experimentation. (See under George Aird for an insight into missile development work.)

More so than aircraft test pilots, engine test pilots are likely to trial a greater number of airframes, because of the variety of types that might be powered by the company's products. As with their aircraft compatriots, establishing reliability, endurance, 'hot and high' performance and many other parameters could lead to many hours airborne – most of these mundane. Much has been written on aircraft engine test-beds, but surprisingly little about engine test pilots and flight test observers. Here, a couple of 'case studies' will have to suffice.

As with aircraft manufacturer test pilots, the trialling of engines and systems has never been without hazard, and personnel have been killed during this exacting form of flying. Thankfully, with the introduction of ejection seats, the toll has diminished. However, the task of making the 'bang seat' a viable and reliable escape method was not without great risk and this chapter concludes with an 'honorary' test pilot, who worked for the pioneering firm Martin-Baker.

Vampires to Vulcans

Unsurprisingly, Rolls-Royce operated by far and away the largest engine flight trials organisation in the UK, although such work now takes place on the other side of the Atlantic. In December 1934 the company established a test centre at the former World War One airfield at Hucknall, just north of Nottingham and about ten miles northeast of the Rolls-Royce headquarters in Derby. The site was considerably expanded both as an airfield, with a 6,800ft southwest-northeast runway post-1945, and as a major test-cell and factory site. Test flying ended at the airfield in 1971, shortly after the RB.211 test-bed Vickers VC-10 was flown – see below – with Filton becoming the new base. Since then, Hucknall has continued as a production facility, but in 2014 the eventual wind-down of the site and its disposal for housing was announced. Hucknall, not Dunsfold or Sydenham, is the birthplace of British jet vertical take-off trials via the curious 'Flying Bedstead' – see 'Jim' Heyworth in Chapter Seven and 'Shep' Shepherd in Volume Two for more.

There are many names that could be chosen to illustrate the work of Rolls-Royce flight test, including some famous ones. As is often the case, the less famous serve to illustrate a point far better, and that is certainly so with Malcom Muir. He was called up for National Service in 1948, aged 19, joining the RAF and excelling in his training. Two years later he was studying aeronautics at Imperial College, London, and flying from Kenley with the University of London Air Squadron. Malcolm joined de Havilland as a production test pilot at Hawarden in July 1953, testing Vampires and Venoms. He also enrolled with 610 (County of Chester) Squadron Royal Auxiliary Air Force, piloting Gloster Meteor F.8s from Hooton Park.

While testing Venom FB.1 WR347 on 20th October 1954 the electrics failed and with that, most of the instruments. Malcolm was flying in cloud and wisely chose to use the Martin-Baker ejection seat. The Venom impacted in open land near Ellesmere Port. 'Bang seats' in those days did not include leg restraint devices and Malcolm landed with both knees dislocated, a broken arm and compression of the spine. Six months of rehabilitation allowed him to resume flying, although walking required the help of a stick for the rest of his life.

In January 1956 Malcolm transferred to the Engine Division at Hatfield where he was involved in Ghost and Gyron turbojet development. During the 1957 SBAC airshow at Farnborough he demonstrated second prototype EE Canberra VN813 fitted with a Gyron Junior in place of the port RR Avon and B.2 WF909 with a Spectre rocket booster in the bomb bay. In May 1958 Malcolm was seconded to Rolls-Royce for development work of the Conway turbofan; this mostly involved piloting Avro Ashton 2 WB491 with a Conway mounted under the centre section. (The forward fuselage of WB491 is preserved at the Newark Air Museum.)

While on Conway test work, Malcolm also briefly flew the prototype Avro Vulcan VX770, which had been converted to act as a test-bed for the RCo.7 version of the Conway in 1957. This aircraft tragically hit the headlines on 20th September 1958 when it flew to Syerston to take part in an airshow. During a low-level pass, the Vulcan disintegrated, killing its crew (Rolls-Royce pilot Keith Sturt, co-pilot Richard 'John' Ford, flight test engineer William Howkins and RAF navigator Flt Lt Raymond Parratt) and three RAF personnel (Sgts E D Simpson and C Hanson and Snr Aircraftsman J J Tonks) on the ground. Post-crash analysis revealed that the leading edges of the delta wing had failed because of the changed loadings brought about by the new and more powerful engines.

Vulcan B.1 XA902 touched down at Hucknall on 17th July 1959, having been fitted with RCo.11s by Avro at Woodford, and Conway testing continued. In 1961 XA902 was taken into the hangars at Hucknall and the inboard Conways were removed and replaced by Spey turbofans for another period of trials. Rolls-Royce chief test pilot Jim Heyworth took it into the air for the first time on 12th October 1961.

Malcolm Muir (white flying suit) and his crew with Victor B.2 XL160 which was used for RCo.17 Conway trials at Hucknall from 1961 to 1962. *via Graham Pitchfork*

Helicopters and Big Fans

Having been seconded to Rolls-Royce from de Havilland Engines, Malcolm Muir was offered a full-time post at Hucknall in 1959 and in 1964 he was appointed deputy chief test pilot under Cliff Rogers. With the acquisition of the aero engine divisions of Bristol and Napier, Rolls-Royce entered the world of helicopters and Malcolm made the transition to rotary winged flight. While endurance testing Gazelle 161-engined Westland Wessex HAS.1 XS118 on 25th May 1965 the turboshaft flamed out at 2,000ft – too low for a re-light – and it crashed at Watnall, just west of Hucknall, amid the construction site for the M1 motorway. Malcolm and flight test observer R Painting were not seriously injured, but the impact did not help Malcolm's general health and in 1967 he stopped flying, having 'clocked' 84 different types.

Malcolm went on to work for the marketing department of Rolls-Royce and was sales manager in the USA for the RB.211 turbofan, which was chosen for the Lockheed TriStar wide-bodied airliner. It was the RB.211 and the TriStar that plunged both Rolls-Royce and Lockheed into chronic financial difficulties in 1971. As part of RB.211 development, Rolls-Royce was given the use of former RAF Transport Command VC-10 C.1 XR809 and this was ferried to Hucknall to have an RB.211 installed, in place of the port pair of Conway 301s. Civil registered as G-AXLR the VC-10 had its maiden flight from a snow-covered Hucknall on 6th March 1970, moving on to Filton to complete certification shortly afterwards. The prototype TriStar took to the air from Palmdale, California, on 17th November 1970. Beyond the TriStar, Malcolm was heavily involved in getting the RB.211 'on board' the Boeing 747, helping to establish the company's major role supplying big fan engines ever since to Boeing and Airbus.

From 1979 Malcolm became chief engineer for the Rolls-Royce flight test department at Filton; he retired in 1987 and died, aged 78, on 2nd August 2008. In his obituary in the *Daily Telegraph* for 25th September 2008 the following words summed up his days with the RB.211: "On his return from a visit to the Lockheed factory at Burbank in March 1971, the American company praised Muir and sent Rolls-Royce a telegram which said, 'Just occasionally the right man comes up at the right time and does the right thing.'"

To bring the Rolls-Royce story up to date, after a period of utilising Airbus or Boeing development airframes to 'hang' new powerplants on, Rolls-Royce took the decision in 2005 to operate a Boeing 747 as a test-bed, adapting the port inner pylon to accommodate a large-fan engine. The 'Jumbo' chosen had last served with Icelandic operator Air Atlanta and was built in 1980 as a series 267B for Cathay Pacific and, naturally, it was RB.211-524C2 powered! The test-bed was tasked with Trent 1000 development, the engine chosen for the Boeing 787 Dreamliner and was appropriately registered N787RR. With a Trent 1000 fitted, the 747 first flew, from Waco, Texas, in June 2007. During October 2014, operating from Tucson, Arizona, and flown by Rolls-Royce test pilot Mark Lewis, N787RR started testing composite fan blades fitted to a Trent 1000 as part of the company's Advance and UltraFan programmes.

Rolls-Royce Hucknall, looking southeast, during the mid-1960s. On the ramp is Airspeed Ambassador G-AKRD used as a test-bed for the Tyne turboprop and a Meteor night-fighter. *Rolls-Royce*

With an RB.211 in place of the port side Conways, VC-10 test-bed G-AXLR charges down the Hucknall runway on its maiden flight, 6th March 1970. *Rolls-Royce*

An Evil Boy

A 19th century forebear of Albert Howley 'Witt' Wittridge was caught stealing a chicken; he looked certain to be 'transported' to Australia, but according to Witt the day the case came up, the judge had a headache and his relative was sentenced to hang. Then there was the kinsman who ran a pub in Carshalton, London, who ended up a chronic alcoholic! Witt wrote about the shadow his 'evil' predecessors cast on him: "...what was to come of Wittridge, a nasty little boy? All the signs were there, up to all sorts of tricks and into all sorts of mischief at first. What was my mum going to have to do to make something worthwhile of me?" Well, a Distinguished Flying Cross in 1945 and a long career with the flight test department at Armstrong Siddeley Motors (ASM) were just *samples* of the 'corrective measures' that Witt undertook. In 2004 he penned his autobiography, *An Evil Boy*. It is an excellent read, right up there with Duke, Lithgow, Waterton and the others: it is well worth seeking out.

Aircraft, or fast cars, were always going to feature in Witt's future. In 1939, aged 17, he told his mother of his plans to join the aircraft industry. In a typical example of his dry humour, Witt wrote in *An Evil Boy* of his intentions in 1939, aged 17: "I wanted to join Hawker Aircraft as a draughtsman apprentice; I correctly felt that they might have enough designers". Sydney Camm could relax; he joined Parnall at Yate instead. By 1941 he was enrolled in the RAF and flying DH Tiger Moths at Booker before sailing the Atlantic to complete his training in Canada on Fleet Finches as Windsor Mills, Quebec, and then NAA Harvards at St Hubert, Montreal. He returned to the UK in October 1942 attending 7 (Pilots) Advanced Flying Unit at Peterborough, on Miles Masters, and then 56 Operational Training Unit (OTU), at Tealing on Hurricanes.

By 1943 he was at Imphal in Burma, flying Curtiss Mohawk IVs with 155 Squadron, before converting to Supermarine Spitfire VIIIs. Witt loved the Mk.VIII, claiming it to be: "Better than the Mk.IX, it had a retractable tailwheel, a stronger mainspar and an extra 24 gallons of fuel in the wings... in my opinion, it was the best model of all the 'Spits' including the later Griffon-engined aircraft I flew". With its Mk.VIIIs fully worked up 155 Squadron became operational at Palel, India, in August 1944. Witt was quick off the mark, on 25th September 1944 he shared in the 'kill' of a Mitsubishi *Dinah* twin and shortly afterwards dispatched a Nakajima *Oscar*.

In April 1944 he left 155 Squadron, bound for Fayid in Egypt and 73 OTU, equipped with Spitfires and Thunderbolts. He joined 213 Squadron at Ramat David in Palestine, at a time of heightened tension between the Arab population and Jewish settlers as the British mandate in the area neared its end. No.213 had Mustang IVs and an undercarriage malfunction on 18th December 1945 nearly put an end to Witt, KM101 was spread across the Ramat-David runway and he had to be pulled from the wreckage. Witt was hospitalised, then put on a ship back to the UK in March 1946. In November he was with 691 Squadron on anti-aircraft co-operation duties flying Martinet Is and Spitfire XVIs, moving in late 1948 to 203 Advanced Flying School at Stradishall, converting to Meteor F.4 jets. His last posting was as a training officer with 616 (South Yorkshire) Squadron at Finningley on Meteor F.4s.

Flt Lt A H 'Witt' Wittridge DFC with the Blackburn YB.1 WB797 prototype behind. Note the 'roller-recorder' in his left hand. *via Graham Pitchfork*

Leicestershire's 'Jet' Dakota

With an eye on his future Flt Lt Wittridge applied in 1949 for the Empire Test Pilots' School at Farnborough "when there were several hundred applicants for 20 places, together with another 15 for overseas applicants". He successfully joined 11 Course on 1st February 1952 and on qualification was posted to 'D' Squadron of the Aeroplane & Armament Experimental Establishment at Boscombe Down. In February 1954 Witt joined Armstrong Siddeley Motors (ASM) at its factory and test establishment at Bitteswell. That year the company employed four test pilots, the 'boss' being Lt Eddie Griffiths RN plus Lt Peter Aked RN, Flt Lt Lyndon 'Pee-Wee' Griffith RNZAF and Witt. (Pee-Wee went on to fly with Aviation Traders as chief pilot – see under Donald Cartlidge and Chapter Seven in Volume Two.) As will be seen from the table, there was a large variety of aircraft to tackle. During the 1954 SBAC display at Farnborough Witt demonstrated the Sapphire-engined Canberra B.2 WD933.

ASM started development of the Mamba turboprop in opposition to the Rolls-Royce Dart in April 1946 and carried out a major campaign to attract users. During this, the company funded the conversion of former RAF Douglas Dakota C.4 from June 1949 to take two of the turboprops, in place of the ubiquitous Pratt & Whitney R1830s radials. This was among the unusual types that Witt flew during his time at Bitteswell. Another was the prototype Blackburn YB.1 WB797 anti-submarine warfare type, powered by the coupled version of the Mamba, the Double Mamba. The YB.1 was not chosen, but the Fairey contender, the Gannet, was hugely successful and also Double Mamba propelled.

Witt also flew several of the Avro multi-engined test-beds: Ashton, Lancastrian and Lancaster. The Lancastrian, VM733, had two Sapphire turbojets in the outer positions, as Witt recounted in *An Evil Boy*: "It was amazing sometimes to formate on BEA DC-3s on the nearby airway, then feather the two Merlins and pull away at great speed on two pure jets!"

Since his early days, Witt had respected the products of Hawker, and he was pleased to discover that ASM's parent company, Armstrong Whitworth, was producing the Sea Hawk naval fighter and Sapphire-powered versions, the F.2 and F.5, of his beloved Hunter at Bitteswell. In March 1954 a Hunter provided a stressful time when after take-off it became clear the powered control to the ailerons had failed to fully engage. This left Witt with no aileron control; he managed to re-join the circuit and land using only the rudder for directional control.

In September 1959, ASM and Bristol's engine division merged to form Bristol Siddeley and Witt relocated to Filton. There he converted to helicopters, and his final testing was carried out on the Westland Scout and Wessex. Most exotic of the types flown from Filton was the Fiat G.91R, a Sabre-esque single-seat fighter, powered by a BSE Orpheus 803 and destined for service with the Italians and West Germans. With the Filton flight test department scaling down, Witt accepted redundancy in 1965 and began a career as a freelance commercial pilot, initially with Imperial Tobacco, flying its Beagle 206S and then BSR Ltd, operating a Bell JetRanger and a HS.125. He retired from flying in 1975, taking up a post in the geography faculty

Armstrong Siddeley and Bristol Siddeley-powered aircraft flown by 'Witt' Wittridge

BP Balliol	1 x Mamba turboprop
HP Hastings TE583	2 x Sapphire Sa.2 turbojets (outers), 2 x Bristol Hercules inners
Avro Lancastrian C.2 VM733	2 x Sapphire turbojets (outers), 2 x RR Merlin inners
Fairey Gannet AS.1 and AEW.3	1 x Double Mamba coupled turboprop
Folland Gnat	1 x Orpheus turbojet
EE Canberra B.2 WD933	2 x Sapphire turbojets
EE Canberra B.2 WK163	2 x Sapphire turbojets and 1 x Viper turbojet under the starboard wing
Blackburn YB.1 WB797	1 x Double Mamba coupled turboprop
Hawker Hunter WB202	2 x Sapphire 6 turbojet with reheat
Westland Wyvern	1 x Python turboprop
Avro Lancaster III SW342	1 x Mamba turboprop in nose, 4 x RR Merlin
	1 x Viper turbojet in rear fuselage, 4 x RR Merlin
Gloster Javelin FAW.1, FAW.7	2 x Sapphire turbojets, including reheat
Hunting Jet Provost T.1, T.3, T.4	1 x Viper turbojet
Douglas Dakota C.4 KJ839	2 x Mamba turboprops
Short Seamew AS.1 XA209	1 x Mamba turboprop
Avro Ashton Mk.4 WB494	1 x Sapphire turbojet under the fuselage, 4 x RR Nene
Fiat G.91R-1 G-45/4	1 x Orpheus turbojet
Vickers Valiant B.1 WP199	1 x Pegasus vectored thrust turbofan under the fuselage, 4 x RR Avon
Canadair Sabre F.4 XB982	1 x Orpheus turbojet
HP Victor B.1	4 x Sapphire turbojets
Westland Scout AH.1	1 x Nimbus turboshaft
Westland Wessex HAS.1	1 x Napier Gazelle turboshaft
Westland Wessex HU.5	2 x Gnome coupled turboshafts

Note: 'Witt' served with Armstrong Siddeley at Bitteswell from 1954, moving to Bristol Siddeley at Filton in September 1959. Types given in 'logbook' order.

Armstrong Siddeley engine test pilots, Peter Aked (left) and 'Witt' Wittridge with a Canberra. *via 'Witt' Wittridge*

An Armstrong Siddeley advert for the company's privately-funded DC-3 conversion; flight tested on Dakota C.4 KJ839.

of Birmingham University as a weather forecaster. Flt Lt Witt Wittridge DFC died on 23rd April 2009, aged 86 having been anything but an 'evil boy'.

Upwardly Mobile

As these words hit the word processor, the counter on the Martin-Baker web-site read 7,463 lives saved in ejections using the world-renowned seats. Each soul represented by that statistic has a lot of people to thank, not least James Martin and Valentine Baker, the founders of the Martin-Baker Aircraft (MBA) company. Chapter Seven gives full details of Valentine and background on MBA. There are two others that need to be remembered, former Spitfire pilot 'Fifi' Fifield and experimental fitter Bernard Lynch. For both of these men, there came a moment when the use of dummies and crude telemetry just would not do; someone would have to try out the system. Bernard is unique in this book; he may be a non-pilot but he certainly deserves 'honorary' status.

After rigs had been tried out at Denham, MBA needed a flying test-bed from which to fire the ejection seat. The Boulton Paul Defiant was the obvious answer; the space previously occupied by the gun turret provided plenty of room for the seat. Mk.I DR944 was transferred to MBA on 11th December 1944 and modified. From 11th May 1945 ejections, using special-weighted dummies were made from DR944 at Wittering; the aircraft moved to Beaulieu six days later and further 'shoots' were carried out. Flying DR944 was Bryan Greensted*, chief test pilot for propeller manufacturer Rotol.

Meanwhile, the rig at Denham was prepared for the next test; firing the development seat with a volunteer strapped to it. Bernard 'Benny' Lynch, working as a fitter in MBA's experimental department, volunteered for the trials. Meanwhile

Powered by a BSE Orpheus 803 turbojet, Italian Air Force Fiat G.91R-1 MM6283 was tested at Filton as G-45/4 during 1960. *Bristol Siddeley Engines*

the pace of the programme was quickening; on 6th November 1945 Meteor III EE416 was allocated to MBA for conversion into the next – and much faster – ejection seat test-bed and by the following year Chalgrove airfield was taken over for flight test purposes. Benny endured a series of blasts up the rig at Denham and a mass of data was gathered. It soon became evident that Benny was the best candidate for the next phase – live firing from the Meteor in flight.

EE416 was ready at Chalgrove by the early summer of 1946 and on the 8th June the first firing of a seat with a weighted dummy was made from the static jet. Then a dozen flying trials were made with the dummy being blasted out at 2,000ft and a speed of about 415mph. The stage was set for the first live British ejection. In 1946, Jack 'Scotty' Scott, former Rolls-Royce development test pilot at Hucknall, chief test pilot for Power Jets and later the National Gas Turbine Establishment, was appointed as MBA's chief test pilot – he held the post until 1960.

Scotty was piloting EE416 out of Chalgrove on 24th July 1946 and strapped in the back was Benny Lynch, although the intention was that the 'passenger' would not be present when the Meteor touched down! At 8,000ft and 320mph, Benny made his debut departure using an ejection seat – he was to carry out another 15. The early seats provided a means of propelling the airman out of the aircraft; it was then up to the ejectee to release himself from the seat, let it fall clear and then pull the ripcord in the conventional manner. The present day seats automate all of these processes. On 29th August 1947 Benny was propelled out at 12,000ft and a speed of 420mph. To mark his courage, he was awarded the British Empire Medal in 1948.

Bernard I Lynch bem died on 13th October 1986; his date of birth seeming to have escaped record. Upon his death, MBA issued a press release and its final words remain a fine tribute to a determined man: "It takes a special kind of courage to fire yourself out of an aircraft when you don't have to; it takes an extra special kind of courage to be the first person to do it. Benny Lynch had that extra special kind of courage."

EE416 carried out over 400 airborne tests for MBA and by August 1953 its replacement – Meteor T.7 WA634 – was ready to take over. The pioneering EE416 was scrapped in 1959 but its all-important modified forward fuselage was presented to the Science Museum. For some time it was displayed at South

A stoic-looking 'Benny' Lynch strapped into Meteor III EE416 at Chalgrove, 1946. *Martin-Baker Aircraft*

Kensington, London, in an 'action' pose with the seat successfully used by MBA's first-ever 'customer', 'Jo' Lancaster who 'banged out' of Armstrong Whitworth AW.52 flying wing TS363 on 30th May 1949 – see Volume Two. Today the forward fuselage of EE416 is proudly on show at Chalgrove.

In 1955 Sqn Ldr John 'Fifi' S Fifield, who had previously commanded an element of the Central Fighter Establishment, joined MBA as a test pilot but quickly discovered that a good way to emphasize with the 'passengers' in the back seat was to try it out personally! As mentioned earlier, Meteor T.7 WA634 was allocated to MBA, on 28th January 1952. As a two-seater already it offered much more space for trial seat installations, and allowed the pilot to also have a 'bang seat' if all went wrong. In

The first live British ejection, 'Benny' Lynch parting company with Meteor III EE416 on 24th July 1946. *Martin-Baker Aircraft*

Sqn Ldr Fifield making the first low-level ejection with an MBA seat from Meteor T.7 WA634 at Chalgrove, 3rd September 1955. *Martin-Baker Aircraft*

1952 Gloster fitted a rear fuselage from an F.8 version among other modifications; because it was a hybrid, it was often referred to as a 'Meteor T.7½'. By this time MBA was developing a seat capable of successfully ejecting at ultra-low level, or even on the ground, and Fifi volunteered to try this out. On 3rd September 1955, Scotty hurled WA634 along Chalgrove's runway at 120mph and the Mk.3 seat shot Fifi 300ft into the air – he was safely back on the ground six seconds later. The following month, Fifi ejected from WA634 from 40,000ft, again with complete success. Meteor T.7 WA634 is presently held in store by the RAF Museum at Cosford. Fifi went on to succeed Jack Scott in 1960; Sqn Ldr J S Fifield OBE DFC AFC retired in 1978.

A fully-instrumented and telemetry-laden dummy blasting through the cockpit of an Aermacchi/EMBRAER AMX in a MBA Mk.10L seat, circa 1982. The forward fuselage was mounted on MBA's rocket-powered sled system at Langford Lodge in Northern Ireland. *Martin-Baker Aircraft*

CHAPTER FIVE

Trials and Tribulations

By far and away the largest number of British tests pilot have been members of the armed forces serving with the research and development agencies and a variety of acceptance and trials organisations. Additionally, the Air Registration Board, established in 1937, and its successor, the Civil Aviation Authority from 1972, have also employed pilots to assess new types. (The work of the ARB and CAA is highlighted in Volume Two.) All of this work is as demanding and risky as that of manufacturer test pilots that form the central part of this book, but the job definition does not include putting the throttle forward for the first time ever on a brand new design.

Lockheed Martin test pilot Bill 'Giggs' Gigliotti took F-35B Lightning II BK-01 ZM135, the first for the UK, on its maiden flight at Fort Worth, Texas, on 13th April 2012. On 23rd July Sqn Ldr Jim Schofield ferried it to Eglin Air Force Base, Florida, for the start of its operational testing and evaluation that may one day see it at Boscombe Down. *Tom Harvey-Lockheed Martin*

That does not mean that there *haven't* been instances of service test pilots taking on a 'first timer' role, a good example being the Royal Aircraft Establishment's Sqn Ldr Jack Henderson. RAE's Aerodynamics Flight ('Aero Flight') was destined to be the operator of the one-off Handley Page HP.115 slim delta research jet and it made sense that one of its personnel should take on the programme from the very beginning. So it was that Jack piloted XP841 on its maiden flight, from RAE Thurleigh on 17th August 1961. Jack and the RAE took on the role that Handley Page would have fulfilled in the normal way of things, signing off the last 'contractor' sortie on 29th September so that it could be 'handed over' to the customer for an extensive and productive flying life. (For more take a look at Jack's entry in Chapter Seven.)

Service test pilots can broadly be grouped in two categories: research and development (the 'trials' of the chapter title) and evaluation leading to acceptance or rejection

Sqn Ldr Jack Henderson of the Royal Aircraft Establishment took the HP.115 XP841 for its maiden flight, from Thurleigh on 17th August 1961. *Handley Page*

by the customer air arm (what manufacturers might regard as 'tribulation'!). The first grouping is the domain of the 'boffin', turning ideas into reality in support of the armed forces or of the industry as a whole. The second should see an aircraft declared 'fit for service', or blown out of the competition altogether. All of this requires the same exacting academic and flying skills as the manufacturer test pilot. In getting an aircraft accepted for service by the armed forces manufacturer and service test pilots work closely together; often handing an aircraft back and forth as the development cycle matures. Many service pilots go on to become manufacturer test pilots, either via bodies such as Boscombe Down or Farnborough or through the Empire Test Pilots' School – see Chapter One.

Much more has been written on the domain of service test pilots than on their manufacturer counterparts; several books are mentioned below (with more detail given in the Bibliography). As service testing is *very* different from that of 'prototyping', this chapter will restrict itself to 'thumb nails' of such establishments while reminding the reader that many of the pilots detailed in both volumes have their roots within these organisations. Government bodies tend to change names frequently and when it comes to the test and trials establishments the lexicon can become labyrinthine. The narrative below makes no claims to be comprehensive; for a master class in the genealogy of service institutions, a copy of *RAF Flying Training and Support Units since 1925* by Ray Sturtivant with John Hamlin really should be on your shelves.

Farnborough, Thurleigh and more

All Fool's Day 1918 saw the birth of two institutions; the Royal Air Force – out of the Royal Flying Corps and the Royal Naval Air Service – and the Royal Aircraft Establishment (RAE) – out of the Royal Aircraft Factory. The 'Factory' at Farnborough had been controversial since its inception because it designed and manufactured *as well* as tested and evaluated – a government body acting as both producer and customer amid a struggling private sector. From 1st April 1918 Farnborough became synonymous with the very best in aeronautical research and development and a vital support

element to the wider industry. It evolved into a complex organisation, eventually operating a series of flights, sub-units and out-stations. Additionally, RAE fostered associated or 'lodger' units, for example the Air Accidents Investigation Branch (AAIB) and the Institute of Aviation Medicine.

On 1st April 1988 the RAE changed its name, if not its initials, becoming the Royal *Aerospace* Establishment. This was the start of many changes to the sign at the main gate. In 1991 it turned into the Aerospace Division of the Defence Research Agency (DRA), adopting the more pendulous moniker Defence Experimental Research Agency (DERA) in 1995 before all of the 'R&D' elements of British aviation were split between the 'Private Public Partnership' QinetiQ and the Ministry of Defence owned Defence Science and Technology Laboratory (DSTL) on 2nd July 2001. Sold off to the private sector in 2006, QinetiQ was rated as the planet's 52nd largest defence contractor at the time of putting this volume together; with sites both in the UK and overseas. The headquarters of QinetiQ remains at Farnborough and research is still carried on there at the Cody Technology Park, although test flying had ceased by the end of the 1990s.

Restrictions in both area and airspace at Farnborough gave rise to the dramatic transformation of the former USAAF Eighth Air Force airfield at Thurleigh and it was opened as RAE Bedford in June 1957. As well as a massive runway and extensive ramp and hangarage facilities, there was an impressive wind tunnel site to the south, close to the former airfield at Twinwood Farm. Thurleigh followed the same naming gymnastics as its founder until airfield site closed in March 1994 although there is still an appreciable QinetiQ presence on the airfield. Other RAE out-stations included Aberporth, Cardington, Cobbett Hill, Larkhill, Lasham, Llanbedr, Newhaven, Oakhangar and West Freugh.

The doyen of all RAE test pilots is Captain Eric 'Winkle' Brown CBE DSC AFC RN and his exploits are recorded in a barrage of books written by him – currently in Crécy Publishing's Hikoki imprint are *Wings of the Luftwaffe*, *Wings of the Navy* and the glorious *Wings of the Weird and Wonderful*. In April 2014 the author was privileged to listen to Eric giving a presentation to the Sywell Aviation Museum and two of the many anecdotes he regaled the audience with will suffice to supply some 'flavour' of the variety of his time with RAE.

While the Airborne Forces Experimental Establishment at Beaulieu (see below) was busy evaluating the Sikorsky Hoverfly helicopter and its applications for the armed forces, RAE also had an interest in the type from a technical and aerodynamic point of view. Helicopters offered enormous potential for the Royal Navy, so Eric's involvement was a certainty. In February 1945 three Hoverflies were available for the RAE and Eric and Sqn Ldr Tony Martindale were despatched to Liverpool Airport, Speke, the following month to learn how to master these devices and ferry them to Farnborough. Hoverflies arriving as cargo at Liverpool Docks were received by 7 Aircraft Acceptance Unit, run by Martin Hearn Ltd at Hooton Park, just across the River Mersey from Speke. (At the time 7 AAU was run by former Handley Page test pilot 'Jim' Cordes – see Chapter Seven.) When Eric and Tony arrived at Speke, several American personnel were carrying out finishing touches to the helicopters. Eric quietly asked who was going to teach them how to fly the devices; the Master Sergeant in charge shook his head, handed over a large booklet and declared: "Here's your instructor, buddy!" That night in the mess, Eric and Tony pored over the manual. Eric asked his colleague how his 'swotting up' was going and Tony replied that it was: "like you are reading your own obituary"! After a lot of "bucking and weaving" at Speke the following morning, the intrepid pair set off – in *very* loose formation – on the multi-stage journey to Farnborough.

Eric is probably most famous for his travels through Germany collecting aircraft and items of interest for examination and trials back in the UK; he had perfect credentials, he was an evaluation test pilot and a fluent German speaker. During this expedition he became the only British pilot to fly the rocket-propelled Messerschmitt Me 163B Komet. He achieved this in a manner typical of how he approached all such sorties, establishing as much detail as he could before hand, and building his experience step-by-step along the way. In this case, he visited the Walter factory at Kiel to study the HWK 509A rocket motor. Eric had many conversations with Luftwaffe Me 163B pilots and he thoroughly digested the flight manual. He then flew a clipped-wing DFS Habicht glider used to familiarise aircrew with the high-speed glide approach and skid-landing made by the Me 163B after the rocket propellant had been expended. An Me 163A-0 glider version of the 'B was located and Eric flew three sorties, towed aloft to 20,000ft by a Messerschmitt Bf 110. At Husum in June 1945 Eric blasted off and in 150 seconds was at 32,000ft! After a brief session assessing the handling, Eric successfully landed the Me 163B, coming over the threshold at 125mph. Looking at his entranced audience in 2014, Eric announced that flying the rocket fighter was "like being in charge of a runaway train!" He had no desire to repeat the experience: "believe me, once was enough!"

On 10th January 1954 BOAC DH Comet 1 G-ALYP disappeared off Elba, Italy, with the loss of all on board. This was tragedy enough but 88 days later another, G-ALYY, crashed into the sea off Naples. A salvage operation was

Captain 'Winkle' Brown, doyen of RAE test pilots, alongside a replica of the Gloster E28/39 at Cranwell in May 2011 for the 70th anniversary celebrations of its first flight. *Ken Ellis*

initiated and the RAE put on full alert, Britain's world-beating jet airliner was under intense scrutiny. A massive and fast-paced investigation brought together two elements at Farnborough, the Accidents Investigation Branch (now the AAIB) and the Structures Department worked to find the cause and, if possible, cure it. On 14th April, just *four days* after G-ALYY had plunged into the Mediterranean, its sister ship, G-ALYS, touched down at Farnborough to start 'live', ground-based trials. The prototype Comet, G-ALVG, was already on site; it had arrived the previous July for a series of tests and was quickly used for metal fatigue experimentation. Having been roaded in, G-ALYU was placed inside a huge water tank on 19th May, beginning four months of intensive pressurisation trials. Meanwhile, *Yoke-Papa* had been retrieved from the deep and was being re-assembled in a hangar. Mk.1A G-ANAV flew in from Hatfield on 24th May and carried out a variety of tests until it was grounded in mid-August. Up to 1957 another *four* Comet airframes were brought by road to Farnborough to join the diagnostic effort.

Cracking under a cabin window led to catastrophic failure of the structure of G-ALYU in the tank, emulating the misfortunes that had befallen its sisters. With much redesign – including the shape of the cabin windows – and strengthening Comets returned to service, but the type's vast sales potential had suffered a mortal blow and competition from Boeing and Douglas reaped the rewards. (See under John Cunningham in Chapter Seven.)

Peter Cooper's *Farnborough – 100 Years of British Aviation* provides a superb level of detail, while Reginald Turnill and Arthur Reed's *Farnborough – The Story of RAE* provides a cracking narrative up to the end of the 1970s.

Sqn Ldr Brian Maloney (seated, fifth from the left), officer commanding RAE Farnborough's 'T' Flight with the unit's civilian and service staff in front of a Gloster E28/29 in 1944. *Peter Green Collection*

Martlesham, Boscombe Down, Flexistowe and Beaulieu

While Farnborough, Thurleigh and others were centres for research and development, the air arms of Britain required a specialist establishment to perfect future requirements for operational types, to evaluate and test aircraft, weapons and other systems intended to meet ministry specifications and competitions and to keep abreast of aviation developments worldwide. The Aeroplane Experimental Station, previously set up as simply the Testing Squadron, at Martlesham Heath was established for this purpose on 16th October 1917. It quickly expanded to take in Orfordness off the Suffolk coast well away from prying eyes and by March 1920 had changed its name to Aeroplane Experimental Establishment (AEE). It took on its most well-known identity, the Aeroplane & Armament Experimental Establishment (A&AEE), on 24th March 1924 and with the prospect of German bombs raining down, de-camped west to Boscombe Down in September 1939.

As with RAE, the initials remained unchanged with the next change, becoming the Aircraft & Armament *Evaluation* Establishment when what remained of the experimental nature of its work was ceded to DRA at Farnborough. By 1993 the Defence Test and Evaluation Organisation was the 'umbrella' body but on 1st April 1996 A&AEE faded away as a name, replaced by the Assessment and Evaluation Centre under the aegis of DERA. The latest iteration of this is the Aircraft Test and Evaluation Centre administered via the Joint Test and Evaluation Group comprising the Ministry of Defence and QinetiQ.

On 18th November 2008 the oldest flying HS Harrier, 1969-built T.2 XW175, retired at QinetiQ, Boscombe Down and it serves as an apprentice training airframe. It richly deserves to be in a museum, but few realise why. In February 1975 the two-seater was delivered to RAE Thurleigh and it was destined to become a phenomenal development and trials platform. During 1977 and 1978 it was used for sea-going trials with the aircraft carrier HMS *Hermes*, helping to develop guidance systems, head-up display symbology and autopilot techniques.

In 1983 RAE Thurleigh entered into a contract with Cranfield Institute of Technology to radically convert XW175 into the Vectored-Thrust Aircraft Advanced Control (VAAC) test-bed. Cranfield acted as the contractor for the transformation which was project led by RAE with inputs from UK industry. The rear cockpit was fitted with a digital fly-by-wire control system, while the front cockpit retained conventional control linkage to provide a back-up. The test-bed was designed to be upgraded with improved control concepts; known as the Bedford 'Unified' system. At the same time the Harrier was updated to make it close to T.4 status. The reconfigured XW175 was re-delivered to Thurleigh in 1986, transferring to Boscombe Down with the closure of RAE Bedford. In September 1998 the Harrier carried out the first ever deck landing using a unified control system, on HMS *Illustrious*.

From 2002 the VAAC Harrier worked on the Lockheed Martin F-35B Joint Strike Fighter (designated Joint Combat Aircraft in the UK) programme to help minimise pilot workload and to perfect the ability to recover to a carrier and then land, both automatically. This culminated with XW175 re-visiting *Illustrious* between 12th and 19th November 2008 when QinetiQ's Justin Paines validated the 'Bedford Array' visual landing aid system which combined inputs from external references and the pilot's helmet-mounted display. Thirty-nine sorties were flown to prove its suitability during the Shipborne Rolling Vertical Landing technique, to the adopted by the V/STOL version of the F-35B. Four years after XW175's final JSF/JCA trials on *Illustrious* the first British F-35B, ZM135, had its maiden sortie at Fort Worth, Texas. Testing and evaluation started at Eglin Air Force Base, Florida, three months later and at some stage, the VAAC's protégé will transfer to Boscombe Down as the latest type to be trialled there.

The Aeroplane and Seaplane Experimental Station was established on the Isle of Grain in May 1918. It was rationalised as the Marine Aircraft Station five months later, then the Marine & Armament Experimental Establishment (M&AEE) in March 1920 before settling on the name Marine Aircraft Experimental Establishment (MAEE) in March 1924; moving to much better facilities at Felixstowe three months

A&AEE's unique hybrid B.2/8 Canberra WV787 was converted by Flight Refuelling Ltd for icing trials, serving as such from the late 1960s to the early 1980s. It is illustrated spraying the third prototype HS.125-1 G-ARYC, operated by Bristol Siddeley Engines. *KEC*

later. Just as A&AEE was evacuated from vulnerable Suffolk, so was MAEE, re-locating to Helensburgh on the Clyde in September 1939. MAEE was back at Felixstowe by August 1945 but the need for a dedicated 'marine' organisation soon vaporised and MAEE was disbanded in 1954.

With Prime Minister Winston Churchill's determination to emulate Germany's parachute and glider-borne troops, the Airborne Forces Experimental Establishment (AFEE) was formed at Ringway on 15th February 1940. It moved to Sherburn-in-Elmet in June 1942 and to Beaulieu in January 1945. AFEE trialled gliders, parachutes and ended up as a centre of excellence for helicopters before being absorbed into A&AEE in September 1950. Airborne radar research was concentred at the Telecommunications Flying Unit (TFU) at Hurn from November 1941, moving to Defford in May 1942. TFU was re-designated as the Radar Research Flying Unit in late 1955 and later became the Radar Research Establishment. RRE consolidated its activities at Pershore in September 1957 and adopted the title Royal Signals and Radar Establishment in March 1976. The following year its facilities were transferred to RAE Thurleigh in January 1977, becoming the Radar Research Squadron.

Sqn Ldr Tim Mason has done more than any other writer to chronicle the vast activities of Martlesham, Felixstowe and Boscombe Down. In turn he has written: *British Flight Testing: Martlesham Heath 1920-1939, The Secret Years, Flight Testing at Boscombe Down 1939-1945, The Cold War Years, Flight Testing at Boscombe Down 1945-1975* and *The Seaplane Years, M&AEE and MAEE* – 'Secret' and 'Seaplane' are currently in print with Crécy Publishing.

Maintenance Unit tribute

An area of test piloting largely overlooked is that of the airmen posted to maintenance units (MUs) in Britain, the Middle East and beyond. In many ways MU pilots played a similar role to the industry's Production Test Pilots – see Chapter Three. Their vital role, working under pressured and difficult conditions, deserves a more substantial tribute. The author is indebted to Air Cdre Graham Pitchfork, who profiled Greek campaign veteran Robert Pearson in his superb *Men Behind the Medals* series in the April 2013 edition of *FlyPast,* for permission to extract from that feature.

Known throughout his time in the RAF as 'Twinkle', Robert W Pearson started his RAF service as an apprentice at Halton before he was accepted for pilot training. In June 1937 he joined 211 Squadron, which was re-forming at Mildenhall with

Close up of the spray boom of Canberra B.2/8 WV787, on the Boscombe Down ramp with A&AEE Beverley C.1 XB261 in the background. Both of these aircraft, WV787 complete and XB261 as a cockpit, are preserved at the Newark Air Museum. *KEC*

Harrier T.2 XW175 making the first automatic touch down on HMS *Illustrious*, in September 1998. *QinetiQ*

Hawker Hinds. The unit moved to Helwan in Egypt in May 1938 and, in April the following year, re-equipped with Bristol Blenheim Is. With war looming, 211 moved forward to El Daba in the Western Desert where it remained until Italy declared war in June 1940; Robert completed 26 'ops' in this theatre.

Italy invaded Greece on 28th October and, together with 84 Squadron, 211 was withdrawn to Ismailia to prepare to re-deploy across the Mediterranean. No.211 was in action from Menidi, near Athens, from late November. On 22nd January 1941, Robert bombed Berat, despite being attacked by an Italian fighter. His aircraft also received a direct hit from flak and was badly damaged, but he managed to return to base.

On 16th March, the crew spotted a Cant Z.506B floatplane and Robert dived to get on its tail, opening up with his two

Blackburn Iris V prototype S1263 on the slipway at MAEE Felixstowe in April 1932 during evaluation. It carries a 209 Squadron badge on the nose, but was not cleared for use by the unit until June. *KEC*

forward-firing guns, then made a series of head-on attacks. When his ammunition was exhausted, he moved to the beam to allow Sgt Chignall to bring his guns to bear from the turret. As they left, the Cant was trailing smoke and flying just above the waves, so they were unable to claim it as destroyed. At the end of March, it was announced that three of 211 Squadron's pilots had been awarded the DFC, among them Twinkle: "In recognition of gallantry and devotion to duty in the execution of air operations". During April, 211 straggled back to Egypt; Robert was one of the few to fly throughout the Greek campaign and survive.

Robert returned to England in 1943 and became the test pilot at 5 MU at Kemble; dealing with a constant supply of aircraft that had been placed in storage and requiring air test. On 7th August 1943, he took off in newly-built Hawker Hurricane IIc LD159. It was seen to climb steeply in a slow turn to 2,000ft and proceeded to carry out a shallow dive over the airfield before levelling at 300ft and repeating the sequence two or three times. On completion of the final dive LD159 was throttled back and banked steeply, first to port and then to starboard with bursts of throttle in between. On the final bank the Hurricane failed to recover level flight, stalled and spun into the ground just outside the airfield boundary.

Flt Lt Ronald 'Twinkle' Pearson DFC was laid to rest in the churchyard at Kemble village. Many years later, his wartime observer, George Riddle, wrote: "I had the greatest respect for 'Twinks' who was one of the best bomber pilots I ever flew with, and I could rely on him to bring the kite just where I wanted it." Having survived the rigours of North Africa and Greece in Blenheims, Robert Pearson tragically proved that a posting to an MU was no sinecure and held its own dangers.

H A Taylor, author of two 'Putnams', *Airspeed Aircraft since 1931* and *Fairey Aircraft since 1915* and co-author (with K M Molson) of *Canadian Aircraft since 1909*, *Flight* magazine columnist, also wrote *Test Pilot at War*. Having learned to fly in 1929, he was an early recruit with the Air Transport Auxiliary civilian-manned ferry service and from May to October 1940, was in command of 3 Ferry Pilot Pool at White Waltham. He was commissioned into the RAFVR in October 1940, becoming a Flight Lieutenant, and was the resident test pilot at 48 MU, Hawarden. From 1942 to 1945 he was an MU Senior Test Pilot, travelling extensively. He was also attached to Supermarine during 1944, production testing Spitfires and Seafires. He ended the war with 1,378 hours in his logbook. Superbly readable, *Test Pilot at War* is worth keeping an eye out for.

'Twinkle' Pearson (left) with his observer with a 211 Squadron Blenheim. *via Graham Pitchfork*

CHAPTER SIX

A Desk Job?

An all-British military jet prototype with sleek, swept wings and plenty of 'stealth' features, sailed into the sky on 10th August 2013. Many readers will be struggling to envisage this important epoch as the last such endeavour was surely nearly *two decades* previously. That was the first UK-assembled Eurofighter Typhoon, DA.2, piloted by Chris Yeo – the author of the Foreword – on 6th April 1994 at Warton.

It took a while for BAE Systems to announce the August 2013 event and confirm that the aircraft was Taranis ZZ250, a prototype unmanned combat air system (UCAS) demonstrator, conceived and built at Warton, and rolled-out there in July 2010. As briefly outlined below, Taranis is not the first British unmanned – or uninhabited – aerial vehicle (UAV) and it certainly will not be the last. The UK Ministry of Defence is looking for what it calls a Future Air Combat System, tentatively for entry into service in 2030, and it is very likely it will have an 'absentee' pilot.

Britain has had 'UAVs' in a basic form since the first gunnery drones, typified by the de Havilland Queen Bee, since the 1930s. The Ministry of Defence still employs indigenous Banshee drones by Meggitt Defence Systems and Italian-built SELIX Galileo Mirach target systems. With the changing world after 9/11 the UK has adopted what it chooses to call Remotely Piloted Air Systems (RPAS), the Thales Watchkeeper based on the Israeli Elbit Hermes 450 surveillance drone being introduced by the Army, and the US-built General Atomics MQ-9 Reaper employed for reconnaissance and strike by the RAF's 13 and 39 Squadrons, headquartered at Waddington. But with Taranis, and the types that have led to it, BAE Systems has pioneered the much more adaptable UCAS with the very real potential to replace present manned strike and reconnaissance assets.

Since Taranis ZZ250 first flew it has become widely accepted that the venue was Woomera, Western Australia. Some time elapsed before BAE turned to the human element and declared that Sqn Ldr Bob Fraser was the commander of the test flight. The BAE Systems 'Newsroom' web-site has provided other material on what is an otherwise 'top secret' project. Bob explained that he was in charge of a team of ten and that as a former captain of large aircraft this was a role he had previously carried out, but with his feet off the ground, not under a desk. He explained that the crew had rehearsed the sortie so many times that when it took place for real there was "an element of routine about it". Despite that, he also noted that he didn't breathe for about 15 minutes and found the experience "probably the most exciting thing I've ever done".

The web-site nominates Wg Cdr Neil Dawson as the pilot within the mission team. (At that point Neil was CTP Unmanned Aircraft Systems and Large Aircraft – more details in Volume Two.) Up to the time of this book going to press, it has not been revealed *where* the test team were located during ZZ250's maiden voyage. Very likely they were also at Woomera, but there remains the tantalising possibility that the flight crew could have been at Warton, or *anywhere*. The public has become used to drones being flown in far away – mostly hot and sandy – places with the controllers sat in air conditioned command centres on the other side of the planet.

Steps to Taranis

The Introduction has declared that UAVs are 'off limits' for the purposes of this book, but as such devices represent the greatest growth potential in military aviation (with high hopes for the civil sector in due course) it would be wrong not to take a fleeting look at what is going on.

When I first saw one of the HERTI prototype UAVs I remarked upon the stencilling on the forward fuselage: 'No Human Occupant'. I said I thought that was self-evident. It was explained that as HERTI had a 'hump' where a cockpit might be expected to be located, the wording was for the benefit of any emergency services on the scene should there have been an

accident. There would be no need for potential rescuers to risk themselves as there was no flesh and blood within. HERTI – High Endurance Rapid Technology Insertion – was BAE's first foray into UAVs. For ease it was based on a Polish-designed light aircraft, the J&AS Aero Design J5 Macro. Fitted with a 'pusher' piston engine, it started trials in late 2004 and was followed by at least four other HERTIs, all of varying format and powerplant. In August 2005 a propeller-driven HERTI 1A carried out the first fully autonomous UAV flight in UK airspace. Other developmental types within the BAE Systems UAV portfolio have included Corax, Kestrel and Raven. On 21st October 2009 Mantis twin-turboprop 'pusher' configured technology demonstrator ZK210 had its debut, from Woomera.

A major step in the wide-ranging BAE Systems UAV development programme involves a *manned* aircraft. After considerable modification BAe Jetstream 31 G-BWWW was transformed into the ASTRAEA test-bed by early 2013. This alphabet soup stands for Autonomous Systems Technology Related Airborne Evaluation and Assessment. This Jetstream is most often referred to as *Triple-Whisky* from its once appropriate registration – it was built at Prestwick in 1983 to the order of the Edinburgh-based Distillers Company! It joined BAe's 'mini-airline' in 1986 and served on factory 'shuttle' flights until nominated for its new role.

ASTRAEA is designed to demonstrate the safe and efficient operation of UAVs within airspace used by 'inhabited' aircraft. It is capable of perceiving bad weather and going around it, sensing and avoiding other air traffic and making an emergency landing on its own. In April 2013, the Jetstream flew a 500-

Draped in covers, Taranis ZZ250 being towed across a wet Warton ready for taxi trials in April 2013. *© 2015 BAE Systems*

mile sortie out of Warton to Inverness and back, totally under the command of a ground-based pilot team and utilising en route air traffic controllers. The on-board crew of three just monitored the proceedings for safety. This was first ever flight in UK shared airspace by an aircraft behaving as a UAV.

Perfect world of autonomy

Powered by a Rolls-Royce /Turboméca Adour turbofan (probably a Series 951), Taranis is roughly the size of a Hawk trainer. Named after the Celtic god of thunder, the programme is reported to have cost £185 million, funded jointly by the UK MoD and UK industry. Team Taranis comprises: BAE Systems, Defence Equipment and Support, GE Aviation (formerly Smiths Aerospace), Rolls-Royce and QinetiQ. Many other UK aerospace and technology companies have acted in support. ZZ250 was formally unveiled in July 2010, although the project had started in 2007. The initial 'power-up' was carried out in late 2010 at Warton. After that the airframe and its complex ground-based systems went through a comprehensive programme of pre-first flight 'milestones'. These included unmanned pilot training, radar cross section measurements and ground station integration. In April 2013 ZZ250 started taxi trials at Warton after which it was airfreighted 'somehwere' for flight test.

The title of this chapter is very much tongue-in-cheek. Taranis Project Pilot Bob Fraser and all of his team are exceptionally experienced flight crew in every sense of the term. Bob joined BAE Systems in 2000 and spent most of his time on the ultimately cancelled Nimrod MRA.4 programme. He also flies for the BAE Systems Corporate Air Travel Team, the 'mini-airline' that connects many of the BAE sites including Farnborough and Munich, in a similar manner to Eric Bucklow, as outlined in Chapter Three. Bob's experience of UAVs has followed the company's steps to Taranis; having flown the HERTI, Mantis and the ASTRAEA Jetstream. He noted ironically in 2012 that he never had the necessary skills to be a fast-jet pilot; the 'desk job' means that he does not need physical agility, his prowess being cerebral dexterity.

When Bob was nominated as Large Aircraft and Taranis Project Pilot for BAE Systems in the summer of 2012 he explained the leap that the company – and test piloting – was about to make. "To get that perfect world of autonomy takes time. The vehicle itself is less important, it's about proving the systems. I think there has been a step change in our thinking during this past year. Everyone is recognising the importance of the complete system – not just the platform that happens to hold it all together and get it where it needs to be." Here's to the future!

Taranis in flight. © 2015 BAE Systems

CHAPTER SEVEN

Throttle Forward – Britain's Test Pilots

In the early 1970s the author's 'A' Level history teacher at Quarry Bank Comprehensive School in Liverpool taught me much, but particularly how to approach *any* piece of writing. He is among a band of people who set me on the road to scribbling about aviators, aircraft and their heritage for a living: Jim Shields, I am indebted to you. The trick is to explain *what* you intend to do and *how* you will do that. If you stick to your self-proclaimed rules, you can't go far wrong. So, here goes...

Chapter One – *What is a Test Pilot?* – defines what a manufacturer's test pilot is for the purposes of this book. Readers should refer there, but to recap: the main rationale for inclusion is at least *one* maiden flight of a type, or significant sub-variant. All known chief test pilots, whether or not they achieved a 'true' first flight, are also detailed. Several other individuals appear by virtue of other exploits or achievements. Sadly, the other criterion for an entry is to have been killed while performing an early test flight. Chapter One also outlines what *sort* of aircraft are dealt with.

Space precludes entries for *all* test pilots and production test pilots, even though their work is very important, not without risk and thoroughly deserving of study. Volume Two provides the *briefest* details. Index I gives test pilots by manufacturer and Index II lists not only types, but who 'first flighted' what as another means of cross-reference. To help keep track of changing names within the UK aircraft industry, Appendix A is a *brief* 'genealogy' of who-became-who of the main players.

The traditional line-up at the Test Pilots' Reunion at Popham, July 2011 in front of Peter Vacher's incredible Battle of Britain veteran Hurricane I R4118 (G-HUPW). The brainchild of the irrepressible Dick Richardson, Popham's manager and vigorously supported by airfield owner Susie Church, Rolls-Royce, Martin-Baker and other elements of the industry, the first reunion was held in 1996 with the curtain being wrung down for the final time in July 2013. Service test and manufacturer test pilots and other worthies are illustrated, those marked with an asterisk (*) are featured in the two volumes that make up *Testing to the Limits*.

Back row, left to right: Keith Dennison* (who had flown in and displayed the Hurricane), Bob Cole, Andy Young, Dave MacKay, Chris Huckstep, Fred Clarkson, Brian Walker, Mike Webber, 'Tommy' Thompson*, Desmond Penrose*, John Brownlow, Alastair Christie, Roger Beazley, Al McDicken*, Iain Young, Dave Southwood, Mike Hindley, Vic Lockwood, 'Johnnie' Walker*, Chris Yeo*, Peter Henley*, John Cockburn*, Tim Mason, 'Murph' Morrison, John Carrodus, Ian Conradi, Peter Sedgwick*, Peter Ginger, John Davis, 'Robbie' Robinson*, Ken Robertson, Alan Merriman, Ian Normand.

Front row, left to right: George Aird*, Duncan Simpson*, Brian Powell*, Chris Orlebar, Doug Gregory, Charles Masefield*, Mike Oliver*, David Lockspeiser*, 'Jo' Lancaster*, Eric Brown, John Farley*, Tony Blackman*, Harry Pollitt, 'Reggie' Spiers, David Bywater, Brian Wilby, John Allam*, Peter Baker*, Dave Eagles*, Graham Andrews, Roger Topp, Tom Gilmore, Clive Rustin, Don Knight*, Heinz Frick*, Jack Sherburn*, Pete Thorne, Peter George. *Photo: Ken Ellis*

Test pilots are listed alphabetically, by 'basic' name, often by nickname. Ranks, full names, decorations/honours, where applicable, are given within the narrative. (Academic or membership qualifications, eg MA, RAeS, etc are *not* given.)

Then, where applicable, a 'log' of that pilot's maiden flights with the following information: date, type (with serial/registration if applicable), number of engines, power and engine name/series. (hp – horse power, to denote piston engines, shp – shaft horse power to denote turboprops and turboshafts and lbst – pounds of static thrust to denote turbojets and turbofans, and rated *dry*, ie without reheat/afterburner.) This is presented by way of a quick guide and to prevent repetition of data within the main narrative, particularly when a lot of prototypes listed. While every effort has been made to make this 'log' comprehensive, in many cases it has

been impossible to get multi-source confirmation. Where a pilot is known to have been a chief test pilot for a particular period, unlike in some publications, no 'blanket' assumptions have been made that *all* significant maiden flights in that timeframe can be attributed to him.

This is followed by *brief* notes on their background, in italics; before a detailed examination of their career as a test pilot is examined. Pilots mentioned within the narrative that have their own section within Chapter Seven in this volume, or in Volume Two are denoted with an asterisk (*) upon *first* mention within each biography. Other than in the 'brief background' notes, abbreviations have been kept to a minimum; those frequently used are given in Appendix B.

'Dizzy' Addicott

Desmond Gerald Addicott, born 1922. Joined RAF 1942, training in Canada. Operational on DH Mosquitos in Far East, with 110 and then 84 Squadrons, up to 1946, as a Squadron Leader. Returned to UK, instructing on Mosquitos and, from 1947, on Vickers Wellington T.10s. Up to 1951 he flew Beaufighters, Spitfires and Vampires with a CAACU. In 1951 he joined Shorts as a ferry pilot. On 13th February 1951, while simulating engine failure on take-off in 762 Squadron Mosquito T.3 VT583 at St Davids, climb-out proved to be impossible and Dizzy executed a force-landing nearby. Both he and his Fleet Air Arm No.2 walked away unhurt; VT583 was written off.

Vickers test pilot 'Dizzy' Addicott flying the Vintage Aircraft and Flying Association-built Vimy replica G-AWAU at Brooklands, June 1969. *KEC*

'**D**IZZY' (a frequent nickname for a Desmond) joined Vickers in 1955, flying from Wisley, mostly for the Guided Weapons Division, but also on Valiant in-flight refuelling development. From 1961 he was with Hunting at Luton, probably seconded from BAC (both Vickers and Hunting had become part of BAC in 1960), as Senior Test Pilot, working on Jet Provosts. For the June 1965 Salon International de l'Aéronautique et de l'Espace at Le Bourget, Paris, Dizzy demonstrated the one-off Hunting 126 jet flap research test-bed XN714, ferrying it to and from its base with the Aero Flight at RAE Thurleigh. (XN714, which was first flown by Stanley Oliver*, is preserved at the RAF Museum Cosford.) Dizzy was back at Wisley during 1965 and involved in Vickers Vanguard, VC-10 and BAC One-Eleven flight testing and, from 1971, flew for company's communications flight from Filton. In his book *Empire of the Clouds*, James Hamilton-Paterson quotes a story, possibly apocryphal, that Dizzy barrel-rolled a VC-10 he was ferrying with minimal crew from North America to the UK. There were no ill-effects to the jetliner, or to Dizzy's employment!

During his time at BAC, Dizzy was deeply involved in the Vintage Aircraft and Flying Association (VAFA) which was based at Brooklands and he became its chairman. Two exacting replicas of Vickers types were built and both had their first flights in Dizzy's hands. The first was FB.5 'Gunbus' G-ATVP which was flown from Wisley on 14th June 1966; it was presented to the RAF Museum in June 1968

and is today on show at Hendon. On 1st June 1969, Dizzy piloted Vimy G-AWAU at Brooklands and five days later flew it to Le Bourget to display it at the Salon. The Vimy was badly damaged by fire at Manchester Airport on 14th July 1969 and was rebuilt to static condition and presented by VAFA to the RAF Museum in 1970; it is also displayed at Hendon.

Along with several other pilots (Les Colquhoun*, Jasper Jarvis, John Judge*, David Morgan*) Dizzy was involved in a series of wet runway braking trials for the Ministry of Supply from 1958 to 1962. Supermarine Swift F.7 XF114 was modified, including the removal of the main undercarriage doors, for the purpose at Wisley. In his excellent book *Swift Justice*, Nigel Walpole notes that in 1962: "Dizzy Addicott carried out landing trials in XF114 on London Airport's 9,300ft No.1 runway, typically landing at 200 knots just before a 3,000ft strip flooded with 6,000 gallons of water, with 'little apparent loss of speed' until reaching the dry area." This Swift still survives, held in reserve for Solent Sky at Southampton.

A long-term motorsport fanatic – on two or four wheels – Dizzy was impressed by the Swift and its 'ground-hugging' abilities. He formulated a scheme to turn a Swift fuselage into the basis of a world land speed record 'car', using a 'tweaked' RR Avon RA7R turbojet and a pair of Bristol Siddeley BS605 rocket motors – the latter mounted on stub 'wings' attached to

Swift F.7 XF114 at Cranfield at the end of the wet runway braking trials. The main undercarriage fairings were removed and the pilot could over-ride the anti-skid gear. The markings on the spine were to aid camera calibration. *KEC*

the rear fuselage to carry the main wheels of the tricycle layout. Dizzy acquired Swift FR.5 WK277 as surplus from 2 School of Technical Training at Cosford for £225 (£4,500 in present-day values) and took it to Wisley for the transformation to be carried out. It was moved to Somerset, but eventually had to be sold. Today, WK277 graces the Newark air Museum in pristine condition.

During his time at BAC, Dizzy also carved a niche as a seasoned pair of hands when demanding film flying was required. Among his credits in front of the lens were: *The Blue*

Max (released 1966, featuring World War One replicas), *The Dirty Dozen* (1967, Junkers Ju 52) and *Mosquito Squadron* (1968, Mosquito TT.35s). After leaving BAC in 1979 he became a well-known performer at airshows and was also at the helm of many of the types operated by aviation film specialists Aces High, including piloting the company's NAA B-25 Mitchell camera-ship N1042B in 1989 for many of the sequences of the remake of *Memphis Belle*. Dizzy stopped flying in 1998 but remained a staunch supporter of motorsport; he died in December 2005.

George Aird in the cockpit of missile trials Sea Vixen FAW.1 XJ476 at Hatfield in October 1964. *Hawker Siddeley Dynamics*

George Aird

George Peter Aird, born 1928. RAF from 1947; operational on DH Vampire FB.5s with 3 and 188 Squadrons in West Germany and from 1951 with 111 Squadron re-equipping with Gloster Meteor F.8s, then Hawker Hunter F.4s and F.6s. George was 'A' Flight Commander on 'Triple-One' and a founder-member of the famous 'Black Arrows' aerobatic team; he was awarded an AFC for his service with 111. Ended his time in the RAF with 229 OCU up to 1959. He flew as a civilian pilot with 3 CAACU on Vampires before moving in 1960 to the Shorts Ferry Unit at Rochester.

GEORGE AIRD started his varied test flying career on 2nd January 1961 with de Havilland at Hatfield. The Propeller Division, established in 1946, had expanded into missiles and operated an extensive trials fleet. (In 1965 the division was renamed Hawker Siddeley Dynamics and, in 1977, it became BAe Dynamics Group.) An early tasking for George was icing trials using a cut-down Bristol Britannia propeller mounted on the port inner Bristol Hercules of the HP Hastings prototype TE580.

DH Comet 1XB XM823 and Short SC.9 XH132, the latter a much-modified EE Canberra PR.9, were used as test-beds for infra-red guidance systems. De Havilland had developed the Firestreak heat-seeking air-to-air missile as the principal armament for the EE Lightning and its own Sea Vixen and was working intensively on its replacement, the all-aspect Red Top. A Meteor NF.12, a Hunter F.6, several Canberras and DH Sea Vixens were also used in missile trials; all of these types were flown by George.

Having mastered the four-engined, 'tail-dragging' Hastings, George was despatched to Warton to pick up a development batch (DB) Lightning F.1 and bring it to Hatfield for missile trials. His first solo on type came on 1st March 1961 and five days later he ferried this machine, XG325, to Hatfield. At least four DB Lightnings (XG313, XG325, XG329 and XG332) operated out of Hatfield on Red Top trials. George claimed that he had launched more Red Tops than any other pilot. He never had a target in sight – that was somebody else's remit.

It is the Lightning that George is most remembered for. In 1962 he was the central point of interest – though

George Aird bringing Lightning F.1 XG325 alongside Comet 1XB XM823 after an infra-red signature trial. *KEC*

unrecognisable – in an amazing photograph. Jim Meade was taking images of the Lightning test fleet and was out in the fields surrounding Hatfield, when George ejected from XG332 at very low level. Jim's fast reactions captured the moment as George was blasted from the cockpit, as the Lightning adopted a near vertical plunge. Jim managed to frame the drama with a farmer on his tractor, looking backwards in horror as he realised what the commotion was behind him.

On the day of the spectacular accident George was air testing XG332 following an engine change. On 13th September 1962, he blasted off from Runway 06 and headed for the south coast for a reheat test up to Mach 1.7 at 36,000ft. (Contrary to at least two other sources, this was *not* Friday the 13th; it was a Thursday.) On the return leg, George intentionally shut down the 'new' engine and it took three attempts to re-light it, but all seemed well once it was eventually up and running again. George was not to know that unvented fuel from the re-lights had pooled via a crack in the jet pipe and had ignited. Suddenly what George called the "Attention Getter" panel warned him of a fire; he checked his instruments, the state of the airframe and his position. He elected to return to Hatfield. He could have jettisoned the belly tank, but was worried that it might hit someone below.

With XG332 seemingly responding as normal, he made a long approach back to base. On short finals to 06, 150ft up and at 175 knots, the fire took its toll of the controls. As the nose reared up, George instinctively slammed the stick forward to counter, but it was no longer connected to the elevators. Up went his hand, down came the handle and blind over his face and the Martin-Baker seat shot him out of the cockpit. The parachute only had moments to fully deploy before George crashed through the roof of a huge glasshouse on the southern boundary of the airfield; he broke both legs in the impact, but was very much alive. It was some time before he was back in the 'office'. Lightning XG332 impacted 50 yards away, in clear ground. It was less than three years old and had 'clocked' about 139 flight hours. This was not the first 'visit' to the greenhouses – see under David Lockspeiser for an 'arrival' the year before.

(Of the aircraft mentioned above, several still survive. The Comet is intact at the RAF Museum Cosford; the cockpit of the Short SC.9 is in private hands in Italy; the cockpit of Sea Vixen XJ476 at the Boscombe Down Aircraft Collection, Old Sarum, and the cockpit of Lightning XG325 is with a private owner near Thetford.)

Jim Meade's sensational image of the moment when George Aird 'banged out' of Lightning XG332 on finals for Hatfield, 13 September 1962. *Jim Meade via Hugh Trevor*

Typical of a test pilot's lot, George also took part in production and development testing of the last Comet 4s to come off the Hatfield line – the final one, for United Arab Airlines flew in February 1964 – and HS Tridents. Additionally, he was often at the helm of the factory communications aircraft: DH Doves and a Heron. In 1967, George was promoted, becoming Chief Military Test Pilot, for Hatfield and the HSA plant at Hawarden.

In 1970 George moved from Hatfield to Hawarden, where the plant was heavily involved in building the world-beating HS.125 executive jet. During George's time at Hawarden, the factory was producing the turbofan Series 700 and working on its replacement, the HS.125-800, which appeared in May 1983. Based at Hawarden was the HSA-owned DH Mosquito T.3 RR299 (G-ASKH) which was flown at airshows and company open days. George made his first solo in it on 5th July 1979. In 1981 George was promoted to CTP at Hawarden; retiring from the role two years later. He went on to fly commercially, retiring from airline flying in 1993.

Left: Aerial view of the crash site of XG332 at Hatfield with the threshold of 06 in the middle. The impact point is just in front of the long run of greenhouses. The point where George crashed through the greenhouses is circled. *de Havilland Aircraft*

Below: Alcock and Brown departing Lester's Field, Newfoundland, at the start of their epic transatlantic flight 14th June 1919. *Rolls-Royce*

John 'Jack' Alcock

John William Alcock, born in Manchester, 1892 – 'Jack' to his friends. Worked as a motor mechanic in Manchester and became fascinated by aviation. Met up with the French pilot Maurice Du Crocq and in 1912 became his mechanic at Brooklands. Du Crocq taught him to fly, Jack gaining Aviators' Certificate No.368 on a Farman on 26th November 1912. He became an instructor with the Avro school at Shoreham and, on 28th May 1913, Jack accompanied 'Freddy' Raynham* when he first flew the Avro 503 floatplane from the nearby River Adur. In 1913 he worked with Frenchman Louis Coatalen developing aero engines for Sunbeam, including the V-8 150hp used on Farmans. Took part in the London to Manchester air race 20th June 1914 in a Sunbeam-powered Farman; he came 3rd at 45mph.

John joined the RNAS in 1914 and, as a Sub Lt, instructed at Eastchurch. By 1917 he was flying Sopwith Camels and Triplanes with 2 Wing at Mudros on the Isle of Lemnos on the Aegean Sea. He was awarded a DFC for a single-handed combat against three Ottoman aircraft. Jack combined airframe components from Camels, Pups and Triplanes to produce the so-called 'Sopwith Mouse' (also known as the Alcock Scout or A.1), powered by a 110hp Clerget. On 30th September 1917 Lt Jack Alcock captained HP O/100 3124, crewed by Sub Lts S J Wise and H Aird on a raid to railway yards near Constantinople. (See John Babington for more on the O/100.) Damaged by anti-aircraft fire, an engine was shut down and they limped back, force-landing in Sulva Bay. They swam ashore and became prisoners of war. While incarcerated, Jack received word that his 'Scout' had flown from Mudros – nothing more is known of this creation.

B Y the spring of 1919 Jack had returned to Britain and was taken on by Vickers at Brooklands, where his experience of large aircraft was recognised and he was appointed chief pilot. That year the *Daily Mail* offered £10,000 for the first direct flight across the Atlantic – that's about £550,000 in present-day spending values.) Vickers realised that the Vimy was ideal to have a crack at this, with Jack as pilot and Arthur Whitten Brown as navigator and pilot's assistant. The 13th Vimy off the Brooklands line was given extra fuel tanks and test flown on 18th April 1919. It was shipped to Newfoundland, Canada, arriving on 26th May. Assembled by a company team at Quidi Vidi, north of St John's, and test flown on 9th June, it settled on Lester's Field, the point of departure for the epic venture. Taking off on 14th June, the pair struggled against the elements over a distance of 1,890 miles for 15 hours 57 minutes, achieving an average speed of 118.5mph, coming to rest at Clifden, County Galway, Ireland. Both Jack and Arthur were knighted for their exploits.

In late 1919 the prototype Viking I, G-EAOV, general purpose amphibian was first flown at Brooklands, perhaps by Jack. Along with Alcock and Brown, Vickers company director Douglas Vickers mp handed over the Vimy to the Science Museum on 15th December 1919. Three days later Sir John William Alcock KBE DSC died, aged 27. On December 18th he was ferrying G-EAOV solo to the Paris Aero Show. Near Rouen he encountered fog and force-landed, he was killed when the stricken aircraft hit a tree and he fractured his skull. He was succeeded at Vickers by Stan Cockerell*.

F Alexander

Apr 1918	Westland Wagtail C4291
	1 x 170hp ABC Wasp

ROYAL Flying Corps officer Captain F Alexander was attached or seconded to Westland during the testing of the Wagtail, the company's second single-seat fighter. Three Wasp-engined Wagtails were built in 1918. Alexander flew the first in April 1918 at Yeovil, soliciting the following from Harald Penrose in *British Aviation – The Great War and Armistice*: "it had been looped on its initial flight, so pleasant were the flying qualities and so rash the pilot". Alexander requested a greatly enlarged cut out in the upper wing centre section and wanted more rudder area. A fire at the factory and problems with the Wasp engine, delayed testing of the Wagtail at AEE, Martlesham Heath. Despite plenty of promise, the Wasp was problematical and the engine was cancelled in late 1918. Two more Wagtails, this time AS Lynx-powered, followed in 1920. By November 1918 Stuart Keep* had become Westland CTP and nothing more is known of Alexander.

John Allam

20 Feb 1959	HP Victor B.2 XH668
	4 x 17,250lbst RR Conway Co.11
18 Aug 1967	HP Jetstream 1 G-ATXH
	2 x 690shp Turboméca Astazou 12
21 Nov 1968	HP Jetstream 3M G-AWBR
	2 x 895shp Garrett TPE-331

John W Allam, born 1924. RAF training at Oklahoma, USA, in 1943. By 1945 he was instructing at Windrush and Little Rissington. He later served with Transport Command, including a detachment flying a VIP Douglas Dakota in Pakistan. He spent two years flying with A&AEE Boscombe Down, including a spell assigned to Vickers at Wisley, flying Boeing Washington B.1s on guided weapons trials. (Three Washingtons, WW349, WW353 and WW354, were used from May 1952 to July 1955 – see also Colin Allen.) He undertook courses at ETPS and the US Navy Test Pilot's School at Patuxent River, Maryland, USA, before ending his 11-year RAF career in 1954 as a Flt Lt.

JOHN ALLAM joined Handley Page at Radlett in August 1954. The company was coming to terms with the loss of the prototype Victor, WB771, which had crashed on 14th July, killing all four of the crew (see 'Taffy' Ecclestone). The second prototype, WB775, took to the air on 11th September and 20 days later John flew it for the first time as pilot-in-command. John had been recruited to carry out the bulk of the flying, leaving CTP Hedley Hazelden* free to concentrate on the Herald airliner. John went on to pilot more examples of the Victor than any other HP 'staffer'.

John was the helm for the debut of the first production Victor, B.1 XA917, on 30th January 1956. The following year,

Very likely Victor B.1 XA930 being rolled at height prior to its appearance at the 1958 Farnborough airshow. *KEC*

he and XA917 hit the headlines. On a routine sortie testing longitudinal stability the aircraft entered a shallow dive and over a wide area the signature double boom of the 'sound barrier' being broken was heard. One of those on the receiving end in Watford was Charles F Joy, who took great personal interest in the disturbance around him: he was the head of the Victor's airframe and systems design team. HP put out a press release the following week, keen to make the most of its supersonic V-bomber and score more than a few points over its rival, Avro. John was quoted as having had his attention diverted momentarily at above 40,000ft when he noticed the Machmeter had reached the magic '1' with a true airspeed of about 675mph. He said that it: "behaved in its customary stable manner". XA917 was the largest aircraft at the time to have gone supersonic and much was made of FTO Paul Langston, seated in the navigator's position, as the first man to travel at Mach one *backwards*! John and 'Spud' Murphy* demonstrated the eighth production Victor, B.1 XA930, at the 1958 Farnborough airshow, 1st-8th September. The pair had been perfecting rolls off the top to highlight the big aircraft's manouevrability.

The Victor programme entered a new era on 20th February 1959 when John took the prototype B.2, XH668, for a 50-minute first flight from Radlett. John ferried XH668 to A&AEE, Boscombe Down, on 17th August and that evening he conducted a conversion sortie with Sqn Ldr R J Moran. Earlier in the month A&AEE pilots had carried out training at Radlett. On 20th August XH668 took off from Boscombe and was never seen again. The V-bomber dived into the sea off Pembrokeshire and the wreckage was not discovered for six months; a massive salvage exercise eventually brought a large proportion of the airframe to the surface for examination. All on board were killed: Sqn Ldr R J Moran (captain), Sqn Ldr G

Publicity image of the prototype Victor B.2 XH668 released on 21st February 1959, the day after John Allam took it into the air for the first time. Initially, it flew without serial numbers on the fuselage or under the wing. *Handley Page*

B Stockman (pilot), Flt Lt N Williams (navigator), Flt Lt R J Hanniford (air electronics officer) all from A&AEE; and Bob H Williams, HP Chief Flight Test Engineer. The sortie was due to take XH668 to around 52,000ft and the crew were to carry out high-speed turns to investigate buffeting. The official report, published by the RAE in 1961, claimed that the starboard pitot tube had shattered leading to excessive speed developing and loss of control. At Radlett, this was not greeted at all well. No 'Mayday' call was received, all of the crew were inside when XH668 hit the Irish Sea, the RR Conway turbofans were at full power on impact and the airbrakes had not been deployed. Crew incapacitation was an oft-cited theory.

Suddenly, the Victor B.2 programme had a huge cloud hanging over it. XH670 was put aside for an intensive investigation programme from August 1960 to February 1961 at RAE Thurleigh, near Bedford, and Radlett carried out by John Allam, Peter Baker* and Harry Rayner. Thinking at RAE was that each flight should be duplicated by John and Peter and that they should present separate reports, with Harry co-piloting each time to provide some consistency. RAE decreed that the initial sorties should have an escort. HP declared that *another* Victor was ideal, but that was unacceptable as it was clear that RAE considered that would be putting two of the V-bombers at grave risk. Don Middleton described in his superb *Tests of Character* the crazy outcome: "Ultimately the Gloster Javelin was chosen. This aircraft would only reach 48,000ft. As the trials would be carried out in periods of 2½ hours, the Javelin's endurance was quite inadequate so a ludicrous situation developed with *three* [author's italics] Javelins in relays staggering along at 48,000ft – up to 50,000ft when light on fuel – whilst the Victor carried out its manoeuvres about a mile above them with no possibility of any useful observations being made." Not surprisingly, the Javelin 'circus' was soon cancelled. John, Peter and Harry went on to prove what was already well known at Radlett – that the Victor was not at fault.

John was in command of B.2 XH673 on 5th December 1960 with Bomber Command's Liaison Officer, Sqn Ldr R N Bates, in the right-hand seat and HP FTOs Ray A Funnell, J P Quinn and J Rudeforth at the 'bench'. Up at 50,00ft the bomb bay doors seized half-way open and it was clear there was a problem with the hydraulics. John elected for the long runway at RAE Thurleigh, but a radio fault prevented him from raising air traffic there. En route to Radlett, a prudent test of the

undercarriage revealed that even the emergency system was not operating. His next destination was Waddington where a foam 'carpet' was laid on the runway. John performed a textbook tail-down, gear up, landing with no injuries. Patched up, XH673 was ferried back to Radlett for repair and was issued to A&AEE late the following year.

Another example of John's life with the Victor is supplied by XH672, which had preceded the errant XH673 down the Radlett production line. Piloted by Peter Baker, XH672 had its first flight on 6th April 1960. In March through to May 1964, XH672 was used to prove the autoland system that the RAF wished to use across the Victor fleet; John and former Royal Aircraft Establishment autoland trials pilot, Alf Camp, carried out an intensive trial, each completing just over 100 landings in about a dozen sorties. All of this activity was to no avail, as the requirement for autoland was cancelled before 1964 was out. In *Tests of Character*, Don Middleton notes that John had explained to him that the Victor's behaviour when on approach almost made autoland pointless: "regardless of the wind, the Victor was capable of making precisely the same firm landing every time at exactly the same point on the runway!" After its autoland trials, XH672 was pulled back inside the factory for conversion to strategic reconnaissance B(SR).2, also known as SR.2, status. It was flown in this guise by John on 10th July 1965.

As noted above, John Allam was appointed as a test pilot by HP to allow CTP Hedley Hazelden to concentrate on the Herald airliner. Nevertheless, John did a lot of development and production flying and demonstrations on Heralds, and was at the controls of G-AODF when it made its first flight in Series 200 guise on 8th April 1961. An important demonstration took place in December 1959 in Herald 100 G-APWA when John let King Hussein of Jordan take control. The Royal Jordanian Air Force went on to order a pair of Series 200s, delivered in January and July 1963.

As HP had refused to become part of either the BAC or HSA combines, it was clear that beyond a contract to convert Victor Mk.2s into K.2 tankers little, if any, work would be forthcoming from the Ministry of Defence. Turning fully to the civilian market, the HP.137 Jetstream twin-turbine feederliner and executive transport was developed. John became CTP in 1965 and in his hands the prototype Jetstream 1 G-ATXH had its maiden flight from Radlett on 18th August 1967. Also on board for the 100-minute sortie were Harry Rayner and FTE

The prototype Jetstream 1, G-ATXH, complete with nose-mounted pitot tube. *Handley Page*

John Coller. The company was rolling all of the dice with the Jetstream and certification delays plus the first examples being over projected weight all strained the finances. Almost out of the blue, HP won the USAF's CX requirement for a light transport, ambulance and general duties aircraft, securing an initial order for 11, designated C-10A. This variant would have the American TPE-331 turboprop plus structural changes and a freight door. Series 3M G-AWBR served as the prototype C-10A and it first flew on 21st November 1968, already way behind the delivery schedule anticipated by the USAF.

Overstretched, Handley Page Ltd went into liquidation on 8th August 1969, to be re-launched nine days later as Handley Page Aircraft Ltd, dramatically slimmed-down to concentrate on building Jetstreams. The USAF cancelled the C-10A programme in October 1969 and on 27th February 1970 one of the most famous names in the British aircraft industry threw in the towel. Terravia Trading Services acquired the rights to the HP.137 and was renamed Jetstream Aircraft Ltd (JAL) as hopes rose that the RAF would acquire the type as a multi-engine trainer. Along with several other key members of HP staff, John Allam joined the new concern and was involved with the test flying from a facility set up at Sywell and demonstrations from Leavesden. In 1972, Scottish Aviation acquired the rights to the design from JAL and production moved to Prestwick. With this, the test piloting days of Flt Lt J W Allam OBE came to an end.

Several aircraft that John test flew are still extant. The cockpits of Victors XA917 and XH670 are with private owners in Scotland and Essex, respectively. Victor XH673 that John brought down for a belly landing at Waddington guards the parade ground at Marham. The South Yorkshire Aircraft Museum at Doncaster is custodian of the cockpit of Jetstream G-ATXH.

As mentioned above, converting Victor Mk.2s to tankers had been devised by HP, but with the collapse in 1970 the contract was eventually taken on by Hawker Siddeley. On 20th March 1974 XH672 touched down at Woodford, to await its turn for transformation and on 14th April 1978 Charles Masefield* carried out a test flight, XH672 being the final example in the programme. Taken on charge by 57 Squadron at Marham on 24th May 1978, it commenced the busy, long-ranging life of a tanker. As a veteran of the black buck raids on the Falklands and the highest-sortie granby Victor tanker during the First Gulf War, XH672 had been requested by the RAF Museum. The runway at Cosford was too 'tight' for a Victor and XH672 was flown to nearby Shawbury on 30th November 1993, making the last-ever flight by the crescent-winged wonder. Four crew members and a passenger climbed down; the latter was John Allam, then President of the Handley Page Association, who had got to know it 33 years before. Dismantled, XH672 made the journey to Cosford early in the New Year for installation in the Cold War hall.

Colin Allen

Colin Allen, born 1924. Joined RAF in 1943, last operational service with 540 Squadron at Benson on DH Mosquito PR.34s. Left RAF 1947 and flew for Central African Airways and then BEA. He enlisted with 604 (County of Middlesex) Squadron RAuxAF flying DH Vampire F.3s from North Weald.

IN 1952 Colin joined Vickers, production testing Valiants and Viscounts from Brooklands and Wisley; additionally he carried out crew-training for Viscount customers. In his autobiography (with Sally Edmondson) Brian Trubshaw describes "a very expensive taxying accident" that befell Colin at Wisley. Discovering a brake problem on a Valiant he was about to test, he returned to the apron but on the downward-sloping taxi track realised the brakes had failed. According to Trubshaw the: "left wing tip clipped the noses of both the B-29 Washington bombers that were used for guided weapons trials, breaking them off like carrots, before embedding his aircraft in the back of another Valiant which was sticking out of the hangar." This most likely relates to 29th July 1955 when Boeing Washington B.1 WW349 was written off in a collision on the ground with a Valiant at Wisley. Vickers had used two others, WW353 and WW354, but only in 1952. The other Washington noted by Trubshaw has not been identified.)

After this, Colin worked for Decca in a ground-based role but was recruited by Jimmy Harrison* to carry out production test with Avro at Woodford in 1960. Colin flew Vulcans, but his airline and crew-training experience made him ideal for that role with the HS.748 programme. Colin made the first delivery of a HS.748 to a customer, departing Woodford in Series 1/105 LZ-PIZ on 18th January 1962 destined for Aerolineas Argentinas. By 1968 Colin had joined the Air Accident Investigation Branch, later going on to fly Douglas DC-8 freighters based in Africa. He returned for a further stint with the AAIB; retiring in the mid-1980s; he died in 2006.

The Jetstream 41 prototype at Prestwick, 1991. *British Aerospace*

Tim Allen

| 25 Sep 1991 | BAe Jetstream 41 G-GCJL |
| | 2 x 1500shp Garrett TPE331-14 |

Timothy N Allen, born 1945. RAF scholarship in 1962, civil pilot's licence at 17, joining RAF as post-graduate in 1966 on fast jets and trainers. No.39 Course ETPS Boscombe Down in 1980 followed by service with A&AEE, including trials and acceptance flying on modifications to Falklands campaign aircraft. Successfully ejected from ETPS SEPECAT Jaguar T.2 XX915 on sortie out of Boscombe Down 17th January 1984. Turbine blade failure in No.1 engine led to engine shut down, followed by engine fire. He left the RAF in 1986, as a Squadron Leader.

TIM ALLEN joined the Regional Aircraft Division of British Aerospace at Prestwick in 1986 as a test pilot, under CTP Len Houston* working mostly on Jetstream 31 twin turboprops. During 1987 he was responsible for certification flying of the Jetstream 32 development. From 1991 Tim became project test pilot for the Jetstream 41 – a dramatic redesign and stretch of the original airframe, accommodating 29 passengers. Tim was at the controls of the prototype, G-CCJL, on 25th September 1991. Tim retired in 1996 going on to a career that included development of simulators and consultancy in the operation of twin turboprops, especially the late-series Jetstreams. By 2012 Tim had flown 71 different types and had accrued over 10,000 flying hours.

Basil Arkell

| 7 Dec 1947 | Fairey Gyrodyne G-AIKF |
| | 1 x 520hp Alvis Leonides |

Basil Henry Arkell, born 1918. Initial RAF service within Coastal Command, followed by Cierva Rota I autogiros with 529 Squadron at Crazies Farm, Henley-on-Thames, on radar calibration duties, as Sqn Ldr. The unit also operated Sikorsky Hoverfly I helicopters from the spring of 1945 until it disbanded in October 1945.

Rare image of Basil Arkell testing Gyrodyne G-AIKF in December 1947 – note the absence of vertical tail surfaces and access door. *KEC*

FAIREY embarked upon a programme to become a leading rotorcraft manufacturer in June 1945. Basil Arkell's rotary wing experience was snapped up. He joined as a test pilot in January 1946 and the Gyrodyne project was made public three months later. 'Gyrodyne' was derived from the somewhat pendulous 'gyratory aerodyne', but is better labelled by a later term, compound helicopter. The Gyrodyne could take off and land vertically, by spinning up the main rotor. In forward flight the rotor free-wheeled, supplying lift while a tractor propeller, mounted on the end of the starboard stub wing provided propulsion and countered the rotor's torque while the wings also took some of the load. It was hoped to make the Gyrodyne tail-less, but early in testing fixed fins and twin rudders were fitted to increase control inputs during autorotative (rotor free-wheeling) flight.

With its single Alvis Leonides radial connected via gearboxes and clutches, Basil carried out extensive ground running of the prototype Gyrodyne (G-AIKF, also allocated the military serial VX591) at White Waltham – a total of 85 hours of engine running and 56 hours of rotor testing, including 'hops' and tethered flying. After a static-only appearance at the SBAC airshow at Radlett in September 1947, Basil carried out the first unrestrained sortie on 7th December 1947. In the spring of 1948, Basil took the second Gyrodyne, G-AJJP, into the air. As experience and confidence grew, it was decided to have a go at the 3-kilometre closed circuit world air speed record. With Basil at the controls, *Kilo-Fox* achieved 124.3mph on 28th June 1948, creating a national and world record. Basil displayed G-AIKF at the SBAC

Part of the static at the 1948 SBAC airshow, the first to be held at Farnborough. Left to right: unflown Cierva Air Horse G-ALCV; second Gyroplane G-AJJP; Bristol 171 VW905. *KEC*

display at Farnborough in September 1948, while G-AJJP was also shown in the static. Basil took part in testing/evaluation of the Cierva Air Horse in early 1949 – see Alan Marsh. On 17th April 1949 Gyrodyne G-AIKF crashed, killing Foster Dixon*, and the programme was terminated. The second machine was radically re-engineered as the Jet Gyrodyne – see John Dennis – but it was not until 1954 that testing began. By early 1950 Basil had left Fairey, going on to fly a wide variety of helicopters, and writing on the subject in magazines; he died in October 2009.

'Joe' Arnold

Joseph Frederick Arnold, born 1910. Served as a civilian flying instructor pre-1939 before joining the RAF and continuing to instruct. Later he served on the transatlantic 'shuttle' service with Transport Command. From 1945 to 1948 he was Chief Flying Instructor for the Luton Flying Club and the associated Hunting Flying Club.

LUTON-BASED Percival Aircraft (Hunting-Percival from 1954) recruited 'Joe' Arnold, from the Luton Flying Club in 1948 and he was involved in Prince/Pembroke, Prentice and Provost testing. On 17th June 1955 he set off from Luton in Provost T.53 378 which destined for the Iraq Air Force. Flying with him was Iraqi Major Mahdi Salih. The Provost crashed locally, killing both occupants; it was said to have failed to recover from a loop. At the time 45-year-old Joe had around 5,600 hours in his logbook.

Saro 'Shrimp' G-AFZS moored on the Clyde at MAEE Helensburgh in March 1941. *Peter Green Collection*

Leslie Ash

Oct 1939	Saro A.37 G-AFZS 4 x 95hp Pobjoy Niagara III
2 May 1940	Supermarine Walrus II X1045 1 x 775hp Bristol Pegasus VI

Apprentice with Sunbeam Motors before joining the RFC going on to fly Sopwith Pups and ending up with Camel-equipped 70 Squadron, RAF. Upon 'de-mob' Sqn Ldr Ash re-joined Sunbeam, becoming a 'rep' for the company in India. By 1924 he was running his own motor business on the Isle of Wight.

IN *Test Pilots*, Don Middleton describes the job at Cowes-based S E Saunders (Saunders-Roe – Saro – from 1928) as a "part-time occupation" as production was sporadic. Leslie Ash is believed to have met founder 'Sam' Saunders during World War One and struck up a friendship. The two 're-discovered' one another on the Isle of Wight in the 1920s and Sam offered Leslie a job as a test pilot under Stuart Scott*. Running his own business, Leslie was not impressed by the payment offered and so he came to an arrangement that boosted his income. He took up a post in the drawing office and carried out flight tests when needed, for an additional fee. He started as a draughtsman, working on the Medina flying-boat, which took to the air in 1926.

Leslie's first flying work is recorded as testing the A.10 single-seat fighter in 1929. He was helping Stuart Scott on sea trials with the prototype London flying-boat, K3560, in 1934. By 1936 Stuart Scott had resigned and Leslie took over full-time. His absence of experience in command of flying-boats explains why In November 1937 he was looking over the shoulder of Frank Courtney* for the maiden flight of the first Lerwick, L7248 from Cowes. Specification R5/39 sought a replacement for the Sunderland, but was quickly jettisoned when it was realised that the magnificent patrol flying-boat had plenty of 'life' left in it. Meanwhile, Saro had launched its S.38 project and embarked upon the build of a half-scale prototype, the A.37, nicknamed the 'Shrimp'. Although its original purpose had gone, Saro completed the A.37 and, civilian registered as G-AFZS (later TK580), it was first flown by Leslie in October 1939. It was issued to the MAEE at Helensburgh in 1941 and later used for development work on the Short-Saro Shetland; it was scrapped in 1949.

With the failure of the Lerwick, Saro spent most of the war building for others, including taking on the bulk of Walrus amphibian production for Supermarine. Saro's Beaumaris, Wales, design office came up with a wooden-hulled Walrus, the Mk.II, in order to minimise the use of strategic materials. Leslie took this version, X1045 a conversion of a Supermarine-built Mk.I, on its first flight in May 1940. Supermarine's George Pickering* assessing it shortly afterwards.

Godfrey Auty

14 Apr 1962	Bristol Type 188 XF923
	2 x 10,000lbst DH Gyron Junior DGJ.10R
1 May 1964	BAC 221 WG774
	1 x 10,150lbst RR Avon RA.28R

Godfrey L Auty, born 1921. Joined the RAF 1940, training in Canada. Operational flying: Mosquito VIs with 21 Squadron and later in the India-Burma theatre with Douglas Dakotas of 62 Squadron and ferry duties after VJ-Day. From 1946 he was a ferry pilot and then as test pilot for 6 MU, Brize Norton.

Godfrey Auty is mostly associated with the problematical 'stainless steel' Type 188 – the only indigenous Bristol turbojet design from Filton to take to the air. Godfrey joined Bill Pegg* and team at Filton in April 1951. He cut his teeth on production test on Type 170 Freighters and Brigands.

In February 1952 Bristol completed the restoration to flying condition of F.2B Fighter D8096 (G-AEPH) ready for presentation to the Shuttleworth Collection at Old Warden, where it is still airworthy. Godfrey flew this machine, possibly on its maiden excursion. He was in command of another classic, this time certainly for its inaugural post-restoration outing, Bulldog IIA 'K2227' (G-ABBB) at Filton on 23rd June 1961 and also for the Shuttleworth Collection. This biplane fighter is today on show at the RAF Museum Hendon.

In July 1957 Bill Pegg retired and 'Bill' Gibb* became CTP with Godfrey as his deputy. On 1st November 1957 Godfrey set off delivering Britannia 302 G-ANCB to Aeronaves de Mexico, starting a three-month crew-training detachment with the airline. The second example, G-ANCC, was flown out commencing on 15th December 1957. Flying with the Mexican airline included route-proving to New York and other US destinations and, during a spell of training at Brownsville, Texas, Godfrey had a close call. All at Bristol were still recovering from the fatal crash of Britannia 301 G-ANCA on 6th November 1957, killing all 15 on board, including test pilot Hugh Statham*. It was established that an electrical fault caused the autopilot to runaway and *Charlie-Alpha* entered a deepening turn, crashing on the approach to Filton. While at Brownsville, Godfrey experienced a similar situation, from which he recovered by disengaging the autopilot.

Bristol also built aero engines for its own products and other manufacturers. From 1959 Bristol and Armstrong Siddeley merged to form Bristol Siddeley Engines with production of powerplants centralising at Filton. The aero

engine organisation had its own flight test department, but occasionally 'borrowed' personnel from the aircraft division. This was particularly so when a new airframe-engine combination was being trialled. This was the case on 3rd July 1958 when Godfrey piloted Canadair-built Sabre F.4 XB982 fitted with an Orpheus 801 turbojet in readiness for the aircraft to serve as a test-bed for the Orpheus 12 the following year. After initial flights, XB982 was handed over to Tom Frost, the engine division's CTP. (See also Chapter Four.)

Godfrey took the helm as CTP in 1960. *Flight* for 7th September 1961 described him as: "A 40-year-old Yorkshireman with a serious expression but a winning smile when it comes." Prior to this, XF923, the first of two Type 188s (another was delivered to RAF Farnborough for static testing) was rolled out at Filton on 26th April 1961. Specification ER.143T had been issued for a research aircraft capable of sustaining speeds beyond Mach 2 to investigate the effects of kinetic heating. Bristol was awarded the contract in February 1953 and design of this very challenging project took the rest of the decade. After many alternatives were ruled out, two DH Gyron Junior DGJ.10R turbojets, capable of 14,000lb st in reheat, were chosen. Special construction techniques had to be developed to create the futuristic-looking Type 188. Among these was a process called 'puddle' (or argon arc) welding to cope with the thin FV.520 stainless steel that the airframe was mostly covered in.

Godfrey embarked upon an intensive spell of flying other types that would increase his experience. This including travelling to the USA to sample the Lockheed F-104 Starfighter at Edwards in California and the Convair F-102 Delta Dagger at Wright-Patterson, Ohio. At RAE Thurleigh, Godfrey flew Avro 707A WZ736 and Fairey FD.2 WG777. As will be seen later, Godfrey was to fly both FD.2s, albeit the other in considerably modified state. At Warton, he flew the Lightning and at Hatfield Javelin FAW.1 XA552 fitted with a reheated Gyron Junior.

Roll-out of XF923 in April 1961 was followed by engine runs and taxying trials but problems with the intakes and the afterburners meant that it remained flightless for the remainder of the year. With a Hunter in the air as chase-plane, Godfrey finally flew XF923 on 14th April 1962 on a 30-minute run down to Boscombe Down where much of the testing was to be carried out. The twin-jet boasted powered flying controls and a pioneering telemetry system; the latter allowing a safety pilot to monitor the health of the aircraft from the ground, greatly lowering the heavy test pilot workload. In the climb-out from Filton a hydraulic problem meant that the undercarriage lowered again after Godfrey selected retraction. A radio snag also caused anxiety, but a safe landing was made at Boscombe. Godfrey displayed XF923 at the SBAC airshow at Farnborough in September and it returned to Filton from Boscombe Down on 15th November 1962.

Godfrey took the second machine, XF926, on its first flight on 29th April 1963 and it reached Mach 1.88 on one sortie. By that time the programme was already regarded as abortive and it was abandoned in January 1964. Engine surge problems dogged the Type 188 from its earliest days and prevented the hallowed Mach 2 from ever being achieved. Fuel consumption was far greater than anticipated and this gave the Type 188 very

Godfrey Auty alongside the starboard intake of the aircraft he is most associated with, the Bristol Type 188. *Bristol*

Released in late June 1962, the first air-to-air of Bristol Type 188 XF923. The pod under the tail on the port rear fuselage holds a parachute for spin recovery. *Bristol*

BAC 221 WG774 at the Farnborough airshow, September 1964. *Roy Bonser*

little endurance – sorties of around 30 minutes were the norm. For a type intended to fly at high speed for sustained periods, these two flaws doomed the enterprise. Only two other pilots flew XF923, Bristol's Ian Williamson* and Paul Millett*, then with the RAE's Aero Flight. Ian Williamson carried out the final flight of XF926 on 11th January 1964, bringing its total flying time to a dismal 26 hours 11 minutes. The whole Type 188 programme had amassed around 40 flying hours in 78 flights. XF923 is today on show at the RAF Museum Cosford.

On 5th September 1959 world air speed-breaking Fairey FD.2 WG774 that had been flown by Peter Twiss* arrived at Filton. Under the Bristol design number 221, it was to be dramatically re-engineered to become a high-speed test-bed for the ogival wing for the BAC/Sud Concorde supersonic transport project. It was not until December 1963 that the aircraft, designated BAC 221, was rolled out. The first flight was made by Godfrey from Filton on 1st May 1964. After this it was flown intensively on development work for Concorde, until it was handed over to the Aero Flight at RAE Bedford on 20th May 1966. Today, the BAC 221 is on show in the 'Leading Edge' exhibition at the Fleet Air Arm Museum at Yeovilton.

Godfrey retired as CTP in 1967 and took the post of Flying Services Manager, running Filton airfield, the communications fleet and other tasks. He left this post in February 1972 and took up a new career selling and developing agricultural machinery. Godfrey Auty died in October 2001.

John Babington

18 Dec 1915	HP O/100 1455
	2 x 250hp RR Eagle II
Sep 1917	HP O/400 3138
	2 x 320hp RR Eagle IV

John Tremayne Babington, born 1891. Joined the Royal Navy 1908. As a Lt, gained Aviators' Certificate No.408 21st January 1913 at the Naval School, Eastchurch, on a 'Short'. With the formation of the RNAS, 1st July 1914, Babington was one of the founder personnel, acting as a Flight Commander under Captain Murray F Sueter. Babington was one of three Avro 504A pilots who bombed the Zeppelin sheds at Friedrichshafen, on 21st November 1914.

IN December 1914 the RNAS embraced what would later be known as strategic bombing and Handley Page responded by building the O/100. Murray Sueter famously said what was wanted was a "bloody paralyser" of an aircraft. With a span of 100ft, wing area of 1,648 sq ft and a maximum weight of around 14,000lb the O/100 was then the UK's largest-ever aircraft. When completed at the Cricklewood factory, the O/100, serial number 1455, was moved by road to Hendon for its first flight. The first O/100 had a fully-glazed, armoured, cockpit at the extreme nose; the engines were equally protected by armour plate and featured very bulky radiators. On 17th December 1915, Lt Cdr John Babington took the helm, with Lt Cdr E W Stedman acting as co-pilot, achieving what was described as a "short straight". In his book *Handley Page Aircraft since 1907* C H Barnes superbly sums up the occasion: "there stood at Hendon, ready to fly, an aeroplane whose span was not much less than the total distance covered by Orville Wright's first flight at Kitty Hawk, twelve years earlier to the day". The pair made a more sustained flight the following day. After modifications, both men took 1455 for another test.

Later the O/100 had the cumbersome, and fragile, glazed cockpit replaced by an elongated nose with side-by-side seating in the open for the pilots. From August 1916 John was the commanding officer of what was simply called the 'Handley Page Squadron' RNAS based at Luxeuil-les-Bains. On the night of 16th-17th March 1917 Babington piloted O/100 serial number 1460 and successfully bombed a railway junction at Metz, France, making the type's operational debut and Britain's first use of a 'heavy'. A total of 46 O/100s were built. From its first outing, the O/100 needed more power and the answer was designated O/400. Babington and Stedman were at the controls when 3138, built as an O/100 but acting as the prototype O/400, first flew at Martlesham Heath in September 1917.

It is possible that Babington joined the staff of Handley Page in 1919, but In January 1920 he took a commission in the RAF, going on to be station commander at Gosport in 1927, Commandant of 1 School of Technical Training at Halton in 1934, among other posts. During World War Two he was Air Officer Commanding Technical Training Command and Head of Mission to the USSR. He retired from the RAF in 1944. Air Marshal John Tremayne Babington KCB CBE DSO died in 1979.

Robert Bager

| 2 Dec 1919 | HP W.8 G-EAPJ |
| | 2 x 450hp Napier IB |

ROBERT BAGER was an early recruit of Handley Page Transport (HPT), the airline established by Frederick Handley Page in June 1919 to capitalise on his parent company's experience in large aircraft and its stock of surplus bombers. In late 1919 the prototype W.8, an airliner combining the best elements of the O/400 and V/1500 bombers coupled with plush cabin fittings, was ready to test. (This machine had been through a painful gestation, including the resignation of HPT's chief pilot, Sholto Douglas – see his entry.) Geoffrey T R Hill* was HP's aerodynamicist *and* test pilot, but was recovering from influenza – a deadly strain of which had become a worrying pandemic. With the Paris Aero Show looming, 20-year-old Robert Bager stepped into the breach and carried out the 20-minute maiden flight of G-EAPJ on 2nd December at Cricklewood. HPT operated a regular service from Hounslow to Le Bourget, Paris, using converted O/400s and the W.8 was intended both as a replacement for these modified bombers and to attract orders from other airlines. Two days after the first flight, Robert took G-EAPJ to Le Bourget in just 110 minutes, *overtaking* the

scheduled HPT O/400 in the process! Geoffrey Hill took over the testing in March 1920.

Robert Bager returned to his duties with HPT. On 14th December 1920 he took off from Cricklewood in O/11 G-EAMA, a transport version of the O/400, with six others on board, bound for Paris. The big biplane hit a tree and crashed into a garden in Childs' Hill, south of Hendon. Bager, engineer J H Williams and two passengers were killed. Three passengers extricated themselves, while Eric Studd caused a press sensation. A search of the burnt out hulk failed to locate him. He was discovered the next day in Paris! He had been in the extreme nose and had been thrown clear in the crash. Concussed, he appears to have been aware that he should go to Paris and got their via the Dover boat-train.

Henry 'Bill' Bailey

28 Dec 1938	Blackburn Botha L6104
	2 x 880hp Bristol Perseus X
May 1940	Blackburn B.20 V8914
	2 x 1,720hp RR Vulture X

Served during World War One as wireless operator on board Submarine Scout 'Zero' type patrol airships. Post-war studied to become a civil engineer, then joined the RAF, becoming a flying instructor and leaving as a Flt Lt.

FLT LT HENRY 'BILL' BAILEY took a post with the Blackburn-owned North Sea Aerial and General Transport at Brough in 1932. Since May 1924 the organisation had been operating an RAF Reserve School for the Air Ministry. Henry instructed on a fleet that largely included Bluebird IVs and, from 1932, B.2s were also being used. In 1935 the Reserve School was renamed as 4 Elementary and Reserve Flying Training School, and in September 1939 it became 4 EFTS. Blackburn was expanding and at times Henry undertook production testing and he became ATP to Flt Lt A M Blake*. From 8-16th July 1935, Henry, along with 'Dasher' Blake, C A Ball and Flt Lt G M Morris – the latter on loan from the RAF – carried out a 100-hour 'soak' reliability and endurance test on Shark torpedo biplane K4364 with the pilots taking turns to fly, only stopping

Botha Is lined up at Brough awaiting delivery, April 1940. *Blackburn*

The ill-fated Blackburn B.20 on the slipway at Dumbarton, March 1940. *KEC*

at night. Henry demonstrated a Shark at the SBAC display at Hatfield in July 1937. With Dasher's death in October 1937, Henry was appointed CTP.

Henry was heavily involved in testing the Skua two-seat shipborne fighter/dive-bomber, taking the second prototype, K5179, into the air for the first time at Brough on 4th May 1938. Blackburn had been awarded a contract for the Botha general reconnaissance/torpedo bomber for Coastal Command and the company tooled up for production at both Brough and Dumbarton. There was to be no prototype as such, the first production example, L6104, was ready at Brough in December 1938. It was a busy month, with Henry detached to the aircraft carrier HMS *Courageous* to assist 800 Squadron with the work-up of the Skua. Because of this commitment, Henry delegated the maiden flight of the Roc shipborne turret fighter, L3057, to Flt Lt Hugh Wilson* on 23rd December. Back from Skua sea trials, Henry flew the Botha from Brough on 28th December. The under-powered Botha went on to earn a poor reputation, with a high accident rate and type was withdrawn from limited operational flying in November 1940.

In the mid-1930s Blackburn's specialist hull and float designer Major J D Rennie came up with a method of avoiding the inherent drag from the deep hulls that monoplane flying-boats required. This was to place the engines as far away from water spray as possible. This format was fine in transport types, such as the pioneering Short C-Class 'boats for Imperial Airways, the first of which appeared in July 1936, as cabin volume was an essential requirement. For a military type, such deep hulls would reduce speed and range. Rennie came up with a retractable hull that provided the 'height' and allowed the aircraft to have the correct wing incidence for take-off and landing and a dramatically reduced cross-section once fully airborne. Rennie also included retractable wing tip floats to further clean-up the airflow. The B.20 flying-boat was pitched at Specification R1/36, which was won by the very conventional Saunders-Roe Lerwick. The ingenious retractable hull was too good an opportunity to pass up and the Air Ministry ordered a B.20 for evaluation by MAEE. V8914 was built at the

Dumbarton plant on the Clyde and Henry carried out the inaugural flight in March or early April 1940. The B.20 was moved westwards up the Clyde to MAEE at Helensburgh where Henry continued testing. During a high-speed trial, with the hull retracted, on 7th April Henry encountered severe vibration and he ordered the crew to bale out. Rolls-Royce FTO Ivan Waller successfully took to the silk, but Blackburn FTO Fred Weeks is thought to have drowned; Henry Bailey was killed as V8914 came down off the Isle of Bute. Some sources quote that two Blackburn riggers were also on board and did not survive.

'Johnny' Baker

| 2-9-55 | Avro Shackleton MR.3 WR970 |
| | 4 x 2,450hp RR Griffon 57A |

John D Baker, born 1924. Joined the RAF in 1941, going on to fly Douglas Bostons and North American Mitchells operationally with 2nd Tactical Air Force. Served with A&AEE and MAEE.

'JOHNNY' BAKER joined Avro in 1948, working on production test on Athenas and Tudor VIIIs. On 17th July 1949 he test flew the last RAF variant of the Anson, T.22 VM306 at Woodford. This was the first of a batch of 33 radio trainers, based upon the post-war C.19. By 1949 Johnny was also involved in development and test flying, backing up CTP 'Jimmy' Orrell*. At the 1949 SBAC display at Farnborough, he made a memorable debut demonstrating the second prototype Shackleton, VW131, which had flown for the first time on 2nd September, only four days before the show started. The pilot's seats were somewhat basic, later being fully adjustable, as were the rudder pedals. Chris Ashworth described Johnny's prowess in *Avro's Maritime Heavyweight – The Shackleton*: "...demonstrating it in a masterly fashion despite being perched up on extra cushions and with wooden blocks on the rudder pedals, necessary because the seat had still to be modified, its current position causing problems for pilots of a short stature".

The prototype Shackleton MR.3, first flown by 'Johnny' Baker. On the nose it carries a Hawker Siddeley Group logo. *Avro*

For the 1953 Farnborough he demonstrated production Shackleton MR.2 WL796 with a Saro-built Uffa Fox Mk.3 air-droppable lifeboat suspended in its belly. Johnny closed his display with a fast run with just the contra-props of the starboard outer Griffon under power, the others being feathered! Johnny was at the controls for the maiden flight of the last major version of the Shackleton, the much redesigned and tricycle undercarriage equipped MR.3. WR970 flew on 2nd September 1955 from Woodford, serving as an aerodynamic prototype, lacking the type's complex detection and weapons systems. In 1958 Johnny took a post at Woomera, South Australia, with Avro's advanced weapons division which was developing the Blue Steel nuclear stand-off weapon. Johnny retired from Avro a decade later and settled in Australia; he died there in 2009.

Peter Baker

Peter P Baker born 1925; joined RAF in 1943. Flew Short Sunderlands 1946 to 1949 with 201, 209 and 230 Squadrons, followed by CFS. In 1953 was on No.12 Course at ETPS Farnborough and went on to join A&AEE 1954 to 1956 flying Vickers Valiants, among others. He was a tutor at ETPS from 1957 to 1959 when he retired from the RAF, as Sqn Ldr Peter P Baker AFC.

PETER BAKER joined Handley Page as a production test pilot in mid-1959 his flying including trials following the loss of Victor B.2 prototype XH668 on 20th August 1959 – see under John Allam*. Peter moved to BAC at Wisley under Jock Bryce* in 1964; working on VC-10s before becoming One-Eleven project pilot. With the tragic loss of the prototype G-ASHG and its crew, including Mike Lithgow*, on 22nd October 1963 Brian Trubshaw* and Peter were engaged on deep stalls with the fifth One-Eleven, Series 201AC G-ASJD, destined for British United Airways. (Brian had flown with Peter on Valiants during their time at A&AEE.) *Juliet-Delta* was the first example to be fitted with a fully-powered elevator and a modified wing leading edge;

Peter Baker with a DH Venom. *KEC*

One-Eleven G-ASJD down on Salisbury Plain, 28th August 1964. Visible above the vehicle near the tail is the housing for the anti-spin parachute. *Vickers-Armstrongs*

60

both brought about by the experience of the prototype. While captaining G-ASJD on 28th August 1964, with T S 'Staff' Harris as co-pilot, Peter had to carry out a forced-landing on Salisbury Plain, north of Boscombe Down, following a control issue. This was the second force-landing in the type that 'Staff' Harris had been through. He had been at the controls of the third machine, Series 201AC G-ASJB, when it suffered a very heavy landing at Wisley on 18th March 1964. Despite hopes to rebuild *Juliet-Bravo*, it was scrapped.

The accident that befell *Juliet-Delta* could have been a mortal blow to the One-Eleven programme, but quickly it became apparent that there was nothing wrong with G-ASJD. During the test, the stall-recovery parachute mounted on the tail was deployed in the belief that a stable stall condition had developed. The jetliner continued to lose speed, resulting in the forced-landing. Investigation revealed that this was not the case and had the parachute been jettisoned, recovery was very likely. (Unlike G-ASJB, *Juliet-Delta* was recovered and rebuilt, ending its days with the Blind Landing Experimental Unit as XX105; it was scrapped in 2011.)

Peter continued with One-Elevens before joining the BAC/Sud Concorde test team, spending extensive time in the simulator at Toulouse, France, and then at the Fairford flight test centre. In his latter days with BAe (as BAC became in 1977) Peter took part in ferrying former British Airways, East African Airways and Gulf Air VC-10s to Filton for the RAF tanker conversion programme. After 19 years with BAC/BAe, Peter left in 1983 taking up a post as test pilot with the Civil Aviation Authority, becoming its CTP in due course. In 1987 he left the CAA, initially as a freelance airline pilot before establishing an aviation consultancy in 1989.

Valentine Baker

Apr 1935	Martin-Baker MB.1 G-ADCS 1 x 160hp Napier Javelin IIIA
6 Feb 1937	Hafner AR.III Mk.2 G-ADMV 1 x 90hp Pobjoy Niagara
3 Aug 1938	Martin-Baker MB.2 M-B-1 1 x 1020hp Napier Dagger III
3 Aug 1942	Martin-Baker MB.3 R2492 1 x 2,020hp Napier Sabre II

Valentine 'Val' (also known as 'Laddie') Henry Baker, born 1888. Enlisted in the Royal Navy 1914, initially as a dispatch rider. Severely wounded on the Gallipoli beachhead, Dardanelles, 1915 – a bullet lodged near his spinal cord – it was decided not to remove it, leaving Val with pain throughout his life. Discharged, he joined the Army, transferring to the RFC and flying 'ops' with 41 Squadron. Post-war he worked for Vickers as a sales representative and instructor, travelling to the Dutch East Indies and, in 1927, to Chile, overseeing delivery and instruction on Type 121 Wibault Scouts. He became an instructor at the Lancashire Aero Club, Barton, then the London Aeroplane Club at Stag Lane and, in 1929, chief pilot for Airwork at Heston.

Built under contract by Martin-Baker for Raoul Hafner's AR.III Construction Company, Val Baker carried out flight tests of the AR.III gyroplane G-ADMV in 1937. *KEC*

VAL BAKER befriended James Martin at Heston and he became a partner in the nascent Martin-Baker Aircraft (MBA) in 1934. The company's website sets the scene: "It was during the designing and the testing of the MB.1, in 1934, that a new figure became associated with the small team at Denham – a man who was to be for the company in the air what James Martin was at the drawing board and the workshop. This was Captain Valentine Henry Baker MC DFC, a well-known flying instructor who Martin had met a couple of years previously. Over the next eight years, a deep and lasting friendship was to develop between these two men, who were in some ways very similar, in others very different, but each with a great respect for the other's considerable skill and ability."

MBA built a two-seat tourer, the MB.1 G-ADCS, of advanced tubular steel construction with many other innovative features. Val tested the MB.1 at Denham in April 1935; it did not go into production. Austrian-born rotorcraft pioneer Raoul Hafner contracted MBA to build his first UK-based design, the single-seat AR.III gyroplane, G-ADMV and Val carried out the first flight, at Denham, in 1937. Hafner went on to create radical designs for AFEE before setting up the helicopter division of Bristol in 1944, resulting in the Sycamore of 1947 – see Alan Marsh.

The MB.2 prototype, P9594, in its May 1939 configuration. Note the extended crash pylon in the rear of the cockpit. *Martin-Baker*

Design features of the MB.1 were put to good use in the MB.2, a simple, single-seat fighter with eight 0.303in machine-guns, pitched as a private venture at Specification F5/34. The MB.2 featured fixed, spatted undercarriage, minimalistic rudder, ease of access to the gun bays in the wing and a retractable crash pylon in the rear of the cockpit to protect the pilot in the event of a roll-over. Wearing the B Condition (or 'trade plate') markings M-B-1, the MB.2 was taken to Harwell, because Denham was too 'tight' for the 1,020hp fighter. Val took it for its maiden flight on 3rd August 1938. In *Ominous Skies*, Harald Penrose wrote that the MB.2 was: "brilliantly demonstrated by Val Baker at Heston on 26th May [1939] during which he dived at 400mph from 10,000ft finishing his pull-out at 150ft above the ground." Evaluation at A&AEE brought criticism of the type's stability and its tail surfaces were enlarged and it re-entered test in May 1939, becoming P9594.

Convinced he could better Sydney Camm's Hurricane, James Martin had Specification F18/39 written around his very advanced MB.3 single-seater with retractable undercarriage and a formidable array of six 20mm cannon in May 1939. With many demands being made of MBA's design capability, work on the MB.3 was protracted and only the first of three prototypes (R2492) was completed. Trials took place at Wing, with Val carrying out the inaugural flight exactly four years after the MB.2. The first two sorties were cut short, due to overheating of the 2,020hp Napier Sabre. In his superb *British Experimental Combat Aircraft of World War Two* Tony Buttler notes that, as testing continued, Baker said that the MB.3 "had excellent flight characteristics, it was easy to fly and highly manoeuvrable, and it handled perfectly with good directional stability." On the tenth flight, 12th September 1942, the engine seized on take-off and Val had seconds to conduct a forced-landing from about 100ft.

Valentine Baker ground-running the impressive-looking MB.3 R2492.
Martin-Baker

Seeing a farmhouse directly ahead, he turned to port to avoid it, R2492 cartwheeled and Captain Valentine Henry Baker MC DFC was killed. His death was a devastating blow to James Martin, who had lost a great friend and a partner in his small company. Work on the MB.4 was not concluded and MBA's last aircraft was the exceptional MB.5 fighter – see under Bryan Greensted. The trauma of Val's death lead James Martin to turn to the development of escape and safety systems and Martin-Baker became world-renowned for its ejection seats. Chapter Four features Bernard Lynch, MBA's 'bang seat' guinea pig.

Peter Barlow

Peter Barlow joined the Royal Navy as an engineering apprentice 1942, attended the RN Engineering College 1946-1948, followed by a posting as an aero engineer on the carrier HMS Victorious. *Transferred to the Fleet Air Arm 1949 and flew operationally on Hawker Sea Fury FB.11s with 804 Squadron from the carriers* Glory *and* Theseus *during the Korean War 1951-1952. Suffered engine trouble north of the bomb line 2nd May 1951 in FB.11 VX610 and force landed, being rescued by helicopter. On No.12 Course, ETPS Farnborough in 1953 and joined A&AEE 1954-1957. RN Volunteer Reserve with 1831 Squadron at Stretton, 1954-1955. Flew Sea Vixen trials on secondment to DH at Hatfield, 1957.*

L**T** C**DR** P**ETER** B**ARLOW** DSC joined de Havilland as a test pilot in 1958 initially on Sea Vixens, including flight refuelling trials on FAW.1s, in late 1959. He also was a PTP on Comets and later HS Tridents (DH became a part of HSA in 1963). At 16:52 hours on 3rd June 1966 at Hatfield Series 1C G-ARPY, the 26th Trident destined for British European Airways, took off from Hatfield on its maiden flight, captained by Peter. His crew comprised former Airspeed test pilot George

Errington*, as co-pilot, flight engineer Edgar 'Brax' Brackstone-Brown and navigator Charles Patterson. Among the tests were stalls in a variety of configurations. With the gear and flaps down, three trials in landing guise – with the centre of gravity well aft – were carried out. During these the stick-shaker and stick-pusher stall warners were employed. For the fourth stall, these devices were switched off to allow the crew to determine the true speeds between stall onset and at its greatest development. This was executed at 11,600ft. At 18:34 a member of the crew calmly announced "We are in a superstall at the moment", it was the last transmission from *Papa-Yankee*. The Trident had dropped a wing and entered a flat spin to starboard; 90 seconds later it impacted in open country near Felthorpe, Norfolk, killing all on board. The Air Accident Investigation Branch report, published in November 1968, noted that Peter had carried out 2,195 stall tests in Tridents, 750 of them as pilot-in-command. The report concluded that decisive recovery action had been delayed too long.

Imperial Airways Argosy I G-EBLF *City of Glasgow* on the apron at Croydon Airport. This was the prototype and first flown by Captain Frank Barnard. *KEC*

Frank Barnard

16 Mar 1926	AW Argosy I G-EBLF
	3 x 385hp AS Jaguar III

Flt Lt Franklyn Leslie Barnard AFC flew with the RAF during World War One. In late 1919 he was retained by shipping magnate Sir Samuel Instone to fly his company's modified DH.4A G-EAMU. By 1920 Barnard was with 24 Squadron from Kenley on 'comms' duties. Left the RAF by 1921, becoming Commodore of the Instone Air Line. He also flew for de Havilland, including pioneering crop-dusting trials in a DH.6 (perhaps G-EAWD) in Kent during 1922. He piloted Instone's G-EAMU in the first-ever King's Cup air race, staged out of Croydon in September 1922, and was the winner, at 123.6mph. Imperial Airways was formed in April 1924 and Barnard became its chief pilot. In July 1925 he was again the winner of the King's Cup at Croydon, flying AW Siskin V G-EBLQ at 151.43mph. From 4th January to 8th March 1926, Barnard and Lt Col F F Minchin (an Imperial captain) flew the Bristol Bloodhound prototype G-EBGG on an engine reliability test for Imperial Airways in between Filton and Croydon. The Bristol Jupiter V engine was sealed to prove it was not tampered with during 226 hours and 25,074 miles.

Nine days after the Bristol Jupiter engine reliability test was completed, Captain Frank Barnard was at Whitley Abbey in the dual capacity of test pilot and representative of the client for a new 20-seat airliner built by Armstrong Whitworth. Imperial Airways had ordered three Argosy I biplanes, later adding another three Mk.IIs in 1928. On 16th March 1926 Frank was at the controls of G-EBLF *City of Glasgow* and flew it several more times in the coming days. He also carried out the maiden flight of the second example, G-EBLO. (In his book, *Armstrong Whitworth Aircraft since 1913,* Oliver Tapper cautions that the 16th is *believed* to have been the date of the Argosy's inaugural flight.) In *British Aviation – The Adventuring Years*, Harald Penrose notes that on the first flight of G-EBLF one of the Jaguar

engines failed after a few minutes. Despite this "Barnard seemed enthusiastic" wrote Harald, who then put the Imperial Airways captain in his place: "...but he was not a test pilot".

During preparations for the 1927 King's Cup, Frank was flying Bristol Badminton G-EBMK, from Winterbourne, near Filton, on 28th July. On the last of three test flights on the 28th, the 510hp Jupiter VI radial failed and the biplane stalled and crashed from 80ft, killing Captain Frank L Barnard AFC.

Harold Barnwell

Early 1913	Vickers EFB.1
	1 x 80hp Wolseley
Sep 1913	Martin-Handasyde Monoplane
	1 x 120hp Austro-Daimler
Oct 1913	Vickers EFB.2
	1 x 100hp Gnome
1914	Vickers EFB.3
	1 x 100hp Gnome
Aug 1914	Vickers EFB.5
	1 x 100hp Gnome
Early 1915	Barnwell Bullet
	1 x 100hp Gnome
Aug 1915	Vickers ES.1
	1 x 100hp Gnome
Aug 1915	Vickers EFB.7
	2 x 100hp Gnome
1915	Vickers FB.16
	1 x 150hp Hart
Nov 1915	Vickers EFB.8
	2 x 100hp Gnome
Jan 1916	Vickers FB.9
	1 x 100hp Gnome
Jun 1916	Vickers FB.12
	1 x 80hp Le Rhône

Jun 1916	Vickers FB.14
	1 x 160hp Beardmore
1916	Vickers FB.11
	1 x 250hp Eagle I
1917	Vickers FB.24
	2 x 150hp Hispano-Suiza
Aug 1917	Vickers FB.26
	1 x 200hp Hispano-Suiza

Notes: To quote Jack Bruce in *The Aeroplanes of the Royal Flying Corps*, "precise details of the line of development of the Vickers gun-carrying biplanes remain disappointingly few and obscure". All of the above took place at Joyce Green, Dartford, except for the Martin-Handasyde and the EFB.2 and EFB.3, which used Brooklands. But, *some* of those noted as having their debut from Joyce Green, *may* have used other flying fields. The chronological sequencing is equally open to debate!

Richard Harold Barnwell, born 1879. Brother to Frank Sowter Barnwell, born 1880. The brothers designed and built a biplane glider and then a small pusher biplane, powered by a 7hp engine, both were tested by Harold and the latter failed to fly. By 1909 they were running the Grampian Motor and Engineering Company in Stirling. In that year they built their third design, a canard biplane with a modified 40hp Hunter Tourist Trophy motorcar engine driving a pair of pusher propellers. With Harold at the helm, this flew on 10th September 1909 a distance of 80 yards, but was damaged in the landing. Their fourth machine appeared in 1911, a single-seat monoplane with an in-house 40hp Grampian two-cylinder engine. In January 1911 Harold was awarded £50 for the first flight by a member of the Scottish Aeronautical Society. On 3rd September 1912, Harold was granted Aviators' Certificate 278 in a 'Bristol' at Brooklands.

Frank Barnwell took up the post of Experimental Designer with Bristol in 1911. Among his masterpieces were the F.2B Fighter, the Bulldog and the Blenheim. Frank F Barnwell OBE AFC was killed at Whitchurch on 2nd August 1938 while testing a single-seat lightplane, Barnwell BSW.1 G-AFID, designed and built by him.

By 1913 Harold Barnwell was instructing at the Vickers School at Brooklands on Vickers monoplanes and company-modified Henri Farman biplanes, known as Vickers 'Boxkites'. One of his pupils was John Lankester Parker*. Another was Noel Pemberton Billing, who went on to found Supermarine. After 25 minutes dual on a 'Boxkite', Harold let 'PB' go solo. Famously, Pemberton Billing managed to get his Aviators' Certificate (No.632, dated 17th September 1913) *before* he took breakfast on the *first* day he had ever flown! Harold took part in the 2nd Aerial Derby at Hendon in September 1913, he came second flying a Martin-Handasyde monoplane at 72mph. He competed again in the 1914 event, but did not finish, flying a Sopwith Tabloid. Harold was involved in testing another Martin-Handasyde the following year.

According to Harald Penrose (*British Aviation – The Pioneer Years*), he was also testing new types for the company. Sharing the tuition load, and *possibly* some test flying, was the founder of the Aviation Department of Vickers, Herbert F Wood*. Vickers closed the Brooklands school in August 1914 and Harold was appointed CTP for Vickers Ltd (Aviation Department), succeeding Leslie Macdonald*.

A 'family' of single and two-seat pusher biplanes, fitted with a machine-gun in the front of the 'bathtub'-like fuselage was developed by Vickers, with the generic nickname 'Gunbus'. The first was the EFB.1 (Experimental Fighting Biplane No.1), known as 'Destroyer', which appeared in early 1913 and crashed on its maiden flight at Joyce Green – not far from the Vickers factory at Crayford. Penrose notes that Harold was testing the second of these, the EFB.2, in October 1913. The two-seat FB.5 and FB.9 (dropping the 'E' suffix as they entered production) were the most well-known, the former being most associated with the name 'Gunbus', while the latter was known within Vickers as the 'Streamline Gunbus'.

In early 1915 Harold tested a single-seat scout biplane that he had designed and built himself, known as the Barnwell Bullet. This suffered an accident on its first flight test, or early on. The company recognised its potential and requested drawing office apprentice Rex Pierson (later to be chief designer and to manage the company through World War Two) to redesign the fighter. Rex already knew Harold and it is very likely he'd given him tuition at the Vickers School; Rex got his 'flying ticket' – No.660 – there in October 1913. This was reborn as the ES.1 – Experimental Scout No.1. By November 1915 Pierson's ES.1 was being tested by Harold and on the 6th he looped it repeatedly over Hendon, presumably to rattle the domestic opposition! With a 110hp Clerget and designated ES.1 Mk.II (some sources quote ES.2) the Bullet was conducting trials with Vickers-developed interrupter gear for the forward-firing machine-gun. A further developed Scout entered production as the FB.19.

The Bullet was not the only tractor biplane type that Harold flew – the FB.11 Zeppelin destroyer, the FB.14 general reconnaissance type and the FB.24 fighter-bomber were also tested. In August 1915 Harold was testing the EFB.7 twin-engined, two-crew heavy fighter. This machine was designed to carry a Vickers one-pounder gun in the nose.

With the FB.12 Vickers embarked on single-seat 'Gunbus' fighters. The last of these was the FB.26 Vampire. While flying

Derived from the Barnwell Bullet, Vickers FB.19 Mk.II A5234 in Palestine, early 1918. *KEC*

the prototype on 25th August 1917 Harold failed to recover from a spin at 2,000ft and was killed; he was 38. In *Vickers Aircraft since 1908*, Andrews and Morgan, record the thoughts of Harold's devoted mechanic, H J Kingsnorth, who provided an insight into a talented and capable aviator. Kingsnorth: "never recovered from the death of his hero Harold Barnwell, who terse of speech and bluff in manner, had played a great part in the early development of British aviation". He was succeeded by Chalres Gordon Bell* at Vickers.

Roland 'Bea' Beamont

13 May 1949	EE A1 (Canberra) VN799 2 x 6,000lbst RR Avon
9 Nov 1949	EE Canberra B.1 VN813 2 x 5,000lbst RR Nene
21 Apr 1950	EE Canberra B.2 VX165 2 x 6,500lbst RR Avon 101
16 Aug 1953	EE Canberra PR.7 WH773 2 x 7,500lbst Avon 109
23 Jul 1954	EE Canberra B(I).8 VX185 2 x 7,500lbst Avon 109
4 Aug 1954	EE P.1A WG760 2 x 8,100lbst AS Sapphire Sa.5
4 Apr 1957	EE P.1B XA847 2 x 11,250lbst RR Avon 210
6 May 1959	EE Lightning T.4 XL628 2 x 11,250lbst RR Avon 210
31 Mar 1962	EE Lightning F.3 XN725 2 x 13,220lbst RR Avon 301
17 Apr 1964	EE Lightning F.6 XP697 2 x 16,360lbst RR Avon 301
24 Sep 1964	BAC TSR.2 XR219 2 x 16,780lbst BS Olympus 22R

Notes: All took place at Warton apart from the B(I).8 which used Samlesbury, the P.1A and TSR.2 which used Boscombe Down and the F.6 flew from Filton.

Roland Prosper Beamont, born 1920. Widely known as 'Bea' (pronounced 'Bee') never 'Roly'. Joined RAF in January 1939, and posted to France with the Hawker Hurricane-equipped 87 Squadron in November. Flying L1963 he downed a Messerschmitt Bf 110, a Dornier Do 17 and a Junkers Ju 88 on 14th, 15th and 17th May respectively. He stayed with the unit after it regrouped from France and flew operationally during the Battle of Britain. He joined 79 Squadron at Fairwood Common, flying Hurricane IIs. In December 1941 he was 'rested' and seconded to Hawker as a PTP – see below. He joined 56 Squadron on Typhoon Is in May 1942, moving to command 609 Squadron – also on Typhoons – in October. In May 1943 he returned to Hawker at Langley for further PTP duties – see the narrative.

In March 1944, as an acting Wing Commander, Bea was at the helm of 150 Wing, with Typhoons and Tempests. With 609, Bea had become a skilled 'train-buster', with 150 Wing (3, 56 and 486 NZ Squadrons), piloting among others Hawker Tempest Vs EJ525 and JN751, both of which carried his initials 'R-P' in place of a unit code, he excelled at intercepting V-1 'doodle-bugs'. In September 1944 the Wing was re-established as 122 Wing (3, 56, 86, 274 and 486 Squadrons), within the 2nd Tactical Air Force, operating in Belgium and then the Netherlands. The following month, Bea was destined to return to Hawker for another spell as PTP until February 1944. On 12th October 1944, Bea was flying 3 Squadron Tempest V EJ710 while attacking Rheine airfield in Germany, and was hit by flak, becoming a prisoner of war. His camp was liberated by Soviet forces in May 1945. He was busy forming up a wing of Tempest IIs to go to the Far East, but the war finished before it could deploy.

Wg Cdr Beamont achieved a tally of nine aerial victories, one shared, two 'probables', four damaged, one destroyed on the ground, an incredible 26 V-1s downed and five more shared. He took up the post of CO, Air Fighting Development Squadron, part of the Central Fighter Establishment, at Wittering. As well as a British DFC and a DSO awarded in 1941 and 1943 respectively (both later with bars), Wg Cdr Beamont was presented with a US DFC and a Belgian Croix de Guerre.

WRITING in Mike Lithgow's 1956 book *Vapour Trails*, Wg Cdr R P Beamont chose the subject 'Typhoon and Tempest' for his contribution dealing, in his delightful prose, with 'ops' on the two fighters. 'Bea' Beamont's first taste of test flying came with secondments as a PTP with Hawker. Bea arrived at Langley in December 1941 and was mostly involved with Hurricanes under CTP Philip Lucas* and Ken Seth-Smith*. Such was the pace that in one day in March 1942 Bea tested eleven separate Hurricanes. He flew two new fighter types, both aimed at Specification F18/37: Tornados P5219 powered by a RR Vulture and HG641 fitted with a Bristol Centaurus. This was his first association with an aircraft called Tornado. The other F18/37 contender was the Typhoon, a type he was to help hone for operations. His maiden 'Tiffie' sortie was in Gloster-built Mk.I R7681 on 8th March 1942. In *Fighter Test Pilot*, Bea explained his initial thoughts: "...it became clear that this big ugly fighter was actually pleasant to fly – if only the pilot could stick his fingers in his ears and could see properly out of it." Shortly after this R7681 was delivered to 609 Squadron, the unit that Bea took command of that October. The vital need for a clear-vision canopy was adopted by Hawker. Bea returned to Langley in May 1943 by which time the much-developed Tempest was under test. Working alongside Bill Humble*, Bea made his first sortie in the Napier Sabre IV-powered Tempest I prototype HM599 on 2nd June 1943. His last flight for Hawker took place at Langley on 17th February 1944 in Mk.V JN730, before returning to active service.

On 20th January 1946, Bea joined Bill Waterton* at the Gloster test airfield at Moreton Valance where he was put to work on Meteor IVs. Beamont and Waterton shared the flying to

Roland Beamont in the cockpit of an 87 Squadron Hurricane I, August 1940. *Peter Green Collection*

An exceptional portrait of 'Bea' Beamont at the helm of Canberra B.2 VX165, July 1950. *English Electric*

establish a new 'red-line' speed for the Mk.IV, using EE455 which had been fitted new nacelles and RR Derwent 5s. An intense series of dives was undertaken in March and April 1946 during which Bea established that the new controllable limit was Mach 0.79. Then came a brief spell with de Havilland as a PTP on Vampires. During this period he conducted the first of many SBAC displays, debuting with Vampire F.1 TG285 at Radlett in September 1946.

Roland took up the post of CTP for English Electric (EE) – a company without an indigenous design in production on the first day of May 1947. From April 1945 the company's Samlesbury plant was building Vampires and this continued to February 1952. This combination of mass production prowess and jets served the company well. In July 1944 EE had signed up the gifted designer William Edward Willoughby Petter, who had left Westland, bringing with him his thoughts on a jet bomber. It was this project, the A1, that tempted Bea and he spent a lot of time on the layout of its instrumentation and cockpit ergonomics. While the A1 was taking shape, Roland engaged in Vampire production testing.

At first, Bea managed to keep up flying as an RAF officer, initially with 609 (West Riding) Squadron, Royal Auxiliary Air Force, with Meteor F.4s (as they had become designated in 1948) at Yeadon, now Leeds-Bradford Airport. From 31st August 1948 to 6th November 1951, Roland was the Commanding Officer of 611 (West Lancashire) Squadron RAuxAF with Meteor F.4s and then F.8s from Woodvale, near Southport, until July 1951 when the unit relocated to Hooton Park on the Wirral.

On 6th August 1947 Bea was back at Moreton Valance, picking up Meteor F.4 EE545 to take it back to EE's newly-established flight test airfield at Warton for a series of high-altitude trials. Between August 1947 and July 1948, he made 47 sorties, some up to as high as 47,200ft. The Meteor trials had been on contract to the Ministry of Supply, but provided a wealth of experience for the forthcoming bomber. A major diversion came in May 1948 when Bea was on a Ministry-sponsored tour of US experimental facilities. This included sampling the prototype North American XP-86 Sabre swept-wing jet fighter, which had had its maiden flight the previous October. He took the XP-86 to Mach 1.01, becoming the first 'Brit' to break the so-called 'sound barrier' in a jet.

During July and August 1948, Bea started a series of in-house high-altitude trials using EE-built Vampire F.3 VT861. On 24th September he sampled the Rolls-Royce operated Avro Lancastrian test-bed VM732 alongside R T Shepherd* from Hucknall, which had an Avon RA.2 turbojet in place of each of the outer Merlins. This gave him throttle experience of the A1's powerplant. All of this was a preamble for Britain's first-ever jet bomber and EE's return to design. A1 prototype VN799 started taxiing at Warton on 8th May 1949 with Roland letting it take increasingly long 'hops' down the runway. Friday 13th provided perfect weather, but Petter was far from happy with the portents of the date; Bea would have none of it. At 10:46 he eased the vitally important prototype, call-sign *Tarnish 1*, into the air, carefully shepherded by Johnny Squier* in a DH Vampire FB.5, for a 27-minute and very successful inaugural flight. The entire envelope was cleared in just 36 sorties. Not long after this, it was revealed that the A1 was to be named Canberra. This aircraft was to alter the fortunes of much of the British industry and propel EE into the dominant military jet manufacturer.

B.1 VN813, powered by the 'insurance' RR Nenes, had its maiden flight with Bea at the controls on 9th November 1949. The prototype of the definitive 'first generation' model, B.2 VX165 followed on 21st April 1950 and Roland carried out the inaugural flight of the T.4 trainer variant, WN467 from Samlesbury on 12th June 1952. EE continued to refine the design and the next 'baseline' variants, the B.6 and PR.7, followed in 1953. Bea took the first PR.7, WH773, into the air on 16th August 1953. The bomber-interdictor B(I).8, with wing hard-points, provision for a belly-mounted weapons pack and a fighter-like canopy was first flown by Bee, from Samlesbury, on 23rd July 1954. By the early 1950s, Roland was assisted by Peter Hillwood*, while production test was led by 'Jock' Still*, supported by Johnny Squier*.

Bea was quickly discovering how agile the Canberra was and EE had great hopes for its debut at the 1949 SBAC display at Farnborough in September. He was determined to show off its fighter-like performance to the full, but management regarded this with some trepidation. On 22nd August Bea took VN799 away from Warton, up to height and thrashed out a routine of loops and rolls. He worked up a polished six-minute routine, which he talked through with Dai Ellis, Head of Flight Test, but kept his intentions quiet from the 'high ups'. On the opening day of the show, 6th September, Bea taxied out ready for his slot, but a mis-management of fuel tanks meant that the port Avon stopped, starved of fuel, while unburnt fuel hit the hot tail pipe shooting a huge billow of grey smoke aft. The jet would need an external start trolley to get it going again. A new 'slot' was permitted for the all-blue bomber – by fluke, Beamont was going to close the show. And he did this in the greatest of style presenting a jaw-dropping performance. *Flight* magazine declared that VN799 was flown: "like no aircraft has been demonstrated before, or is ever likely to be demonstrated again".

The ability to cooly assess the potential, or isolate the quirks of an aircraft and to show it off in a lively, but safe, style made Bea in demand not only for flight test, but for demonstration flying. Often he acted as an ambassador for EE, doing much to make the Canberra programme an unparalleled success story. In February 1951 Roland flew B.2 WD932 in a crucial fly-off at Andrews Air Force Base, Maryland, that could see the Canberra adopted by the US Air Force. Martin's three-jet XB-51 was the rival, but a Douglas A-26 Invader (twin-piston), North American B-45 Tornado (four-jet) and North American AJ-1 Savage (twin-piston plus single turbojet) were to be flown for comparative purposes. Ransom and Fairclough's superb *English Electric Aircraft and their Predecessors* described the contest which comprised: "one flight by each of the five types, during with the aircraft had to perform a set sequence of manoeuvres within a time limit of ten minutes. All four American types failed to complete the manoeuvres inside the time limit. However, after Beamont had taken the Canberra through the complete sequence, he found that 3½ minutes remained... Beamont then performed two extra manoeuvres, after which he landed with a minute... to spare". While its XB-51 was thoroughly outclassed, Martin was in a win-win situation, the company built the Canberra under licence as the B-57.

With Bea in command, D A Watson as navigator and R H T Rylands as radio operator, B.2 WD940 was delivered to the

English Electric's pioneers, group in front of VN799, the prototype Canberra, 1949. Left to right: F D Crowe, chief structure designer; D L Ellis, chief aerodynamicist; H C Harrison, production design; A E Ellison, assistant chief designer; W E W Petter, chief engineer; R P Beamont, chief test pilot; D B Smith, project administration; F W Page, assistant chief designer; H S Howat, Ministry of Supply technical officer. *British Aerospace via Peter Green*

USA on 31st August 1951 to act as a pattern for the Baltimore, Maryland, production run. Flying from Aldergrove to Gander, WD940 set a new point-to-point world record of 4 hours, 18 minutes at 481.12mph. Better was to come, on 26th August 1952, using B.5 prototype VX185 Bee, Peter Hillwood and D A Watson, achieved the first-ever out-and-back across the Atlantic in a day. With Roland captaining, VX185 flew Aldergrove Gander in 4 hours 33 minutes, averaging 454mph, turned around in two hours and, with Peter in command, came back in 3 hours 25 minutes at 605mph. Total time for the 4,144 miles was 10 hours, 3 minutes; average speed 412mph. (B.5 VX185 later became the prototype B(I).8 and the original – record-breaking – cockpit is preserved at the National Museum of Flight Scotland, East Fortune.)

Ransom and Fairclough provided an insight into the demands of coping with the surge of Canberra orders; five additional PTPs being taken on during the 1950s and early 1960s. "Four pilots were normally engaged in production flight test work, each making up to four flights a day. Most aircraft were cleared in about five flights, which usually totalled about four flying hours. However, sometimes ten or more flights were necessary, particularly for aircraft fitted with special equipment."

Roland Beamont at the helm of the B.2 prototype, VX185. *English Electric*

'Bea' flying the A1, VN799, captured prior to his breath-taking display at the 1949 Farnborough display. *English Electric*

As part of the preparation for EE's second product, the P.1 supersonic interceptor, Shorts was commissioned to build a slow-speed, highly-swept jet, the SB.5, flown by Tom Brooke-Smith* on 2nd December 1952. The SB.5's wings could be adjusted for sweep (but *not* in flight) and with them set at 60-degrees, Bea sampled WG768 in August 1953 and in the spring of 1954 in its definitive 'Lightning' format, with 60-deegrees of sweep and low-set tailplane. The first P.1A, WG760, was moved by road to Boscombe Down where Roland carried out an uneventful 33-minute maiden sortie on 4th August 1954. With this event, the UK industry had made a massive leap forward in capability. On its third outing on the 11th Bea took WG760 to 30,000ft and in level flight – it did not have after-burning, that was available from January 1956 – the Mach meter clocked 0.98. Analysis discovered that this was in error, Bea had reached Mach 1.02. This was the first faster-than-sound turbojet flight in controlled, level attitude. Bea took the second P.1A, WG763, into the air on 18th July 1955, this time from Warton. Both P.1As are extant: WG760 at the RAF Museum, Cosford, and WG763 at the Museum of Science and Industry, Manchester. In August 1955 the canopy blew off WG760 and insulation material within the cockpit began to disintegrate in the 575-knot maelstrom, Roland was temporarily blinded but regained control and made a safe landing. This worrying phenomenon was to occur two more times, both to Desmond de Villiers* who, along with Peter Hillwood, was sharing the load of test flying.

The programme was extensive, three P.1B interim machines and then 20 development batch Lightning F.1s took part in getting the type ready for service. In 1954 Bea was awarded the OBE and the following year became EE's Manager, Flight Operations and was elected to the board in 1960 as Special Director. Roland flew the first P.1B, XA847, on 4th April 1957 and on 25th November 1958 took it to Mach 2 (1,280mph) in level flight over the Irish Sea. This was the first UK-built machine to travel at twice the speed of sound.

(P.1B XA847 is preserved by a private owner in Suffolk.) The prototype two-seat trainer, T.4 XL628 also had its debut in Bee's hands, on 6th May 1959.

In-flight refuelling trials in the summer of 1961 involved sorties flown behind Vickers Valiant B(PR)K.1 WZ376, which was used for trials out of Wisley by Vickers and at A&AEE. Brian Trubshaw* flew WZ376 and describes, in his autobiography with Sally Edmondson, an incident in which Beamont: "set up a closing speed that was much too high, clouted the drogue which caused the hose to whip and smartly removed the end of his probe." This resulted in a typically down-played transmission from Beamont: "I seem to have lost my probe"!

In 1960 BAC was formed as the result of a forced marriage between EE, Bristol and Vickers – later taking in Hunting. 'Jock' Bryce* was appointed as CTP for BAC, with Beamont becoming his deputy. By this time, the design office at Warton was dominated by plans to replace the Canberra; this was to emerge as the TSR.2, the glittering prize promised from the merger. Even today, hackles rise when the TSR.2 is discussed. It was axed on 6th April 1965, the prototype having flown 192 days previously. The merits of the machine, or of the decision to terminate, will not be debated here. The prototype, XR219, left Warton by road and arrived at Boscombe Down on 6th March 1964 and Bea started taxying trials on 2nd September 1964. With navigator/systems operator Donald Bowen in the back seat, at 15:28 hours on 27th Bea lifted XR219 off the runway for a 13 minute, 50 second test flight. 'Jimmy' Dell*, in Lightning T.4 XM968, and John Carrodus in Canberra B.2 WD937, shadowed the prototype. In his company report, Roland wrote: "In this first flight configuration and under the conditions tested, this aircraft could be flown safely by any moderately experienced pilot qualified on Lightning or similar aircraft, and the flight development programme can therefore be said to be off to a very good start."

Bea piloted XR219 again on the last day of 1964 and another eight times. It was not until the fifth sortie, on 14th January 1965, that the undercarriage was cycled. The port main leg refused to tuck in and its twin-bogie dangled, forward wheel lowest. Bea re-cycled the gear and the starboard leg assumed the same pose. While the legs looked down-and-locked, the bogies were clearly unlocked, making landing *very* difficult, if not impossible. Bea announced that he would attempt a landing and Don Bowen declined the implied offer to 'bang out'. Roland brought the prototype down for the gentlest of 'greasers' and the bogies obligingly assumed their usual position. Bee's penultimate sortie was on 22nd February 1965 bringing XR219 to Warton, via its first transonic dash over Colwyn Bay when it reached Mach 1.12. His last TSR.2 flight came four days later.

Jimmy Dell first experienced XR219 on 15th January 1965 at Boscombe Down with the gear locked down; it was the tenth flight before the undercarriage cycling was cured. Jimmy was the last to fly the machine, on 31st March from Warton, his 12th sortie. Don Knight* was the third and final pilot to sample the TSR.2, flying it twice, on 10th February at Boscombe and on 27th March, from Warton. As well as Don Bowen, two other 'back-seaters' flew in XR219: Brian McCann and Peter Moneypenny.

The second of nine development aircraft, XR220 was built at Brooklands and taken by road to Boscombe Down on 9th September 1964. The low-loader jack-knifed on the apron and the fuselage fell off, requiring considerable attention from a working party from Warton. With repairs complete, XR220 started ground-running on 22th February 1965. The ministerial axe fell on the very day that it was planned for Bea to fly XR220. The one and only 'flyer', XR219, became a static ballistics target at the Proof and Experimental Establishment, Shoeburyness. Airframes on the production line, the jigs and all sundries including mock-ups were scrapped or burned with great haste. Two examples managed to survive the cull: XR220 at the RAF Museum, Cosford, and the fourth airframe, XR222, at the Imperial War Museum, Duxford.

In the post-TSR.2 restructuring of BAC, in November 1965 Roland became Director of Flight Operations, and deputy to CTP Brian Trubshaw. Roland 'traded in' his OBE for a CBE in 1969. Bea became heavily involved in the Anglo-French SEPECAT Jaguar programme, the first Warton-built prototype taking to the air on 18th August 1969 in the hands of Jimmy Dell. Six months prior to that, Panavia had been formed to oversee the development of the Anglo-German-Italian Multi-Role Combat Aircraft, which became the Tornado and the next major Warton project. Bea was appointed Panavia's Director of Flight Operations in 1971 and relinquished his BAC directorship to clear the decks; although his office continued to be at Warton. Paul Millett* became Manager, Flight Operations at Warton and Dave Eagles the CTP. The first Tornado flew on 14th August 1974; Bea was involved in flying and assessing both the Jaguar and Tornado.

Roland retired on 31st July 1979, but he was to keep his hand in flying for a long time beyond that. He enjoyed light aviation and for a decade was President of the Popular Flying Association. On 21st June 1969 he was at the helm of another

maiden flight, though not a first of type – Gardan Minicab G-AWEP built by BAC engineer Stan Jackson. Beyond that Bea frequently used *Echo-Papa* to commute between Samlesbury and Warton. He attended several fly-ins and rallies in G-AWEP and during 1980 and 1981 was its owner. Bea presided over the maiden flights of two other Warton-built light aircraft, both in 1979: Practavia Sprite G-BCWH built by BAC engineers Parry Parkinson and Roy Tasker on 23rd February and Procter Petrel G-BACA built by Warton apprentices on 25th May. (*Echo-Papa* and *Whisky-Hotel* are still flying, in the skies of Lincolnshire and Norfolk, respectively.) From the early 1970s, Bea piloted several of the treasures at the Shuttleworth Collection, Old Warden, including the Bristol F.2B Fighter – arguably the Canberra of its day. In the 1990s, he was to be found putting the throttle of a pair of Avons forward – but not *too* far – as the guest of the Lightning Preservation Group at Bruntingthorpe. LPG keeps F.6s XR728 and XS904 'in steam' with regular taxying days up and down the Leicestershire airfield's long runway.

A genial character and a supremely talented pilot, Bea became a gifted writer of many articles and books. His autobiography, *My Part in the Sky*, was published by Patrick Stephens in 1969 and other titles included: *English Electric Canberra* (1984), *English Electric Lightning* (1985), *Flying to the Limit*, *Fighter Test Pilot* (1986), the much sought-after *Phoenix into Ashes* (1968), *Testing Early Jets*, *Testing Years*, *Typhoon and Tempest at War* and *The Years Flew Past* (2002). Edward Lanchbury's biography *Against the Sun – The Story of Wg Cdr Roland Beamont* was published by Cassell in 1955. Wg Cdr Roland Beamont CBE OBE DSO* DFC* died on 19th November 2001, aged 81.

This is a good place to pay tribute to the work of James Longworth and all of the team at the BAE Systems Heritage Department. From 2012 to 2104, the three-volume *Test Flying in Lancashire – Military Aviation at the Leading Edge* appeared, charting with incredible depth yet great readability, the legacy of Samlesbury and Warton airfields from World War One to the present day. An inspirational series; if *all* test pilots and their exploits were chronicled in this manner, the book you have before you would never have been needed!

The first P.1A, WG760, during a strip-down inspection at Warton, 1955. *Peter Green Collection*

Flaps down, air brakes out, P.1B XA847 turning for finals at Warton, with the Ribble estuary below. *English Electric*

TRS.2 prototype XR219 on a sortie out of Warton, 1965. *British Aerospace*

'Bea' climbing on board the Shuttleworth Collection's Bristol F.2B Fighter, ready for a display at Old Warden, July 1972. *Peter Green*

Warton-built Practavia Sprite G-BCWH, first flown by 'Bea' Beamont in 1979. *Ken Ellis*

'ENGLISH ELECTRIC'
Canberra

The only jet bomber in squadron service with the Royal Air Force
Also in production for the Royal Australian Air Force and the United States Air Force

SUPER PRIORITY

POWERED BY ROLLS-ROYCE AVON ENGINES   *Designed and built by* THE ENGLISH ELECTRIC COMPANY LIMITED

Mid-1950s advert for the Canberra – with the RAF, the RAAF and USAF as customers, this was a powerful message.

'Bill' Bedford

21 Oct 1960	Hawker P.1127 XP831 1 x 11,300lbst BS Pegasus 2
7 Mar 1964	HS Kestrel FGA.1 XS688 1 x 18,000lbst BS Pegasus 5
31 Aug 1966	HS Harrier GR.1 (DB) XV276 1 x 19,000lbst BS Pegasus 6

Alfred William Bedford, born 1920. Served an electrical apprenticeship with Nottingham-based Blackburn Starling Ltd. Joined the RAF in 1940, flying Hawker Hurricanes with 605 Squadron in 1941 before transfer to India, Ceylon and Burma, with 135 Squadron on Hurricanes. Seriously injured in a road accident; hospitalised for six months. During 1944, he was serving with 65 Squadron, flying North American Mustang IIIs; awarded AFC. Final service was with CFS 1945-1949. As a Squadron Leader, he graduated from ETPS Course No.8, Farnborough 1949, staying on as an instructor before 'crossing the field' to the RAE. In both cases he taught or carried out trials on spin recovery of swept wing aircraft.

BEFORE we outline the career and achievements of the master of the spin and vertical take-off, a moment of diversion. 'Bill' Bedford was also a highly accomplished glider pilot and an authorised test pilot and instructor for the British Gliding Association. Taking off from Odiham in an EoN Olympia 2B sailplane on 24th July 1950 he achieved the British Gain of Height record, reaching 19,120ft. He wasn't finished with altitude, the following month there was more. Towed out of Farnborough by an Auster on 24th August Bill and the Olympia were released at 4,300ft. He reached 21,338ft and landed at Driffield – 193 miles away. For his final record-breaking flight, Bill turned his attention to distance. On 2nd May 1951 he and the Olympia travelled 257 miles from Farnborough to Newcastle to snatch the British distance record.

Bill joined Hawker at Dunsfold in 1951 and succeeded Neville Duke* as CTP in October 1956. He participated in a dwindling amount of Sea Hawk work and sustained Hunter development and production. Duke had flown the prototype two-seat Hunter T.7 XJ615, on 8th July 1955 and after an extensive development programme, it was decided to hit some headlines as the type had good prospects for orders. On 20th October 1956 Bill had a crack at the London to Rome Class C1/I point-to-point record, flying XJ615. He achieved this in 94 minutes with a speed of 556.1mph. Five days later he reversed the process and clinched Rome-London in 100 minutes at 533.93mph.

The Hunter that is most associated with Bill Bedford is also one that brings a sigh of admiration to most fans of Camm's exceptional swept wing fighter: the private venture two-seater G-APUX, universally known as 'Pucks'. The scarlet-and-white one off T.66A which was an amalgam of sections from a Belgian F.6, RAF F.6s and a T.7 cockpit previously used for static displays. Bill took the civil registered G-APUX into the air from Dunsfold on 12th August 1959. From his days at RAE, Bill had become *the* source of spin recovery techniques and at the 1959 and 1960 Farnborough SBAC displays he

Bill Bedford (standing, centre) with colleagues from 'A' Flight, 135 Squadron, Mingaladon, Burma, January 1942. Tropical filter-equipped Hurricane behind. *Sqn Ldr W J Story via Andy Thomas*

spellbound the audience with up to a dozen spins from height. *Uniform-Xray* attended the 1961 and 1962 events before earning its keep on loan to Iraq from 1963 with David Lockspeiser* detached on instructor duties, then Jordan and Lebanon until late 1965. 'Pucks' was refurbished as a T.72 for Chile in 1967, retiring in 1995 and is extant at the National Aviation Museum in Santiago.

The latter half of the 1950s was devoted to creating the latest Hawker project, which became the incredible V/STOL P.1127, the Kestrel 'transition' and the world-beating Harrier. Sir Sydney Camm died in March 1966, but he had spent much time on the concept of what became the P.1127. Along with his deputy, Hugh Merewether*, Bill prepared for a very demanding, and different, maiden flight. The pair learned how to fly a helicopter on a civilian Hiller 360. NASA's Ames Laboratory in California offered up its Bell X-14 twin-jet to give Bill and Hugh some experience. This open cockpit machine first took to the air in 1957, using deflectors to drive the efflux from a pair of nose-mounted turbojets either

backwards for thrust or down for lift. Hugh was first to have a go, succeeding in bending its undercarriage when he could not correct a roll due to its slow control response. Then they visited Shorts at Sydenham to try out the VTOL SC.1 XG900. Great emphasis had been placed on well harmonised, simple, manual controls on the P.1127; so the clumsy X-14 and the auto-stabilized SC.1 were not much help in 'prepping'.

The BSE Pegasus was bench run in September 1959 and the first of six private venture prototype P.1127s, XP831, was rolled out at Dunsfold in July 1960. A special gridded area was readied at Dunsfold for a careful, step-by-step, series of ground runs and tethered hovers from late 1960. Things had to be taken in a cautious manner, between them Hawker and BSE were testing a new method of flight and the first-ever vectored thrust turbofan all at once. (It was as late as 11th March 1963 before test-bed Vickers Valiant B.1 WP199 flew with a Pegasus 3 in its belly.) In the run up to the first 'hops', Bill suffered a second vehicle accident in which he was a passenger (the first was in 1944, see his introduction above). With a leg in plaster, it looked as though a delay was inevitable, but Bill convinced the P.1127 team that for tethered flying, his impaired state would not matter. With the nozzles locked into the vertical, Bill made the initial tethered hover on 21st October 1960 above the grid. This was a momentous moment, but needs further description. He managed an 'altitude' of about a foot and the 2-minute 'flight' consumed 35 gallons of fuel! Three days later, Hugh carried out a similar 'hop'. On the 19th November, the 21st test, Bill achieved a free, untethered, hover.

The P.1127 was roaded to RAE Thurleigh and on 13th March 1961 Bill carried out the type's inaugural sortie as a conventional jet. He flew it back to Dunsfold on the 25th. As the hovers increased in complexity and piloting experience grew, on 12th September 1961 in four sorties Bill and then Hugh took XP831 from a vertical take-off to a conventional landing and then from a 'normal' take-off to a vertical landing. As Hugh climbed out, completing XP831's 99th flight – the P.1127 concept was proven!

Bill Bedford made demonstrating – and spinning – Hunter T.66A G-APUX an art form: SBAC Farnborough September 1962. *Roy Bonser*

The first P.1127 hovering at Dunsfold, with Bill Bedford at the controls, November 1960. The wing-tip mounted outriggers are fitted with temporary extensions from XP831's time hovering over the special grid. The wire attached to the starboard outrigger is a radio connection. *Hawker Aircraft*

Kestrel FGA.1 prototype XS688 displaying at Farnborough, September 1964, in Tripartite Evaluation Squadron colours. Bill Bedford and Hugh Merewether shared the flying at the show. *BAe*

A 1962 brochure highlighting the P.1127 and the possibilities it offered. The rear cover declared: 'Any field ...an airfield'.

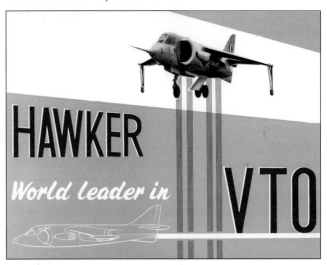

Bill flew the second P.1127, XP836, conventionally on 7th July 1961 and the pace of the programme increased. On 12th December Bill was exploring the top end of the P.1127's performance envelope and XP836 went supersonic in a swallow dive. Two days later Bill and XP836 were in trouble, the port 'cold' (front) vectored thrust nozzle fell off and he tried for a conventional, and very much emergency, landing at Yeovilton. On selecting flap at 300ft, he lost control and it rolled violently, Bill triggered the ejector seat and escaped unscathed, XP836 was destroyed.

At the September 1962 SBAC display at Farnborough XP831 and the fourth prototype, XP976, were demonstrated by Bill and Hugh. On 8th February 1963 the future was graphically illustrated when Bill flew XP831 on and off the aircraft carrier HMS *Ark Royal*. He took XP831 to Le Bourget, Paris, on 13th June to demonstrate the P.1127 at the Salon Aéronautique trade show. On the 16th the display ended in a cloud of dust and a very public accident; XP831 was badly damaged, Bill was relatively unhurt. Foreign object damage had jammed a nozzle actuating motor – another lesson learned. XP831 was rebuilt and today is displayed in the Science Museum in London.

After the six P.1127s, a batch of nine partially militarised Kestrel FGA.1s was built. The V/STOL fighter concept had galvanised the Americans, attracted the West Germans and 'sold' the RAF. Bill took the first Kestrel, XS688, into the air on 7th March 1964, by which time Hawker Aircraft had morphed into HSA. A unique organisation, the Tripartite Evaluation Squadron, was established at West Raynham in late 1964 and perfected tactics and capabilities until November 1965. Kestrels carried a complex design of roundel and fin flash, combining the national markings of the three participating nations: Germany, UK and USA. Meanwhile, the main event was under development, the fully-operational Harrier GR.1, which the design department regarded as 90% new from the pioneering P.1127. Bill carried out the maiden flight of XV276, the first of the development batch of Harrier GR.1s on the last day of August 1966.

Bill was awarded an OBE in 1961. He retired from test flying in 1967 with 6,800 hours to his credit and was succeeded by Hugh Merewether. He became HSA's sales manager from 1968 and, from 1977, a marketing manager for BAe until 1986. He set himself up as a freelance consultant, specialising in V/STOL applications and was attending special events into 1996. Alfred William 'Bill' Bedford AFC OBE died on 20th October 1996, aged 75.

Charles Gordon Bell

19 Jul 1912	Martin-Handasyde Monoplane 1 x 75hp Chenu
30 Nov 1917	Vickers FB.27 (Vimy) B9952 2 x 200hp Hispano-Suiza
Dec 1917	HP R/200 N27 1 x 200hp Hispano-Suiza

Charles Gordon Bell, born 1889. (Some sources hyphenate Gordon-Bell.) In 1910 he was flying from Brooklands, trying a powered version of the Weiss glider (see Gordon England), then a Triplane with the Roe school before moving to the Hanriot school. He qualified for Aviators' Certificate No.100 on 4th July 1911 on a Hanriot and tried out the rebuilt Humphreys 'Elephant' monoplane and a Martin-Handasyde monoplane. He became the chief demonstration pilot for the French REP (Robert Esnault-Peterie) company and moved to Buc, France. R Dallas Brett in his History of British Aviation *notes him as the: "first English pilot to be employed by a foreign manufacturer". He also instructed at Buc, one of his pupils being 'Tiny' Scholefield*. In early 1912 he was flying the REP Monoplane* Ordu *in Istanbul, Turkey and training Ottoman pilots. In spring 1912 he returned to Brooklands and flew a Blériot.*

WITH a lot of flying experience behind him Charles Gordon Bell (CGB) established himself as a freelance test pilot, becoming well known for his stammer and for the monocle he sometimes wore. He flew and instructed for Hanriot (England) Ltd in 1912 and was in demand at the Military Aeroplane Competition, held at Larkhill starting that July. There he flew a Gnôme-powered British-built Deperdussin and a similarly powered Hanriot monoplane. On the 19th at Brooklands he carried out the maiden flight of Martin-Handasyde's entrant, a monoplane fitted with a Chenu engine which proved to be particularly troublesome. After the trials, this machine was fitted with a 65hp Antoinette and finally a 120hp Austro-Daimler. On 13th June 1913 with Lt J R B Kennedy RN as a passenger, CGB was seen to 'shoot up' Brooklands and crashed, Kennedy was killed and Bell was badly injured. He was censured by the Royal Aero Club for his recklessness in this incident.

By April 1913 CGB was testing Tractor Seaplanes for the Short brothers at Eastchurch and Sydney Pickles* was recruited to take his place while he convalesced from the crash. CGB was back at Eastchurch by September 1913 and on 2nd October test flew the specially commissioned S.80 two-seater pusher biplane floatplane. By January 1914 CGB was testing Short 'Folders', predecessors of the famous Type 184 floatplane, ready for handing over to the RNAS. That July he took Type 184 No.121 to Calshot, along with a mechanic and overseen by Oswald Short, for torpedo dropping trials. With a 14in diameter 810lb torpedo slung under the fuselage, CGB took off in the late evening of the 27th and dropped it successfully into the Solent. This was the first-ever launch of a torpedo from an aircraft in the UK.

In August, 2nd Lt Gordon Bell joined the RFC and his place with Shorts was taken by Ronald Kemp*. He ferried Royal Aircraft Factory RE.1 No.608 to France for 2 Squadron,

based at Le Cateau on the 23rd. CGB flew with 10 and 41 Squadrons. With 10 Squadron, based at Chocques, he became the highest-scoring Bristol Scout pilot of the war, downing five enemy aircraft (thee LVGs and two Albatroses) between 19th September and 30th November to become an 'ace'. By the end of the year ill health had forced him to return to 'Blighty'.

With the death of Harold Barnwell* in August 1917, Vickers took CGB on as a test pilot and he took the prototype FB.27 bomber – later named the Vimy and made famous by Alcock* and Brown – for its maiden flight at Joyce Green, Dartford. In *British Aviation – The Great War and Armistice*, Harald Penrose put it this way: "The FB.27 was tested by the flamboyantly dressy and stuttering Gordon Bell on the last day of November." The following month he carried out the first flights of the initial HP R/200 two-seat naval scout biplane floatplanes, N27 and N28. This took place from the Welsh Harp, a stretch of water named after its shape and now known as the Brent Reservoir. French Motor manufacturer Darracq, based at Suresnes, had a licence from Vickers to build a version of the FB.16 biplane fighter, the FB.16E with a 275hp Lorraine-Dietrich. CGB was killed in an FB.16E at Villacoublay on 29th July 1918.

Henri Biard

Mar 1922	Supermarine Sea King II G-EBAH 1 x 300hp Hispano-Suiza
Jun 1923	Supermarine Sea Eagle G-EBFK 1 x 360hp RR Eagle IX
25 Mar 1924	Supermarine Swan N175 2 x 360hp RR Eagle IX
21 May 1924	Supermarine Scarab M-NSAA 1 x 360hp Eagle IX
11 Sep 1924	Supermarine Sparrow I G-EBJP 1 x 35hp Blackburne Thrush
10 Mar 1925	Supermarine Southampton N9896 2 x 470hp Napier Lion V
25 Aug 1925	Supermarine S.4 N197 1 x 680hp Napier Lion VII
21 Jun 1927	Supermarine Nanok 99 3 x 430hp AS Jaguar IV
9 Jan 1928	Supermarine Seamew N212 2 x 238hp AS Lynx IV
Feb 1930	Supermarine Air Yacht G-AASE 3 x 490hp AS Jaguar VI

Notes: All from the waters off Woolston apart from the Sparrow, which flew at Hamble.

Henri Charles Biard, born 1892. Started flying with Grahame-White Aviation Company on Blériots, Farmans in 1911, became an instructor. Gained Aviators' Certificate No.218 on 4th June 1912 in a Howard-Wright at Hendon. Joined RFC and served with the CFS at Upavon. By 1916 was back with the Grahame-White school, instructing. At about this time, he took the Irish playwright George Bernard Shaw for his first flight. Post-war he joined Supermarine, flying with the company's coastal resort 'joy-riding' operation and in the autumn of 1919 a service from Southampton to Le Havre was briefly operated and Henri was engaged on this venture.

In his chapter in Mike Lithgow's *Vapour Trails*, Henri Biard summed up his own progress and that of aviation in the first paragraph: "The first time I ever took an aircraft into the air was from Hendon in the autumn of 1911. The last time I flew an aircraft was again from Hendon in 1944. In the comparatively short space of those 33 years almost incredible changes had taken place in aviation. In 1911 the speed of an aeroplane was between 40 and 50mph. Machines had no airspeed indicator, oil pressure gauge, or instruments of any kind, and people taught themselves to fly often in machines they had built themselves."

British-born, Anglo-French Henri Biard is best remembered for his Schneider Trophy exploits and clinching a world speed record in the S.4, but he also developed a close relationship with Reginald Joseph Mitchell, making the maiden flight on the Swan, the designer's first multi-engined flying-boat for the company, in 1924. By 1920, Henri was the only pilot on the pay roll with the fledgling flying-boat airline run by Supermarine and the role of test pilot was a simple evolution.

Among the flying-boats that Henri took skyward for the first time, was a diminutive landplane, the Sparrow I, Mitchell's one and only foray into light aviation. Powered by a Blackburne Thrush 3-cylinder, the biplane was aimed at the Air Ministry Two-Seater Light Aeroplane Trials, to be held at Lympne in September 1924. The engine proved to be temperamental and Biard and G-EBJP were unplaced. It was rethought for the *Daily Mail*-supported 1926 competition, appearing as the Sparrow II parasol monoplane with a Bristol Cherub III. Again, the Sparrow did not fare well, Biard having to force-land near Beachy Head, where the machine was blown over.

Supermarine managing director, Hubert Scott-Paine, was resolved that the Italians would not win the sixth Schneider Trophy contest, to be staged at Naples in August 1922. At Venice in 1920, the Italians had a walk-over with the Savoia S.12 and at the same venue a year later competed against themselves in a variety of Macchi types. As laid down by armaments magnate Jacques Schneider, any country winning three times in a row, would secure the trophy in perpetuity and the competition would be at an end. As a company embarking on the production of flying-boats, success at Schneider would be a major boost for Supermarine. Joining Scott-Paine in this private venture were Napier, Shell and Wakefield Oil. Mitchell set to modifying Sea King II G-EBAH, fitting a 450hp Lion, and Henri took the 'boat into the air for the first time in July 1922 – only to have the engine fail at about 200ft, necessitating a hasty return to the

Above: R J Mitchell's first multi-engined flying-boat for Supermarine, Swan N175 was first flown by Biard in March 1924. *Supermarine Aviation Works*

Top: Passengers disembarking from Sea Eagle G-EBFK – Henri Biard carried out its first flight in June 1923. *Supermarine*

Left: Cigarette in hand, Henri Biard in front of a Farman at Hendon, circa 1917-1918 while engaged with the Grahame-White Aviation Company. *Peter Green Collection*

Blackburne Thrush-powered Sparrow I, wearing its Lympne competition number '9', 1924. *Supermarine Aviation Works*

waters of the Solent. Soon Biard was flying G-EBAH at over 150mph and he could roll and spin it; Britain had a winner on its hands. And so it was, on 12th August 1922 Henri beat off three Italian Macchis and won at 145.72mph.

As the winner, Britain was to host the next competition and this was to be staged at Cowes on the Isle of Wight, across the Solent from the Supermarine works. The 1922 winner was polished into the Sea Lion III but on 28th September 1923, Biard was outclassed by the two sleek American Curtiss CR-3 biplane floatplanes, which were around 20mph faster. The eighth race was to be staged in Chesapeake Bay, Baltimore, in October 1925 and Mitchell used the time to develop the radical S.4 floatplane. The British government backed the Gloster III and the S.4. Taking it for its first flight before it was crated and shipped to the USA, Henri was not happy about the new creation. In his autobiography, *Wings*, published in 1934 by Hurst and Blackett he wrote: "I knew there was trouble coming in that machine. It didn't feel right. Besides, the visibility from the cockpit was perfectly dreadful. The wings were right in the way." Despite this, on 13th September flying over Southampton Water, Henri clinched a world air speed record of 226.75mph in the S.4. Portents for the race offshore in Maryland were not good. Henri broke his wrist on the voyage across and then was struck by the flu. On 23rd October, Henri was seen to sideslip violently and the S.4 plummeted into the water. He was swiftly rescued, suffering a re-fracture of his wrist. One of the first on the scene was fellow test pilot Hubert Broad*. In November 1928 Vickers bought out Supermarine, although the company continued to trade in its own name, first flights became the domain of 'Mutt' Summers*. Henri Biard died on 18th January 1966, aged 74.

'Harry' Blackburn

Dec 1912	Blackburn Single-Seat Monoplane 1 x 50hp Gnome
Aug 1913	Blackburn 'Type I' Monoplane 1 x 80hp Gnome

Harry Blackburn at the helm of a Blackburn Monoplane, circa 1912. *Peter Green Collection*

Harold 'Harry' Blackburn, born 1879 – no relation of the aircraft pioneer Robert Blackburn. Gained Aviators' Certificate No.79 at the Bristol school, Brooklands, 9th May 1911 on a 'Bristol'. In September 1912 Robert Blackburn opened up a school at Hendon, with Harold as its instructor. When the school closed, Robert moved to Leeds, flying for Robert Blackburn.

OUTPUT by the Leeds-based manufacturer Robert Blackburn was sporadic and limited in 1912 and 1913, so 'Harry' Blackburn filled in his time with demonstration flying and seeking opportunities for publicity, for example delivering stocks of the *Yorkshire Post* in July 1913. With the advent of the so-called 'Type I' two-seater, which Harry first flew in August 1913, 'joy rides' became a major part of his post. With sponsorship from the *Yorkshire Evening Post*, Harry took part in a race that was dubbed 'The War of the Roses' a race between the Type I and its Lancashire rival, the prototype Avro 504. Staged on 2nd October 1913, the 100-mile course ran from Leeds to York, Doncaster, Sheffield, Barnsley and back to Leeds. Harry flew with the Type I's owner, M G Christie, while for Avro, 'Freddy' Raynham* had A V Roe's younger brother Humphrey as passenger. Avro and Blackburn were neck and neck until poor weather forced Raynham to make a precautionary landing near Barnsley. The day was Blackburn's!

The Shuttleworth Collection's Blackburn Monoplane performing at Old Warden, it was first flown by Harold Blackburn in December 1912. *Alf Jenks*

Harry was not to realise it, but his maiden flight of the one-off Single-Seat Monoplane in December 1912 was to have major significance much later on. In 1937 Richard Ormonde Shuttleworth acquired the dilapidated remains of this machine in 1937 and today it flies with the collection that bears his name at Old Warden – now a centenarian, it is the oldest *airworthy* British aeroplane in the world.

Harry joined the RFC in 1914 and is known to have flown and fought in Palestine against Ottoman forces; he was awarded the Military Cross. The RFC became the RAF on 1st April 1918 and in that year Harry added an AFC to his MC. Staying with the RAF after the Armistice, Harry was based at Henlow in the early 1920s. His last post was as Officer Commanding A&AEE from September 1924 to November 1928; he retired the following year. Wg Cdr Harold Blackburn MC AFC died in 1959, aged 80.

Tony Blackman

Anthony L Blackman, born 1930. Two year national service started in 1948, joining the RAF as ground-based instructor. Changed to flying course, with 6 FTS at Ternhill, soloing in 1950. In 1951 joined 11 Squadron on DH Vampire FB.5s then 5 Squadron on DH Venom FB.1s, both West Germany. Leading a flight of two FB.1s 21st August 1953 from Wunstorf he encountered severe vibration on take-off, Tony force-landed WE329 and walked away from it; Plt Off A L Schlesinger suffered likewise and also crashed, WE306 caught fire, Schlesinger escaped. ETPS Course No.13 Farnborough February 1954, graduating and moving to A&AEE December 1954.

Tony joined Avro, having been recruited by Roly Falk*. His first sortie was on 8th August 1956 in the second prototype Vulcan, VX777, which was being prepared to become the aerodynamic prototype for the much improved B.2. Routine work included production and development testing of Vulcan B.1s and Shackleton MR.3s. In the spring of 1961 he was involved in tests with Vulcan B.2s XH537 and XH538 fitted with dummy Douglas GAM-87 Skybolt ballistic missile. Tony flew with two and then one missile – to determine asymmetric characteristics – on the underwing pylons. In 1965 the name Avro was dropped and Hawker Siddeley was adopted. On 31st July 1967 he captained the second prototype Nimrod, Avon-engined

Tony Blackman in his office at Woodford, circa 1970. *BAe*

development airframe XV147 on its maiden flight, having been converted from a DH Comet 4 airframe. Tony was to spend a lot of time on Nimrod and HS.748 development work and, in the case of the latter, considerable hours on demonstration flying. With the retirement of Jimmy Harrison*, in 1970 Tony was appointed CTP and a major task was the ferrying of Victor B.2s from the former Handley Page plant at Radlett to Woodford, in readiness for conversion to K.2 tankers. A fascinating assignment in December 1972 was to give 67-year-old American multi-millionaire Howard Robard Hughes a 'taste' of handling the HS.748. The first session, on the 10th, was in demonstrator Series 2A G-AZJH and on the 27th in Rousseau Aviation Series 2A F-BRSU, both out of Hatfield. Tony clearly made an impression on Hughes, who requested he accompany him on two flights in July 1973 in HSA-owned HS.125-403 G-AYOJ. As part of the run-up to the Nimrod AEW project, Comet 4 XW626 was delivered to Woodford on 2nd April 1976 for conversion into a radar test-bed. This fusion of Nimrod and Comet gave the aircraft the nickname 'Nimet' when it was rolled out in March the following year. Tony was in command of the first flight of this unusual-looking aircraft, on 28th June 1977.

HSA became BAe in 1977 and in 1978 Tony retired after 22 years with 'Avro'; he was succeeded by Charles Masefield*. As an avionics expert, he moved on to 15 years with Smiths Industries, including work on the head-up display for the Hawk jet trainer. Tony followed that with four years as a technical member of the Civil Aviation Authority Board. Anthony L Blackman OBE is now a writer, aviation titles including: *Vulcan Test Pilot* (2007) *Test Pilot – My Extraordinary Life in Flight* (2009 – based on his first book *Flight Testing to Win*), *Nimrod – Rise and Fall* (2011) and *Vulcan Boys – True Tales of the Iconic Delta V-Bomber* (2014), all published by Grub Street, as well as several technical books and five novels.

John Blair

20 Aug 1976	SAL Bullfinch G-BDOG
	1 x 200hp Lycoming AEIO-360

John Blair, born 1916. Worked for Blackburn at Brough from 1933, in a non-flying capacity. Joined RAF in November 1940 and flew Consolidated Liberators with Coastal Command. QFI course at CFS Upavon 1943, then to Canada as an instructor. Returned to Blackburn briefly in 1946. Became a commercial pilot, joining Scottish Airlines (an off-shoot of Scottish Aviation) flying Douglas Dakotas and Liberators out of Prestwick.

JOHN BLAIR joined Scottish Aviation (SAL) from its Scottish Airlines division in 1955 and was involved in final flight testing and deliveries of Pioneers to Ceylon from Prestwick. He followed this up with development and production testing of Twin Pioneers. He succeeded Noel Capper* as CTP in 1956 and saw the Twin Pioneer programme through to its last example (of 87 built) in June 1963. After this he was involved in flight testing aircraft under major overhaul by SAL.

The year 1970 witnessed the renaissance of SAL in terms of manufacture. In December 1969 Beagle ceased trading and the design rights to the Bulldog military trainer were acquired by SAL. 'Pee Wee' Judge* had flown the prototype Bulldog in 1969 but John flew the second, fully militarised, example (G-AXIG) at Prestwick on 14th February 1971. The Bulldog became a huge success, more than 300 examples being delivered until production ended in 1980. *India-Golf* is displayed at the National Museum of Scotland in Edinburgh.

On 20th August 1976, John carried out the maiden flight of a radical rethink of the Bulldog, the four-seat, retractable undercarriage Bullfinch. This was aimed at two markets, as a civilian 'tourer' and, as the Bulldog 200, for military trainer/liaison. During the third test flight, G-BDOG's undercarriage would not lower and it looked as though the planned appearance at the SBAC display at Farnborough the following month would be scrubbed because of a wheels-up landing. Deputy CTP Len Houston* came alongside in a Bulldog and eventually, the gear was persuaded to come down and to lock. John displayed *Oscar-Golf* at Farnborough; he had flown the Shoreham-built Bulldog G-AXEH at the 1970 event. Now referred to as a Bulldog 200, G-BDOG is privately owned and airworthy at Netherthorpe, Yorkshire.

The one-off SAL Bullfinch G-BDOG, as first flown by John Blair, was still airworthy at Netherthorpe in 2014. *Ken Ellis*

To return to 1970... SAL had been working on a potentially lucrative sub-contract building Jetstream wings for Handley Page. In February 1970 HP collapsed and, via Jetstream Aircraft, SAL acquired the rights; completing a batch of Jetstream T.1s for the RAF in 1976. SAL became a part of BAe in April 1977. John's last flight for SAL was the delivery of HP-built Jetstream N510F from the USA to Prestwick in December 1978. This machine became the prototype 'second-generation' Jetstream, Series 31 G-JSSD, in 1980, piloted by John's successor, Len Houston. John retired in March 1979 but kept up a marketing post with BAe. John Blair died on 2nd November 2003, aged 87.

'Dasher' Blake

23 Feb 1929	Blackburn Bluebird IV G-AABV [1]
	1 x 100hp DH Gipsy I
28 Dec 1929	Blackburn T.7B
	1 x 625hp Hispano-Suiza 51
9 Feb 1931	Blackburn Segrave I G-ABFP [2]
	2 x 120hp DH Gipsy III
10 Dec 1931	Blackburn B.2 G-ABUW
	1 x 120hp Gipsy III
4 Apr 1932	Blackburn CA.15 G-ABKV [3]
	2 x 400hp AS Jaguar IVC
30 Sep 1932	Blackburn Ripon V B-4 [4]
	1 x 650hp AS Tiger I
8 Mar 1933	Blackburn M1/30 S1640
	1 x 825hp RR Buzzard IIIMS
10 Jun 1933	Blackburn CA.15 G-ABKW [3]
	2 x 400hp AS Jaguar IVC
24 Aug 1933	Blackburn Shark B-6
	1 x 700hp AS Tiger IV
9 Feb 1937	Blackburn Skua I K5178
	1 x 650hp AS Tiger I

Notes: All first flights took place at Brough. [1] Bluebird IV was a complete redesign, with all-metal construction. [2] See under Stuart Scott for more on this twin. [3] There were two versions of the CA.15, G-ABKV a monoplane, G-ABKW a biplane. [4] The Ripon V was the prototype Baffin.

Alfred Montague 'Dasher' Blake, born 1889. Learned to fly in 1912 at the South Coast Flying School. Moved to Russia in 1914 to work with the aircraft department of the Baltic Waggon Works in Petrograd. Returned by October 1914 and joined the Aircraft Inspection Department. Granted a commission in the RNAS, posted to Chelmsford, teaching night flying. In 1916 he was transferred to 2 Wing in the Eastern Mediterranean. By 1918 he was a flight commander at 2 School of Special Flying, Redcar. He stayed on post war, as a Flt Lt; leaving in 1926 to work with the Air Survey Company in Rhodesia. He took up a post as personal pilot to Charles Blackburn for long-distance flights in a Bluebird in 1927.

'Dasher' Blake piloting the Blackburn Ripon in 1932. This machine served as the prototype for the Baffin torpedo-bomber. *Blackburn*

The prototype Blackburn Skua naval dive-bomber; first flown by 'Dasher' Blake in February 1937. *Rolls-Royce Bristol*

'DASHER' BLAKE was engaged by Blackburn as CTP in 1927, taking over from Henry Worrall*, and served for a decade. He was engaged in all aspects of landplane testing, development and demonstration with the Brough-based company. During his tenure, Blackburn capitalised on its series of torpedo-bomber biplanes with the Ripon, Baffin and Shark. His last maiden flight was the Skua dive-bomber – the Navy's first operational monoplane – which entered large scale production in 1938.

His most unusual type was an example of 'tested, but not flown'. The F7/30 prototype K2892 was aimed at an RAF fighter requirement that stipulated the RR Goshawk III with evaporative cooling as powerplant. The competition solicited a wide range of entries, both officially sanctioned and private-venture. The Goshawk proved to be a troublesome cul-de-sac and the RAF defaulted to the Gloster Gladiator to meet its needs. The Blackburn F7/30's low wing was *below* the fuselage with the bulky radiator nestled between the fuselage and the lower centre section. 'Dasher' started initial taxying on 20th July 1934 and commenced 'hops' and 'straights' on 17th August. The Goshawk constantly overheated and flight was not attempted; the deadline for ministry trials came and went and the ungainly biplane did not take to the skies. In *British Aviation – Widening Horizons*, Harald Penrose quoted 'Dasher' telling him: "The little beast has no future".

Alfred Montague 'Dasher' Blake AFC died at his home in Hull on 16th October 1937 – he was 48. He was succeeded by Henry 'Bill' Bailey*. In its obituary, *Flight* noted that Blake's: "calm and deliberate attention to details and amazing memory for facts and figures were of the greatest service to the company".

The Blackburn F7/30 got no further than 'hops' at Brough in the summer of 1934. *KEC*

John Bolton

John W A Bolton: RAF from 1966, mostly on fast jets, including HS Harriers. ETPS Course No.33 Boscombe Down in 1974. From 1985 to 1988 was OC ETPS as Wg Cdr. Left RAF in 1993.

JOHN BOLTON became CTP for BAe Regional Aircraft, initially at Prestwick in 1993, working on the Jetstream 31, 32 and 41. In 1998 he transferred to Woodford, overseeing development and production test of the RJ series all-digital version of the HS.146 jetliner. In 2000 he joined Airbus undertaking production and development flying from Hamburg, Germany. He became a flight test operations consultant from 2006.

John Booth

16 May 1957	Saro SR.53 XD145
	1 x 8,000lbst DH Spectre 1A
	and 1 x 1,640lbst AS Viper 8

John Stanley Booth, born 1919. Joined RAF 1938, deployed to France with 59 Squadron on Bristol Blenheims October 1939. Wounded and evacuated May 1940; awarded DFC. Served as instructor in UK and then in Canada. Briefly with Ferry Command mid-1943. Converted to DH Mosquitos and serving operationally with 125, 151 and 239 Squadrons; awarded a Bar to his DFC. From October 1944 he served with A&AEE, then ETPS Course No.3 Boscombe Down in December 1945. From February to October 1946 he worked for Power Jets on turbojet development.

JOHN BOOTH became a production test pilot for Shorts in November 1946. He left in February 1949, joining Saunders-Roe (Saro) as deputy CTP to Geoffrey Tyson*. He carried out development work on the SR.A/1 jet flying-boat fighter and was second pilot to Tyson for the maiden flight of the giant Princess commercial flying-boat on 22nd August 1952. From 1954, John was heavily involved in the design and construction phase of the SR.53 single-seat mixed-power interceptor and succeeded Tyson as CTP in February 1956. The SR.53 was only the second landplane fighter to be built

The first SR.53 mixed powerplant interceptor. The Viper turbojet was installed above the Spectre rocket in the rear fuselage. *Peter Green Collection*

BAE Systems CTP, Mark Bowman. © 2015 BAE Systems

by Saro, the previous example being the A.10 biplane of 1929. The concept of the SR.53 was to use a DH Spectre rocket motor to give it spectacular climb to intercept, coupled with a Viper turbojet to bring it back after the rocket was expended. While it could fly and land using the Viper alone, it could only achieve take-off using *both* powerplants.

In 1957, the notorious Defence White Paper from Conservative Minister of Defence, Duncan Sandys, cancelled all fighter projects other than the EE P.1 and the SR.53 was destined to be a research platform only. The prototype SR.53, XD145, was taken by road to Boscombe Down and John began ground runs of the Spectre rocket on 16th January 1957, with the Viper firing up for the first time in April. John took XD145 for its debut on 16th May 1957. XD145's tenth flight was to Farnborough on 1st September where John demonstrated it with dummy Firestreak air-to-air missiles attached at the wing tips. The second SR.53, XD151, was on show in the static, having been brought in by road. John's display on 5th September was cut short when a flash fire forced him to cut the Spectre rocket motor and abort the sortie.

John took the second SR.53, XD151, into the air for the first time, from Boscombe Down, on 18th December. During the take-off roll on XD151's 12th flight on 5th June 1958 he called "Panic stations!" following that seconds later with "Come and get me" and the drag 'chute was deployed. The aircraft over-ran, hit obstructions and exploded, killing John. Just what happened on that flight – John's 34th on type – is still a topic of debate. The Spectre rocket had either failed, or John had cut it in readiness for an aborted take-off. Peter 'Sheepy' Lamb* took over as Saro CTP and carried out more flights in XD145 during 1959: it is now on display at the RAF Museum Cosford. Sqn Ldr John S Booth DFC* was posthumously awarded a Queen's Commendation.

Mark Bowman

Mark N Bowman, born 1960. Achieved an Air Cadet scholarship and got his PPL at 17 (months before his driving licence!) and was a cadet entrant, joining the RAF after a degree in Aeronautical Engineering, in 1981. Operational flying: 1 Squadron Harrier GR.3s from 1985, 4 Squadron on

GR.3s from 1988. ETPS Course No.49 at Boscombe Down 1990 led to a tour at A&AEE as HS Harrier and SEPECAT Jaguar Project Test Pilot. As Sqn Ldr, returned to frontline flying on Harrier GR.7s with 3 Squadron, 1993 to 1998 engaged in operations in the Gulf and the Balkans.

MARK joined British Aerospace at Dunsfold in 1998 as Harrier Project Pilot. With the closure of Dunsfold in September 2000 he transferred to Warton. During 2002 he carried out the first test flight of the Harrier GR.7A upgrade (September 2002) and converted to the Typhoon. On 3rd February 2005 he was the first pilot to fly a Typhoon across the Atlantic, soon after becoming Typhoon Project Pilot. Mark succeeded Paul Stone* as CTP in March 2010. As this volume went to press, one of the major projects in Mark's 'in-tray' was development of the Striker II helmet-mounted display system with night vision capability.

'Brackles' Brackley

22nd May 1924 English Electric Kingston I N168
2 x 450hp Napier Lion

Herbert George Brackley, born 1894. With 7 Squadron RNAS captained HP O/100 3130 25th September 1917 to bomb a bridge at Namur. By October 1918 was serving with RAF 214 Squadron, flying O/400s. Awarded DSO and DSC. Was to have captained HP V/1500 F7140 on transatlantic flight from St John's, Newfoundland, but pipped at the post by Alcock and Brown in June 1919. Instead, flew the V/1500 to New York October 1919 for publicity flights.*

Became chief pilot for Handley Page Transport 1920 and attempted to fly O/400 G-EAMC to Cape Town, but suffered a force-landing near Khartoum 25th February 1920. In 1923 he was appointed Air Superintendent for Imperial Airways.

HERBERT GEORGE 'BRACKLES' BRACKLEY DSO DSC was commissioned by English Electric (EE) to test the Kingston patrol flying-boat. The prototype, N168, was launched into the River Ribble at Lytham St Anne's on 22nd May 1924. After seaworthiness trials and some 'taxi' runs; Brackles along with C J Blackburn and W A Bannister as observer and engineer respectively, started the take-off, but this ended in the 'boat hitting something in the water and coming to rest, nose down – the three crew were rescued unscathed. An order for four more Kingstons followed and Brackles tested the third and fourth. In late 1924 EE appointed Marcus Manton* as CTP.

With Imperial Airways, in 1929-1930 Brackles helped to compile the specification that gave rise to the Handley Page HP.42 airliner. During World War Two he returned to the RAF, gaining high office and a CBE in 1941. Post-war he took a major post with BOAC and then with British South American Airways. He was a great advocate of the Saro Princess project. In late 1948 Air Commodore H G Brackley CBE DSO DSC was drowned in an accident off the Copacabana beach, Rio de Janeiro, Brazil. The following year W G de Lara Wilson self-published *Brackles – A Memoir* as a tribute to a great aviator.

'Reggie' Brie

Reginald Alfred Charles Brie, born 1895. Joined the Army 1914 and by 1915 was an artilleryman at the Somme. Transferred to RFC late 1917, becoming an observer with 104 Squadron, on DH.9s. Shot down on a raid to Mannheim 1918 and taken prisoner; repatriated December 1918. Left RAF 1922 and worked for Shell-Mex. Gained a Commercial Licence 1929 and joined Cierva in November 1930 as a demonstration pilot on a temporary basis.

'REGGIE' BRIE took to autogiro flying and by the autumn of 1931, he had over 400 hours on rotary wings in his logbook. During 1931 he toured the UK in a *Daily Mail*-sponsored 'circus' flying Cierva C.19 Mk.III G-AALA. He took up the post of CTP for the Cierva Autogiro Company, succeeding 'Dizzy' Rawson* and was assisted by Alan Marsh*. In May 1932 he established an autogiro flying school at Hanworth on behalf of Cierva. In that year he was the pilot when rotorcraft pioneer Raoul Hafner, later to design the Bristol Sycamore, made his first autogiro flight. Reggie flew long distances – bit-by-bit – on demonstration and delivery; eg in June 1932 C.19 Mk.IV G-ABUD to Denmark for demonstrations and 5th January 1934 a C.30P (*probably* G-ACIM) to an owner in France. On 6th August 1932 he piloted the DH-built C.24 G-ABLM (see Cierva's own reference) in the Brooklands to Newcastle race, averaging 103.5mph. In 1934 Reggie wrote *The Autogiro and How to Fly It*.

With the outbreak of World War Two, he re-joined the RAF and became a champion of using autogiros for radar calibration and helped to establish 1448 Flight, Reggie flew with this unit

as a Squadron Leader, then commanded it, as a Wing Commander. In June 1943, 1448 Flight was re-numbered as 529 Squadron and its CO throughout was none other than Sqn Ldr Alan Marsh. By September 1943, Reggie was at Bridgeport, Connecticut, USA, learning to fly the Sikorsky Hoverfly I (USAAF designation YR-4B) helicopter, with him was 'Jeep' Cable*. The first British Hoverfly, FT833, had been damaged at Sikorsky's Bridgeport plant, in July 1943 by a US Coast Guard pilot and Reggie started acceptance trials of the repaired machine in late September; only to roll it on landing, smashing the rotors and cabin – Wg Cdr Brie was unharmed.

In 1945 Reggie left the RAF and was briefly with Fairey as it established its helicopter division. On 14th March 1947 he gained Helicopter Aviators' Certificate No.1 and went on to establish the BEA Helicopter Experimental Unit at Gatwick. On approach to Sembawang airfield, Singapore, on 26th October 1948, Supermarine Spitfire FR.18 TP376 of 28 Squadron encountered difficulties and crashed. Its pilot, Fg Off Graham C A Brie – Reggie's son – was killed. Reggie retired from BEA in 1957 and joined Westland on the technical side and helped in the planning and commissioning of Battersea Heliport, which opened in 1959. Awarded the MBE in 1963, he retired from Westland in 1973. Wg Cdr Reginald Alfred Charles Brie MBE died in 1988, aged 93.

Alan Bristow

5 Oct 1948	Westland WS-51 Mk.1A G-AKTW
	1 x 520hp Alvis Leonides 50

Alan Edgar Bristow, born 1923. Joined the Merchant Navy, aged 16, on the outbreak of World War Two. Twice in 1942 he had ships sunk from under him: Japanese aircraft despatched the SS Malda *on 6th April and the German submarine U-214 took out the SS* Hatarana *on 18th August. This may have encouraged him to join the Fleet Air Arm in 1943! Pilot training in Canada was followed by conversion to Sikorsky XR-4 helicopters in 1944.*

AT one of the tremendous test pilot reunions staged by Dick Richardson and his team at wonderful Popham aerodrome, globe-trotting entrepreneur and helicopter zealot Alan Bristow was greeted by one-and-all with warmth and respect. It was 2006 – a then serving Boscombe Down test pilot, who did not want to be named, summed up Alan. "The best helicopter test pilot we never had. [Staying with Westland] would have delayed, or even prevented, his name becoming synonymous with helicopters as a reliable, vital, tool of industry." Alan was known for a quick temper that, in his youth, could be linked with clenched fists – a skill learned in his merchant marine days. In 1949 the Westland CTP struck the company's sales manager and his two-year career came to an instantaneous end.

After that flash of angst Alan embarked on a meteoric rise to create what is now a Texas-based multi-national organisation with hundreds of helicopters still proudly bearing its founder's name – Bristow Helicopters, now the Bristow Group. In April 1985 Alan fronted a consortium – Bristow Rotorcraft – in a £90 million bid to acquire his then ailing former employer; the offer was later withdrawn.

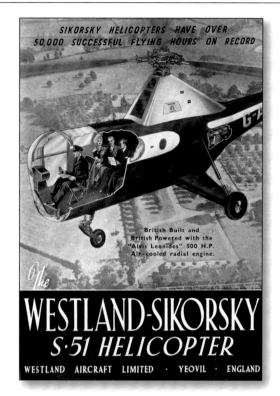

SIKORSKY HELICOPTERS HAVE OVER 50,000 SUCCESSFUL FLYING HOURS ON RECORD

British Built and British Powered with the "Alvis Leonides" 500 H.P. Air-cooled radial engine.

The WESTLAND-SIKORSKY S·51 HELICOPTER

WESTLAND AIRCRAFT LIMITED · YEOVIL · ENGLAND

Westland faced a considerable 'education' programme in introducing helicopters into civil aviation; this 1948 advert typifying the approach. Alan Bristow's spirited and imaginative demonstrations helped put the new enterprise on the map.

Having made the visionary decision to become a helicopter manufacturer, Westland set about establishing a small venture centred upon a licence to build and re-engineer the Sikorsky S-51. In 1947 Lt Alan Bristow (aged 24) was taken on as helicopter test pilot under CTP Harald Penrose*. Re-engined and re-thought, the prototype WS-51 – the Dragonfly – was first flown by Alan at Yeovil on 5th October 1948 and a world-beating helicopter dynasty was born. That WS-51, G-AKTW, was rebuilt to Widgeon status in 1955 and was one of a batch bought by Bristow Helicopters – Alan became a major Westland customer.

As Westland geared up for production, the most important requirement was to show the world's armed forces and industry the value of this novel form of aviation. Alan set to this with gusto. On 7th February 1948 he and Westland hit the headlines when he piloted S-51 G-AJHW to re-supply the beleaguered lighthouse keepers on Wolf Rock, off Land's End. In a 'combined operation' by Bristol, Gloster and Westland, on 30th September 1948 Sir Frederick Wells delivered a message from the Lord Mayor of London to the Deputy President of the Municipality of Paris in 46 minutes 29 seconds. Eric Swiss* flew the second prototype Bristol 171 VL963 (later named Sycamore) from a car park behind St Paul's cathedral to Biggin Hill in 9½ minutes. There, Sir Frederick boarded Gloster's two-seat demonstrator Meteor T.7 G-AKPK and was flown by Bill Waterton* to Orly Airport, Paris, in 27½ minutes. Then Alan whisked the passenger to the Place des Invalides in 8½ minutes in a WS-51. It was not a sizzling city-to-city time, but a superb statement about the capabilities of helicopters. Alan was back in Paris in late April

and early May 1949 for the Paris Salon and he carried out demonstrations within the city.

Not long after this came the punch and the dismissal; Alan was succeeded by Ken Reed* at Yeovil. Alan flew for French agency Helicop-Air, braved Antarctic conditions to pioneer whale spotting by helicopter before founding Bristow Helicopters, the first operator dedicated to supporting the offshore oil and gas industry. Alan was awarded the French Croix de Guerre in 1950 and an OBE in 1966. The French honour was for a daring rescue of French soldiers under fire in 1949. Alan was demonstrating a Hiller and realised both the humanitarian and commercial value of showing what a rotorcraft could do. The soldiers were saved and an order for six Hillers was placed by France! Alan Edgar Bristow OBE CDG died on 26th April 2009, aged 85.

Hubert Broad

30 Jul 1923	DH DH.50 G-EBFN 1 x 230hp AS Puma
1 Oct 1923	DH Humming Bird G-EBHX [1] 1 x 6.5hp Douglas
19 Jul 1924	Gloster II J7504 1 x 585hp Napier Lion VA
6 Dec 1924	HP Handcross J7498 1 x 650hp RR Condor III
17 May 1925	DH Hyena J7780 1 x 385hp AS Jaguar III
28 May 1925	DH Highclere G-EBKI 1 x 650hp RR Condor IIIA
29 Aug 1925	Gloster III N194 1 x 700hp Napier Lion VII
10 Feb 1926	HP W.10 G-EBMM 2 x 480hp Napier Lion IIB
24 Apr 1926	HP Harrow I N205 [2] 1 x 500hp Napier Lion VA
30 Sep 1926	DH Hercules G-EBMW 3 x 420hp Bristol Jupiter VI
17 Nov 1926	DH Hound G-EBNJ 1 x 530hp Napier Lion VIII
24 Jun 1927	DH Tiger Moth G-EBQU [3] 1 x 85p ADC Cirrus II
Dec 1927	DH Giant Moth G-EBTL 1 x 450hp Bristol Jupiter VI
Oct 1928	Parnall Pipit N232 1 x 495hp RR F.XI
7 Dec 1928	DH Hawk Moth G-EBVV 1 x 200hp DH Ghost
27 Jan 1929	Saro A.10 K1949 1 x 480hp RR F.XI

9 Sep 1929	DH Puss Moth E-1 1 x 120hp DH Gipsy III
11 Jul 1929	DH DH.77 J9771 1 x 300hp Napier Halford H
26 Oct 1931	DH Tiger Moth E-6 [4] 1 x 120hp DH Gipsy III
29 Jan 1932	DH Fox Moth G-ABUO 1 x 120hp DH Gipsy III
24 Nov 1932	DH Dragon E-9 2 x 130hp DH Gipsy Major I
14 Nov 1933	DH Tech School TK.3 E-3 1 x 120hp DH Gipsy III
14 Jan 1934	DH DH.86 E-2 4 x 200hp DH Gipsy Six
17 Apr 1934	DH Dragon Rapide E-4 2 x 200hp DH Gipsy Six
8 Sep 1934	DH Comet E-1 [5] 2 x 230hp DH Gipsy Six R
3 Apr 1937	Carden-Baynes Bee G-AEWC 2 x 40hp Carden Ford SP.1
May 1937	CW Cygnet G-AEMA 1 x 90hp ADC Cirrus Minor

The first DH.66 Hercules G-EBMW in Egypt in Imperial Airways service as 'City of Cairo', 1931. *KEC*

Notes: All flew at Stag Lane, apart from: Gloster II and III at Felixstowe; Handcross, W.10 and Harrow at Cricklewood; Pipit at Yate; A.10 at East Cowes; Dragon Rapide and Comet at Hatfield; Bee at Heston; Cygnet at Hanworth. [1] The wreckage of the prototype DH.53 is stored at Old Warden by the Shuttleworth Trust. [2] First use of the name Harrow, for a torpedo-bomber biplane, see under James Cordes for the bomber-transport Harrow. [3] First use of name Tiger Moth, single-seat monoplane, see 25th October 1931. Cirrus used for initial trials only, then fitted with 135hp Gipsy. [4] Second use of name, see 24th Jun 1927 above and narrative. [5] First use of name, DH.88 twin-engined long-distance racer.

Hubert Stanford Broad, born 1897. Aged 19 learned to fly at the Hall School at Hendon, on a Caudron. By the end of 1915 he was in the RNAS at Eastchurch, moving to Cranwell. Joined RNAS 'Naval 3' Squadron at Dunkirk, then lent to RFC 3 Squadron on Sopwith Pups. While flying N6203 in spring 1917 he claimed an Albatros but was shot in the neck in combat on 11th May 1917. Once recovered, he instructed at Chingford, joining 46 Squadron on Sopwith Camels in France late 1917. By 1918 he was instructing again at Fairlop. By 1920 he was with the Avro Transport Company on joy-riding duties in Avro 504s and travelled to the USA to fly in a similar venture in New York State on Avro 504 floatplanes.

HUBERT BROAD joined de Havilland at Stag Lane in October 1921 as test pilot, although the company founder and designer, Geoffrey de Havilland* (GDH) continued to take command of some maiden flights. Hubert flew the entire spectrum of types produced by DH during the golden years that turned the company from workshop to industrial giant. He was at home with types like the Hercules and DH.86 airliners, the challenging DH.77 fighter and the DH.88 racer, but it was his prowess with light aircraft that made him such a great asset to DH. Hubert would break records, win races, tirelessly liaise with aero clubs and private owners about the virtues of the latest DH type. As will be seen from the 'log' above, Hubert also managed to squeeze in the occasional test for other constructors.

His first work for another company, Gloster, nearly proved to be his undoing. He was chosen as one of the pilots for the company's entry for the eighth Schneider Trophy contest, to be held in Baltimore, Maryland, in October 1924. The Gloster II floatplane was taken to Felixstowe for trials. On its first flight, Hubert found it to be very promising, but upon alighting it started to porpoise and a float strut shattered. The floatplane disappeared in a plume of water and capsized. Hubert was drenched but unharmed. With no Italians in contention, the Americans were faced with a walkover, but cancelled the competition instead. Next year, Hubert flew the even more powerful and refined Gloster III at Felixstowe in August, pronounced it acceptable and it was shipped to Baltimore. At Chesapeake Bay on 26th October 1925, Hubert came second at 199.17mph; Lt 'Jimmy' Doolittle taking the honours in a Curtiss R3C-2 at 232.56mph.

Having taken the Handley Page W.10 into the air in February 1926, Hubert was well prepared for the first flight of the DH Hercules, ordered by Imperial Airways, seven months later. As a prestige commission, the whole of Stag Lane was allowed out to watch the event. Hubert took the tri-motor biplane up, flew past his audience on two engines, followed by another run on just *one*!

Prototype Hawk Moth, G-EBVV, de Havilland's first foray into the cabin monoplane market. *De Havilland*

Bearing the legend 'Tiger Moth' on the nose, the first DH.60T in 'B-Condition' (or 'trade plate') markings as E-5, 1931. *Peter Green Collection*

First flown by Geoffrey de Havilland, the prototype Hornet Moth. Troubles with its flying characteristics may have played a part in Hubert Broad's dismissal. *BAe Hatfield*

GDH was at the controls for a momentous occasion in the history of his company, on 22nd February 1925 he flew G-EBKT, the prototype DH Moth. More than happy with its performance, and mindful he was not the CTP, he came back in and beckoned Hubert to join him for the next sortie. As the Moth evolved, Hubert was to master each nuance and his demonstrations became legendary. In 1928 he took part in an incredible feat of endurance. With tankage for 80 gallons squeezed into Moth G-EBWV, he took off from Stag Lane at exactly 5:30pm on 16th August and, to quote Harald Penrose in *British Aviation – The Adventuring Years*: "remained aloft 24 hours during which he read three novels as relaxation". He touched down at 5:30pm on the dot on the 17th. He still had 12 gallons available to him; he had flown 1,440 miles. Also in 1928, he came first in the King's Cup, a hard-fought contest centred upon Hatfield, piloting Moth G-EBMO at an average of 90.4mph. The Moth airframe evolved into a military trainer, Hubert flew the first of these, DH.60T E-5 (later G-ABNJ) in May 1931 and in its definitive form as the first DH.82 E-6 (later G-ABRC) on 26th October. *Both* of these can claim, in their own way, to be the prototype Tiger Moth.

Hubert already had a DH Tiger Moth in his logbook. In June 1927 he first flew the diminutive single-seat *monoplane* DH.71 Tiger Moth, the interior of which had been more or less built around his equally small frame. On 24th August Hubert set two world records for a light aircraft, using the DH.71. Over a closed circuit, he clocked 186.47mph and took just 17 minutes to reach 19,191ft. DH moved out of Stag Lane in 1934, having started the migration to Hatfield in stages from 1930. It was from the latter that Hubert piloted the first DH.88 Comet racer airborne on 8th September 1934. Returning after the maiden sortie, Hubert ran low along the airfield, worrying onlookers that he might land with the novel retractable undercarriage in the 'up' position. What he was doing was checking the Comet's shadow, to see if the gear was down, as the undercarriage position indicator had yet to be installed.

Then in 1935 came a hammer blow, with no inkling of what was coming Hubert was dismissed after 14 years. He was 38, so age was not a factor. In *British Aviation – The Ominous Skies*, Harald Penrose wrote of an assessment made years afterwards from talking with members of the DH management, Hubert "uncritically corrected handling deficiencies and this failed to be sufficiently analytical to help the designer". Harald hinted

that a development problem with the DH.87 Hornet Moth two-seat cabin biplane was the tipping point. The prototype, with slightly tapering wings and rounded wing tips, gave way to the DH.87A with classic DH elegant, tapered and pointed wing tips in 1935. It was discovered that this format gave a pronounced wing drop at the stall, making it challenging for the average pilot – the very market base that DH aimed at. Production standardised on the DH.87B with square-cut wing tips that restored benign characteristics. DH.87A owners could opt for the new wings. Penrose claimed that 50 sets of the complex DH.87A wings had been built in anticipation of sales and it would seem that this state of affairs was laid at Hubert's door.

Hubert freelanced, including production testing HP Harrows at Radlett, and flew for the Air Registration Board and then RAE. He was involved in another light aircraft in 1937, testing the innovative CW Cygnet. This design was adopted by General Aircraft and Hollis Williams* considerably redesigned it and test flew in, as the Cygnet II, in 1939. Hubert became Chief PTP for Hawker at Langley in 1940, managing the relentless shaking down of Hurricanes, the few Tornados built, Typhoons, Tempests and early Furies. Neville Duke* arrived at Langley in January 1945 and in his book *Test Pilot* describes Broad as: "one of my boyhood heroes. It was a great moment to meet him for the first time." Hubert retired from Langley in 1946 and by 1948 had taken up a post with undercarriage and propeller specialist Dowty. Hubert Stanford Broad MBE AFC achieved over 7,500 flying hours on about 200 types. He died on 30th July 1975, aged 79.

Ground-handling the first DH.88 Comet, G-ACSP 'Black Magic' at Mildenhall at the start of the Robertson Trophy race to Australia, October 1934. *KEC*

Tom 'Brookie' Brooke-Smith

28 Aug 1950	Short SB.3 WF632 2 x 1,475shp AS Mamba
10 Aug 1951	Short Sperrin VX158 4 x 6,000lbst RR Avon RA2
14 Jul 1951	Short SB.1 G-14-5 glider
2 Dec 1952	Short SB.5 WG768 1 x 4,850lbst BS Orpheus
4 Oct 1953	Short SB.4 G-14-1 2 x 350lbst Turboméca Palas
2 Apr 1957	Short SC.1 XG900 [1] 1 x 2,130lbst RR RB.108
23 May 1958	Short SC.1 XG905 [2] 5 x 2,130lbst RR RB.108

Notes: [1] Conventional flight only, from Boscombe Down. [2] First hover, at Sydenham

Thomas William Brooke-Smith, born 1918. Studied at the Chelsea College of Aeronautical Engineering 1934 and learned to fly at the Brooklands School of Flying, going solo at the age of 17. Owned and operated DH Puss Moth G-AAVA 1935-1936. Started work with Continental Airlines, Croydon, on basic ground duties, while gaining commercial licence. Flew with a joy-riding concern, then for Air Dispatch. From 1940 worked with the Air Transport Auxiliary. From 1942 was based at Rochester, delivering and overseeing the delivery of Stirlings.

A jubilant Tom Brooke-Smith climbing down from one of the two Short SC.1s.
Short Brothers and Harland

WHILE ferrying Stirlings from Rochester, Thomas Brooke-Smith (TBS) came to the attention of Shorts director of flight operations, and former CTP, John Lankester Parker* and he appointed the 24-year-old as junior test pilot. ('Brookie' was *born* the year John became CTP for Shorts!) TBS graduated from No.6 Course ETPS at Farnborough in 1947 and became CTP in March 1948, succeeding Harold Piper*. Work centred on development of the second Shetland flying-boat, Sealand amphibians, Sturgeon target-tugs and Solent flying-boats. Rochester closed in July 1948 and TBS moved to Sydenham, nestled within Belfast's dockland. Other than one type, all of the aircraft first flown by TBS were for trials and research. The exception was his first maiden fight, the SB.3 airborne early warning picket, which was defeated by the Fairey Gannet AEW.3 which entered production.

Much was hoped for the SA.4 Sperrin aimed at Specification B14/46 and seen as 'insurance' for the complex Vulcan and Victor V-bombers. However, the Valiant was seen as a better alternative. The order for two Sperrins stood; they would be used for trials work. The Sperrin's four RR Avons were mounted as pairs, one above the other on each wing. TBS flew the first Sperrin, VX158, single-handed, using the longer runway at Aldergrove (now Belfast Airport). He shared development trials with 'Jock' Eassie and Walter Runciman*.

Professor Geoffrey Hill*, in semi-retirement in Northern Ireland from 1948, co-operated with Shorts chief designer David Keith-Lucas to develop the swept-back aero-isoclinic wing, which included rotating wing tip-mounted elevons, similar to those pioneered on Hill's pre-war Pterodactyls. As a private venture, Shorts built a glider as a scale version of a planned four-engined jet bomber. TBS flew the SB.1 at Aldergrove from a winch-launch in July 1951. Sixteen days later, he was towed behind Sturgeon TT.2 VR363, flown by Jock Eassie. TBS found this very difficult, probably caused by the twin-engined Sturgeon's contra-rotating propellers. The same combination took to the air again on 14th October, with a longer tow rope, which TBS hoped would solve the turbulence and lack of control. Far from it, he was forced to abort the tow and the SB.1 crashed back on to the runway. Brookie suffered crushed spinal vertebrae and was hospitalised. He made it plain that the only way he would return to aero-isoclinic wings was with the addition of power! With a new fuselage and a pair of small Turboméca turbojets, TBS flew the SB.4 in October 1953 at Aldergrove. The test-bed was given the semi-official name Sherpa – standing for Short and Harland Experimental Prototype Aircraft. As the lightest of the Shorts test pilots at the time, much of the SB.4 flying was carried out by Jock Eassie!

'Brookie' piloting the SB.1 glider on one of its three sorties. The black stripes were to alert other traffic in the Aldergrove circuit that it was unpowered. *Short Brothers and Harland*

The second Sperrin, VX161, first flown by Tom Brooke-Smith on 12th August 1952. *Short Brothers and Harland*

English Electric's P.1 supersonic interceptor programme, which blossomed as the Lightning, faced plenty of design challenges and Shorts responded to a requirement for a simple, fixed-undercarriage, jet to try out the proposed highly swept wing in the low speed regime and to help determine if the P.1 should have a low-set tailplane or a 'T-tail'. The sweep of the main wings could be changed, but only after 'surgery' on the ground – the SB.5 was not a variable geometry ('swing-wing') aircraft. TBS took WG768 on its maiden fight from Boscombe Down in December 1952. At this point, it was in 'T-tail' configuration and with 50-degrees of sweep. In June 1953 it was flown at 60-degrees and the following month Roland Beamont*, EE's CTP, sampled it. The next metamorphosis was tested in January 1954 when WG768 flew with the low-set tailplane and 69-degrees of sweep.

The remainder of Brookie's test career was to be dominated by vertical take-off and landing, which he described as "learning to ride a bicycle again". With the success of the Thrust Measuring Rig – the 'Flying Bedstead' – Rolls-Royce started development of a purpose-built lift jet, the RB.108. Requirement ER.143T was issued and Shorts was awarded a

contract for two rotund delta SC.1s. Four RB.108s were mounted in an upright position within the centre fuselage; these could tilt 35-degrees forwards or backwards to provide some directional thrust as well as lift. In the tail was another RB.108 providing propulsion.

In the run up to tackling the SC.1, TBS took a helicopter conversion course at A&AEE Boscombe Down in 1954. He was in good hands, the OC 'D' Squadron, Ron Gellatly* had him going solo within 24 hours! TBS piloted XG900 on its maiden, conventional, fight from Boscombe Down on 2nd April 1957. At this point, it was only fitted with the rear RB.108; XG905 was to be the first with the full five powerplants. Ground-running of XG905 commenced in September with TBS at the controls. Its first tethered 'hops' were made using a huge rig, called the 'Goal Post', at Sydenham on 23rd May 1958. The tethers were discarded on 25th October. Moved to RAE Thurleigh, XG905 carried out the inaugural transition from vertical to horizontal fight, and back again, on 6th April 1960. Brookie demonstrated this publically the Farnborough airshow that September. (At Long Kesh, the Ulster Aviation Collection is restoring the SB.4; the SB.5 is displayed at the RAF Museum, Cosford; the Science Museum in London has SC.1 XG900 on show and its sister, XG905, is as the Ulster Folk and Transport Museum near Belfast.)

The second SC.1, XG905, in hovering mode. *Short Brothers and Harland*

Dramatic view of the SB.5 WG768, in1960 with the wing set at 69-degrees and low-set tailplane. *Rolls-Royce*

THE SHORT S.A.4

Long range, High level, 4 jet bomber now
undergoing special trials for the development
of some of Britain's latest secret equipment

Shorts

By 1952, the SA.4 Sperrin had been sidetracked to a life of test and trials, but could still provide a powerful message of the capabilities of Shorts. From late 1947, the company announced it was to be known as Shorts. This was explained as not being plural, or possessive, but as a contraction of Short Brothers.

TBS was due to retire before the Farnborough display of September 1960, but he was the only available current pilot and so displayed at the show. Succeeded by Denis Tayler*, Brookie joined Fight Refuelling Ltd in public relations and sales. Thomas William Brooke-Smith died in 2004, aged 84.

'Tommy' Broome

Feb 1923	Vickers Vixen G-EBEC
	1 x 450hp Napier Lion

F C 'Tommy' Broome DFC served with 151 Squadron in France flying Sopwith Camels, with Stan Cockerell as his flight commander; they became friends. By 1920 he was working with Cockerell at Brooklands.*

WITH Jack Alcock* heavily involved in preparations for the famous Atlantic crossing in a Vimy from April to June 1919, Stan Cockerell was brought in to fly the Vimy Comercial variant. With the death of Alcock in December 1919, Stan took over the task of chief pilot for Vickers at Brooklands. He turned to his colleague and friend from his 151 Squadron days, 'Tommy' Broome, to assist him. In 1920, *The Times* chartered Vimy Commercial prototype G-EAAV to carry zoologist Dr P Chalmers Mitchell for a flight from Cairo, Egypt, to Cape Town, South Africa, with Stan and Tommy as pilots and two ground crew. The flight departed Brooklands on 24th January, reaching Heliopolis, near Cairo, on 3rd February. Beset with problems, making at least two force-landings, engine failure on take-off from Tabora in Tanganyika on 27th February wrecked G-EAAV and the adventure came to an end. Both Stan and Tommy were awarded AFCs for the endeavours. Back at Brooklands, Tommy assisted with testing the expanding portfolio of Vickers types but in February 1923 he was at the controls for the first flight of the Vixen two-seat general purpose military biplane. The Vixen was developed into a family of similar types, built in small numbers up to the late 1920s: Valparaiso, Venture, Vivid and Valiant. Tommy Broome shared test flying duties with H J Payn* from 1923 until the arrival of 'Tiny' Scholefield* as Vickers CTP in mid-1924 and he does not appear to have not been involved beyond that point. Tommy was sales manager for Vickers by 1938.

'Duggie' Broomfield

1 May 1950	HP HPR.2 WE496
	1 x 385hp AS Cheetah XVIII

Douglas J P Broomfield served in Bomber Command during World War Two and was awarded the DFM. He qualified from No.4 Course ETPS at Cranfield in 1946 and later served with A&AEE.

'DUGGIE' BROOMFIELD joined Handley Page as a test pilot in 1948, on Hastings and Hermes development at Radlett and from the newly-acquired Reading facility – the former Miles plant at Woodley, where he tested and delivered Marathons. In May 1950 he was at the helm at Woodley for the maiden flight of the HPR.2 prototype – aimed at an RAF

The second of two Handley Page HPR.2 trainer prototypes, as tested by 'Duggie' Broomfield. *Handley Page (Reading)*

9 Jan 1941	Avro Manchester III BT308 [2] 4 x 1,145hp RR Merlin X
26 Nov 1941	Avro Lancaster II DT810 4 x 1,650hp Bristol Hercules VIs
5 Jul 1942	Avro York LV626 4 x 1,620 RR Merlin T34
9 Jun 1944	Avro Lincoln PW925 4 x 1,1750hp RR Merlin 85

Notes: All from Woodford other than the Manchester, Manchester III, York and Lincoln, which used Ringway. [1] The first of a military trainer family, including the Tutor and the Type 626. [2] See the narrative.

Harry Albert Brown, born 1896. Joined the Army in 1914. After the Somme, he transferred to the RNAS and learned to fly at Vedome, France, on Caudrons and later instructed at Redcar. In 1919 he worked for the Avro Transport Company, joy-riding with Avro 504s from the beach at Blackpool and, later, at Rhyl. He moved to Barcelona in 1920, instructing for the Spanish naval air arm. He returned to the UK in 1926 to replace Neville Stack* as the CFI at the Lancashire Aero Club, Barton.

requirement to replace the Percival Prentice trainer. On take-off, the sliding canopy blew off, but Duggie was able to continue with an abbreviated circuit. Only two HPR.2s were built, Percival getting the contract with the exceptional Provost. With a party of VIPs on board on 5th June 1951, he flew the turboprop Hermes V G-ALEV from Heathrow to Orly, Paris, in 46 minutes, with a ground speed of spot-on 300mph.

On 23rd August 1951, Duggie ferried crescent wing test-bed HP.88 VX330 from Carnaby to Stansted. (For details of the HP.88 see 'Sailor' Parker.) At the Essex airfield, Duggie was due continue trials, make a demonstration to representatives of the Ministry of Supply and work up a routine for the imminent SBAC display at Farnborough. After being airborne for around 15 minutes on the 26th, Duggie returned at high speed down the main runway; the single-seat jet started to pitch violently then disintegrated, killing Flt Lt Douglas J P Broomfield DFM instantly.

'Sam' Brown

early 1929	Avro Avian IVM G-AACV 1 x 90hp ADC Cirrus III
Sep 1929	Avro Trainer G-AAKT [1] 1 x 155hp AS Mongoose III
1929	Avro Five VP-KAE 3 x 105hp AS Genet Major
1931	Avro Mailplane G-ABJM 1 x 525hp AS Panther IIA
May 1932	Avro Cadet G-ABRS 1 x 135hp AS Genet Major
Feb 1934	Avro 642/4m G-ACVF 4 x 215hp AS Lynx IVC
1934	Avro Commodore G-ACNT 1 x 215hp AS Lynx IVC
1935	Avro 636 A14 1 x 460hp AS Jaguar VIC
25 Jul 1939	Avro Manchester L7246 2 x 1,760 RR Vulture I

WHILE instructing at Barton with the Lancashire Flying Club, 'Sam' Brown more and more found himself being called upon to help Avro at Woodford production testing Avians. He very likely got his nickname from the military belt invented in the 19th century by Sam Browne. Sam developed another nickname during his Woodford days, to the junior pilots and ground crew he was 'Cappo' as a considerable mark of respect. In February 1928 'Bert' Hinkler* gave up his test piloting post at Avro and Sam became the company's first CTP at the age of 31. His inaugural maiden flight was the metal-framed Avian IVM, followed by the Trainer, the first of a 'family' that became a major production programme. On 19th October 1929 Sam's career was nearly cut short, or even terminated. He was test flying the second Avro Avocet, N209, which had returned from Martlesham Heath for modifications. (Note that one source quotes this incident as taking place in a Tutor.) The Avocet dived into the ground; Sam was badly hurt but was back in harness by May 1930.

With some test pilots there are stand-out types that dominate their portfolio. From 1939 Avro had been using the airfield at Ringway – now Manchester Airport – as the base for experimental flying, away from the increasingly manic PTP work being carried out at Woodford. As well as Ansons – Woodford was busy with a large batch of Bristol Blenheim Is; Sam flew the first of these, L6594, in September 1938. During the spring of 1939, the prototype of gifted designer Roy Chadwick's heavy bomber was assembled at Ringway. On 25th July 1939, with Bill Thorn as second pilot, Sam flew Manchester L7246. Quickly it was discovered to be directionally unstable; this was fixed by fitting a third tail fin. What couldn't be cured quickly were the unreliable Vulture engines, which looked set to ruin the prospects of an otherwise excellent airframe. On 5th January 1941 Roy Chadwick signed the clearance to fly for BT308, the four-engined evolution

The prototype Avro Commodore, a development of the Cadet/Tutor family. *HSA*

Sam Brown in the front seat of the prototype Avro 636, which was the first of four for the Irish Air Corps, delivered on 16th October 1935. *via Donal MacCarron*

The prototype Manchester vividly demonstrated the problems with the Rolls-Royce Vulture powerplants – it was force-landed three times: on delivery to Boscombe Down in Staffordshire on 29th November 1939; on 12th December (illustrated) and 23rd December it came down close to the Boscombe circuit. *Rolls-Royce*

of the the Manchester, officially called Manchester III. On the document, the historic name 'Lancaster' appeared and a legend was born. Sam went on to clear hundreds of 'Lancs' for service. The combination of Brown and Thorn were at the controls again in November 1941 when the Hercules-powered Lancaster II took to the air for the first time. In July 1942 and June 1944 Sam presided over the maiden flights of two Lancaster developments, the York transport and the Lincoln bomber.

During the run up to the famous 'Dams' raid of 16th-17th May 1943, Sam was at the helm on one of the test drops of what was then referred to as a 'mine' off the coast of Reculver, Kent, in April. With him was the Vickers CTP, 'Mutt' Summers* but he left the flying to Sam, as he was intent on observing how the 'bouncing' bomb reacted upon hitting the water. In this case, fragments went everywhere, some impacting the 'Lanc'. On 22nd June 1943, Sam was among those celebrating Chadwick's CBE. The mood of euphoria was shattered with the news that Sam's son, who had finished his tour with Bomber Command, decided to accept one more 'op' because of illness on his unit. All of the crew fell victim to a German night-fighter and perished; ironically they were in a Lancaster when they met their deaths.

In the spring of 1945, Sam's career came to an abrupt end. He was due to fly a photographic sortie out of the Avro factory at Yeadon – now Leeds-Bradford Airport – in Lancaster III RE172. To quote from the superb *Avro Lancaster – The Definitive Record* by Harry Holmes: "With higher-than-normal blood pressure and an impending medical check, Sam drove over to Yeadon for the photographic sortie. His intuition proved to be correct; he was permanently grounded after the medical." Bill Thorn took over. Harry Albert Brown was awarded the OBE in 1946; he died in 1953.

It fell to 'Sam' Brown to plan and recruit pilots to test the vast output of Lancasters from the giant Avro Chadderton factory and Woodford final assembly and flight test airfield. *BAe*

PW925, the prototype Lincoln at Hucknall, 1945. *KEC*

'Jock' Bryce

4 Sep 1953	Vickers Valiant B.2 WJ954
	4 x 9,500lbst RR Avon RA14
21 Jan 1959	Vickers Vanguard G-AOYW
	4 x 4,985shp RR Tyne 506
29 Jun 1962	Vickers VC-10 G-ARTA
	4 x 21,000lbst RR Conway 540
20 Aug 1963	BAC One-Eleven 200 G-ASHG
	2 x 10,410lbst RR Spey 506
7 May 1964	Vickers Super VC-10 G-ASGA
	4 x 22,500lbst RR Conway 550

Note: All took place at Brooklands, other than the One-Eleven, which flew from Hurn.

Gabe Robb Bryce, born 1921, joined the RAF in 1939, training as a navigator at Prestwick. He served initially with a Bristol Blenheim Special Duties Flight, followed by 172 Squadron at Chivenor with Vickers Wellington VIIIs – one of his colleagues was John Derry*. Re-mustered as a pilot, he trained in Canada then joined Ferry Command, based at Dorval. He transferred to 232 Squadron in India, flying Douglas Skymasters and Consolidated Liberator transports. His final posting was with the King's Flight, on Vickers Vikings – also on the unit was Brian Trubshaw*. In Test Pilot, *Brian relates a sortie in King's Flight DH Dominie on 11th November 1946 with Flt Lt Bryce at the helm. Due to fuel starvation, Jock had to force-land it near Benson and RL951 was written off. 'Jock' left the RAF after this.*

As a Scotsman, it was inevitable that Gabe Robb Bryce was nicknamed 'Jock' by his colleagues. He joined Vickers in 1947, under 'Mutt' Summers*. He was second pilot to Mutt on the first flight of the Viscount (16th July 1948) and the Valiant (18th May 1951) and was heavily involved in development work on both types. In 1951 Mutt retired and Jock became CTP. Jock flew the first Viscount 700, G-AMAV, from Brooklands on 28th August 1950 and he and it had their airshow debut at Farnborough the following month.

Jock's first taste of large jets came with Nene-engined Viking VX856 and the twin Tay-powered Viscount VX217, both of which provided much experience ready for the Valiant V-bomber. (All three of these had their maiden flights at the hands of Mutt.) While flying the prototype Valiant, WB210, on 12th January 1952 a fire developed in the starboard wing after an unsuccessful engine relight. This severed an aileron and Jock ordered the 'back room boys' – Roy Holland, John Prothero-Thomas and Jan Montgomery – to bale out, as they did not have ejection seats. With the trio safely out, Jock and Bomber Command liaison officer Sqn Ldr Brian Foster 'banged out'. Tragically Foster hit the fin on exit and died; the remainder of the flight test team survived. It was Jock that flew the much-modified 'Target Marker' Valiant B.2, with stretched fuselage, the undercarriage relocated into fairings in the wings; this was his first 'true' maiden flight.

The VC-10 team come down the steps at Wisley after the first flight of G-ARTA, 29th June 1962. Top to bottom: Ernie Marshall, senior design project engineer; Bill Cairns, flight engineer; Brian Trubshaw, co-pilot; 'Jock' Bryce, pilot. *BAC*

The prototype Vanguard, G-AOYW; it was followed by another 43 examples. *Vickers*

The follow-up to the highly successful Viscount, the Vanguard, proved to be a disappointment and much time was lost in protracted development trials. In his history of BAC, Charles Gardner summed up the risks: "This combination of green engine, green engine/airscrew match and a green airframe was to prove costly. With its runway limited to just 1,300 yards, Brooklands could not be used for testing and nearby Wisley was utilised for this purpose. First flights tended to be very brief affairs: out of Brooklands then 3 miles due south to Wisley, the 'record' time being just 2 minutes, 40 seconds! For the inaugural flight of the prototype Vanguard, *Yankee-Whisky*, Jock was joined by his former King's Flight colleague Brian Trubshaw as co-pilot; he had joined the Wisley test team in May 1950. A 'hop' was intended, but as things seemed all well, the sortie was extended to 20 minutes. On approach to Wisley there was excessive flap buffet and then a flap fell off. A successful landing was achieved, but it was a portent of what lay ahead; including over 2,000 stalls while the airliner's violent stall characteristics were corrected and smoothed out.

In 1960 Vickers became BAC, but the next airliner to fly from Brooklands kept the 'Vickers' label. While it had a much easier development, the much loved VC-10 also failed to meet expected production figures. Crew for the maiden flight of the prototype, G-ARTA was Jock, Brian Trubshaw as co-pilot, flight engineer Bill Cairns and senior design project engineer Ernie Marshall. Before the crew went down the steps at Wisley to meet the press, Jock made an announcement to the team: "I'd like to thank you all for the tremendous help you've been to me in the last 20 months and especially in the last 20 minutes." Jock was in command of the inaugural flight of the stretched Super VC-10, G-ASGA, which took to the skies in May 1964. His last prototype was the BAC One-Eleven twinjet, Jock flying G-ASHG from the new final assembly facility at Hurn – today Bournemouth Airport.

Jock was awarded an OBE in 1957. He retired as CTP in 1964, handing over to Brian Trubshaw. He continued with BAC as a sales director until 1975, becoming a vigorous supporter of the Brooklands Museum. Gabe Robb 'Jock' Bryce OBE died on 7th May 2014, aged 93.

Series 1103 VC-10 G-ASIX blasts off the 1,300 yard runway at Brooklands on 17th October 1964, destined for Wisley, just a short hop away. *BAC*

A 1966 advert summing up the later years of testing for 'Jock' Bryce – VC-10 and BAC One-Eleven.

the long-haul **VC·10**

NEW STANDARDS OF AIR TRAVEL COMFORT
are being pioneered throughout the world by British Aircraft Corporation's two rear-engined jet airliners, the magnificent VC10 intercontinental airliner and the short-haul BAC One-Eleven

the short-haul **ONE·ELEVEN**

BOTH BUILT BY BRITISH AIRCRAFT CORPORATION
100 PALL MALL LONDON SW1

A G Bullmore

13 Jun 1951	R&S Bobsleigh VZ728
	2 x 145hp DH Gipsy Major 8

As a Flying Officer, A G Bullmore had been the CFI of 7 Elementary and Reserve Flying Training School (later 7 EFTS), operated by Reid & Sigrist (R&S) at Desford, in 1939. As Sqn Ldr A G Bullmore DFC he was back at Desford by at least 1951 when he carried out the maiden flight of the RS.4 Bobsleigh prone-pilot test-bed. In 1939 R&S revealed its first foray into aircraft, the RS.1 Snargasher twin-engined trainer – see George Lowdell. The war interrupted any development of the Snargasher, but R&S were convinced that the concept was a winner. On 9th July 1945 RS.3 Desford G-AGOS was flown for the first time – see C F French. In May 1949 the RS.3 was bought by the Air Council and R&S was commissioned to convert it so that a pilot lying prone in the nose could fly the aircraft – hence the name Bobsleigh. During flight testing at Desford, Sqn Ldr H A Howes tried out the cramped forward cockpit. With the military serial VZ728 the RS.4 was delivered to RAE Farnborough in August 1951. (It still survives, stored by Leicestershire Museums.) The idea was that a pilot lying down would be able to resist greater 'g' forces and it would reduce the cross-section of a fighter and hence its radar 'signature'. The Bobsleigh paved the way for the Armstrong Whitworth-converted Gloster Meteor F.8 – see Eric Franklin.

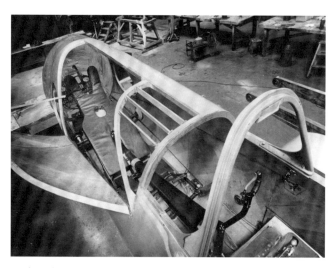

Work on the nose section of the Bobsleigh, 1950. To the right is the original cockpit and control column. The 'couch' for the prone pilot has been installed in the new nose section. *KEC*

The one-off Bobsleigh at Desford in 1951, showing the prone pilot cockpit grafted on to the nose. *KEC*

'George' Bulman

6 Sep 1923	RAE Aero Club Zephyr G-EBGW
	1 x 17hp Douglas
Sep 1923	RAE Aero Club Hurricane G-EBHS
	1 x 17hp Douglas
summer 1924	Blackburn Cubaroo N166
	1 x 1,000hp Napier Cub
1925	Hawker Horsley J7511
	1 x 665hp RR Condor IIIA
1925	Hawker Heron J6989
	1 x 455hp Bristol Jupiter VI
17 Apr 1926	Blackburn Ripon N203
	1 x 467hp Napier Lion V
24 Apr 1926	Blackburn Sprat N207
	1 x 275hp RR Falcon III
Jun 1926	Hawker Hornbill J7782
	1 x 698hp RR Condor IV
1927	Hawker Harrier J8325
	1 x 583hp Bristol Jupiter VIII
Mar 1927	Hawker Hawfinch J8776
	1 x 450hp Bristol Jupiter VII
18 Feb 1928	Blackburn Beagle N236
	1 x 460hp Bristol Jupiter VIIIF
Jun 1928	Hawker Hart J9052
	1 x 525hp RR Kestrel IB
Aug 1928	Hawker F20/27 J9123
	1 x 450hp Bristol Jupiter VII
Nov 1928	Hawker Tomtit J9772
	1 x 150hp AS Mongoose IIIC
Apr 1929	Hawker Hornet J9682 [1]
	1 x 480hp RR F.XI
6 Nov 1935	Hawker F36/34 K5083 [2]
	1 x 1,029hp RR Merlin C
14 Feb 1936	Hawker Hector K3719
	1 x 805hp Napier Dagger IIIMS
10 Mar 1937	Hawker Henley K5115
	1 x 1,030hp RR Merlin F

Notes: All took place from Brooklands, apart from: the RAE Aero Club machines, flown from Farnborough and the Blackburn types at Brough. A look through this reveals that 'George' first flew only single-engined types; in the entire history of Hawker, the company *only* produced aircraft with one engine! [1] The Hornet became the Fury. [2] F36/34 was named Hurricane in the spring of 1936.

Paul Ward Spencer Bulman, born 1896. Joined the Honourable Artillery Company, before transferring to the RFC in 1917, flying operationally in France with 46 Squadron on Sopwith Pups and 3 Squadron on Sopwith Camels. Awarded the MC *and AFC. Stayed on with the RAF post-Armistice, initially acceptance testing Royal Aircraft Factory SE.5as and Sopwith Snipes, and ferrying HP O/400s and DH.10s. From his work with SE.5s George met Roderic Hill*, in charge of the Research Flight at Farnborough, and he was offered a post with the Engine Flight. He joined RAE on 19th October 1919. Flying was not restricted to engine development; he carried out many trials in spin recovery, particularly on Camels.*

PAUL BULMAN took on the nickname 'George' as a reminder of his own inability to recall people's names; even though his up-take of technical detail, often under frantic conditions, was exceptional. When he couldn't put a name to a face, he would use 'George' instead. His RAF colleagues retaliated by referring to *him* by that name, and it stuck.

George's meticulous observational and piloting skills led him to join the RAE Aerodynamic Flight at Farnborough, as noted above. There he honed his evaluation prowess while flying a wide range of aircraft, including the pioneering, but ill-fated, Brennan helicopter in 1922. He also became chairman and chief pilot of the RAE Aero Club. In the latter role he found himself at the helm of a Hurricane in 1923 and it very nearly brought his career, and potentially his life, to a premature end. (Hold hard – *1923*? This is *not* a typo – read on...) Designed by S Childs and built by club members two single-seat aircraft were created for the 1923 Light Aeroplane Trials at Lympne. The Hurricane was a monoplane with 23ft wingspan, empty weight a mere 375lb and a maximum speed getting up to 58mph. The Zephyr was a pusher biplane with the pilot in a 'pod' ahead of the wings, looking like a throwback to the fighter designs of the early years of the Great War.

En route to Lympne, concerned that he would miss the cut-off time for entrants, George found that the diminutive 600cc converted Douglas motorcycle engine had failed and his altitude was less than 1,000ft. George quickly established that the fuel cock had closed; this was *under* and *behind* the very basic instrument panel. While juggling to find it, George also needed to enter a slight dive to re-fill the carburettor so he could re-start the engine. This did not solve the problem; he had to repeat the process all the way to Kent. It was a close run thing! So ended George's first spell of 'classic' test piloting and he was to return to Lympne before long.

'George' Bulman flying Hurricane PZ865 'The Last of the Many', July 1944. *Peter Green Collection*

The RAE Aero Club Hurricane at its birthplace, Farnborough, 1923. *KEC*

In 1925 George, aged 29, was seconded from RAE to Hawker, taking over from 'Freddy' Raynham* who had taken the post on a freelance basis after the death of Harry Hawker*. George quickly became a permanent member of the staff and resigned his RAF commission. At Brooklands, he started with the huge Horsley two-seat day bomber and the Heron single-seat fighter. The year before he had been loaned out to Blackburn at Brough to carry out the debut of the Cubaroo torpedo-bomber; RAE and A&AEE test pilots were frequently deployed to help out manufacturers. George returned to Brough in April 1926, carrying out two maiden flights in eight days on the Ripon carrier-borne torpedo-bomber and the Sprat advanced trainer, and again in 1928 for the Beagle high-altitude two-seat bomber. These three sessions were courtesy of the Hawker 'boss', Thomas Sopwith*; one of his many goodwill gestures.

George returned to Lympne in 1926, taking part yet again in the Light Aeroplane Trials, this time representing Hawker. Sydney Camm's first design for the company was the Cygnet two-seat biplane aimed at the 1924 contest. Two examples were built, tested by Freddy Raynham, and flown in the competition by Fred (G-EBMB) and W H Longton (G-EBJH). Both Cygnets were back for the 1926 trial, which was sponsored by the *Daily Mail*, offering £3,000 (£165,000 in present-day values). G-EBMB was entered by Hawker director Fred Sigrist and flown by Bulman and 'JH by the RAE Aero Club. George was awarded the main prize on 26th September 1926. Cygnet G-EBMB is today on show at the RAF Museum, Cosford.

First Hawker fighter flown by 'George' Bulman as CTP – the Heron prototype, J6989, 1925. *KEC*

Hawker Cygnet G-EBMB, flown by Bulman to victory at Lympne in 1926, is displayed at Cosford. *Ken Ellis*

George took the Hart day bomber for its inaugural flight, from Brooklands, in June 1928. At a stroke, this magnificent aircraft transformed the RAF, Hawker and was to set the tenor for the remainder of its CTP's career. In a hotly-fought competition with the Avro Antelope, the DH Hound and the Fairey Fox, the Hart came out the winner. Camm's system of construction allowed for a very robust airframe, relatively easy and economic to build and the ability to create a 'family' from essentially the same design 'base'. Thus, from the Hart came the Demon (two-seat fighter), Osprey (fleet spotter/recce), Audax (army co-operation and its Hartbees South African version), Hardy (general duties) and the Hind which was the ultimate in 'family planning' – an interim Hart replacement. The Hector was also a Hart descendent, but its Napier Dagger made it a very different beast. The sleek single-seat Hornet, which became the

The second of two Dantorps for Denmark. This was a special export version of the huge – 56ft 5in span – Horsley. *Rolls-Royce*

Pewter tankards in hand, jubilant Hawker test pilots in the 'hack' Hart G-ABMR en route to the 1932 Hendon display. Left to right: 'George' Bulman, 'Gerry' Sayer and Philip Lucas. *Hawker Siddeley*

Atmospheric image of the Hawker biplane 'family' at work: Audax of 28 Squadron, based at Ambala, India, 1937. *KEC*

exceptional Fury interceptor, spawned the Nimrod fleet fighter. Prototype J9682 was powered by the revolutionary Rolls-Royce F.XI 12-cylinder 'vee', which gained fame as the Kestrel. This powerplant was a constant with most of the 'family', although Camm was prepared to accommodate other engines for export customers, including radials that ruined the smooth lines of the breed. Orders poured in from home and overseas; at times the RAF was referred to as the 'Hawker Air Force'!

Hawker invested in several development airframes and by far the most well-known of these was an aircraft that George flew more than any other of the Hart dynasty. Civil registered as G-ABMR, this Hart worked hard. It was used as a Kestrel test-bed, a demonstrator, development airframe for many 'tweaks' and armament options, photo-platform and general duties 'hack'. From 1930 to 1936 'MR visited 15 European countries and, clad in camouflage, during the war ferried pilots all over the UK. Post-war it flew on with the Hawker 'circus' at airshows and in air races until it was presented to the RAF Museum. Today it is on show in the 'Milestones of Flight' gallery at the RAF Museum, Hendon.

In June 1935 Hawker acknowledged the vital role that George Bulman was playing in the expansion and success of the company by making him a director. By then, George was heavily involved in helping to prepare another prototype that would have an even greater effect on the fortunes of Hawker, and indeed the country. Sydney Camm and his team had conceived a 'Fury Monoplane' multi-gun fighter with fixed undercarriage and a Rolls-Royce Goshawk. Thankfully, as the design process moved on, the new fighter adopted the new Rolls-Royce V-12, soon to be named Merlin, increased firepower and a retractable undercarriage. Specification F36/34 was written around this

The prototype Hornet in 1929 – it was soon to gain fame as the Fury. *Hawker*

K5083, the prototype Hurricane with two-blade fixed-pitch wooden propeller, hinged mainwheel covers and braced tailplane. *Hawker*

private venture and the name Hurricane was given to it in the spring of 1936. On 6th November 1935 George carried out the maiden flight of K5083 – his *second* Hurricane. After that sortie, carried out with the undercarriage left down as George was not happy with the hand-crank mechanism, he is reported to have turned to Camm and said: "Another winner, I think!"

The Hurricane suffered engine problems, undercarriage, canopy and other quirks, but these were soon ironed out and it was widely regarded as a massive leap forward. Unlike the Spitfire, it was easy to 'industrialise' and it rolled off the Brooklands line in numbers sufficient to transform the UK's prospects should a battle for air supremacy develop over the homeland. For Hawker and the RAF, the monoplane fighter era had dawned. Ironically, George's next inaugural was a biplane, the Napier Dagger-engined Hector, four months later. This was the last extrapolation of the Hart, although the Hurricane was the summation of all of the design and construction knowledge gained from that biplane lineage.

George's final 'first' was the Henley, a light bomber that was essentially an enlarged Hurricane that eventually found a niche as a target-tug. George also had a 'last' flight. Rolled out with due ceremony at Langley on 27th July 1944, Mk.IIc PZ865 bore the legend *Last of the Many* under the cockpit. It was indeed the last of 10,030 Hurricanes built by Hawker and the last of 12,780 built in the UK. There was only one man who could do the honours that day, the pilot who had taken the prototype into the air for the first time in November 1935. PZ865 was retained by the company and flown as part of its post-war 'circus' from Langley and then Dunsfold. It was presented to the Battle of Britain Memorial Flight in March 1972 and, based at Coningsby, continues to grace the sky.

Flown three months after the Hurricane had heralded the monoplane era, the prototype Hector with H-format Napier Dagger. *Hawker*

In 1937, at the age of 41, George had handed over the post of CTP to his deputy, Philip Lucas*, and took on the role of chief of test flying. By 1943 this had expanded to be chief of test flying of the Hawker Siddeley Group, but he kept his hand in with production Hurricanes, Typhoons, Tempests and early Sea Furies. George was temporarily seconded, with the rank of Group Captain, as the Head of the Test Branch, British Air Commission, Washington DC, during 1941 to 1942. He led a delegation of Ministry of Aircraft Production pilots liaising with US manufacturers regarding test flying and acceptance standards. In May 1943 George published *Piloting Techniques at Compressibility Speeds: Some Notes on What to Expect and How to Cope*. At the end of 1945 Bulman left the company and resigned his directorship. It seems that in retirement he dropped all links with Hawker and aviation. Gp Capt Paul Ward Spencer 'George' Bulman CBE MC AFC died on 6th May 1963, aged 67. Eleven days later, John Yoxall provided a eulogy in the weekly magazine *Flight*. John, a professional photographer, had worked closely with George and between them they were famed for the 'head on' images they achieved. John wrote: "Although at Brooklands he had a fine team of mechanics, every alteration from a previous test flight was most carefully checked by himself before taking off again... He was patient with those who tried, but would tear to pieces the imposter or the lazy."

Right: Magnificent image from the days when advertising was an art form. The prototype Hurricane zooming out of the racetrack-cum-airfield at Brooklands.

William R Burton

Assistant to Handley Page CTP Hedley Hazelden*, William Burton was involved in development testing of the Hermes airliner series. On 10th April 1951, William was piloting Hermes V G-ALEU when it suffered a *triple* engine failure. He did extremely well to coax the remaining 2,490hp Bristol Theseus 502 turboprop to a wheels-up landing just short of Chilbolton airfield. Analysis determined that the engines had suffered fuel starvation caused by acceleration. Hazelden had first flown *Echo-Uniform* on 23rd August 1949. It was salvaged to the airfield, but was determined a write-off and broken up for spares. William went on to fly on the Victor programme.

Vernon E G Busby

25 May 1918	HP V/1500 B9463
	4 x 300hp RR Eagle VIII

"All test flights are a tense occasion to the designers and builders of any prototype aeroplane, particularly of something so huge as the V/1500 on which such high hope was centred. Pilots seem less concerned." With these words, Harald Penrose introduced the 126ft span, 17,600lb empty weight Handley Page V/1500 bomber to the readers of *British Aviation – Great War and Armistice*. A keen motorcyclist in his youth, Vernon Busby served in the RFC and RAF during the Great War and then AEE at Martlesham Heath, generating a lot of time on heavy twins. In May 1918 the latest and largest HP bomber, V/1500 B9463, was ready to test at Cricklewood by Vernon. It had been built by Harland & Wolff in Belfast and shipped to England. Starting in the traditional manner with 'straights' up and down the field, he took it fully into the sky, with four others on board, on the 25th. Upon his return he was well critical; the ailerons were heavy and worse, it suffered

from poor stability in pitch and yaw. Modifications were made to the rudders and tail surfaces accordingly.

On B9463's thirteenth flight, Busby plus five others climbed on board and off it went. Quickly it was seen to be in difficulties. Some report that all four engines – arranged in pairs, two pulling, two pushing – cut out. It stalled and crashed close to the aerodrome, bursting into flames. All perished other than the Air Board's Colonel Alec Ogilvie who was in the rear gunner's position – he suffered injuries but recovered. (Ogilvie had achieved Aviators' Certificate No.7 in his own Short-Wright biplane at Camber on 24th May 1910.) It fell to Clifford Prodger* to flight test the second example.

Edward 'Ted' Busk

30 May 1914	Royal A/c Factory BE.2c 602
	1 x 70hp Renault

Edward Teshmaker Busk, born 1886. Graduated in Mechanical Sciences at Cambridge 1907, following up with post-grad studies into self-regulating carburettors, then investigations into stresses in tension wires and gusting effects. Joined the Royal Aircraft Factory in June 1912. Assisted scientist F Short during the August 1912 Military Trials on Salisbury Plain fitting each competing aircraft with a Trajectograph, a pioneering 'black box', or flight recorder, that Short had invented. Busk developed his own, photographic paper-based Ripograph which improved data recording.

Mervyn O'Gorman, Superintendent of the Royal Aircraft Factory, was persuaded by his Assistant Engineer/Physicist 'Ted' Busk that the best way he could put his theories on stability to the test was in the air, at the controls of an aircraft. O'Gorman agreed and turned to the Factory's chief pilot, Geoffrey de Havilland (GDH), and asked him to teach Busk to fly. Paul Hare, in *The Royal Aircraft Factory* notes that Ted: "steadfastly refused

RAF personnel provide scale to an operational HP V/1500. With the wings folded back, the 'push-me, pull-you' arrangement of the four engines is evident. *KEC*

to wear a helmet, preferring to feel the wind in his hair". In mid-1913 the two-seat RE.1 biplane, No.607, designed using inputs from GDH, Henry Folland and Ted, started flight testing. Ted used this machine considerably in his research. A series of modifications to the rudder, the wing 'stagger' and the incorporation of ailerons instead of wing warping allowed Ted, on 25th November 1913, to fly an RE.1 for seven miles without touching the ailerons, turning purely on the rudder. He had created the first inherently stable aircraft. This knowledge allowed him, again with GDH and Folland, to redesign the BE.2b and create the much evolved BE.2c. Busk took modified BE.2b 602 for its first flight as a BE.2c on 30th May 1914. Trials of 602 proved it to be a superb aircraft, ideal for patrol, training and much more. Large orders were placed and the type became the backbone of the RFC as it went to war. On 27th September 1914, while testing an RE.3, the engine failed and Ted crashed on Farnborough Common, thankfully he was unhurt. While the sun was setting and GDH was flying near Farnborough on 5th November 1914 he saw a BE.2 in difficulties, it caught fire and plunged down, crashing on Laffan's Plain. This was the demise of 28-year-old Ed Busk; BE.2c 601 is believed to have suffered a leaking fuel tank. Edward Teshmaker Busk was buried in Aldershot Military Cemetery, close to that of S F Cody.

Henry 'Harry' Busteed

15 Apr 1913	Bristol-Coanda Seaplane 120 1 x 80hp Gnome
Feb 1914	Bristol Scout 206 1 x 80hp Gnome

Henry Richard Busteed, born in Australia, 1887. Built and raced motorcycles with his friend, Harry Hawker*. Harry, Hawker and other friends Eric Harrison and Harry Kauper all moved to England, hopefully to find work in aviation, arriving in May 1911. Harry gained Aviators' Certificate No.94 on 13th June 1911 at the Bristol School, Larkhill. Flew for Bristol instructing and demonstrationing, mostly on Boxkites, and from this he gravitated to occasional test piloting work for the company.

UNDER great secrecy, Australian 'Harry' Busteed and a team from British and Colonial Aeroplane Co (Bristol) were at

Dale, on the shores of Milford Haven in Pembrokeshire ready to test a revolutionary form of marine aircraft in May 1912. This was the X.2, designed by navy Lt C D Burney and built by Bristol. A monoplane, it featured a 'sealed' fuselage and wings, allowing it to alight on the water. At the bottom of the main undercarriage legs was not a float, but a propeller, each of which was powered via a clutch from an 80hp Canton-Unné rotary, that also powered a conventional tractor propeller. Burney referred to this propeller-drive undercarriage as 'Hydropeds'. Despite many attempts by Harry, the X.2 failed to escape from the waters of Milford Haven; Lt George Bentley Dacre RN took over as Harry had another commission to carry out. Dacre was soaked on 21st September when the X.2 lifted out of the water, while under tow from a motor torpedo boat, stalled and crashed into the estuary. By September 1913 Harry was back at Dale, this time to test a floatplane version of the Bristol TB.8 biplane and have a crack at the Bristol-Burney X.3, apparently much improved over the flightless X.2 and featuring counter-rotating propellers at the bottom of the Hydropeds. These trails came to nothing and at the beginning of the third session in June 1914, the X.3 hit a sandbank and the project was abandoned.

The 'other commission' that brought Harry away from the X.2 was that he had been selected as one of several pilots engaged by Bristol for the company's assault on the Military Aeroplane Competition, staged on its own turf at Larkhill in July 1912. Harry flew Bristol-Coanda Military Monoplane '14' and succeeded in sharing the third prize. In March 1913 Harry moved to Cowes on the Isle of Wight in readiness for the maiden flight of a two-seat military floatplane designed by Henri Coanda and fitted with floats designed by Oscar Gnosspelius. Trials on the River Medina were disappointing as the floats took in so much water. A new set was commissioned from Sam Saunders' nearby boatyard and on 15th April all was ready. On take-off the Gnome overheated with the result that Harry and the floatplane impacted the water heavily; the aircraft sank, Harry was thrown into the Medina but was not rescued until 30 minutes later.

During Harry's frustrating time at Dale in 1913, Harry and Bristol designer Frank Barnwell devised a small, single-seat biplane for use as a scout, having been impressed with Sopwith Tabloid. (For more on Frank, see the section on his brother, Harold Barnwell.) They adapted the unfinished fuselage of Coanda's SB.5 monoplane, coupled it to new tail surfaces, small-span wings and an 80hp Gnome. The result was nicknamed the

Harry Busteed in front of the 'Baby Bristol' at Larkhill, February 1914. *Peter Green Collection*

The ill-fated Bristol-Burney X.3 at Dale, 1914. *Peter Green Collection*

'Baby Bristol' and Harry took it for its first flight by February 1914. It was developed into the Bristol Scout, which became a pioneering fighter for both the RNAS and the RFC.

Harry joined the RNAS in 1914, becoming the officer commanding (OC) at Hendon until 1915. By 1916 he was at Eastchurch working on new developments for the RNAS, including arrester gear and shipborne take-off techniques. By 1919 he was an RAF Wing Commander and the OC of the Marine Aircraft Experimental Station, Isle of Grain (renamed MAEE in 1920), staying until 1921. From 1923 until late 1925 he was involved in the commissioning of the aircraft carrier HMS *Furious* before retiring in 1930. With the outbreak of World War Two Harry, by then an Air Commodore, was working in Balloon Command, finally retiring in 1943. Air Cdre Henry Richard Busteed CBE AFC died on 14th June 1965, aged 78.

'Jeep' Cable

Frederick John Cable, born 1915. Worked as a telegraph messenger boy and via an aircraft enthusiast's club formed by Geoffrey Dorman (see below) was invited by Juan de la Cierva* to learn to fly an autogiro at his company's school at Hanworth with tuition from Alan Marsh*. Aged 17 'Jeep' gained his Royal Aero Club aviators' certificate on 21st September 1932, becoming the first pilot ever in the UK – and very likely the world – to qualify as rotary-winged without any fixed-wing training. He was taken on a by Cierva Autogiro as resident pilot shortly afterwards.

In his landmark 1950 book *British Test Pilots*, Geoffrey Dorman affectionately wrote of 'Jeep' Cable. Both he and Jeep worked for a telegraph company, although he declines to be specific, and Geoffrey formed a club for aviation enthusiasts among the workforce, with the aim to get members flying as often as possible. Dorman believed the 'Jeep' moniker came from the curious animal to be found in the earlier *Popeye* cartoons; which, by shaking its tail, could send messages, called 'Jeep-o-Graphs'. He also noted that this was 1931 and the nickname 'Jeep' well pre-dated the ubiquitous American military vehicle. The author thinks the telegraphy link valid, but the origin of F J Cable's nickname was much simpler, facially he had more than a passing resemblance to the on-screen character.

Jeep was taken on as a pilot by the Cierva Autogiro Co, working under Alan Marsh and its CTP Reggie Brie*. By 1936 Jeep had gained his engineering licences and in April 1939 was endorsed as an autogiro instructor. Commissioned in the RAF on New Year's Day 1941, Jeep served under Reggie and Alan at Duxford, flying Cierva C.30s and Avro Rotas with 1448 Flight and, from June 1943, with 529 Squadron. Reggie and Jeep travelled to the USA during the summer of 1943, going to the Sikorsky factory at Bridgeport, Connecticut, to convert to the Hoverfly helicopter. Three Hoverfly Is, FT833, FT834 and FT835 were loaded on the MV *Daghestan*, which arrived at Liverpool in January 1944. Jeep became the first pilot to fly a Hoverfly in Britain, ferrying one of the trio off the deck of the ship to Liverpool's Speke airport. Early in February, Jeep made the first British helicopter cross-country taking a

Hoverfly to General Aircraft at Hanworth where the Helicopter Unit was established to train pilots, with Jeep as an instructor. Jeep was at the controls of FT835 when it crashed at Hanworth on 8th May 1944 – he was fine, the helicopter was relegated to ground instructional duties.

During 1944 Jeep was appointed as commanding officer of the Ministry of Aircraft Production-run Rotary Wing Unit at Hanworth, which by January 1945 moved to Beaulieu, working within the Airborne Forces Experimental Establishment, Jeep suffered his second Hoverfly accident, much more serious than the 'prang' of May 1944, at Beaulieu in January 1945. Boscombe Down pilot Sqn Ldr H G 'Pat' Hastings AFC AFM was P1 and encountered difficulties, Jeep took over, but at about 700ft control was impossible and the helicopter plummeted down; both pilots were lucky to escape with their lives. In August 1947 Sqn Ldr F J Cable AFC took up the wholly civilian post of CTP for the Ministry of Supply, still stationed at Beaulieu. On 13th June 1950 Jeep was flying as P2 to the man who had taught him to fly, Alan Marsh, in Cierva Air Horse VZ724 near Eastleigh when one of the rotors suffered structural failure at 400ft. Jeep, Alan and flight test observer Joseph Unsworth all perished. By this point, Jeep Cable had amassed 2,000-plus hours – not a lot by fixed winged standards but it represented vast experience in rotary-winged flight. And not *one* of those hours was as pilot-in-command of a fixed-wing aircraft.

Geoffrey Cairns

23 Aug 1983	Trago Mills SAH-1 G-SAHI
	1 x 115hp Lycoming O-235-L2a

Born 1926, Geoffrey Cairns joined the RAF in 1944, serving with 43 Squadron on Supermarine Spitfires, 73 Squadron on DH Vampires and 72 Squadron on Gloster Meteors. From 1953 to 1956 he was Adjutant to the Royal Hong Kong Auxiliary Air Force. ETPS Course No.15 Farnborough 1956 and then served with A&AEE. A posting to CFS Rotary Wing at Ternhill, before returning to A&AEE as Superintendant of Flying from 1968 and he was back again, this time as Commandant, 1972-1974. Finally served as Chief of Staff at 18 Group, becoming Air Vice-Marshal, retiring in 1980 to become an avionics consultant.

During 1981 Geoffrey Cairns took up a directorship with Mike Robertson's Trago Mills retail organisation, establishing its Aircraft Division. The company was backing the construction of a new training/touring light aircraft, designed by Sydney A Hollaway, the SAH-1. Geoffrey was the test pilot for the prototype (G-SAHI (from its designation, with the 'I' to be read as a '1') from Bodmin on 23rd August 1983. He demonstrated it at the 1984 Farnborough display and saw it through its certification which was gained in 1985. *Hotel-India* was the only example built under the aegis of Trago Mills, marketing it under the name Orca but failing to find an outlet. In late 1991 the design rights were acquired by FLS Aerospace with construction at undertaken by the company's Lovaux Ltd subsidiary at Bournemouth. Re-designated the FLS Sprint, another four examples were built, the last two appearing in

The attractive-looking SAH-1 with Geoffrey Cairns in the right-hand seat, 1983. *Trago Mills (Aircraft Division) Ltd*

Having been in a flat spin, the Bristol Type 133 was very recognisable when it 'arrived' at Longwell Green, near Bristol on 8th March 1935. *via Don Middleton*

1998. (G-ASAHI is still airworthy, operated by a group in Bedfordshire.) AVM Geoffrey Cairns CBE AFC retired from flying in 1994; he died on 5th February 2009, aged 82.

'Jock' Campbell

By 1921 Wg Cdr Thomas Wight Campbell (TWC), known as 'Jock', was an instructor with the Bristol-operated school at Filton. As was so often the case, he was asked to carry out tests when the need arose and by 1923 he was assistant to CTP Cyril Uwins*. A look through the maiden flights performed by Cyril will reflect the work carried out by TWC during his time at Filton and provide more detail on the types mentioned here. On 23rd November 1923, TWC was flying the prototype Jupiter Fighter G-EBGF (a version of the famous F.2B with a Bristol Jupiter IV radial) when the engine seized at 20,000ft. He managed to force-land safely, but G-EBGF was written off. During preparations for the 1924 Lympne Light Aircraft Trials, TWC fouled telephone wires while flying Brownie G-EBJK; he managed to limp back to Filton. The Brownie was repaired and TWC shared flying in the contest with Uwins. Jock flew the prototype Bristol Bloodhound G-EBGG in the Croydon-based 1925 King's Cup air race, but did not finish.

By 1927 the very successful Bulldog fighter was demanding many hours of test, along with its development the Bullpup from 1929. TWC was on a boat bound for Chile in September 1930, along with a Bulldog, for a 'fly off' against a Curtiss Hawk biplane for a potentially lucrative order from the air force. The demonstration went well and an order for 20 was placed, but the finances fell through. Testing of the Type 133 monoplane fighter prototype, R-10, was nearly complete and it was ready to go to Martlesham Heath for evaluation in early March 1935. It featured 'trouser' fairings below the wings and the novel retractable undercarriage tucked into these. TWC took R-10 up for general handling on 8th March 1935 and at 14,000ft put it into a spin to starboard. He'd forgotten the undercarriage was still in the 'down' position and this configuration turned a benign spin into a potentially lethal flat one. The Bristol Mercury radial failed and TWC was in serious trouble. Down to around 6,000ft Jock tried to bale out, but one of his feet was caught by the control column. He was down to about 2,000ft before he freed

himself, parachuting to safety. R-10 impacted in a field close to houses at Longwell Green, south of Kingswood, Bristol; nobody was hurt on the ground. Hopes at Filton for an order from the hotly-contested Specification F7/30 were dashed, Gloster was the winner with the Gladiator.

Alan Campbell-Orde

3 May 1930	AW Aries J9037 [1] 1 x 400hp AS Jaguar IV
1930	AW XVI S1591 1 x 560hp AS Panther IIA
6 Jun 1932	AW Atalanta G-ABPI 4 x 340hp AS Serval III
26 Feb 1934	AW AW.19 A-3 1 x 810hp AS Tiger VI
4 Jun 1935	AW AW.23 K3585 2 x 810hp AS Tiger VI
17 Mar 1936	AW Whitley K4586 2 x 795hp AS Tiger IX

Notes: All took place at Whitley Abbey. [1] Improved Atlas – see Frank Courtney – only one built.

Alan Colin Campbell-Orde, born 1898. Joined RNAS and fought in Belgium and France, ended his naval service as a Flt Sub-Lt. Absorbed into RAF April 1918 and awarded AFC in 1919. He last served with 1 Communications Squadron using modified DH.4s (among others) to fly dignitaries to the peace conference at Versailles, near Paris, becoming a Flying Officer. This provided superb credentials to work for Aircraft Transport & Travel Ltd in 1919, Britain's first commercial airline, also operating DH.4s. AT&T was wound up in December 1920 and Alan instructed in China, perhaps under contract to Vickers.

Until 1930 when Alan Campbell-Orde (ACO) was appointed as Armstrong Whitworth's CTP, it had been company practice to use the chief flying instructor of the AW-run flying school, which also occupied the airfield at Whitley Abbey. ACO, described by Harald Penrose as "a handsome, somewhat

A famous image of Alan Campbell-Orde wearing his test piloting gear for a publicity shot in 1930. Note the stopwatch, knee-pad 'notebook' and barometer. *AWA*

The one-off AW.19 general purpose biplane of 1934. *AWA*

inscrutable man" in *British Aviation – Widening Horizons*, joined the AW school in 1924. Prior to ACO's appointment most of the testing had been the domain of freelancer Frank Courtney*. The last AW instructor to test fly had been Douglas Hughes* who was killed in a Siskin in July 1927. ACO's testing career started with the Aries and Type XVI single-seat biplanes, the latter a prototype

naval fighter. The two-seat AW.19 was a private venture aimed at Specification G4/31 to replace the Wapiti as a general-purpose warplane. It was unsuccessful, Vickers taking the prize with the monoplane that was eventually named Wellesley.

It was multi-engined types that crowned ACO's time with AW, also providing experience for his later duties with British Airways and BOAC. The company had established a good relationship with Imperial Airways with its Argosy biplane airliner of 1926 and it offered its first monoplane design for a requirement issued in 1930 for a nine-passenger type for use on the West and South African routes. ACO was at the controls of the first of eight Type XVs, G-ABPI *Atalanta*, named after a Greek mythological maiden, on 6th June 1932. Imperial usually adopted the name of the first example as the class name for the fleet hence the Type XV became the Atalanta. The prototype exhibited few problems although the servo-tab enhanced rudder was found to induce oscillation at high speeds. This was damped out by fitting springs and designer John Lloyd found a way by which he could observe the rudder's behaviour. A hole was cut in the upper fuselage over the toilet cubicle; by standing on the 'loo' Lloyd could pop his head out into the airstream and monitor the errant rudder! On 20th October 1932 a take-off in G-ABPI went very wrong when all four Serval ten-cylinder, two-row radials failed due to an air lock in the fuel system. ACO had little option but to force-land the airliner on a hill to the west of the airfield. ACO was unhurt but his co-pilot, Don Green, was so injured that his test flying career was curtailed. G-ABPI was rebuilt and entered service with Imperial Airways.

AW's response to Specification C26/31 for a RAF bomber-transport resulted it the company's first retractable undercarriage type. AW.23 K3585 had its maiden flight on 4th June 1935 but the production contract went to the Bristol Bombay. (The AW.23 went on to be used for flight refuelling trials – see George Errington.) All was not wasted as the design office already had its eyes on B3/34 for a long-range twin-engined bomber. The AW.23's mainplanes and tail surfaces were utilized in the Whitley, ACO taking the first example, K4586, skywards from the airfield it was named after on 17th March 1936. Along with the Hampden and Wellington, the Whitley became Bomber Command's backbone during the early years of World War Two; 1,466 examples were built up to mid-1943.

'Atalanta', the prototype Type XV airliner. Note the spatted main wheels. *KEC*

A 1936 advert showing the capabilities of AWA, with the Whitley bomber, top, and the AW.53 bomber-transport.

During early 1936 all staff at AW busied themselves moving to the much-enlarged factory site and airfield at Baginton. ACO was the first to fly from the new airfield, flying a Scimitar biplane there on 26th May 1936. Later that year, he gave up the post of CTP to become the operations manager of British Airways – the first use of that name. He was succeeded by Charles Turner-Hughes*. From 1940 he was Operational Director for BOAC and was awarded a CBE in 1943. ACO finished his career with BOAC as Development Director in 1957, retiring to become a consultant. Alan Colin Campbell-Orde CBE AFC died in 1992, aged 94.

Chris Capper

1 Jun 1962	DH Sea Vixen FAW.2 XN684 2 x 11,230lbst RR Avon 208
13 Aug 1962	HS HS.125-1 G-ARYA 2 x 3,000lbst BS Viper 20

Alan Christopher Capper, born 1923. Completed RAF flying training in Canada 1943, staying on to instruct, before operations on DH Mosquitos. By August 1945 he was a test pilot at 308 MU Bamhrauli, India. Final positing was with 4 Squadron, on Mosquito FB.VIs in West Germany. No.7 Course ETPS, Farnborough 1948, followed by extensive flying with the Aero Flight, RAE Farnborough; types flown included the DH.108. During his time at RAE he was awarded the AFC; leaving in 1951.

The prototype HS.125, G-ARYA, rolled out at Hatfield, August 1962. Note the 'DH 125' lettering. *DH*

A gathering at Hatfield early in 1965 as RAF 'brass' inspect the first two Dominie T.1s, XS709 and XS710. Left to right: Sqn Ldr Trevains, John Cunningham, AVM Ayling, Chris Capper, Richard Blyth (HSA Military Sales Manager) and AM P H Dunn, C-in-C Flying Training Command. *HSA*

BY 1951 Chris Capper's RAF career looked set only to 'fly a desk' and he sought other options, joining Bristol as a PTP, mostly testing Sycamores. With the death of John Derry* at Farnborough in September 1952 de Havilland CTP John Cunningham* offered Chris a post as test pilot. Chris was at the controls when the second prototype Sea Vixen, DH.110 WG240, with a new flight control system installed, was first flown. Under 'Jock' Elliot*, Chris was put in charge of output from Christchurch – the former Airspeed plant – with maiden flights of Sea Vixens ending at a new test facility at Hurn. Chris piloted FAW.1 XJ475 out of Christchurch on 28th June 1957, landing at Hurn. Three days later while shaking it down at Hurn, the main undercarriage failed to lock and it collapsed on touchdown; Chris was unhurt and XJ475 was back in the air by August. From 1960 Sea Vixen debuts concluded at Hatfield and Chris continued to oversee them. Sea Vixen FAW.1 XN684 was the first of two built as FAW.1s on the Christchurch line that were converted to act as prototypes of the extensively redeveloped FAW.2. Chris carried out its maiden flight at Hatfield on 1st June 1962.

John Cunningham had a new programme for Chris by 1961. Hatfield was involved in the creation of two major types, the HS.125 corporate jet and the HS Trident jetliner. John planned to devote himself to the latter and make Chris project test pilot on the '125. (It had been initially designated DH.125 and was to have been named Jet Dragon, but this was dropped. In 1963 DH was merged into Hawker Siddeley.) Chris flew the prototype HS.125-1 G-ARYA at Hatfield with FTO John Rye, a regular companion from his Sea Vixen days, on 13th August 1962 for a 50-minute sortie. Waiting for Chris on his return was John Cunningham. It was a momentous moment; Chris had started a programme that ran to 360 Viper-powered HS.125s. After the two prototypes, production was carried out at Hawarden, near Chester, and in 1966 Chris became CTP there. Among his many tests at Hawarden, Chris was at the helm of Dominie T.1 XS709 on 30th December 1964, the first of 20 navigation trainers for the RAF. (XS709 is preserved at the RAF Museum, Cosford.)

One of Chris's responsibilities at Hawarden was the HSA-owned Mosquito T.3 RR299 (G-ASKH) which was displayed at airshows and company open days. It was in this 'Wooden Wonder' that Chris elected to have his last flight, in August 1981, nearly 40 years since he flew the type on 'ops'. His days with de Havilland and HSA were not yet over, as he took up the post of airfield manager at Hatfield, finally retiring in 1988. Alan Christopher Capper AFC died in 2007, aged 84.

Noel 'Cap' Capper

5 Nov 1947	SAL Pioneer I VL515 1 x 240hp DH Gipsy Queen 32
25 Jun 1955	SAL Twin Pioneer G-ANTP 2 x 540hp Alvis Leonides 503/8

Noel John Capper, born 1908. Joined RAF, going solo in 1929, by 1932 was with 12 Squadron at Andover on Hawker Harts. Left the RAF in 1934, as a Flying Officer, working for Hillman's Airways and Imperial Airways. From 1935 he was CFI of 12 EFTS at Prestwick, which was run by Scottish Aviation. Re-joined the RAF in 1939 as an instructor, leaving again in 1946, as a Wg Cdr. Re-joined SAL in 1947, initially as Flight Manager.

The cover of a Scottish Aviation Pioneer brochure, showing the prototype, G-AKBF.

W ITH the advent of the Prestwick Pioneer short take-off and landing utility aircraft, Noel 'Cap' Capper was appointed as CTP for Scottish Aviation Limited (SAL) in 1947. (The 'Prestwick' prefix was dropped when the Twin Pioneer was conceived.) Early in 1947, Cap and several engineers crossed the Atlantic to Buffalo, New York, the home of Bell Aircraft. There they undertook a conversion to the Bell 47 helicopter, SAL intending to market the type, and possibly build it, in the UK. The prototype Pioneer, VL515, was first flown on 5th November 1947 and Cap demonstrated its incredible short-field flying characteristics at the 1948 SBAC display at Farnborough. Civilian registered as G-AKBF, the aircraft was re-engined with a 520hp Alvis Leonides and flown in this guise by Cap in June 1950. SAL's first venture into aircraft design and manufacturing was reasonably successful, with a total of 59 being built. Greater sales were forecast for a more capacious twin-engined version and Cap was at the helm of the first Twin Pioneer, G-ANTP, on 25th June 1955. Wg Cdr Noel John 'Cap' Capper AFC OBE retired from SAL in 1965; he died in 1985, aged 77.

Proudly 'flying' the Scottish saltire on the central fin, the prototype Twin Pioneer, G-ANTP, on a sortie out of Prestwick. *SAL*

Leonard Carruthers

May 1942	Percival Proctor IV LA586 1 x 210hp DH Gipsy Queen II
31 Mar 1946	Percival Prentice TV163 1 x 250hp DH Gipsy Queen 32
9 May 1947	Percival Merganser X-2 2 x 296hp DH Gipsy Queen 51

Leonard Turnell Carruthers (LTC), born 1899. Joined the RFC 1917, training in Egypt. Operational flying on the Western Front in autumn 1918. Posted to 1 Aircraft Acceptance Park, Coventry, to test DH.10s, among others. Serious accident circa 1919 when the Avro 504 LTC was piloting spun in – he was invalided out of service. Despite this, it seems he kept his hand in, albeit unofficially. He managed

to re-join the RAF in 1926, going on to fly Vickers Virginia VIIs with 9 Squadron, then on 'ops' in Iraq with 55 Squadron, on Westland Wapitis; ending as an instructor circa 1934. LTC freelanced beyond that, including time with Cobham's 'circus' in its last season, 1935. While piloting Westland Wessex G-ADFZ over Blackpool on 7th September 1935, Avro 504N G-ACOD struck the underside of the tri-motor, ripping into the fuselage and knocking out two of its engines. LTC managed a forced-landing using the remaining engine. He and his passengers survived, G-ADFZ was a write-off; the two occupants in the 504 perished. He then instructed at the Reid & Sigrist-operated 7 E&RFTS at Desford, under George Lowdell*, moving in 1940 to the Bristol Wireless Flight, a sub-unit of 2 Radio School, at Yatesbury. Here he was recruited by Cyril Uwins* as a TP, but this was not taken up and LTC was transferred to 24 EFTS at Luton in August 1940.

Indian Air Force Prentice T.20 HV903 on air test out of Luton in late 1950. *Percival Aircraft*

JUST a couple of months into his spell as an instructor with 24 EFTS at Luton, Leonard Turnell Carruthers (LTC) was offered the post of CTP to Percival Aircraft, also sited at the Bedfordshire airfield. The 41-year-old had big shoes to fill, as Edgar Percival*, who did much of the testing, had left the company he founded in the spring of 1940. As LTC started work, Proctor production was running down, with F Hills and Sons at Barton, Manchester, taking over from the spring of 1941. Percival turned to building Airspeed Oxford crew trainers and, from 1944, DH Mosquito XVIs and PR.34s and LTC oversaw the small band of PTPs carrying out flight tests. In the spring of 1944 LTC piloted the first Luton-built Mosquito XVI (the batch started at PF379) on its maiden flight in the spring of 1944 but on return discovered that the retractable tailwheel refused to come down. He carried out a very gentle landing, slowing carefully to minimise the damage when the lower rear fuselage started to scrape along; there was little damage and it was soon back in the air.

Percival was not finished with the Proctor; in response to Specification T9/41 the Mk.IV – practically a new design – wireless operator trainer was created. Leonard flew the prototype

and a small batch before the Barton production line took over. The Proctor IV formed the basis of the purely civilian Proctor 5 which kept LTC and his team busy from late 1945 to 1948.

Specification T23/43 sought a replacement for the Tiger Moth as an elementary trainer for the RAF and the Percival design was declared the winner. LTC first flew the Prentice at Luton on 31st March 1946 and 474 were ordered for the RAF and export, including India. Much work was needed to ready the Prentice for RAF service. It suffered from lateral stability problems, even a gentle turn could result in early examples inverting. Distinctive up-turned wing tips cured this. Spin recovery was difficult and several formats were trialled in 1947 to overcome this. The tailplane and elevators were mounted higher up the fin on second prototype TV166 and the first production example, VN684, sprouted twin fins and rudders before strakes were fitted at the base of the fin. All of this took many hours of testing.

The final prototype flown by LTC was the five-passenger twin engined Merganser which took to the air in May 1947. This did not go into production, it was considerably redesigned and enlarged emerging as the Prince the following year, but this was in the hands of the next Percival PTP, 'Sandy' Powell*. With around 8,000 hours in over 60 types to his credit, Leonard Turnell Carruthers retired from Percival in 1948; he died in 1973, aged 74.

Unpainted and unmarked, the Merganser ground-running at Luton, early 1947. *Percival Aircraft*

Larry Carter

May 1923	Gloster Grebe J6969 1 x 350hp AS Jaguar III
Jul 1923	Gloster I G-EAXZ 1 x 530hp Napier Lion
Oct 1923	Gloster Gannet G-EBHU 1 x 32hp Carden
Feb 1925	Gloster Gamecock J7497 1 x 398hp Bristol Jupiter IV

The demonstrator Grebe II G-EBHA, flown by Larry Carter in the 1923 King's Cup air race. *Peter Green Collection*

Line-up of a dozen Gamecock Is of 23 Squadron. *KEC*

Larry L Carter, born 1898. In 1919 he was a pilot with Britain's first commercial airline, Aircraft Transport & Travel Ltd. In November 1921 he ferried reconditioned Bristol M.1C M-AFAA from Filton via Croydon to Spain for its customer. By May 1922 he was working for Handley Page Transport and flying Bristol Ten-Seater G-EAWY on the Paris-London service. On take-off from Le Bourget it was noticed that one of the main wheels was hanging down in a manner that would threaten the landing. A message was sent to Croydon to warn Larry of his predicament. He was contacted by wireless and made a superb touch down, damaging only a wing tip. Continuing his association with Bristol on 7th August 1922 he competed in the Hendon Aerial Derby, flying M.1D G-EAVP, winning the race at 107.8mph.

LARRY CARTER became the Gloucestershire Aircraft Company's test pilot in April 1923, succeeding 'Jimmy' James*. (The company was re-named Gloster Aircraft in 1926: this book refers to its products as 'Gloster' throughout.) During his brief time with the company Larry helped to establish the biplane fighter dynasty of designer Henry Folland. Larry flew the prototype Grebe, a development of the experimental Grouse, in May 1923. With the Grebe, Gloster was established as a major supplier of fighters to the RAF all the way through to the Gladiator and again in the jet era with the Meteor, concluding with the Javelin. Acceptance was swift, Larry testing the first production Grebe II in August 1923. Gloster built Mk.II G-EBHA for demonstrations and trials. Having already established his racing prowess (see above) Gloster entered Larry and G-EBHA in the King's Cup, staged from Hendon, in July 1923. In the hands of Frank Courtney* the rival AW Siskin took the honours, but Larry won £100 for the fastest circuit.

Also in July 1923 Larry tested Gloster I G-EAXZ, a high performance biplane extensively rebuilt from the Mars I, or 'Bamel'. (Jimmy James had made the debut in this machine in its original form.) Larry was back at Hendon on 6th August, this time with G-EAXZ, again winning the Aerial Derby, at 192.4mph. This was an incredible 84.6mph faster than his achievement the year before in the Bristol M.1D. Then he had 140hp from a Bristol Lucifer, for 1923 the Gloster I boasted 530hp from a Napier Lion. Beyond this triumph, pneumonia laid Larry low, but he was able to test fly the diminutive 18ft-span Gannet powered by a 750cc two-cylinder designed by John Carden in October 1923. This was the company's entry in the *Daily Mail*-sponsored Light Aeroplane Trials at Lympne. The little two-stroke proved problematical and Larry only managed to fly it once during the competition, on the 10th.

The Grebe was further developed and, powered by the more reliable Bristol Jupiter and named Gamecock, was flown by Larry from Hucclecote in February 1925. Following a spirited demonstration in Helsinki in March 1927 by Howard Saint*, Finland licence-built the type as the Kukko. In May 1925 Larry was at Cranwell to flight test the second prototype Gloster II J7505. Hubert Broad* had flown the first example, as a floatplane, in July 1924 in readiness for that year's Schneider Trophy but it was wrecked in October and the contest postponed. The second machine was completed as a landplane to try out new features for the next Gloster Schneider design and the huge all-grass airfield at Cranwell was considered ideal for such a high-performance biplane. After two flights, on 10th June disaster struck. Flying at about 40ft above the airfield and at around 240mph Larry encountered elevator flutter. He managed to switch off the engine, thankfully the biplane did not roll over on impact but Larry suffered a fractured scull and a broken leg. Larry did not fly again, for a while he liaised with

The ill-fated Gloster II at Cranwell in June 1925. *Peter Green Collection*

RAF Grebe squadrons on behalf of Gloster; his place as CTP was taken by Howard Saint. Larry attended the light aircraft trials at Lympne in September 1926 but was rushed to hospital and died, aged 28, having succumbed to meningitis.

Don Cartlidge

| 21 Jun 1961 | ATEL Carvair G-ANYB |
| | 4 x 1,450hp P&W R2000-7 |

Donald Brian Cartlidge, born 1928. Course No.15 ETPS Farnborough 1956. From 1959 was personal pilot to Edward J Stanley, 18th Earl of Derby, flying Piaggio P.166 G-APVE to horse racing events etc from its base at Speke.

DON CARTLIDGE was appointed as senior pilot for Freddie Laker's Aviation Traders (Engineering) Ltd (ATEL) in September 1960 to test fly and assist in the certification of the ATL.98 Carvair, a radical conversion of the well-established Douglas DC-4/C-54 Skymaster airliner. The Carvair – derived from 'Car-via-Air – was intended to replace Bristol 170 car ferries and to act as a bulk item transport. Under ATL chief designer A C Leftley, a brand new nose was grafted on to the DC-4 airframe. The flightdeck was placed above the cabin and freight or cars could be loaded directly via a hinged door in the extreme nose. The nosewheel retracted into a fairing under the forward fuselage so that it did not impinge the cargo floor. The Carvair was 9ft 3in longer than the DC-4, this and the 'keel effect' of the bulbous nose was countered by a much enlarged, DC-7 style, fin and rudder. Up to five cars could be accommodated plus 25 passengers; or combinations thereof in the car ferry role. In pure freight configuration, the Carvair offered a 75ft cargo floor.

With Don as captain, *Yankee-Bravo* embarked on a 120-minute test flight from Southend on 21st June 1961. Co-pilot was Robert 'Bob' Langley, managing captain of launch customer Channel Air Bridge; ATL's flight test engineer Ken W Smith was also on board. ATL had two senior pilots, the second being Lyndon Griffith who flew a Cessna 310 chase-plane with the designer, A C Leftley, among others, observing. (Griffith was also ETPS-trained, having attended No.10 Course at Farnborough in 1951 and latterly had been flying for Armstrong Siddeley – see Chapter Four.) *Yankee-Bravo* was the first of 21 Carvairs the last one taking to the air in

1968. After his time with ATL, Don went on to fly with Shannon Air, Boeing 707s with Lloyd International and finally Britannia Airways. Donald Brian Cartlidge died on 15th August 2010, aged 82.

Peter Chandler

| 14 Jun 2013 | Airbus A350-941 F-WXWB |
| | 2 x 83,000lbst RR Trent XWB |

Air Training Corps then aeronautical engineering degree at Southampton. Joined RAF 1975, streaming to fast-jets and later posted to USAF Test Pilot School at Edwards Air Force Base, California. On return to the UK, he flew at Boscombe Down and as an instructor. He left the RAF in 1994 becoming a commercial pilot, mostly on Airbus A340s.

IN one form or another, the UK has been a part of the Airbus consortium since its formation in December 1970. Unlike the bulk of the events listed in this book, first flights take place in Toulouse, France, or Hamburg, Germany, or Seville, Spain. Throughout the incredible success story that is Airbus, the UK has been a centre of excellence for wings, with the major construction sites at Hawarden, near Chester, and Filton, Bristol. Depending on the programme, Rolls-Royce and other UK aerostructures companies have also been involved. As a major partner in the huge operation, it would be wrong to leave Airbus out of the coverage.

It was not until 2009 that a 'Brit' got to command the inaugural flight of an Airbus product when Ed Strongman* piloted the prototype A400M airlifter. Prior to this, Airbus first flights had been captained as follows: A300 28th October 1972 by Max Fischl; A320 22nd February 1987 by Pierre Baud; A340 25th October 1991 also Pierre Baud; A330 2nd November 1992 by Etienne Tarnowski and A380 27th April 2005 by Jacques Rosay. Throughout these and countless other development flights, British co-pilots and flight test engineers have been involved.

The first captaining of an Airbus airliner by a British test pilot was carried out amid great publicity by Peter Chandler when he took the prototype A350 wide-body twin-jet into the air from Toulouse-Blagnac on 14th June 2013. All eyes were on this because it was the first over-ridingly composite Airbus airliner; as this book closed for press there were 780 orders for the type.

The eleventh Carvair conversion, G-APNH 'Menai Bridge' in service with British United, 1965. *Roy Bonser*

Peter Chandler (left) with some of the A350 first flight crew. *Courtesy and © 2015 Airbus-H Goussé*

View of Airbus A350 F-WXWB from the chase aircraft during the first flight, 14th June 2013. *Courtesy and © 2015 Airbus-P Maselet*

Peter joined Airbus and became CTP Civil Programmes, in 2008. He was in the right-hand seat for the first flight of the A380 'super-jumbo' at Toulouse in April 2005. Crew with Peter on the first, 2 hours, 48 minute A350 flight were as follows: Guy Magrin, Project Test Pilot; Pascal Verneau, Project Test Flight Engineer; Patrick du Che, Head of Development Flight Tests; Emanuele Costanzo, Flight Test Engineer and Fernando Alonso, Head of Flight Operations. Commenting on his first flight, Peter said: "I am very lucky and very privileged," adding: "After the first few minutes, it didn't feel like we were doing a first flight. It felt like we were flying an aeroplane at the end of a test programme... it was so relaxed and so predictable."

Charles Chilton

| 4 Jul 1929 | Saro Cutty Sark G-AAIP |
| | 2 x 105hp Cirrus Hermes I |

Charles Edward Chilton, born 1906. Joined the RAF in 1924, training at Cranwell. After a flying-boat course at Calshot in 1926, he was posted to MAEE in May 1927.

D URING 1929 Fg Off Charles 'Chilly' Chilton was seconded by MAEE Felixstowe to Saunders-Roe (Saro) to test fly the prototype Cutty Sark four-seat general purpose amphibian, from the Medina River at Cowes. After successful evaluation at Felixstowe in late August, Charles took it to the seaplane rally at La Baule in France the following month. With him on this venture was none other than Sir Sefton Brancker, the Director of Civil Aviation. While only a dozen Cutty Sarks were produced, the amphibian was a turning point in the fortunes of the company.

Chilly learned how to pilot aircraft catapulted from a ship at RAE Farnborough and in November 1929 he was being hurled

off the deck of HMS *Ark Royal* in a Fairey IIIF. He handed responsibility for catapult development to Fg Off Frank Whittle, who should need no introduction but if you need a refresher see 'Gerry' Sayer in Volume Two. Fg Off Chilton became 209 Squadron's Navigation Officer in September 1931, equipped with Blackburn Iris, Short Singapore and Supermarine Southampton flying-boats. A posting to CFS was followed by an exchange to the South African Air Force from 1935. In May 1937 he joined Bomber Command as Navigation Staff Officer, becoming a Squadron Leader. By 1943 he was Officer Commanding Chivenor and in the teeth of Coastal Command's U-Boat war. Air Marshal Sir Edward Chilton KBE CB was appointed Air Officer Commander-in-Chief Coastal Command In June 1959. Retiring from the RAF in 1962, he took up a post with IBM UK until 1978; he died on 20th August 1992, aged 86.

The prototype Saro Cutty Sark G-AAIP on the beach of St Aubin's Bay, St Helier, Jersey in 1929. It is almost certainly on its way to, or returning from, the seaplane rally at La Baule, France, with C E Chilton piloting. *Peter Green Collection*

Juan de la Cierva

23 Oct 1928	Cierva C.17 Mk.I G-AABP [1] 1 x 95hp Cirrus III
Jul 1929	Cierva C.19 Mk.I G-AAGK [2] 1 x 80hp AS Genet II
Sep 1931	Cierva C.24 G-ABLM [3] 1 x 120hp DH Gipsy III
20 Apr 1932	Cierva C.25 G-ABTO [4] 1 x 80hp Pobjoy Cataract
Apr 1933	Cierva C.30 G-ACFI [5] 1 x 105hp AS Genet Major
May 1933	Cierva C.28 [6] 1 x 40hp Douglas Dryad
4 Feb 1935	Cierva-Lepère CL.20 G-ACYI [7] 1 x 90hp Pobjoy Niagara III

Notes: [1] Also designated Avro 612, Avian III fuselage, flown from Hamble. [2] Also designated Avro 620, flown from Hamble. [3] Built by de Havilland, flown from Stag Lane. Owned by the Science Museum, this machine is displayed at the de Havilland Aircraft Museum, London Colney. [4] Built by Comper Aircraft at Hooton Park. First attempt at flight 20th March 1932 resulted in rotor failure, re-flown as shown. [5] Assembled at Hanworth by National Flying Services; flown at Hanworth. Later built by Avro as the Type 671 and known as the Rota I in RAF. [6] Built by G and J Weir at Cathcart, also designated Weir W.1. Flown at Hanworth. [7] Two-seater, flown with Alan Marsh at Yeovil.

Additionally there were three 'nearlies': February 1928 Cierva tested the Parnall-built C.11 G-EBQG (120hp ADC Airdisco) but it was wrecked. On 25th April 1930 he tested the float-equipped C.17 'Hydrogiro' (100hp Avro Alpha) on Hamble Water, but it failed to airborne. In the spring of 1934 repeated attempts to get the Westland-built C.29 K3663 airborne at Yeovil failed.

Also Juan first flew *at least* the following European-built examples: 23rd May 1929 the Cierva C.12 (also designated Loring C.XII, powered by a 22hp Wright Whirlwind J-5) near Cuatro Vientos, Madrid, a very significant flight for him, in his homeland. In the spring of 1931 he carried out the debut of the 95hp Renault 4Pb-powered Weymann CTW.200 in France. In November 1932 he first flew the Cierva C.27 (also designated Cierva-Lepère CL.10, powered by a 85hp Pobjoy Cataract) at Orly, Paris.

Señor Don Juan de la Cierva Codorníu, born in 1895 in Spain. Influenced by Blériot's Channel crossing of 1909 and the appearance of a Blériot XI in Spain the following year in 1910-1911 he, his brother Ricardo and friends built a pair of gliders, neither of which were successful. Studied engineering at Madrid from 1911, graduating 1917. In 1912, Juan, Ricardo and Pablo Diaz designed and built the two-seat BCD-1 El Cangrejo (Crab) biplane powered by a 50hp Gnome; tested by Frenchman Jean Mauvais in August 1912 it was the first Spanish-built aircraft to fly. This was followed by the BCD-2 monoplane of December 1913. In

The trans-Channel Cierva C.8L, G-EBYY, is displayed at the Musée de l'Air et Espace at Le Bourget. *Alan Curry*

1913 Juan responded to a government competition for a military aircraft and he designed and built the C.3 tri-motor bomber; this crashed on its first flight 8th July 1919.

From then on Juan started investigations into slow flight and then wingless flight. His initial patents using a wind-milling rotor were lodged in July 1920 and the word 'Autogiro' was coined by him. Autogiro No.1 (retrospectively designated C.1) with a 60hp Le Rhône and a fuselage from a 1911 Deperdussin monoplane featured counter-rotating rotors and was tested in October 1920 but did not fly. This was followed by the No.3 (C.3) with a 50hp Gnome and was extensively trialled from June 1921. No.2 (C.2) did not enter test until 1922, but was not satisfactory. On 17th January 1923 Lt Alejandro Gómez Spencer made the world's first controlled gyroplane flight in No.4 (C.4, 110hp Le Rhône) which featured hinged rotor blades and started intensive trials, developments and refinements. The C.5 – the first to carry the C-series designations – appeared in 1923 and in February 1924 the C.6 (also 110hp Le Rhône) with the fuselage from an Avro 504K first flew; followed by the much refined C.6bis.

With the C.6, Juan de la Cierva was really getting the attention of governments and manufacturers. Vickers made approaches for him to come to the UK but it was an invite from British Air Ministry to come to the RAE that he responded to. (He will be referred to throughout as Juan to avoid confusion with the Cierva Autogiro Co Ltd which he founded in March 1926, with James G Weir as its chairman.) The C.6A was assembled at Farnborough on 1st October 1925 and was to have been flown by experienced Autogiro pilot Captain Joaquín Loriga, but he was ill and RAE engaged Frank Courtney* to carry out the trials. Ironically, the long-delayed and hugely expensive Brennan Helicopter was wrecked for the second and final time at Farnborough on 2nd October 1925 in the hands of Bob Graham*; Cierva's timing was inspired. Frank Courtney achieved his first sorties in the C.6A just ten days after this mishap, making the inaugural sustained rotary winged flight in Britain. Air Ministry and industry interest was high and Juan appointed Frank as his test pilot and made plans to move to England.

As Juan settled in Britain he did so as a gifted and pioneering designer; he was not a pilot and had been a

The de Havilland-built C.24 cabin Autogiro, tested by Juan de Cierva in September 1931. *De Havilland Heritage Centre*

spectator whenever his creations flew. He was determined to master his own creations and Alan Marsh* taught him to fly at Hanworth, the Spaniard receiving his aviator's certificate in January 1927. In his superb book *Cierva Autogiros – The Development of Rotary-Wing Flight*, Peter Brooks notes that this wish added to the increasingly tempestuous relationship with Courtney. On 7th February 1927 Frank was injured when the C.6C crashed at Hamble and the two parted company. Immediately Bert Hinkler* was brought in and he served until January 1928, but increasingly during 1927 Juan took over the testing of new machines, leading to his debut with a new type, the C.17 in October 1928. Despite his growing experience, Juan was never without a CTP to run his test flight office and particularly for demonstration flying as the prospects for customers and licence production ballooned. Beyond Bert Hinkler his CTPs were, in order: George Thomson*, 'Dizzy' Rawson*, 'Reggie' Brie* and Alan Marsh*.

Forever honoured as the man who gave the world practical rotor-borne flight, Juan de la Cierva seldom gets a mention as a test pilot. As can be seen from the notes to his 'flight log' above, Autogiro development was fraught and included several false starts. The study of Cierva rotorcraft is challenging with a large number of variants and a variety of constructors as well as through his company, sited in the former Avro premises at Hamble. During 1928 Avro, Hamble-built C.8L Mk.II G-EBYY powered by a 180hp AS Lynx IV was used for an extensive tour of British aerodromes before Juan, with the editor of the French magazine *L'Aeronautique* as his passenger, flew from Croydon to Le Bourget, Paris, on 18th September to complete the first-ever rotary-wing crossing of the English Channel. After demonstrations in Paris, Juan picked up 'Dizzy' Rawson and they went on to Brussels and then Berlin in early October. This adventure helped to 'normalise' the Autogiro in the eyes of potential operators. After the tour, the C.8L stayed on in France and today is displayed at the Musée de l'Air et Espace at Le Bourget.

The first of Cierva's designs intended for 'club' use – by everyday pilots – was the two-seat C.19 and Juan flew the prototype in July 1929 and it became the first Cierva design to enter series production. Much development work lay ahead to render the Autogiro truly a 'people's aeroplane'. Initially fitted with conventional aircraft controls, flying an Autogiro at low speed in experienced hands was no problem, but not so with novices. The answer

was what Juan called 'direct control', the ability to tilt the rotor disc to suit the flight regime. By allowing the rotor hub to tilt in all directions and providing a control stick that could be accessed from the cockpit, the responses of the C.19 were greatly enhanced. Juan began testing this on C.19 Mk.V G-ABXP from March 1932. The following year Juan commenced a process that was to continue through to 1938; the ability to achieve a 'jump' take-off by spinning up the otherwise free-wheeling rotor directly from the engine. In August 1933 G-ACFI, the prototype of the most prolific of his designs, the C.30, was trialled by Juan. By October that year Alan Marsh was able to wind up the rotor on G-ACFI after which it would leap 10 to 12ft into the air from which he could commence his climb-out. This work produced the Autodynamic rotor in the summer of 1936.

In collaboration with D Rose, Juan wrote the influential *Wings of Tomorrow* which was published in New York, in 1931. It was a detailed examination of his steps to the Autogiro, its aerodynamic challenges and its possibilities for the future.

At a fog-shrouded Croydon, Juan boarded the already delayed KLM flight to Amsterdam on 9th December 1936. Douglas DC-2 PH-AKL of KLM took off but its pilot became disoriented and the airliner hit houses on the perimeter and crashed in flames. Two of the 16 on board survived, by a miracle nobody on the ground was killed. One of those who perished was a 41-year-old Spaniard; one can only guess at what might have been achieved by Señor Don Juan de la Cierva Codorníu had he survived. Frank Courtney's autobiography *Flight Path* highlights the irony of Cierva's death: "He had devoted his life to the creation of an aircraft that could not stall, and he lost it in a plane that stalled on take-off."

A colour-enhanced postcard of Avro-built C.30A G-ACWF. This machine was used by the Cierva Autogiro Company at Hanworth from 1934 for training and demonstration. *Peter Green Collection*

Ron Clear

Ronald Edward Clear, born 1917. Aged 14 he joined the Portsmouth and Southsea Gliding Club and experimented with several gliders of his own design and construction, but was not successful. Took a post as an apprentice with Wiltshire School of flying at High Post, trading work for lessons. He gained his engineer's rating, went solo after 150 minutes and gained his PPL in February 1934. By 1937 Ron was working as an engine fitter on Oxfords at Airspeed, Portsmouth. In January 1938 he was appointed as RAF liaison officer on Oxfords, which included a trip to Canada in 1940.

RON CLEAR became an ATP with Airspeed in 1940 and from August 1941 was cleared to test all types going through the Portsmouth, and from 1941, the Christchurch factories. Working initially under 'Percy' Colman* and then George Errington*, Ron went on to test about 1,400 Oxfords, more than a quarter of the number built by Airspeed. From 1942, Ron was also involved in Horsa assault glider development and production testing the 122 DH Mosquito VIs and B.35s built at Christchurch. Ron graduated from No.3 Course ETPS at Boscombe Down in 1945 and returned to Airspeed, joining George Errington on the Ambassador airliner from late 1947. Ron acquired Comper Swift G-ACTF in May 1949, flying it until mid-1955 from Portsmouth – today it is

part of the Shuttleworth Collection. This machine has strong Portsmouth and test pilot connections, having been owned by Ron's former 'boss', George Errington, 1934 to 1936 and it was then with Francis Luxmoore* until the end of the war. (See under Neville Duke for another Shuttleworth machine with strong test pilot links.)

On 13th November 1950 Ron was captaining the third Ambassador, G-ALFR, out of Christchurch to establish new forward centre of gravity (CG) limits. On finals, Ron realised that there was insufficient elevator movement and he gunned the throttle to initiate a go-around. Both of the 2,625hp Bristol Centaurus 661s failed to interpret this as an urgent requirement and stuttered. Before the power kicked in the aircraft made a *very* heavy landing: on-board instrumentation recorded a force of 14g. Don Middleton's *Airspeed, the Company and its Aeroplanes*, takes up the story: "The result of this excessive loading was that the engines parted company with the nacelles and just went straight ahead. In Ron Clear's memorable words: 'the glider climbed over them [the engines] to a height of some 40ft with the control column now on the forward stop and the CG well aft of the aft limited.' A safe landing was eventually made before he reached the edge of the airfield, with all the tyres flat and the aircraft some four tons lighter." *Fox-Romeo* was soon back in the air with modified elevators. At a works dinner, George Errington presented Ron with a 'trophy' to commemorate his

Ron Clear with a Mosquito B.35 at Christchurch. *BAe Hatfield*

skilful handing of what could have been a disaster: he handed over a model of a ship's engine room telegraph lever, set at 'Finished with Engines'! (By 1955 G-ALFR was a test-bed with Napier – see Chapter Four.)

Airspeed had been acquired by de Havilland in 1940 but continued to trade under its own name. In June 1951 it was wholly absorbed into the parent, with Christchurch producing DH Vampires, Venoms and Sea Vixens. Ron worked under DH CTP John Cunningham* running flight test at Christchurch. With the wind down of the factory, Ron moved to Hatfield in 1960 and began testing Comet 4s before moving on to play a major role in the development of the HS Trident, including the Autoland system. He was actively involved in delivering Tridents to CAAC in China, the last one heading out of Hatfield in the summer of 1978. Ron retired as a test pilot that year, taking on the role of airfield manager. He made his last flight in the HSA-operated Mosquito T.3 RR299 (G-ASKH) in September 1980, the type having been his favourite since his Christchurch days. Departing Hatfield in 1982, Ron went on to a long retirement; he died on 3rd June 2004, aged 87.

Sir Alan Cobham seated in a Tiger Moth, 1932. *KEC*

Alan Cobham

| 26 Mar 1922 | DH DH.34 G-EBBQ |
| | 1 x 450hp Napier Lion |

Alan John Cobham, born 1894. By 1909 he was an apprentice in a wholesale business, moving on to farming by the age of 18. In August 1914 he joined the Army Veterinary Corps, serving in France looking after horses at the front line, becoming a Staff Sergeant. Transferred to the RFC early in 1918, going solo at Manston on 1st June 1918; he trained as an instructor, ending up as a 2nd Lt. 'Demobbed' in February 1919 he was part of the group that set up the 'joy-riding' business Berkshire Aviation Co, which started operations with an Avro 504K in May 1919. In 1920 he joined the Aircraft Manufacturing Co (Airco), establishing its Airco Aerials photography side-line. Airco folded, but Alan transferred to a similar role when Geoffrey de Havilland founded a company in his own name at Stag Lane, Edgware, in September 1920.*

Best known for his long-range flights surveying routes for airlines, the National Aviation Day 'circus' and most of all for the pioneering of in flight refuelling (IFR), Sir Alan Cobham had a brief period flying for de Havilland. The exploits of the company he founded, Flight Refuelling Ltd brought about an entirely new form of test flying and this is dealt with in depth in the second volume of *Testing to the Limits*.

With a nascent company in an uncertain economy, Geoffrey de Havilland was keen to diversify, Alan was busy taking aerial photographs for newspapers and other clients while Frank Barnard* experimented with crop-dusting in a DH.6. A charter service made great sense and in 1921 the Aeroplane Hire Service was established, offering rates of two shillings (10p in present-day coinage) a mile. This greatly appealed to Alan and others, as noted in C Martin Sharp's *DH – A History of de Havilland*: "Pilots began to invade the place. One had a habit of shedding tailskids and became known as

the tailskid bloke, but his name was Alan Cobham. He was as keen as mustard on charter flying and was taken on to fly a couple of DH.9s..." As with many small organisations, job definitions were flexible and in March 1922 Alan carried out the debut flight of the DH.34 two-pilot, nine-passenger biplane at Stag Lane. A dozen of these were built, helping to establish de Havilland as a serious manufacturer and not reliant on refurbishing and reconfiguring wartime types.

On 30th July 1923 Hubert Broad* flew the prototype DH.50 G-EBFN, a four-passenger biplane powered initially by a 230hp AS Puma. The first two DH.50s played a major part in Alan's developing career. Four days after its maiden flight, Alan flew G-EBFN to Gothenburg, Sweden, to take part in the International Aeronautical Exhibition. This event involved several competitions and the DH.50 won the main award, for a practical commercial aircraft. De Havilland gleaned licence production contracts in Australia, Belgium and Czechoslovakia as well as building another 16 examples at Stag Lane helped greatly by the international recognition at Gothenburg. In August the following year, Alan flew G-EBFN to victory in the Martlesham Heath-based King's Cup air race, averaging

The prototype DH.34 G-EBBQ, first flown by Alan Cobham in March 1922, was delivered to Daimler Hire Ltd at Croydon later in the year. *British Airways*

106.6mph. The second DH.50, G-EBFO, powered by a 385hp AS Jaguar radial, departed Croydon in November 1925 with Alan piloting and a support crew of two. He flew to the Cape of Good Hope and was back in March the following year. Then fitted with floats, he took it to Melbourne, Australia, in June 1926 returning to alight outside the Houses of Parliament in October. His fame as a long-distance aviator was cemented.

On 8th December 1923 Alan took single-seat Humming Bird G-EBHX to Brussels direct from Lympne, a journey of 150 miles, taking four hours and costing 10 shillings in fuel. (That's 50p in modern coin.) On the return flight a very dispirited Alan watched a freight train comfortably overtake G-EBHX; he landed and requested Stag Lane send help so it could be dismantled and brought home on the ferry! After this Alan expressed his belief that the production run of DH.53s that had been initiated was not the way to go, he insisted that the ability to take a passenger, some luggage and range to get to, say, Paris, from the Home Counties was essential. Via the DH.51 of July 1924, de Havilland came up with the game-changing DH.60 Moth in February 1925 – both flown for the first time by the company's namesake. (DH.53 G-EBHX joined the Shuttleworth Collection in 1960; tragically it was involved in a fatal accident at Old Warden on 1st July 2012.) Alan delivered the eighth production DH.60 from Stag Lane to its new owners, the Lancashire Aero Club at Barton, on 29th August 1925, as the Air Ministry-sponsored clubs began to take their allocations of Moths. This machine was G-EBLV which today flies with the Shuttleworth Collection, on loan from BAE Systems.

Alan was knighted for his exploits in long-range flying in 1926 and during 1927 he set off on a tour of the USA. Increasingly his vision was taking him away from the 'day job' with de Havilland and he left in May 1927 to form Alan Cobham Aviation Ltd. Much of his work continued to be surveying routes and likely locations for aerodromes for the airline industry. In 1931 he established the National Aviation Days, a touring 'circus' to raise awareness in aviation. His first IFR experiments took place in 1932 with a DH.9A receiver and a Handley Page W.10 tanker. Among the pilots involved in this early work was Geoffrey Tyson*. Flight Refuelling Ltd was formed on 29th October 1934 and as Cobham plc it is still a world force in IFR and other technologies. Sir Alan John Cobham KBE AFC died on 21st October 1973, aged 79. His autobiography, *A Time to Fly*, was published in 1978.

Carrying the race number 34, DH.50 prototype G-EBFN, piloted to victory in the 1924 King's Cup by Alan Cobham. *KEC*

John Cochrane

John Cochrane, born 1930. Gained cadetship and trained at Cranwell, graduating in 1952. He served with 617 Squadron on EE Canberras, then 214 and 90 Squadrons on Vickers Valiants as a Squadron Leader. No.19 Course ETPS at Farnborough; he resigned his commission to work for BAC as a test pilot.

JOHN COCHRANE joined flight test at BAC Weybridge in September 1960, under 'Jock' Bryce* and Brian Trubshaw* from 1964, working on Vickers VC-10s. In 1966 Brian invited John to join him at Filton to prepare for Concorde and two years later he was appointed as deputy chief test pilot on the supersonic airliner. John's path to commanding Concorde had him flying Lightings and French Air Force Mirages, plus the BAC 221 and Handley Page HP.115 test-beds. He also spent a lot of time in the simulator at Toulouse and was quite critical about how useful it was, generating some characteristics that were not reproduced in the real thing. John was co-pilot to Brian on the debut of 002, G-BSST, the UK prototype on 9th April 1969. He later commented: "My main memory of the first flight from Filton to Fairford was how uncomfortable it was, as we were decked out in safety equipment – hard hats, parachutes and the like."

John was extensively involved in the development phase and testing production examples. He took pre-production 01 (G-AXDN now with the Duxford Aviation Society) to Tangier, Morocco, in 1974 for intake control system trials. In *Test Pilot*, Brian Trubshaw wrote: "John Cochrane was the spearhead of these tests and did a wonderful job. During tests 01 reached Mach 2.23. On one flight all four engines surged which prompted John to say: 'I thought I had been sent for...'" On another sortie in 1974, his co-pilot put the undercarriage down during a tight turn which resulted in damage to the port main gear bogie. John

John Cochrane in the P2 seat of a museum Concorde. *via Graham Pitchfork*

alerted Fairford that he was returning with a problem and carried out a gentle touch down on the starboard bogie first, before settling on to the suspect undercarriage member safely.

Brian and John were back at the controls of G-BSST on 4th March 1976 when they delivered it to Yeovilton for display at the the Fleet Air Arm Museum, under Science Museum ownership. Along with Brian and Peter Baker*, John was involved in ferrying the VC-10s used in the initial RAF tanker contract to Filton for conversion in 1977 and 1978. By this time John was pretty disillusioned with the prospect of test flying with what had become British Aerospace, there being no programmes on the horizon, and he resigned in 1980. He joined Cyprus Airways on BAC One-Elevens and from July 1983 was project pilot introducing Airbus A310s into the fleet. He retired in 1990, staying on Cyprus and working in aviation insurance. He was on the flight deck of one of the British Airways Concordes on 24th October 2003 when the last ever flights, to preservation in Barbados, New York and Filton, were made. Sqn Ldr John Cochrane died in Cyprus, aged 76, on 4th November 2006.

John Cockburn

John Jeremy Cockburn, born 1937. Joined the RAF 1956, becoming a Flt Lt and flying EE Canberras with 139 and 12 Squadrons. He left the RAF in 1961, to join the Ferranti Flying Unit at Turnhouse on radar and avionics development, alongside Len Houston. Work included EE Lightning AIRPASS radar work, using Canberra B.2/8 WJ643 and Gloster Meteor NF.11 WD790. During this work he was seconded to BAC at Warton, via a Lightning course at 226 OCU, Coltishall. He left Ferranti in July 1966 to work for BAC.*

JOHN COCKBURN is an example of a specialist-within-specialists test pilot, devoting much of his time to avionics development. Starting with BAC at Warton in July 1966 he worked as a PTP on Canberras, later moving on to Saudi Lightnings and weapons fit trials. On 4th September 1968 he took off from Warton in Saudi Lightning F.53 53-690, just over six minutes into the sortie there was an explosion in one of the Avons followed by a fire. He tried to get back to Warton, but realising that was not possible, he pointed 53-690 out to sea and 'banged out'. He landed safely, the Lightning impacted near Pilling on the coast northeast of Fleetwood, thankfully without harm to those on the ground. Ten days later he was demonstrating F.53 G-AWOO (53-687) at the SBAC display at Farnborough. By 1970 he had converted to Jaguars and in 1975 to the Tornado and was appointed as Senior Avionics Development Test Pilot for the latter. John retired in 1979, farming for while before accepting a part-time post with Ferranti, going full-time in 1987. In early 1990 he joined BAe (from 1999 BAE Systems) and among his tasks was Project Director of the NATO Flying Training School in Canada, equipped with Hawks. He was awarded an OBE in 2002.

Stan Cockerell

13 Apr 1919	Vickers Vimy Commercial K-107 [1] 2 x 360hp RR Eagle VIII
Mar 1921	Vickers Valentia N124 [2] 2 x 650hp RR Condor IA
May 1922	Vickers Vulcan G-EBBL 1 x 360hp RR Eagle VIII
22 Aug 1922	Vickers Victoria I J6860 2 x 450hp Napier Lion I
24 Nov 1922	Vickers Virginia I J6856 2 x 450hp Napier Lion I
mid-1923	Vickers Viget G-EBHN 1 x 6.5hp Douglas

Notes: [1] Vimy Commercial flown from Joyce Green, Dartford, later registered as G-EAAV and used for the Cape Town attempt. [2] The Valentia flying-boat had a hull built by S E Saunders at Cowes and was test flown from the River Medina, Isle of Wight. Others flown from Brooklands.

Stanley F Cockerell, born 1895. Volunteered in July 1914, becoming a despatch rider with the RFC. By 1915 was a mechanic and in 1916 he completed flying training. Flew operationally in France with 24 Squadron on DH.2s, converting to DH.5s in April 1917. During this time he downed six enemy aircraft, two of them shared. He returned to Britain for home defence duties with 50, 112 and then 78 Squadrons. He returned to France, joining 151 Squadron on Sopwith Camels in the summer of 1918. His final victory was a Gotha on 2nd August 1918. While with 151 he was flight commander to 'Tommy' Broome and they became friends. Awarded Chevalier of the Order of the Crown (1917) and Croix de Guerre (1918) by Belgium.*

WITH Jack Alcock* heavily involved in preparations for the famous Atlantic crossing in a Vimy from April to June 1919, Stan Cockerell was brought in to debut the Vimy Commercial. This was essentially a Vimy bomber fitted with a new, oval-section fuselage to take ten passengers. After the prototype, another 42 were built along with 55 of the essentially similar Vernon for the RAF. With the death of Alcock in December 1919, Stan took over as chief pilot for Vickers at Brooklands and he turned to his friend from his 151 Squadron days, 'Tommy' Broome*, to assist him. See under Tommy for details of the attempted flight to Cape Town via Cairo in the Vimy Commercial prototype of January-February 1920. Both Stan and Tommy were awarded AFCs for this adventure.

From 6th February 1921 Stan piloted Viking III G-EAUK on a series of route-proving flights from the River Thames to the River Seine, linking the city centres of London and Paris. He tested the large Valentia flying-boat, co-built with S E Saunders, from the Medina three months later. The portly Vulcan eight-seater biplane was an attempt to build on Vimy Commercial experience, but only nine were manufactured. The other two debuts in 1922 became major money-spinners for Vickers. The Virginia was a large night bomber and it was much

The prototype Vimy Commercial, first flown by Stan Cockerell in April 1919 and flown to Africa in 1920. *Vickers*

The first Vickers Vulcan, G-EBBL, in Instone Air Line markings, named 'City of Antwerp'. The pilot sat in an open cockpit in front of the leading edge of the top wing. *Vickers*

developed, ending up with the all-metal Mk.X staying in frontline service until 1937. The Victoria was a transport version that exhibited similar longevity and the family was extended to the Valentia (second use of the name) for use in the Middle East and the purely civilian Vanguard. The Viget single-seater biplane was the company's unsuccessful entrant in the 'Motor Glider Competition' staged at Lympne in early October 1923 where Stan put it through gentle aerobatics. At this point, Stan appears to have retired from test flying, Tommy Broome sharing duties with H J Payn* until the arrival of 'Tiny' Scholefield* as Vickers CTP in mid-1924. Along with daughter Kathleen (aged 6), Stanley F Cockerell AFC (aged 45) was killed at Sunbury on Thames on 29th November 1940 during an air raid.

Virginia III J6993 wearing the 'new types park' No.7 for its debut at the Hendon display in June 1924. *Vickers*

'Percy' Colman

26 Jun 1934	Airspeed Envoy G-ACMT 2 x 185hp Wolseley AR.9
19 Jun 1937	Airspeed Oxford I L4534 2 x 375hp AS Cheetah X

Cyril Henry Arthur Colman, born 1906 or 1907. Joined the RAF in January 1927, going on to fly fighters operationally, ending his service at the Armament & Gunnery School, Eastchurch, as a Flt Lt, and electing to stay on the Reserve List. By 1933 he was flying for Midland and Scottish Air Ferries from Renfrew.

IN June 1933 'Percy' Colman was sent to Portsmouth to pick up brand new Airspeed Ferry G-ACFB, the second of two ordered by his employer, Glasgow-based Midland and Scottish Air Ferries. It seems that Airspeed co-founder, Nevil Shute Norway was impressed with the young RAF officer's flying skills and offered him the post of test pilot. The small company had moved from York to Portsmouth the previous March and in the April its Courier monoplane had its maiden flight. George Stainforth* had been brought in to do this, but the company was as yet without a regular pilot. Percy – perhaps so called from the American baseball player – accepted the job having been offered an annual salary of £400. (That's £22,000 in present-day values; in its 1933 context when the average salary was just over £180.)

With its retractable undercarriage the Courier was an advanced and promising design but it was felt there was a far greater market for a twin using the same radical concept. This was the Envoy and Percy took the prototype on its maiden flight from Portsmouth in June 1934 and six days later flew it to Hendon for the SBAC display, where it raised more than a few eyebrows! G-ACMT was followed at Portsmouth by another 49 examples and a one-off version, the Viceroy. In 1935 George Errington* joined Airspeed to assist Percy with the increasing workload. During January and February 1937 Percy ferried Envoy G-AERT to China and was back at Portsmouth by June. On the 11th George carried out the first flight of the Queen Wasp – see under his section for more – while Percy took the prototype Oxford crew trainer on its debut eight days later. Both machines were on show at Hendon

With a pitot tube in the nose and portions of the port cowling unattached, the first Envoy at Portsmouth, probably in June or July 1934. In the left background are Hawker Fury Is of Tangmere-based 1 Squadron and to the right Vickers Virginia Xs of 58 Squadron, from Worthy Down. *via Don Middleton*

The in-house *Airspeed Gazette* paid tribute to 'Percy' Colman on his departure to re-join the RAF in 1939 with a superb caricature of him 'riding' an Oxford. *via Don Middleton*

Les Colquhoun

Leslie Robert Colquhoun, born 1921. Joined the RAF at 19 and after training was posted to 603 (City of Edinburgh) Squadron on Supermarine Spitfire IIs as a Sergeant in October 1941. Transferred to 1 PRU at Benson in February 1942. Ferried a Spitfire PR.IV to Malta April 1942 and was seconded to 'ops' with 69 Squadron at Luqa, at one time one of only two pilots with the unit; he stayed on the island for eight months and was awarded the DFM. By October 1943 he was with 682 Squadron in Tunisia and later Italy, flying Spitfire PR.XIs and XIXs. Returned to the UK to instruct with 8 OTU at Haverfordwest.

Unlit cigarette in hand, Les Colquhoun with one of the 36 Attackers for the Pakistan Air Force, 1951. *Vickers-Armstrongs via Peter Green*

on 28th June 1937. L4534 was the first of 8,586 Oxfords, 4,411 of which were churned out at Portsmouth. The second Queen Wasp, K8888, was completed as a floatplane and Percy took it into the skies for the first time in late 1937. This event was remarkable as Percy had not been at the helm of a seaplane or flying-boat until that sortie.

With the advent of war, despite the demands of mass production by Airspeed, Percy elected to return to the RAF and George took over as CTP. On the night of 3rd/4th January 1941 Percy was flying a Bristol Blenheim If of 23 Squadron back from an intruder operation against Dieppe. The aircraft failed to return, coming down in the English Channel. Crew members F/Sgt D W Mathews and Sgt H I MacRory were never found and are commemorated on the Runnymede memorial. Sqn Ldr Cyril Henry Arthur Colman's body was washed ashore at Worthing and he is buried at St Andrew's Church at Tangmere.

The second Queen Wasp provided Percy Colman with his first taste of a seaplane. *Portsmouth Libraries*

Les Colquhoun was involved in the testing of both of the elegant Seagull ASR.1s – first example PA143 illustrated. *Vickers-Armstrongs*

INSTRUCTING was not high on Les Colquhoun's list of satisfying duties so when he was told in February 1945 that he was being seconded to Supermarine and to get to High Post, near Salisbury, and report to Jeffrey Quill* he was delighted. Testing late-series Spitfires straight off the production line was his initial task. Flt Lt Leslie R Colquhoun DFC DFM was 'demobbed' in April 1946 and to quote Les from Geoffrey Dorman's *British Test Pilots*: "The only difference that made to me was I arrived one day for normal work in uniform, and the next day in civvies as a complete civilian on the test pilot staff of Supermarines." In 1947 Jeffrey Quill retired and Mike Lithgow* became CTP.

Early work included Seafire F.47 testing and in 1948 he was flying Seafang F.32 VB895 and assisting Lithgow on Seagull amphibian development. His first taste of jet trials came with Attackers and Swifts. On 23rd May 1950, Les was detailed to carry out high-Mach number and dive-brake trials on the first production Attacker F.1, WA469. He took off from South Marston and after two dives at 400kts, the next reached 430kt and the aircraft began to pitch forward and back. Suddenly there

was a loud and disturbing bang. A rapid scan of the instruments was followed by a look outside to see the starboard wing in its *folded* position! He booted hard port rudder to counteract, chopped the throttle and quickly assessed the situation. Apart from the asymmetric load, the ailerons were effectively out of action: indeed half of the starboard one was behaving more like a *fin* than an aileron! Les discovered that he could control WA469 and by making turns with only the rudder he brought the Attacker safely back to South Marston. What could have been a disaster resulted in just bursting the port tyre and WA469 was back in the air within three months. For this incredible exploit, Les was awarded the George Medal.

During trials of the ultimately unsuccessful Seagull ASR.1, Les clinched a world airspeed record for amphibians. He was competing in an air race in the second Seagull, PA147, at Sherburn-in-Elmet on 22nd July 1950 and averaged 241.9mph. Along with David Morgan*, Les flew Type 535 Swift VV119 for sequences used in the David Lean 1952 film *The Sound Barrier*. Les took part in wet runway trials with Swift F.7 XF114 in the late 1950s – see under 'Dizzy' Addicott. His final flying with Supermarine was shaking down Scimitar F.1s straight off the South Marston line, Les taking the last example into the air in December 1960. Beyond that, he became involved in the hovercraft programme of the parent organisation, Vickers. This included captaining the VA.3 during the world's first passenger service, from Wallasey to Rhyl, August to September 1962. It was a logical step to become the operations manager of Hoverloyd (later Seaspeed) on cross-Channel services from 1966 before he retired in the late 1960s. Flt Lt Leslie Robert Colquhoun GM DFC DFM died in July 2001, aged 80.

Attacker F.1 WA506 of 803 Squadron on the deck of HMS *Eagle* in September 1952, showing the wing fold. *KEC*

Derrick Colvin

12 Nov 1952	Westland WS-55 Srs 1 G-AMJT
	1 x 600hp P&W R1340-40

Derrick Albert Sandison Colvin, born 1922. Served in the RAF 1940 to 1946, flying Supermarine Spitfires operationally with 64 and then 249 Squadrons. He went on to command 249, in Italy and was awarded a DFC in May 1944. He flew for Scottish Airlines (part of Scottish Aviation) at Prestwick and piloted a helicopter for the first time in 1948 (perhaps at Prestwick, see Noel Capper).

Derrick Colvin's helicopter experience came to the eye of Harald Penrose* and he was recruited as a test pilot for Westland in 1949. He flew both fixed wing, under Penrose, and helicopters for Ken Reed*. On 3rd November 1950 Derrick was testing the prototype two-seat Wyvern T.3 conversion trainer VZ739 on a sortie out of Yeovil, with Bob Page as observer. At 1,500ft a bearing seized in the AS Python I contra-rotating turboprop and Derrick had very little time to select a site for a wheels-up landing. VZ739 slithered to a stop on the mud flats of the River Axe close to where it meets the sea on the south Devon coast alongside Seaton. Both occupants were unhurt, but after several attempts at salvage the T.3 was a write-off.

Westland's future lay with helicopters and the wise decision to captialise on the established experience of Sikorsky was made. The first Anglicized WS-55 Series 1, G-AMJT, was ready for intial testing on 12th November 1952 and Derrick completed three hovers. After this came an intensive period of ground runs to fully 'soak test' the British-manufactured transmission and systems. This machine emerged to fly again on 15th August 1953 as the first Whirlwind HAR.1 for the Fleet Air Arm, XA862. At this time Harald Penrose retired and handed over to 'Slim' Sear*. (The cockpit of XA862 is preserved by the Yorkshire Helicopter Preservation Group at the South Yorkshire Aircraft Museum, Doncaster.) The Whirlwind was destined to become the backbone of the rebirth of Westland. Derrick was involved in production testing through to the second major product, the Wessex, flight testing naval HAS.3s in the late 1960s. When not testing helicopters Derrick was keen on motor racing, he entered his Cooper 500 at Silverstone 1958 to 1960. Sqn Ldr Derrick A S Colvin DFC died in 1986, aged 64.

The prototype Wyvern T.3 VZ739 at Yeovil before it was taken for its maiden flight by Harald Penrose on 11th February 1950. Ten months later, it was skilfully force landed by Derrick Colvin. *KEC*

Nick Comper

14 Sep 1924	Cranwell CLA.2 G-EBKC
	1 x 32hp Bristol Cherub
Jul 1925	Cranwell CLA.3 G-EBMC
	1 x 32hp Bristol Cherub
Aug 1926	Cranwell CLA.4A G-EBPB
	1 x 36hp Bristol Cherub III
Jan 1930	Comper Swift G-AARX
	1 x 40hp ABC Scorpion II
1933	Comper Mouse G-ACIX
	1 x 130hp DH Gipsy Major
1934	Comper Kite G-ACME
	1 x 90hp Pobjoy Niagara
12 Apr 1934	Comper Streak G-ACNC
	1 x 145hp DH Gipsy Major

Notes: Cranwell types all first flew at Cranwell, the Swift had its maiden flight at Hooton Park, the others at Heston.

Nicholas Comper, born 1897. Apprentice draughtsman at the Aircraft Manufacturing Co (Airco), Hendon, from the summer of 1914, working under the chief designer, Geoffrey de Havilland (GDH). He left in 1915 to enlist in the RFC and in July 1916 was a 2nd Lt pilot, joining 9 Squadron flying Royal Aircraft Factory BE.2s (designed by GDH). He returned to Britain in April 1917 for undetermined duties. Took a commission, studied aeronautical engineering at Cambridge from 1920, going to the RAF College Cranwell in October 1922. He was promoted to Flt Lt in June 1923.

Nick Comper's zeal for aviation, particularly its lighter side, drove him throughout his life; he became a designer-pilot in the mould of the great names of the 1900s and 1910 (see Chapter One). Having established his own company, he followed a path trod by others before him – and since – striving to keep a grip on the drawing board, the flight test office *and* the board room. Typically, it was only in the first two that he excelled but it was the latter that was his undoing.

Once established at Cranwell, Nick formed the Boys' Wing Glider Club in January 1923, which became the Cranwell Light Aeroplane Club (CLAC). With Nick as the chief designer, CLAC built a small biplane to compete in the 1924 light aeroplane trials at Lympne, the CLA.2. Nick carried out the first

The prototype Swift in 1930, showing off its clean lines courtesy of the ABC Scorpion – Avro 504N behind. *Peter Green Collection*

flight and shared the flying with Flt Lt E P Mackay during the competition. The CLA.3 and CLA.4A were entered for the next two Lympne contests. Captain Douglas Pobjoy became the Boys' Wing Education Officer in 1924 and, impressed with CLAC, started to develop a 7-cylinder radial for its use but his Pobjoy P was too late to fit to the CLA.4A in 1926.

In November 1926, Nick was posted to the Marine Aircraft Experimental Establishment at Felixstowe and straight away formed the Felixstowe Light Aeroplane Club, although no full-scale types were built. By 1929 Nick's mind was on the future and in March he formed the Comper Aircraft Company – with himself as Managing Director and Chief Designer – and resigned his commission the following month. Hooton Park on the Wirral was chosen as the base because one of his financial backers owned the aerodrome and Pobjoy, who had formed Pobjoy Airmotors in 1928, was in the process of moving there. Nick set about creating one of the most charismatic sporting aircraft of the era, the CLA.7 Swift, its designation paying homage to its Cranwell heritage. The prototype had an ABC Scorpion but many in the production run of 41 adopted the 85hp Pobjoy R. A Swift fuselage was used as the basis for the Comper-built Cierva C.25 autogiro, this was wrecked on its first test in the hands of Juan de la Cierva* in March 1932. Repaired, he successfully flew it the following month.

In the spring of 1933, Nick moved the company to Heston, but orders for the Swift were drying up. He countered with three types: the Streak low wing single-seat envisaged as a replacement for the Swift; a two-seat version, the Kite; and the Mouse two-seat cabin monoplane. All had retractable undercarriage and did not get beyond the prototype stage. Comper Aircraft folded in August 1934 with some of its assets being taken over by Heston Aircraft. By December, Nick was in talks with Blackburn

The Shuttleworth Collection's Pobjoy Niagara II-powered Swift G-ACTF was owned and flown by three test pilots: George Errington 1934 to 1936, Francis Luxmoore* 1936 to 1945 and Ron Clear 1949 to 1955. *Ken Ellis*

The Comper Mouse, one of three designs that Nick Comper hoped would change the prospects of his ailing company. *KEC*

Aircraft regarding his role as consultant engineer supervising the construction of a helicopter to the design of Austrian Oskar Asboth – nothing came of this. In December 1936 Nick formed Comper Aeroplanes Ltd promoting concepts for long-range airliners. He also designed the CF.1 Scamp, created in association with Gerard Fane, and commenced construction courtesy of the College of Aeronautical Engineering at Brooklands. (This did not see the light of day until 1940 by which time it was designated the Fane F1/40, G-AGDJ.) Injured in a street altercation in Hythe, possibly caused by a misinterpretation of Nick's well established ability to be a prankster, 42-year old Nicholas Comper died on 18th June 1939. His obituary in the *Times* summed up his endeavours perfectly: "It was his true boast that he never produced a bad aeroplane, although the markets for each successive design were continually being swept away from him by the winds of the world depression".

'Jim' Cooksey

James Reginald Cooksey, born 1912. Joined the RAF in 1928 as an apprentice. Re-trained in 1936 as a pilot, serving operationally throughout World War Two; finally with 74 Squadron as CO, flying Gloster Meteor IIIs 1945-1947.

QUICK reactions have always been a vital to test pilots. Faced with the likelihood that his next posting within the RAF would be a desk, as an operational Meteor pilot, Sqn Ldr 'Jim' Cooksey approached Gloster about a job. The interview went well enough but he was told there were no vacancies. On his way home he heard that a Gloster test pilot had died in a crash; this was 'Jimmy' Bridges, killed in Meteor IV RA394 on 22nd April 1947. Jim Cooksey shot off a telegram and was taken on as a production test pilot. Gloster was working hard to produce an improved Meteor and in October 1948 Jan Zurakowski* took the first F.8, VT150, up for its debut. Development of the F.8 was far from straightforward and Jim was heavily involved in trials; it was not until December 1949 that the first examples were issued to RAF service. Gloster was always striving to cut costs and Jim examined production 'shake down' testing procedures, normally set over 17 sorties, and brought the average down to 2½ flights.

With the F.8 in RAF service, Gloster embarked upon a publicity programme to stimulate export sales. Jim was elected to have a crack at the 1,000km closed-circuit speed record, which was held by the USA, in a Lockheed P-80 Shooting Star, established on 3rd June 1946. The F.8 did not boast the greatest of range and Jim had to spend a lot of time working out how to maximise the speed while eking out the endurance. He practised 'dead stick' landings at the Gloster test airfield of Moreton Valence in case he ran the tanks dry. On 11th May 1950, Jim took F.8 VZ496 up for the attempt and had no need to turn it into a glider; he clinched the record at 510.9mph. Jim was at the helm of a much-modified version of the F.8 for its maiden flight on 4th September 1950. This was the private venture Meteor Ground Attack Fighter (GAF), sometimes called the Reaper. Flying initially with the B Condition ('trade plate') identity G-7-1, it was later civilian registered as G-AMCJ and painted in Gloster 'house colours' of carmine red with ivory trim. With tip tanks, the potential to have rocket-assisted take-off rockets attached to the rear fuselage and bombs or rocket projectiles under wing the Meteor GAF failed to attract orders.

On 9th April 1954 Jim strapped himself into F.8 WL191 and piloted it off the small runway at the Hucclecote factory for the short flight southwest to Moreton Valance; it was the last Meteor built by Gloster. Jim retired that year, having clocked about 4,900 hours, 2,200 of them in Meteors. By 1957 he had put his RAF apprentice training to good use and transformed his career, working for the diversification subsidiary Gloster Vending, designing and building milk vending machines. He left Gloster In 1962 and freelanced as a vending machine designer. He was tempted back into the industry in 1968, working as a facilities engineer at BAC's Concorde test centre at Fairford until 1974. His final job, up to 1978 was developing mouldings for large load-bearing plastic structures. Sqn Ldr James Reginald Cooksey died in 2001, aged 89.

Aubrey Corbin

19 May 1947	Cunliffe-Owen Concordia Y-0222
	2 x 550hp Alvis Leonides 4M

In 1937 tobacco magnate Sir Hugh Cunliffe-Owen was attracted by the ideas of American Vincent Burnelli, pioneer of the 'wide-body' flying wing. This featured a deep aerofoil section for a much-widened fuselage which also provided lift and accommodated passengers *across* the fuselage, not *down* it. Burnelli was way ahead of his time, since then McDonnell-Douglas, Boeing and Airbus, among others, have all come up with similar design studies. One aircraft, OA-1 G-AFMB, was built under licence by Cunliffe-Owen Aircraft (COA) at Eastleigh and flew in 1938. Overtaken by the war, the OA-1 was not followed up and the company built Seafires and other sub-contract work during the war. The dream of building airliners lingered and COA embarked on a twin-engined ten-seater with tricycle undercarriage, the Concordia. Hopes were high and a batch of six was commenced prior to flight of the prototype. Aubrey G Corbin took Y-0222 (B Condition or 'trade-plate' markings, before it was registered as G-AKBE) on its maiden flight from Eastleigh in May 1947 amid announcements that the Nawab of Bhopal had acquired the second example (G-AKBF) and that BEA was keen and a sales tour was pending. The factory was also engaged in work on the unfortunate Air Horse under contract to Cierva. With no orders and the banks jittery, all production was stopped and with that, Corbin, the Concordia and Cunliffe-Owen faded into history.

'Jim' Cordes

12 Jun 1930	HP Heyford J9130
	2 x 575hp RR Kestrel III
21 Jun 1932	HP HP.43 J9833
	3 x 590hp Bristol Pegasus IM3
8 May 1935	HP HP.51 J9833
	2 x 700hp AS Tiger IV
21 Jun 1936	HP Hampden K4240
	2 x 1,000hp Bristol Pegasus XVIII
10 Oct 1936	HP Harrow K6933
	2 x 980hp Bristol Pegasus X
25 Oct 1939	HP Halifax L7244
	4 x 1,130hp RR Merlin X

Note: All at Radlett other than the Halifax which first flew from Bicester

James Lucas Brome Hope Cordes, born 1895. Served as a company commander in the 2nd Battalion, Gloucester Regiment, and wounded in Salonica fighting Bulgarian forces, 1916. Transferred to the RFC, learning to fly in Egypt on Farman Shorthorns. Converted to the Bristol F.2B in England, flying with 48 Squadron in France and accounting for two enemy aircraft. His final operational flying came with 39 Squadron, also on F.2Bs, on home defence duties at North Weald. After an instructor's course in 1921 at CFS he served on until 1928.

MAJOR JAMES – 'Jim' or 'Jimmy' to most – joined Handley Page (HP) as a test pilot early in 1928, working for Tom Harry England*. Harald Penrose* referred to him as "the debonair Major" and with his white flying overalls and monocle he was a memorable character, not least because he was known for speaking his mind. In March 1928 Jim was sent to Woodford to pick up Air Ministry Avro Avian III J9182 (powered by a 80hp AS Genet radial) and bring it to HP factory at Cricklewood for auto-slot (see below) work. The ferry flight was carried out in marginal conditions; Cordes admitted defeat at Radlett, 10 miles northwest of Cricklewood and spent the night with a local farmer. When he finally arrived, Jim noted that he'd found a good potential airfield and factory site as Cricklewood was incapable of expansion. By mid-1929 the company was busy setting up Radlett airfield and a factory at Colney Street.

Tom Harry England (THE) could see the potential in Jim and on 8th February 1929 he let his deputy fly the all-metal version of the Hinaidi bomber, Mk.II J9478, at Cricklewood. There were more exotic plans for Jim... As well as aircraft, HP and Gustav Lachman (later HP's chief designer) had combined talents to pioneer the leading edge slot and an automatic version was destined to transform aircraft safety. Income from patents provided vital cash flow for HP in the 1920s. In response to the Safe Aircraft Competition staged by the Daniel Guggenheim Fund for the Protection of Aeronautics, HP built the two-seat HP.39 biplane featuring full-span leading edge

The one-off Concordia prototype in flight in 1947. The fairing in front of the fin housed an anti-spin parachute. *Cunliffe-Owen Aircraft*

'Jim' Cordes demonstrating slow and high angle-of-attack approaches at Cricklewood in the Gugnunc, June 1929. *Rolls-Royce Bristol Engine Group*

The prototype Heyford, J9130, first flown by Jim Cordes on 12th June 1930. The '12' on the fuselage side is the 'New Types Park' number for the June 1932 Hendon SBAC display. *KEC*

The unsuccessful HP.43 tri-motor transport of July 1932. It fuselage was used in the HP.51 monoplane. *KEC*

slats and full-span flaps: today, it would be called a 'technology demonstrator'. The Guggenheim Competition Biplane, G-AACN, was flown by THE on its debut on 30th April 1929. He then handed it over to Jim to perfect slow, hands off and – to use another modern-day term – high angle-of-attack flying. The *Daily Mirror* children's strip cartoon *Pip, Squeak and Wilfred* featured a 'word' regularly uttered by Wilfred – 'Gugnunc'; this quickly replaced the cumbersome name Guggenheim Competition Biplane. In September Jim and the Gugnunc – the latter in crates – crossed the Atlantic and by mid-November, Jim had out-flown all of the opposition including the Curtiss Tanager, at Mitchel Field, Long Island, New York. Frederick Handley Page, also at the contest, was

enraged to find that the Tanager had slotted wings, without having paid any royalties for the privilege. The prize, an eye-watering $100,000, went to the Tanager. Glenn Curtiss and Frederick had sparred before and the 'Brit' mobilised the lawyers while Jim found himself marooned as the Gugnunc was impounded. A Curtiss injunction of 1920 had banned *any* HP types from the USA! By May 1930 Jim and the Gugnunc were back in the UK and eventually Curtiss and 'HP' backed down. (G-AACN was presented to the Science Museum in 1934 but rarely exhibited. In 2015 its somewhat reclusive existence was due to end with it going on show in a new presentation at South Kensington.)

Unlike the Hinaidi II, which was a remodelling of an existing type, Jim took his first 'real' prototype into the air in June 1930, the Heyford, J9130. With its *lower* wing separate from the fuselage, the spatted main undercarriage anchored to the leading edge of this wing and its centre section acting as a bomb bay, the Heyford was radical-looking. Jim's 'boss' was back in command on 14th November 1930 for the first flight of the iconic HP.42 airliner, with Jim as co-pilot. The HP.42 concept led to the HP.43 military transport which Jim took on its debut in June 1932. It was not a success, but HP deemed its fuselage had further life, re-formating the aircraft as a twin-engined monoplane, the HP.51 of May 1935. This also remained a one-off but paved the way for the Harrow. This morphing meant that Jim had *two* maiden flights in *two* very different aircraft, *both* with the serial J9833!

On 31st August 1934 Tom Harry England left HP, and Jim became CTP. Two years later, Jim presided over two maiden flights, both of which were of great importance to the company. The first was the HP.52, soon to be named Hampden, which he piloted on 21st June 1936, before taking it to the Hendon display, the SBAC show at Hatfield and a gathering of new types for King Edward VIII to inspect at Martlesham Heath on 6th July – an intensive 16 days. After a demonstration of the new bomber, C G Grey, the over-blown and sarcastic editor of *The Aeroplane* and *Jane's All the World's Aircraft* button-holed Jim and exclaimed: "It looks like a flying suitcase!" Jim, who made a habit of looping Hampdens, was unfazed and countered: "Oh yes, it's a perfect revelation!" The other 1936 debut was in October, the bomber-transport Harrow, derived from the HP.51.

On 5th November 1936 the undercarriage warning buzzer failed on Hampden prototype K4240 and, as another would take time to create and Jim was in the middle of a test sequence, one further flight was authorised. Jim and FTO R S Stafford went airborne again but on returning to Radlett, the starboard gear collapsed and the bomber skidded along on its belly. Jim later recounted that Stafford, seemingly unaware of the drama, declared: "There's a hell of a strong smell of grass in here!" The prototype was repaired and Jim was at the helm again on 13th January 1937. Heading north back to Radlett, near to Elstree, there was a cataclysmic bang from the starboard 'Peggie', which had been replaced after the undercarriage collapse, and the engine shed its propeller. There was no fire and Jim made a perfect single-engined landing. He was concerned that the prop had plummeted into housing and was at pains to direct police to its likely landing place. Thankfully, it had impacted in a field.

Radlett was considered too small to test fly the next HP bomber prototype, so Halifax I L7244 was taken to Bicester and assembled in October 1941. While waiting for L7244 to be cleared for flight, Frederick Handley Page was wearing thin the patience of his flight crew and the technical team. Don Middleton in *Test Pilots* provides a fine example of Jim's directness, even with the 'top man'. Frederick offered Jim a lift across the airfield in his pride-and-joy Rolls-Royce; the test pilot declared that it: "Looks like a bloody hearse!" On 25th October 1939 Jim and FTO E A 'Ginger' Wright took L7244 into the air for a successful, undercarriage locked down, test flight.

From April 1939 Gustav Lachman was involved in the design of a tail-less aircraft, the HP.75, a test-bed for a possible format for a future long-range heavy bomber. Jim referred to it from the start as the 'Manx' after the tail-less cats of the Isle of Man and the name stuck. He began fast taxi trials of the Manx on 29th February 1940 and in March, along with 'Ginger' Wright, more were carried out. It fell to 'Jamie' Talbot*, Jim's successor, to fly this unusual machine. Jim left HP on 31st July 1941 to run the Martin Hearne-operated 7 Aircraft Assembly Unit at Hooton Park. Among the facility's many tasks was the erection and flight testing of Canadian-built Hampdens – Jim could indulge in looping them again! No.7 AAU was also the receipt centre for Sikorsky Hoverfly helicopters and Jim gained a 'chopper' rating at Hooton. This was only the second in the UK, the first being 'Jeep' Cable*. Major James L B H Cordes gave up test flying at the end of the war. He died in 1980, aged 85.

The Harrow bomber-transport prototype, K6933, flown by 'Jim' Cordes on 10th October 1936.

'Jim' Cordes flying production Hampden I L4159 on an air test out of Radlett, early 1939. *Handley Page*

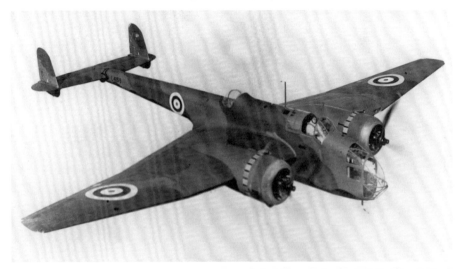

First flown from Bicester, the prototype Halifax, L7244. *KEC*

Frank Courtney

late 1917	Kennedy Giant 2337 [1] 4 x 200hp Salmson	N
Mar 1918	B&P Bobolink C8655 1 x 230hp Bentley BR.2	M
late 1918	B&P P.6 X25 [2] 1 x 90hp RAF Ia	M
Mar 1919	Airco DH.11 Oxford H5891 2 x 320hp ABC Dragonfly	H
1919	B&P Bourges IA F2903 2 x 230hp Bentley BR.2	M
Apr 1919	B&P Atlantic 2 x 450hp Napier Lion	M
1919	Siddeley Siskin C4541 1 x 320hp ABC Draonfly	R
1920	Airco DH.18 G-EARI 1 x 450hp Napier Lion	H
25 Jun 1921	AW Sinaia J6858 2 x 500hp AS Tiger	F
1922	B&P Bodmin J6910 2 x 450hp Napier Lion	M
Apr 1922	Central Centaur IIA G-EAHR 2 x 160hp Beardmore	N
Sep 1922	B&P Bolton J6584 2 x 450hp Napier Lion	M
9 Dec 1922	Handasyde H.2 1 x 350hp RR Eagle III	B
7 May 1923	AW Siskin II J6583 [3] 1 x 325hp AS Jaguar III	W
28 Jun 1923	AW Awana 'J6860' [4] 2 x 450hp Napier Lion	W
30 Jun 1923	B&P Bugle J6984 2 x 400hp Bristol Jupiter II	M
19 Jan 1924	AW Wolf J6921 1 x 350hp AS Jaguar III	W
10 May 1925	AW Atlas G-EBLK 1 x 400hp Jaguar IVC	W
4 Jun 1925	Parnall Peto N181 1 x 135hp Bristol Lucifer IV	Y
Jun 1925	Westland Yeovil J7508 1 x 650hp RR Condor	YV
Jun 1926	Saunders Valkyrie N186 3 x 680hp RR Condor IIIA	C
Sep 1926	Westland Westbury J7765 2 x 450hp Bristol Jupiter	A
10 Dec 1926	Parnall Perch N217 1 x 270hp RR Falcon III	Y

3 Mar 1927	Parnall Pike N202 1 x 450hp Napier Lion V	Y
14 Oct 1938	Saro A.33 K4773 4 x 830hp Bristol Perseus XII	C
Nov 1938	Saro Lerwick L7248 2 x 1,375hp Bristol Hercules	C

Notes: [1] A 'technicality', see the narrative below. [2] Courtney is *believed* to have made its first flight. [3] Siddeley Deasey came under the Armstrong Whitworth banner from 1919. [4] Serial wrongly painted on airframe ; it was actually J6897. Airfields decode: A – Andover, B – Brooklands, C – Cowes, ie from the River Medina, F – Farnborough, H – Hendon, M – Mousehold, N – Northolt, R – Radford, W – Whitley Abbey, Y – Yate, YV – Yeovil.

Frank T Courtney, born 1894. By 1912 he was a bank clerk in Paris and spoke fluent French. He wrote to Claude Grahame-White* in 1913 and was given a non-paying apprenticeship, training under designer John D North. Freddy Dunn* and Frank Goodden* shared his lodgings. Many more 'names' were to share Frank's life – read on. He learned to fly with the Grahame-White school, again at his own expense, gaining Aviators' Certificate No.874 in 20th August 1914. His short sight prevented him enlisting in the RFC, his interview lasting just seconds with Major Hugh 'Boom' Trenchard – later Marshal of the Royal Air Force (MRAF) Hugh Montague Trenchard, Viscount Trenchard Bt GCB OM GCVO DSO). Frank settled for a mechanic's course, assured that his Aviators' Certificate would inevitably lead to flying duties.

Frank was mustered as a pilot and posted to Farnborough, moving to the Western Front, as Sgt Courtney, to serve with 3 Squadron, flying Morane Type Ls and BBs by June 1915. Working as a mechanic with 3 Squadron was 'Jim' McCudden – later to re-train as a pilot, becoming Major James Thomas Byford McCudden VC DSO* MC* MM fighter 'ace' and author of Five Years in the RFC*). An observer who occaisionally crewed-up with Frank was Lt Charles Portal – later MRAF Charles Frederick Algernon Portal, Viscount Portal of Hungerford KC GCB OM DSO* MC. Frank was shot down in a Morane, by French anti-aircraft fire; Courtney and his observer walked away from the wreck. He crashed another Morane at the end of a night-time artillery 'shoot' flight; again both he and observer Lt 'Hoppy' Cleaver. On 21st October 1915 while flying a Morane with Sgt George Thornton in an attempt to down a German kite balloon they were shot down by a Fokker E.III, Frank was hospitalised until late January 1916: Thornton was only slightly injured. Portal told them that their assailant was 'Lt Max Inglemann' – none other than Max Immelmann, exponent of Germany's 'Fokker scourge'. He returned to Farnborough, testing for the Royal Aircraft Factory with much work put in on the FE.2d. He went back to France, joining 20 Squadron on FE.2ds in mid-1916 before transferring to 45 Squadron and 70 Squadron, both on Sopwith 1½ Strutters. He was awarded the French Croix de Guerre with Palm. Back in England by mid 1917, as a*

Captain, he instructed at London Colney with 56 Training Squadron. He had returned to Farnborough for more flight testing by late 1917 and early the following year was seconded to Boulton and Paul.

Erecting the ungainly Kennedy Giant at Northolt in 1917. This huge machine was Frank Courtney's first commission; note the 'push-pull' arrangement of the engines. *Peter Green Collection*

DUBBED by the British aviation press as: "The man with the magic hands," Frank Courtney, the famous freelancer seemed to be able to fly any sort of aircraft. This image was perpetuated in the USA, where a magazine article describes him as the "airplane doctor". As ever Harald Penrose provides a good pen-sketch of the man in *British Aviation – The Adventuring Years*: "In the hands of tall [he was 6ft 3in] Frank Courtney of the wavy black hair, clipped moustache and pince-nez glasses..." Frank's secondment to Boulton and Paul at Mousehold gave him the taste for test piloting and he began to devise his future career. Gordon Kinsey in *Boulton and Paul Aircraft* provides a glimpse of Frank's potential revenue: "...it is interesting to record that his standard fee for three hours' test flying was £50". Calibrating the relative *value* of money is never easy. In present-day figures that would be £2,750 with the national median gross salary for 2013 coming in at £26,884. So, Frank would 'only' need nine three-hour sessions to be Mr Average income! He'd require a lot of commissions to come up to a 'professional' level or similar and he was embarking on a career at the same time as Britain was taking a slide into deep depression. On a starker note, it is best remembered that an agricultural worker had an annual income of £117 (£6,435 present-day) in 1920 and that was set to *halve* by the end of the decade.

With such a varied career, the chronological narrative adopted for the rest of the book has been dropped in favour of a company-by-company approach for Frank. It is also important to note that his commissions roamed into Europe, for example he flew the prototype Koolhoven FK.31 two-seat parasol fighter from Waalhaven in the Netherlands in June 1923.

While at Farnborough, he was asked to test Handley Page O/100 3117 fitted with four 200hp Hispano-Suizas mounted back-to-back: two pulling, two pushing. He flew this 100ft-span biplane in October 1917, but the engine combination was not a success. This experience led to an even bigger beast and – at Frank's insistence, or at least that of his lawyer – his first maiden flight. This was the Kennedy Giant 2337, with a wingspan of 142ft and four 200hp Salmsons arranged in the same manner as the 'Hissos' on 3117. Designed by C J H Mackenzie-Kennedy along the lines of Igor Sikorsky's mammoth flown in Imperial Russia, the Giant was built by Fairey Aviation and the Gramophone Company under sub-contract. It was assembled at Northolt and as Frank carried out 'straights' up and down the airfield, he found it to be well underpowered and with an inadequate rudder. Before he washed his hands of it, Frank demanded payment as he had managed to get it off the ground as requested – as proven by the tracks of the mainwheels in the grass which stopped for a distance, the recommenced. Only after recourse to the law did he get his fee, hence it's place in the 'flight log' above!

Two commissions were carried out for the Aircraft Manufacturing Co (Airco) at Hendon, which built the designs of Geoffrey de Havilland* and he was asked to act as a reserve

pilot for the associated Aircraft Transport and Travel. The first was the Oxford day bomber powered by problematical ABC Dragonflies and destined to remain a one-off. Frank's autobiography, *Flight Path*, explains in his relaxed style, how the pressure was piled on for this debut. Major General Sefton Brancker, a director of ABC, insisted on joining Frank on the first flight, in the co-pilot's seat. Frank takes a delicious half-page to describe the event, but here's the short version: "I had reached about a couple of hundred feet over the railroad line bordering the field [Hendon] whe, with no warning, the starboard engine shattered its intestines and stopped dead. ..."I had just about got headed, downwind, back toward the field when the port engine developed bronchitis and coughed itself down to idling power. ...[I] kept going to make one of my best Gosport-style downwind landings." Brancker, an RFC veteran, was unruffled and grinned: "Good show, old boy. We'll put in the spare engines and take another crack at it." The DH.18 of 1920 was an eight-passenger commercial biplane which became a casualty of Airco's collapse but helped set up the newly-independent de Havilland at Stag Lane, Edgware. (It is possible that from March 1919 when Frank flew the DH.11 to 1920 and the DH.18, he was 'on the books' of Airco: in *Flight Path* he writes about the need to "venture into freelance work".)

Frank was brought in to fly the Central Aircraft Company's six-passenger twin, the Centaur IIA, G-EAHR, in July 1919. It was remodelled to put the fare-payers in an enclosed cabin and this machine, G-EAPC, was flown by Frank at Northolt in May 1920 and, job done, he moved on to other clients.

The Boulton and Paul P.6, which bcame Frank Courtney's personal runabout. *Boulton Paul plc*

The prototype Sikin, first flown in 1919. *Armstrong Whitworth Aircraft*

During September to November 1920 an airline called Air Post of Banks operated a pair of Westland Limousine biplanes out of Croydon to Paris. Frank was its chief pilot, but the concern was wound down by December. George Handasyde designed a six-seater tricycle undercarriage monoplane, the H.2, for an Australian customer and contracted Air Navigation and Engineering Co (ANEC) to build it and for Frank to test it. He took the unregistered prototype into the air at Brooklands in December 1922; it remained a one-off.

As well as testing the four-engined O/100 in 1917, Frank carried out at least one other task for Handley Page. He was

The Armstrong Whitworth Sinaia, fown by Frank Courtney on 25th June 1921. The serial is not painted on the fuselage, but on the massively extended engine fairing containing a gun position. *Armstrong Whitworth Aircraft*

The private venture Atlas prototype G-EBLK. *Armstrong Whitworth Aircraft*

to deliver the slotted-wing test-bed HP.20 J6914 from the factory at Cricklewood to Farnborough in September 1921. This machine, a parasol monoplane using a Westland-built DH.9A fuselage, had been first flown by HP's Arthur Wilcockson*. While familiarising himself with the HP.20 Frank deployed the full-span leading edge slats on approach which produced a very steep 'arrival' and a cracked longeron, putting the machine back in the factory. It was February 1922 before it was issued to Farnborough.

From his second posting to Farnborough, Frank was seconded to Norwich-based Boulton and Paul, testing the Sopwith Camels the company was building. Here he met up again with John North, his mentor at Grahame-White, Hendon, from 1913. In March 1918 he tested B&P's contender for a Camel replacement, the Bobolink. It was unsuccessful and instead B&P manufactured the winner, Sopwith's Snipe. Frank almost certainly was at the helm of the two-seat P.6 biplane in late 1918 which led to the larger P.9 that provided B&P with its first civilian work and exports (to Australia); eight were built. Frank either acquired or arranged to have the use of the P.6, registered as G-EASJ, and he based it at Croydon commuting to his commissions in it until about 1924.

In 1919 Frank flew the first of three Bourges twin-engined three-crew day bombers, each varying in format. Frank looped and rolled it, as well as happily flying it with an engine shut down. At the 1923 Hendon RAF Pageant while flying a Bourges, Frank was 'attacked' by Nieuport Nighthawk fighters, only to engage in aerobatics to shake them off! The second Bourges was badly damaged in a crash at Mousehold and parts were used to create the much-developed P.8 Atlantic, designed to have a crack at the *Daily Mail*'s £10,000 prize for a non-stop crossing of the Atlantic. On the first flight the P.8's port engine failed on take-off; Frank and his observer miraculously escaped serious injury, the P.8 was badly damaged. The Air Ministry was very interested in what was called the 'engine room' layout – placing powerplants within the fuselage using shafts to drive the propellers. B&P was contracted to build two Bodmins with two Napier Lions in the fuselage, driving via shafts and gearboxes four propellers, two pushing and two pulling – a layout that Frank was well acquainted with! The Bodmins were followed by B&P's inaugural all metal design, the one-off Bolton, and the Bugle day bomber which entered limited production.

Another company with which he had a long association was Armstrong Whitworth. Frank started off with Siddeley Deasy, which was taken over by AW in 1919. He flew the Siskin prototype for Siddeley Deasy in early 1919 and had considerable input in what was to become an exceptional fighter, establishing AW as a major forcet. The Mk.II, which Frank first flew in May 1923, was AW's first all-metal design. Between 1922 and 1924 Frank conducted sales tours in a Siskin V to Belgium, France, the Netherlands, Romania, Spain and Sweden. Frank also piloted the prototype Atlas, the RAF's first dedicated army co-operation type. Other AW designs he trialed included the Wolf reconnaissance biplane, the Sinaia day bomber which had gun positions in extensions from each engine nacelle and the Awana military transport. None were adopted for production.

While delivering an aircraft to Cuatro Vientos, Madrid, Spain in the summer of 1925, Frank was shown what he called a "crazy looking" contraption in a hangar. He thought no more of it until a Spaniard called Juan de la Cierva* telephoned him explaining he had been recommended as a test pilot by the Air Ministry. Cierva had no English and Frank no Spanish, but they were delighted to find they both spoke French. As related under Cierva's section, Frank demonstrated the Spanish-built C.6A autogiro at Farnborough in October 1925, becoming only the second 'Brit' to achieve rotary-winged flight – the first being Bob Graham*. In March 1926 the Cierva Autogiro Company was formed, Frank serving as its technical manager. With Cierva resident in the UK, the pace of development accelerated: on 19th June Frank flew C.6C J8068 and on 29th July the C.6D, both had been built by Avro at Hamble. The C.6D was the first ever two-seater autogiro and the day after its debut, Frank took Juan up, thus he became the inaugural rotorcraft passenger. While piloting J8068 at Hamble on 7th February 1927 a rotor blade detached and the 'giro plummeted to the ground. Frank was hospitalized, but was fit enough by 3rd March to fly the Parnall Pike – see below. With the accident Frank and Juan parted company; Bert Hinkler* took his place.

The output of Parnall Aircraft at Yate was so small that a 'standing' test pilot was a luxury and to meet this sort of need was exactly why Frank was in business. Frank flew three Parnall designs all destined to remain prototypes: the Peto two-seat floatplane, the Perch naval trainer and the Pike 2/3-crew naval reconnaissance type. Of these the diminutive Peto could be folded so it could be kept within a water-tight hangar on a submarine's deck, launching when the vessel surfaced. While flying Pike N202 at Yate on 30th June 1927 with designer Harold Bolas along for the ride, Frank found that modifications to the tailplane meant that he could not raise the nose sufficiently to flare in the normal manner. He tried a fast approach but nosed over, the Lion engine breaking through its mountings and pinning Frank in the cockpit. To quote from *Flight Path*: "I suffered my regular damage – a couple of skinned shins".

By 1925 at least Frank's rates had gone up! Westland was readying the 59ft 6in Yeovil two-seat day bomber for its debut at the airfield of the same name. The Air Ministry decided that resident test pilot Laurence Openshaw* lacked currency on larger machines and Frank was brought in, charging £100. The following year Frank was again engaged by Westland, this time from the large open spaces of Andover, for the debut of the Westbury three-seat 'bomber destroyer' in September 1926. He found its characteristics to be acceptable and the following day Openshaw flew it to its birthplace at Yeovil.

Frank was no stranger to competitive flying. By March 1920 he was working again for Grahame-White at Hendon, though it is not known in what capacity. He competed in the fifth Aerial Derby at Hendon that July, winning in the Martinsyde Semiquaver G-EAPX at 153.4mph, but over-turning the machine on landing; he climbed out unharmed. At the *Daily Mail*-sponsored gliding competition at Itford Hill in 1922 Frank flew the Sayers SCW. In Siskin II G-EBEU he won the second King's Cup air race, staged out of Hendon, at 149.0mph. For the 1925 Lympne Light Aeroplane Trials Frank raced Parnall Pixie II G-EBKM and in the following year's contest – the last

to be staged – he piloted the two-seat Pixie III G-EBJG.

The attempt to fly the Atlantic had come to nought in April 1919 when the twin-engined B&P P.8 had crashed on take-off. Frank had not finished with ideas of flying across the forbidding ocean. Frank had cultivated the son of Canadian millionaire Edward B Hosmer and through him acquired in March 1927 an Italian-built Dornier Do J Wal (Whale) which was registered G-EBQO. History was repeating itself, the Wal was twin-engined, one pulling, one pushing! The flying-boat was re-engined in Genoa with two 450hp Napier Lions and prepared for an Atlantic flight. Frank and crew departed Calshot on 2nd September 19127 but had to force-land off Corunna, on the coast of Spain the following day. Determined not to be defeated, the tried again the following year, reaching the Azores in G-EBQO on 28th June. On the first day of August he took off with the attention of flying direct to Newfoundland. Once again he was forced down, this time in high seas, Frank, Edward Hosmer, engineering F Pierce and radio operator H Gilmour where picked up by a westbound liner. By a miracle, G-EBQO proved to be very resilient, it was found damaged but 'seaworthy' by a ship and put under tow bound for Portugal. The Dornier was sold in Germany in late 1928.

Frank crossed the Atlantic again in 1928, by ship. He moved to the USA to become a technical assistant for the newly-established Curtiss plant in St Louis, Missouri (which became part of the Curtiss-Wright Corporation from 1929). He competed in the Cleveland National Air Races in 1929, in a DH Gipsy Moth. Frank designed a five-seat amphibian with a retractable tricycle undercarriage and this flew for the first time in 1935 as the CA-1. ('CA' standing for Courtney Amphibian.) At first glance this was a tractor biplane, the cowled 365hp Wright 975E being placed at the leading edge of the upper wing, but it drove a pusher propeller *behind* the trailing edge via an extension shaft. Two, or three, were built, all going to Japan. During 1936 Frank returned to the UK, offering his services as a flying-boat test pilot.

Frank returned to Britain in 1936, offering his services as a consultant/test pilot specialising in marine aircraft. Apart from the CA-1, he'd piloted the Saunders Valkyrie tri-motor biplane flying-boat from the River Medina on its maiden flight in June 1926. In 1928 S E Saunders became Saunders-Roe and in 1938

Frank Courtney flying the Cierva C.6C J8068 at the RAF Pageant at Hendon, July 1926. *KEC*

once again the company turned to Frank's expertise. Saro had responded to Specification R2/33 with the radical A.33 four-engined parasol monoplane with fuselage-mounted sponsons to eradicate the need for wing tip floats – in the same manner as the Dornier Wal. Saro's resident test pilot, Leslie Ash*, was lacking in large flying-boat experience and Frank captained the debut in October 1938. He found the A.33 reasonable in the air, but it had unacceptable porpoising tendencies in the water. On the 25th the A.33 hit the wake of a ferry boat and the porpoising became more pronounced, then the starboard side of the wing failed and twisted. The unfortunate aircraft was towed back and ultimately axed; the Sunderland winning the requirement. The following month, Frank took the prototype Lerwick airborne – see under Leslie Ash for more.

Returning to the USA in 1940, Frank joined Consolidated Aircraft (later Convair) at San Diego, California, as a PTP and engaged on the ferrying of Liberators and other types to Europe. In his autobiography, Frank describes his last test flying activity as co-piloting a four-engined jet transport. He's not specific, but given his associations with Convair, the author wonders if this would be the CV-880 which first flew on 27th January 1959. Frank ended his aviation career as a consultant for Boeing. In 1972 he wrote *Flight Path – My Fifty Years of Aviation*, published by Kimber in the UK and by Doubleday in the USA as *The Eighth Sea* (beyond the seven seas there is another, the sky). Frank T Courtney died in December 1982 in San Diego, California, aged 88.

Parnall Peto N181 naval floatplane. *KEC*

The Saunders Valkyrie flying-boat, tesed by Frank Courtney in June 1926. *Saro*

John 'Tiny' Crosby-Warren

1939	Parnall Heck III J-1
	1 x 200hp DH Gipsy Six

John A Crosby-Warren, born 1911. Studied at Cambridge and learned to fly with the Cambridge University UAS. Joined Bristol Aeroplane as an apprentice, at the same time he was reported to have enrolled with the 'Bristol Squadron' of the Auxiliary Air Force – 605 (Warwick), or 614 (Glamorgan) Squadrons were the nearest.

"The flight testing of production aircraft is a vocation which should not be followed by any pilot unless he feels himself to be really interested in turning 'green' or raw aircraft into live things which will not only fulfil their purpose, but give pleasure to those pilots and crews who eventually receive them." So wrote John Crosby-Warren in his 1943 book *Flight Testing of Production Aircraft*, as quoted in Constance Babington Smith's exceptional tome, *Testing Time*. At 6ft 8in tall, John was not of typical pilot stature and inevitably was called 'Tiny'. Despite the windscreen, John was always further into the slipstream of open cockpit aircraft than his contemporaries and his use of a Russian-style fur hat to compensate made him very distinctive. His first test piloting job was the Parnall Heck III, a development of the Heck 2 tourer, aimed at replacing the Magister. The Heck III remained a one-off and it turned out to be the last Parnall design to fly; the company went on to become a major airframe sub-contractor and manufacturer of gun turrets.

In late 1940 John joined Gloster as a PTP, working initially on Henleys, Hurricanes and Typhoons from the Hucclecote factory under 'Gerry' Sayer* and, from October 1942, Michael Daunt*. By 1943 John was heavily involved in experimental testing on the blossoming jet programme and on 3rd May 1943 he ferried the second Gloster E28/39 W4046 to Farnborough. On 26th July 1943 he flew F9/40 Meteor prototype DG202 (now at the RAF Museum) and this *probably* was his first sortie in the type. John wrote on a variety of topics in *Flight* magazine, under the pen name 'Sparrow'. On 27th April 1944 John was piloting the second F9/40 to fly, DG205, investigating aileron instability when a trim tab detached and it went into a dive. It was seen to be recovering when it half-rolled and crashed on the golf course at Minchinhampton, near Stroud. John A Crosby-Warren, aged 33, was killed instantly. The obituary in *Flight* for 4th May 1944 paid fine tribute: "A superb pilot, he could make the flying of a machine like a piece of poetry, yet his technical knowledge was very extensive."

The one-off Parnall Heck III trainer. *Peter Green Collection*

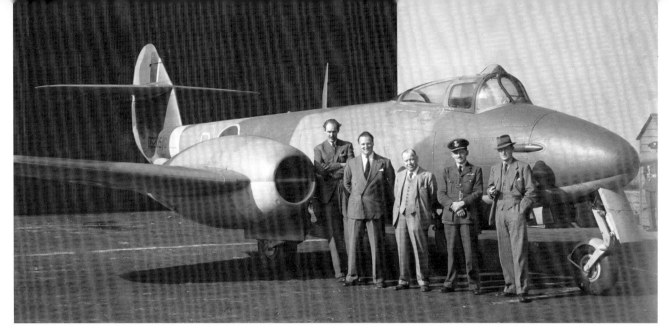

At 6ft 8in John Crosby-Warren (left) dominates this august line-up: Michael Daunt, Gloster CTP; F McKenna, Gloster general manager; Gp Captain Frank Whittle; W George Carter, Gloster chief designer. Behind is DG205/G, the second F9/40 Meteor prototype to fly, the first with Whittle engines and in which John was killed in April 1944. *KEC*

Lindsay Cumming

1 Jun 1981	Short 360-100 G-ROOM
	2 x 1,424shp P&W PT6A-67R

Lindsay Logan Cumming, born 1929. National service in the Royal Engineers in Kenya, followed by an engineering degree at Edinburgh. Learned to fly with Edinburgh UAS; wrote off DHC Chipmunk T.10 WB603 when it hit telephone wires on approach to Turnhouse, 26th April 1952. Joined the RAF 1952, serving with 76 Squadron on EE Canberra B.2s, later B.6s. Deployed to Christmas Island, Pacific, to monitor UK atom bomb tests 1956-1957. Squadron Leader in 1960 and became CO of Queens UAS, Sydenham. Left the RAF in 1968.

LINDSAY CUMMING started work for Shorts at Sydenham, Belfast, in 1968 as a production test and demonstration pilot on Skyvans and, from 1974, on 330s. He succeeded Don Wright* as CTP on 17th December 1976 and in June 1981 was at the helm for the debut of the enlarged and developed 360 twin turboprop commuter airliner. Tasks remained much as before, flight test, demonstrations, deliveries and communications work. He retired on 19th October 1984, handing on to Allan Deacon*. Settling back in his native Scotland, he continued to fly for the RAFVR until 1994. Sqn Ldr Lindsay Logan Cumming died on 4th February 2007, aged 77.

The tenth production Short 360 N715NC, for Newair of New Haven, Connecticut, USA, was first flown at Sydenham 28th March 1983 and delivered the following month. *Shorts*

John Cunningham

27 Jul 1949	DH Comet 1 G-5-1
	4 x 4,450lbst DH Ghost 50 Mk.1
26 Sep 1951	DH DH.110 WG236
	2 x 6,500lbst RR Avon RA3
16 Feb 1952	DH Comet 2X G-ALYT
	4 x 6,600lbst RR Avon 502
9 Jan 1962	HS Trident 1 G-ARPA
	3 x 10,400lbst RR Spey 505
23 May 1967	HS Nimrod XV148
	4 x 12,160lbst RR Spey 250

Notes: All took place at Hatfield except for the Nimrod, which took off from Hawarden, landing at Woodford.

John Cunningham, born 1912. Enrolled at the de Havilland Aeronautical Technical School at Hatfield 1935 and helped to build its second original design, TK.2 G-ADNO of August 1935. He also joined 604 (County of Middlesex) Squadron Auxiliary Air Force, learning to fly on Avro 504Ns at Hendon, going on Hawker Demons.

AFTER his course at the Aeronautical Technical School, John Cunningham started his long career in 1938 with de Havilland with the light aircraft division. He worked for Geoffrey de Havilland jnr as an assistant test pilot and an early task was clearing the Moth Minor two-seater for airworthiness. There were high hopes for the Minor as it was seen as the new DH.60 Moth. A special long-distance coupe Moth Minor, E-2, was intended for a record flight by John to Baghdad; a venture supported by 'DH Senior' but overtaken by the outbreak of war. While testing the prototype, E-4, on 11th April 1939 Geoffrey and John were investigating spinning characteristics with the centre of gravity set well aft. Try as they might they could not recover from a spin and both took to the silk; the stricken aircraft plummeting past them to crash near Wheathampstead. In the *Ominous Skies*, Harald Penrose writes that the pair lunched in a

Jimmy Rawnsley (left) with John Cunningham in front of a night-fighter Mosquito. *Peter Green Collection*

hostelry with hardly a mention of their first use of parachutes. In a similar manner to the Tiger Moth, strakes fitted immediately forward of the fin/tailplane junction solved the problem.

As a member of 604 Squadron, John was mobilised in August 1939, the unit flying Blenheim Is and switching to the night-fighter role. Conversion to Beaufighter Is started the following month. On the night of 19th/20th November 1940, John opened his 'account', by downing a Junkers Ju 88. Late in 1940 John was re-united with Sgt C F 'Jimmy' Rawnsley, who had been his gunner during 604's Demon era and had re-mustered as a radar operator. The two became a formidable force: by 1943 they were the RAF's top-scoring night-fighter team. (This accolade was later taken on by Mosquito 'ace' Wg Cdr Branse Burbridge.) This fame led to John receiving the nickname 'Cat's Eyes' which, while he understood its appeal to the press and the public, he greatly disliked. John became commanding officer of 604 in August 1941, he and Jimmy moving to the Mosquito-equipped 85 Squadron in January 1943, with John as its leader. The pair set off for Burma in mid-1945, but the surrender of Japan allowed them to turn around and return to the UK. Ending the war as a

Wing Commander, John achieved a total of 20 'kills', 3 'probables' and 7 damaged. He was always at pains to praise his radar operators, especially Jimmy; the two having made an exceptional combination. Sqn Ldr Jimmy Rawnsley DSO DFC DFM* went on to write *Night Fighter* with Robert Wright, with a foreword by John. It first appeared in 1957 and has been in print more or less ever since. As soon as he could, John re-joined de Havilland as a test pilot. He again became CO of 604 Squadron, by then with Spitfire XVIs, but pressures of work at Hatfield meant that he had to give this up.

When Geoffrey de Havilland jnr was killed in DH.108 TG306 on 27th September 1946, John was delivering a Vampire to Switzerland. (See under Geoffrey's section for more.) In the worst of circumstances John was appointed as CTP, his duties included overseeing flying at all of the de Havilland sites, including the Airspeed subsidiary. James Hamilton-Paterson in his exceptional *Empire of the Clouds* quotes John's salary, circa 1948 as £1,500 which in present-day values would be £45,000. A third DH.108, VW120, much revised in the light of experience with the first two, was flown by John from Hatfield on 24th July 1947. Part of the original concept of the DH.08 was to investigate swept wings for the DH.106 Comet jetliner programme.

Vampire development and preparing the way for the Comet took up most of John's time. Some concern was expressed about the shape of the nose of the jetliner, the configuration of the flight deck windows and especially the view from the latter in poor weather. An ingenious solution was found to test this: the Airspeed Horsa II assault glider had a cockpit section that hinged to the side, allowing Jeeps and field guns to be loaded. Harris Lebus-built TL348 had its cockpit removed and a wooden replica of the Comet nose grafted on. John piloted this incredible test-bed, towed aloft by a Halifax, giving the tug pilot instructions to find poor weather so that he could assess visibility. (To go off on a tangent, when Sud Aviation was designing its Caravelle twin-jet, the French adopted the layout of the Comet's nose in its entirety... hopefully with some remuneration heading towards Hatfield!) English Electric-built Vampire F.1 TG278 was converted into a test-bed for the Ghost

The third, and much modified, DH.108 was first flown by John Cunningham in July 1947. *British Aerospace*

turbojet that was to power the Comet. Its wingspan was increased by 8ft to 40ft and it was given a strengthened canopy with just small 'portholes' for sideways vision. In this guise John took it to 59,446ft on 23rd March 1948, setting a world altitude record. (See 'Wally' Gibb for the next to hold this record.)

John was at the helm of the world's first jet airliner, Comet 1 G-ALVG at Hatfield on 27th July 1949, which happened to be his 32nd birthday! On board for the 31-minute flight were co-pilot John Wilson*, flight engineer Frank T Reynolds, electrics flight engineer H 'Tubby' Walters and FTO Anthony J Fairbrother. The prototypes featured single wheel main undercarriage; production versions were fitted with four-wheel bogies. There are many sorties in the Comet captained by John that could be highlighted, but the Tripoli, Libya, 'to-and-back' was jaw-dropping for the world's press and illustrated what the 'jet age' would mean to air travel. Lifting off from Heathrow at about 06:30 on 25th October 1949 G-ALVG was flown to Castle Benito, turned around in about two hours and was back 'home' at 15:20 – 6½ hours of flying nearly 6,000 miles travelled at an average speed of around 450mph.

John was also the captain of Comet 2X G-ALYT on 16th February 1952 out of Hatfield. This was the first Rolls-Royce Avon-engined version, with a slightly longer fuselage. After the Comet disasters of 1954 – see Chapter Five – the programme was brought to a halt while investigations were carried out. Much re-thought, re-designed and stretched, the prototype 'second generation' Comet 3 G-ANLO was flown by John and Peter Buggé on 19th July 1954. Four days previously at Boeing Field, Seattle, Washington, USA, Alvin 'Tex' Johnston had taken the Model 367-80 into the air for the first time. The 'Dash-80' as it was known, was the prototype of the Boeing 707 and it brought about a seismic change in the jetliner market, rapidly eclipsing the Comet.

The twin-engined, twin-boomed DH.110 WG236 was taken on its maiden flight by John on 26th September 1951, with FTO Tony Fairbrother (who had been with him on the Comet's first sortie). John and Tony paired up for most of the tests up to January 1952 when John Derry* took over the majority of the programme. The DH.110 was adopted by the Fleet Air Arm as the Sea Vixen. John then concentrated on Comet testing and deliveries; flying the first Series 4, G-APDA, on 2nd February 1958.

The prototype Trident, G-ARPA, took to the air at Hatfield shortly after noon on 9th January 1962 for an 81-minute sortie. Captaining *Papa-Alpha* was John, with Peter Buggé as P2, 'Brax' Brackston Brown as flight engineer, Tony Fairbrother (Hatfield flight test manager and FTO to John on the Comet and the DH.110) and two FTOs, John Johnston and John Marshall. While cycling the undercarriage, the starboard main gear snagged semi-retracted but this was soon solved by Brax who depressurised that element of the hydraulics and the jam was cleared. With 'three greens' on the panel, a low run across Hatfield with the undercarriage down allowed for a visual inspection for confirmation and was followed by a textbook touchdown. Post-flight John declared that G-ARPA was "superb to fly".

For John's final prototype, he was returned to his Comet roots. To replace the Shackleton maritime patroller, Hawker

Horsa II TL348 fitted with a mock-up Comet nose section was tested by John Cunningham. *British Aerospace*

Siddeley had devised a much-modified version of the Comet, the HS.801 Nimrod. (DH became part of HSA in 1963.) From late 1957, Comet 4s began to be assembled and flight tested at Hawarden, to help free up space at Hatfield for Trident production. Two unfinished Series 4 airframes held in store at Hawarden were reconfigured to act as Nimrod prototypes. One, XV147, was completed as a Comet 4C and ferried to Woodford, where new-build Nimrods would be produced, on 25th October 1965. There it was converted to Nimrod status, but retained Avon turbojets and was used from 31st July 1967 as the systems flying test-bed. Meanwhile, the other airframe, XV148, was fitted with Spey 250 turbofans to act as the 'full' Nimrod prototype. As this was a Woodford project, its CTP 'Jimmy' Harrison* would have been the expected choice for the maiden flight. Given John's extensive Comet experience, Jimmy made the 75-minute test flight from Hawarden on 23rd May 1967 in the right-head seat, with John as captain and instructor; the sortie landed at Woodford. John handed the project over to Jimmy nine days later.

The world's first jetliner, Comet 1 G-ALVG. *Key Publishing collection – www.keypublishing.com*

The one-off Series 3 G-ANLO served as the prototype for the 'second generation' Comet. *De Havilland*

John captained the maiden flight of the stretched Trident 3B prototype, G-AWYZ, from Hatfield on 11th December 1969. Prominent among the export Trident customers was the Civil Aviation Administration of China which eventually ordered 35, mostly Series 2Es plus a pair of 3Bs. The first, B-2201, was delivered by John in December 1970 and CAAC made it a condition that John play a prominent part in the programme. On 20th November 1975, John was the captain of company HS.125-600B G-BCUX – less than a year old – and was to take a party of seven Chinese visitors from Dunsfold to Hatfield. Seconds after rotating *Uniform-Xray* from Runway 07 John, then 58 with 11,848 hours in his logbook, encountered a huge flock of birds and the Viper 601 turbojets surged and lost power. With amazing presence of mind, John got the jet back on the runway, but it careered through the airfield boundary, hit a car on A281 and came to rest in countryside. John, his co-pilot and his passengers escaped before the 125 erupted in flame. Tragically, all six in the car died. John suffered some spinal damage, but was back in the air within a year.

John, who had been appointed as a director of de Havilland on 1st December 1958, retired in October 1980 with around 13,000 flight hours to his credit. He was succeeded by Mike Goodfellow*. Gp Capt John Cunningham CBE DSO** DFC* (who also had the Soviet Order of the Patriotic War First Class and the US Silver Star among other awards) died on 21st July 2002, aged 84.

Top left: Distinguished by the retention of its airliner windows and the lack of MAD-boom at the tail, the prototype Nimrod XV148, as flown by John Cunningham. *Hawker Siddeley*

Left: John Cunningham (at the base of the air stairs) with the rest of his test flight crew, after the first flight of the first Trident 3B, G-AWYZ, December 1969. *British Aerospace*

Below: The prototype Trident, G-ARPA, airborne from Hatfield. *British Aerospace*

Ken Dalton-Golding

Kenneth William Dalton-Golding, born 1922. Joined the RAF in 1941, serving in Coastal Command. By 1949 he was with 45 Squadron at Tengah, Singapore, converting from Bristol Beaufighter TF.10s to Brigand B.1s. He flew the Brigand's first combat sortie, 19th December 1949. ETPS No.10 Course, Farnborough followed by service with A&AEE.

KEN DALTON-GOLDING joined Handley Page (HP) as an experimental and development test pilot as deputy to Hedley Hazelden* in July 1952. The company was gearing up for the first flight of the prototype Victor, WB771, which Headley achieved on Christmas Eve 1952 at Boscombe Down. Ken became the second to pilot a Victor on 22nd February 1953. The previous month the first of a batch of 75 EE Canberra B.2s to be built by HP was flight tested at Radlett and this consumed time not occupied on the Victor programme. On 25th February 1954, Ken and FTO Michael Goodridge took B.2 WJ622 on its second shake-down flight from Radlett. On return, the Canberra was observed to invert, assume a nose-down attitude and impact on a railway embankment on the eastern boundary of the airfield. Michael (21) and Flt Lt Kenneth William Dalton-Golding DFC (33) were killed instantly. As news of the crash spread through the Radlett plant, there was confusion as to what had happened, as Hedley was also airborne at the time. Investigations revealed that elements of the powered flight controls had failed on WJ622. Ken's death left Hedley as the only test pilot at Radlett until he recruited 'Taffy' Ecclestone*.

Michael Daunt

| 5 Mar 1943 | Gloster F9/40 DG206/G |
| | 2 x 2,000lbst Halford (DH) H1 |

Neil Michael Daunt, born 1909 to Irish parents. Studied engineering at Cambridge and learned to fly with Cambridge UAS at Duxford. Terminating his degree course, he joined the RAF in 1930 and served with 25 Squadron on Hawker Fury Is at Hawkinge. He left the RAF in 1935 and became a flying instructor at de Havilland, Hatfield.

CHOOSING to be known by his middle name, Michael Daunt became a production test pilot for Hawker at Brooklands in 1936, having got to know CTP 'George' Bulman* during the latter's visits to Hawkinge. Michael's stay with Hawker was brief, he moved to Gloster – part of the Hawker Siddeley Group from 1935 – as a PTP under 'Gerry' Sayer* in 1937, later becoming his deputy. On 27th May 1941 Michael flew Typhoon I R7576, the first Gloster-built example, at Hucclecote.

Specification 43/37 brought about a remarkable aircraft that both Gerry and Michael were involved in and took an almost instant dislike to. Henry Folland's company won the contract for a dedicated engine test-bed that could easily have different piston-engined powerplants attached to the firewall. This was the Folland Fo 108 and construction of the first two of a batch of a dozen started at Eastleigh in 1940, with Folland moving his factory to Staverton later that year. Lacking a test pilot, Henry Folland turned to Gloster for help; he had been

the company's designer, from Gamecock to Gladiator. The prototype Folland 43/37, P1774, powered by a Napier Sabre first flew at Eastleigh around August 1940 with Gerry most likely at the controls. Once established at Staverton, Gerry and Michael shared testing. Michael was flying P1777 on 19th May 1942 when the tailplane failed, followed by the propeller parting company with the Bristol Centaurus engine. Wisely electing to bale out, Michael came down in a Gloucestershire field; he'd broken his collar bone and a wrist, among other injuries. First on the scene was the local clergyman, who in his zeal to move the downed pilot hurt him so much that Michael thumped him! Michael was taken to hospital and it was six months before he was fully back at work. Describing the Fo 108 as "bloody dangerous", Michael dubbed it the "Folland Frightful" – and the nickname stuck. While pilot's loathed the machine, flight test observers had nothing but praise for it as it had a purpose-designed, spacious cabin behind and below the cockpit, whereas normally FTOs were squeezed in wherever possible.

While flying a Typhoon on a liaison visit to 1 Squadron at Acklington on 21st October 1942, Gerry Sayer was killed in what is believed to have been a collision. Michael, in turn, became CTP for Gloster. In May of the previous year, Gerry had made the first-ever flight of a British jet, the Gloster E28/39 and was the only pilot to have flown it. Thankfully, he'd kept Michael abreast of its qualities and vices. Michael became the second British jet aviator when he took the E28/39 into the air on 6th November 1942 at Edgehill. John Crosby-Warren* and John Grierson* were quickly introduced to the new technology so as increase the number who were current on the type.

Cranwell had been the venue for the maiden flight of the E28/39 and the large grass airfield was again chosen for its twin-engined successor, the F9/40, soon to be named Meteor. Prior to dismantling the Halford H1-engined DG206 for the journey to Lincolnshire, a full-throttle ground run at Bentham, close to the Hucclecote factory, nearly ended in tragedy. Michael, standing close to the leading edge, bent forward and was sucked into an intake. Whoever was in the cockpit reacted like lightning and chopped the throttles, while technicians grabbed Michael. He was extremely shocked – not to mention lucky – and spent a couple of days getting over it. Whenever he was asked about it the incident, Michael's wry sense of humour would gloss over the seriousness with his claim to be the only test pilot to have "pranged himself on a ground run". Specially-made grills were fitted for all ground runs after that and in Michael's honour they were called 'Daunt Stoppers'.

On 5th March 1943 Michael was at the helm of DG206 for its truncated debut at Cranwell. He encountered considerable directional stability problems – 'snaking' – and the sortie lasted just 210 seconds. Despite this, the pace of the programme increased, Michael flew DG205 on 12th June 1943 and 42 days later DG202; both fitted with Whittle W2B/23s and flown from Barford St John. (DG202 is displayed in the 'Milestones of Flight' hall at the RAF Museum, Hendon.) Michael flew the first pre-series Meteor I EE210, complete with cannon in the nose, on 12th January 1944. He had to force-land DG203, the fourth Meteor to fly and powered by a W2B/500, on 22nd April 1944. He skilfully brought it down in a potato field. Again Michael's

The prototype Folland 'Frightful' P1774, probably at Staverton, August 1941. *D Napier and Sons*

Michael Daunt adjusting his leather helmet before the first flight of F9/40 DG206/G at Cranwell, 5th May 1943. Just visible inside the nacelle of the port engine are the grills of a 'Daunt Stopper'. *via Don Middleton*

Michael Daunt re-united with DG202/G and a Whittle W2B at the RAF Museum, Cosford. *via Don Middleton*

name was associated with another 'product', someone declaring the Meteor to be the 'Whittle-Daunt Potato Lifter'. In *Testing Time*, Constance Babington Smith quotes, Michael's response to this description, declaring it was: "Not just a potato *lifter*; they were chipped and cooked as well as delivered!" As work was in hand to salvage and repair DG203, tragedy struck on the 27th when John Crosby-Warren was killed in DG205.

Aged 55, Michael retired from Gloster in June 1944; Eric Greenwood* taking the helm. He became a farmer, then a sales engineer and for ten years he was chief technician at a Kidney unit in a Birmingham hospital. Neil Michael Daunt OBE died on 26th July 1991, aged 82.

J E Davies

APPOINTED CTP for British Aerospace at Woodford in 1998, succeeding Al McDicken*. Major work centred on the flight testing of the RJ series of jetliners, a refined version of the HS.146. His tenure was short, passing on the baton to John Bolton*.

Allan Deacon

| 30 Dec 1986 | Short Tucano T.1 ZF135 | 1 x 1,100shp |
| | Garrett TPE331-126 | |

H W Allan Deacon, born 1932. Joined the Fleet Air Arm in 1955 and by 1957 was with 891 Squadron on DH Sea Venom FAW.22s, then 892 Squadron on DH Sea Vixen FAW.1s. Graduated from ETPS Course No.20 at Farnborough in 1961, followed by a tour with A&AEE. In 1965 he joined the Buccaneer S.2 trials unit, 700B Squadron; ending his FAA service with 801 Squadron, also on Buccaneer S.2s. Served as a pilot with Rolls-Royce at Hucknall 1966 to 1970. He joined executive jet operator McAlpine Aviation at Luton in 1970.

ALLAN DEACON joined Shorts at Sydenham in 1977 working as a PTP on Skyvans, 330s and 360s. He succeeded Lindsay Cumming* as CTP in October 1984 and was soon involved in the much-modified version of the Brazilian EMBRAER EMB.312 Tucano to replace the RAF's Jet Provost. The initial Garrett-engined prototype, PT-ZTC, was built in Brazil and tested there on 14th February 1986. It was shipped to Sydenham and flown by Allan with the B Condition ('trade plate') marking G-14-007 on 11th April 1986. It became G-BTUC in June 1986 and is today preserved by the Ulster Aviation Collection at Long Kesh, Northern Ireland.

Alan flew ZF135, the first Sydenham-completed Tucano T.1 in December 1986, and the majority of the RAF order for

Tucano T.1s of 7 Flying Training School, Church Fenton, in June 1990. The unit had accepted the first Tucanos for RAF service the previous December.
Cpl Lee Palman-RAF Church Fenton

130. While clearing the first Kenyan T.51, ZH203, for weapons carriage on 22nd February 1990 the tail section suffered a catastrophic failure due to flutter. Allan successfully ejected off Rathlin Island on the Northern Ireland coast, but he drowned in heavy seas; Lt H W A Deacon MBE was 58.

The last Short 360 twin-turboprop flew in 1991 and the final new-build C-23 Sherpa (USAF version of the Short 330) followed in 1992: these were the last Shorts-designed aircraft to fly from Sydenham. The last Tucano maiden flight was T.1 ZF516 on 23rd December 1992, the last of a long line of Short types. When Allan Deacon took ZF135 aloft in December 1986 he could directly trace the lineage of his job back to 1910 and the first-ever British test pilot, Cecil Grace*.

Sir Geoffrey de Havilland

8 Jun 1911	Royal A/c Factory SE.1 1 x 60hp ENV
16 Aug 1911	Royal A/c Factory FE.2 1 x 50hp Gnome
4 Dec 1911	Royal A/c Factory BE.1 1 x 60hp Wolseley
1 Feb 1912	Royal A/c Factory BE.2 1 x 60hp Renault
3 May 1912	Royal A/c Factory BE.3 1 x 50hp Gnome
Feb 1913	Royal A/c Factory BS.1 1 x 100hp Gnome
Mar 1913	Royal A/c Factory FE.3 1 x 75hp Chenu
Jan 1915	Airco DH.1 1 x 70hp Renault
1 Jun 1915	Airco DH.2 1 x 100hp Gnome
1916	Airco DH.3 2 x 120hp Beardmore
Aug 1916	Airco DH.4 3696 1 x 230hp BHP
Jun 1917	Airco DH.9 A7559 1 x 230hp BHP
4 Mar 1918	Airco DH.10 Amiens 2 x 230hp BHP
5 Jul 1921	DH Doncaster J6849 1 x 450hp Napier Lion IB
1 Jul 1924	DH DH.51 G-EBIM 1 x 90hp RAF 1A
22 Feb 1925	DH Moth G-EBKT 1 x 60hp ADC Cirrus I
21 Aug 1931	DH Swallow Moth E-7 1 x 80hp DH Gipsy IV
27 May 1933	DH Leopard Moth E-1 1 x 130hp DH Gipsy Major
9 May 1934	DH Hornet Moth E-6 1 x 130hp Gipsy Major 1
22 Jun 1937	DH Moth Minor G-AFRD 1 x 90hp DH Gipsy Minor

Notes: Royal Aircraft Factory designs, all first flown from Farnborough. FE.3 designed by S J Waters, all other Royal Aircraft Factory types listed designed by GDH. All Airco – Aircraft Manufacturing Company – types designed by GDH and flown from Hendon. DH Doncaster to Leopard Moth all first flown at Stag Lane, Edgware; Hornet Moth and Moth Minor from Hatfield.

Sir Geoffrey de Havilland OM CBE AFC. *British Aerospace*

Geoffrey de Havilland (GDH), born 1882. Studied at Crystal Palace Engineering School 1900-1903. In 1903 he joined Williams and Robinson in Rugby, manufacturers of engines – he designed and built his own motorcycle, including the engine, during this period. From 1905 worked in the design office of the Wolseley Tool and Motor Car Company moving to the Motor Omnibus Construction Company in 1906, both in London. He befriended Frank Hearle, working for a rival concern as an engineer. With financial help from his grandfather, GDH and Frank combined their talents, jacked in their jobs, so that they could build a flying machine. They created what became known as the Biplane No.1, a single-seater powered by a 45hp four-cylinder also designed by GDH and built on commission by the Iris Motor Co. The engine drove two pusher propellers via shafts. No.1 was built in Fulham and moved in May 1909 to a shed at Seven Barrows, near Newbury, for assembly. On its first flight in December 1909, No.1 got to a height of about 15 to 20ft and crashed; GDH was only slightly hurt. Undaunted, GDH designed a two-seater biplane with the engine from No.1 driving a single pusher propeller. On 10th September 1910 Biplane No.2 flew for about a quarter of a mile at Seven Barrows. Geoffrey de Havilland was in the aeroplane business.

A VIATION history has benefitted from the vision and zeal of many families. Britain has had its share, names such as Barnwell, Miles and Short among others, but there is no dynasty like de Havilland, where a father had to suffer the loss of two sons in flight test tragedies: Geoffrey Raoul de Havilland* and John de Havilland*. As related in Chapter Two,

as a pioneer Geoffrey de Havilland does not initially qualify as a *test* pilot, he was a designer-pilot. When he joined the Balloon Factory at Farnborough in February 1911, his job description included the word 'pilot' as well as 'designer'. This was also the case when he worked for Airco at Hendon. With the establishment of his own business, GDH continued in the role of designer *and* test pilot until he dropped both to concentrate on management. Geoffrey de Havilland – Sir Geoffrey from 1944 – will be referred to throughout this entry as GDH to avoid confusion with his company.

After successfully flying Biplane No.2, GDH met Frederick 'Fred' Michael Green at the Olympia Motor Show in November 1910. In the previous January Fred had been appointed as Engineer-Designer to the Balloon Factory at Farnborough. Fred suggested that the formidable Mervyn Joseph Pius O'Gorman, superintendent of the factory since 1909, would be interested in meeting GDH and seeing his creation fly. At Farnborough on 14th January 1911 GDH showed that his biplane could meet the requirement of staying airborne for an hour – although it was so perishing cold that he was allowed to alight every 20 minutes or so to thaw out! O'Gorman was convinced and arranged for Biplane No.2 to be bought by the War Office for £400 – £44,000 in present-day values. More importantly GDH was taken on as designer and pilot – effectively *test* pilot – and his colleague Frank Hearle took up a post as an engineer; both men reporting to Fred Green. (The Balloon Factory was renamed the Royal Aircraft Factory on 26th April 1911.)

Biplane No.2 was given the factory designation FE.1 – Farman Experimental No.1. The system of nomenclature adopted by 'The Factory' was deliberately vague to get around a War Office ban on Farnborough designing or building aeroplanes. As Britain's independent aircraft industry was rapidly expanding and becoming more experienced, a government-owned rival would be very unwelcome. Farnborough could repair and modify aircraft, but not *originate* – which made pointless the post of designer! This explains the subterfuge over GDH's first 'Factory' design to fly, the SE.1 which adopted the canard layout of his unsuccessful Biplane No.1. The designation stood for Santos Dumont Experimental No.1 and was a nod to the 'tail-first' machine designed and flown by Brazilian-born Alberto Santos-Dumont in France in 1906. To the War Office, this was a rebuild of an unfortunate Blériot XII that came to grief on Salisbury Plain around September 1910. The Blériot's flying characteristics were reflected in its nickname, *The Man-Killer*. As GDH pointed out in his autobiography *Sky Fever*: "The only vestige of the *Man-Killer* in the new canard, the SE.1, was the engine [a 60hp ENV]".

O'Gorman's assistant, Lt Theodore J Ridge, set about learning to fly on the FE.1 and on 15th August 1911 he crash-landed it, very likely ending its flying days. Undaunted, he went to Salisbury Plain and succeeded in getting his 'ticket', Aviators' Certificate No.119, on a 'Bristol' on the 17th. The very next day, he was badgering GDH to let him have a go in the SE.1 but was advised that it was no machine for a novice. *Sky Fever* provides the conclusion: "It had no effect. He was a religious fanatic and believed Providence looked after his every action. He had only been in the air five minutes when he stalled and spun into the ground, dying within minutes. So the tradition of *Man-Killer* was sustained."

Geoffrey de Havilland's successful Biplane No.2 shortly after it was purchased by the War Office in 1911, under the designation FE.1. *British Aerospace*

GDH carried out the maiden flight of the FE.2 on 16th August, the day *after* Theodore wrecked the FE.1 (alias the Biplane No.2). Yet the 'Factory' maintained that the FE.2 was no more than a *rebuild* of the FE.1! The FE.2 two-seat pusher was a major step forward; it was soon flying in floatplane guise from Fleet Pond and later carried a Maxim gun in the nose. While flying this machine GDH was granted Aviators' Special Certificate No.4 on 1st September 1912 for sustained distance and altitude. The FE.2 was refined and enlarged in 1913 and the definitive FE.2a family – really a brand new type – appeared in January 1915 becoming a practical bomber and was widely produced. Designed by a team led by S J Waters, the bizarre FE.3 two-seat pusher was an example of GDH serving solely as test pilot to the 'Factory', having no input in its formulation.

After the pusher FEs and the SE.1, GDH turned to the tractor format and began the steps that created the first practical military aircraft, the incredible BE.2 (Blériot Experimental) family. Once again, the wool was pulled over the eyes of authority by declaring the BE.1 as a 'rebuild' of The Duke of Westminster's wrecked Voisin, yet only its Wolseley engine was utilized. The BE.1 was what can now be regarded as a 'classic' biplane, a tandem two-seater with docile flying characteristics setting the format for decades to come. GDH was at the helm in December 1911 – his third 'first' of the year – and all the richer for an extra two shillings and sixpence (12½p in current coin) bonus for flying a prototype. The more refined BE.2 flew on 1st February 1912 the following year. As O'Gorman was one of the judges at the military aeroplane trials held on Salisbury Plain in August, the clearly ground-breaking BE.2 was not eligible for consideration. The archaic-looking Cody Military Biplane (see Chapter Two) was the victor. To emphasize the BE.2's qualities, GDH and Major F H Sykes climbed to 10,560ft in the early hours of 12th August to set an altitude record. The BE.2c was so much further refined that it can be considered virtually a new type – see under 'Ted' Busk for details. The BE.2 was mass produced by no less than 16 manufacturers.

The canard pusher SE.1, Geoffrey de Havilland's first design for the Royal Aircraft Factory. *RAE Farnborough*

The BE.3 and its follow-ons, the BE.4, 5 and 6 general purpose two-seaters, commenced testing in May 1912, all flown and created by GDH. In February 1913 he began testing the world's first single-seat scout, a type soon to be widely referred to as a 'fighter': the BS.1 – Blériot Scout. With assistance from Henry Folland and S J Waters, GDH produced a sleek biplane which could reach 91mph and climb at 900ft per minute on just 100hp. (Folland created the SE.5 in 1916, then worked for Gloster before going on to establish his own company in 1937.) The rudder of the BS.1 was too small and a 'fix' had been designed, but on 27th March 1913 during an evening test, GDH banked at about 100ft and the BS.1 entered a flat spin. GDH was sent to hospital in Aldershot with a broken jaw, other facial injuries and a badly damaged ankle. In classic 'Factory' procedure, the BS.1 re-emerged almost totally rebuilt as the SE.2 (Scout Experimental) in October 1913 by which time its principal designer was well recovered and testing it.

Ground crew working on Boulton & Paul-built FE.2d A6429 on the western front, circa 1916. *KEC*

Geoffrey de Havilland pre-flighting the prototype BE.1 at Farnborough, 1912. *FAST*

Towards the end of 1913 the Aeronautical Inspection Directorate (AID) was formed and great pressure was put on a very reluctant GDH to take up the post of Inspector of Aircraft. It seems he had no option and GDH's employment at Farnborough came to an end and Ronald Kemp* took over testing. AID was important work, but a criminal waste of GDH's talents and he started to consider alternatives. The very nature of GDH's job put him in touch with designers and managers of Britain's aircraft industry, including the ambitious and perceptive George Holt Thomas of the Aircraft Manufacturing Company (Airco) at Hendon. The pair came to a deal on 23rd May 1914 and probably the most gifted and experienced designer (not to mention pilot) in Britain was engaged by Airco for a minimum period of a year. The annual salary was £600 and – something

GDH never had at 'The Factory' – commission on sales, and life insurance. Airco was about to be transformed from essentially a licence builder of French designs and by the end of the war it claimed to be the largest aircraft manufacturer in the world.

While GDH settled down to design the DH.1 – of which more anon – the political situation in Europe was slipping inexorably into the abyss of war. In March 1913 GDH had signed up as a special reservist and on the day that Britain declared war on Germany, 4th August 1914, he was mobilised and soon despatched to Montrose in Scotland, to fly a Blériot XI on coastal patrol. All of this was rescinded on the 26th and GDH flew the frail 50hp monoplane to Farnborough – taking just over 10 hours of flying time, a very credible achievement. GDH kicked his heels test flying at the 'Factory' while Holt Thomas campaigned to have Captain de Havilland back at Hendon.

Holt Thomas got his way and GDH settled down to create some of the most important types of the conflict. The DH.1 two-seater and the DH.2 scout both reverted to the pusher format because it was the only way at the time to provide a forward-firing machine-gun, prior to the adoption of the interrupter gear enabling bullets to fire through the propeller arc. The DH.3 and DH.10 twin engined bombers saw little success. The DH.6 was designed as a docile trainer capitalising on GDH's experience with the BE.2. It was widely used and must have helped formulate ideas that gave rise to the DH.51 and the DH.60 Moth. It was the DH.4 day bomber that was the major contribution to the war effort and indeed it provided the means for early commercial services in Europe and general purpose military use well into the 1920s. Comparison with World War Two's Mosquito is not inappropriate, the DH.4 evolving from day bomber, to fighter, recce, and many other roles. As well as Airco, it was built by six other British manufacturers and produced in the USA. The refined DH.9 and its Eagle-powered DH.9A derivative were also mass produced including in the USA. GDH conducted the bulk of Airco prototype testing at Hendon, while production flying was carried out by many – mostly anonymous – pilots. Other first flights and development work was undertaken by 'Benny' Hucks* from 1916 and then Frank Courtney*.

Airco was one of the many casualties of the return to peace, despite George Holt Thomas rapidly recognising the potential of civil aviation. As early as October 1916 he had established yet another company within his empire – Aircraft Transport and Travel (AT&T). On 25th August 1919 AT&T operated the world's first scheduled international service, using a DH.4A passenger conversion to fly to Le Bourget, Paris. In 1920 Holt Thomas bowed to the inevitable and sold Airco to the Birmingham Small Arms Company which was only interested in the industrial capacity, not the products.

GDH set to finding the finance to establish his own company and on 25th September 1920 the de Havilland Aircraft Company became a reality. It was established at Stag Lane, Edgware, starting work with two unfinished DH.18 eight-passenger transports from Airco's Hendon factory. The 1920s and 1930s witnessed a gradual, and inevitable, transition of GDH's roles from designer-pilot to industrial magnate. Design responsibility was increasingly transferred to Arthur Ernest Hagg, who had worked in the Airco drawing office. In

1921 Hubert Broad* was appointed as CTP, but Geoffrey kept his hand in, mostly with the light aircraft. The exception to this was the 54ft-span DH.29 Doncaster research monoplane for the Air Ministry which gave GDH a challenging maiden flight in July 1921. On getting the tail up, GDH discovered that the 450hp Napier Lion just in front of his open cockpit blasted him, blew away some of the hatches and stripped fabric covering off the upper fuselage and inner wings. He brought it round for a landing, appreciating that the rudder was far from satisfactory which was confirmed when the 16ft 6in high airframe whipped around into a ground loop as the speed decreased on touch down. W K MacKenzie occupied the second pilot's seat from the next sortie onwards, acting as a flight test observer. The Doncaster required considerable redesign; only one other was built.

Father of the Moth dynasty was the DH.51, intended as a practical, affordable three-seater. Hand-in-hand with creating a mass market biplane was the engine and the Royal Aircraft Factory 1A, while cheap, proved impossible to certificate without considerable expenditure. Only three DH.51s were built; the last survives in airworthy trim at the Shuttleworth Collection. Frank Halford of the Aircraft Disposal Company (Airdisco) came up with the solution, slicing a 120hp V-8 into a four-cylinder in-line with a new crankcase to create the 60hp Cirrus. The DH.60 was a single-bay biplane, unlike the DH.51, and its folding wings would save on hangarage or even allow for it to be trailered home. As related under Hubert Broad, GDH took the prototype Moth, G-EBKT, for its maiden flight before returning to beckon his CTP to join him for the second sortie. While Broad went for an endurance record in a Moth, GDH took his wife, Louie, up to establish a height record on 26th July 1928 of 19,980ft.

GDH flew the prototype Leopard Moth three-seater monoplane in B Condition ('trade plate') markings as E-1 in May 1933 – the final 'first' from Stag Lane as the company completed the move to Hatfield in January 1934. Hatfield played host to the King's Cup air race in July 1933 and GDH and his company could ask for no better outcome than his winning the prestigious trophy at an average speed of 139.5mph in the first Leopard Moth, by then registered as G-ACHD.

Geoffrey de Havilland's last designs and his final maiden flight were both concerned with replacing the biplane Moth with an aircraft of similar performance and practicality, but as a wing-folding monoplane. The first foray into this market was the DH.81 Swallow Moth, which GDH took for a brief circuit of Stag Lane in August 1931. Eventually fitted with a cabin, the two-seater seems to have been flown exclusively by GDH and it was quietly retired the following February, being declared as only experimental. Lessons learned and with the economy in far better trim, GDH's refined thinking on a 'Moth replacement' was the DH.94 Moth Minor and he flew the prototype at Hatfield in June 1937. Flight testing was handed on to Geoffrey jnr and his assistant John Cunningham*. The onset of World War Two put an end to the incredible prospects of the Moth Minor.

Geoffrey and Louie had three sons, Geoffrey Raoul (born 1910), Peter Jason (1913) and John (1918). Geoffrey jnr and Peter are detailed below. In his autobiography, *Sky Fever*, published in 1961 GDH explained his policy in what he

An Airco-built DH.2. *KEC*

The DH.3 prototype at Farnborough. *British Aerospace*

The prototype DH.4, 3696, in 1916. It was the first of a long line of variants. *British Aerospace*

proudly regarded as a company with a family atmosphere, declaring that no relative or friend: "has ever suggested I should use any influence on his behalf, and they have retained their jobs on merit alone. Geoffrey and John, for example, were obvious pilots of great skill; and Peter, my surviving son, after doing some years of very useful flying, joined the sales side where his knowledge of French was, and is today, a big asset." *Sky Fever* remains an exceptional work, a human insight to an amazing enterprise. Mention should also be made of Martin Sharp's *DH – A History of De Havilland*, which first appeared in 1960 and GDH praised in *Sky Fever*; it is an impressive chronicle. Sir Geoffrey de Havilland OM CBE AFC died 21st May 1965 aged 83; his ashes were scattered at Seven Barrows, where the adventure began.

Above: DH.29 Doncaster J6849 in its original form at Martlesham Heath. *British Aerospace*

Left: Miss Kenya, the third DH.51 before delivery to Africa in 1925. Today it flies, as G-EBIR, from Old Warden. *KEC*

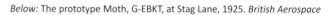

Below: The prototype Moth, G-EBKT, at Stag Lane, 1925. *British Aerospace*

Flown for a short period, 1931-1932, the one-off Swallow Moth in cabin configuration. *British Aerospace*

The prototype Leopard Moth in which Geoffrey de Havilland won the 1933 King's Cup air race. *KEC*

Below: High-powered, multi-lingual advert emphasizing the stature of the de Havilland 'empire', 1936.

THE SIGN OF A GREAT INDUSTRY

The de Havilland Aircraft Co., Ltd., Hatfield, Hertfordshire, whose premises cover 739 acres, are engaged in the quantity manufacture of private, commercial and military aircraft of all types, the famous Gipsy range of aero engines, also controllable pitch airscrews.

The organization embraces military and civil flying schools, apprenticeship training, and the world wide distribution and servicing of both aircraft and engines.

Visitors to England interested in aviation are cordially invited to visit the new de Havilland factory at Hatfield.	Auslandsbesucher in England die sich für das Luftwesen interessieren sind herzlichst eingeladen die neuen Havilland-Werke in Hatfield zu besuchen.
Les étrangers se rendant en Angleterre qui s'intéressent à l'aviation sont cordialement invités à visiter la nouvelle usine de la maison de Havilland à Hatfield.	Los extranjeros visitando Inglaterra que se interesan en aviación quedan cordialmente invitados de visitar la nueva fabrica de la casa de Havilland en Hatfield.

THE DE HAVILLAND AIRCRAFT CO. LTD., HATFIELD, HERTFORDSHIRE, ENGLAND

Close to the roaring A34 road south of Newbury is a memorial at Seven Barrows noting the first successful flight of Geoffrey de Havilland's Biplane No.2. *Ken Ellis*

Geoffrey de Havilland jr

28 Dec 1938	DH Flamingo G-AFUE 2 x 890hp Bristol Perseus XII
25 Nov 1940	DH Mosquito E-0234 2 x 1,460hp RR Merlin 21
20 Sep 1943	DH Vampire LZ548 1 x 2,700lbst DH Goblin 1
28 Jul 1944	DH Hornet RR915 2 x 2,070hp RR Merlin 130
15 May 1946	DH DH.108 TG283 1 x 3,000lbst DH Goblin 2

Geoffrey Raoul de Havilland, born 1910 first son of Louie and Geoffrey de Havilland – aged eight weeks he flew, cradled in his mother arms, in his father's Biplane No.2 at Seven Barrows, near Newbury. In 1916 he more fully experienced flying, with his younger brother Peter (then aged 3) again flown by his father, in a DH.6 from Hendon. He joined de Havilland as an apprentice at Stag Lane in 1928 and learned to fly at the company-run 1 E&RFTS, moving to Hatfield in 1930. He was briefly engaged in air survey work in South Africa, before taking up a post as an instructor at Hatfield.

To many personnel at Hatfield, Geoffrey Raoul de Havilland was 'Young DH', for *this* entry he will be referred to as Geoffrey. As with many manufacturers of the era pressures in the flight shed meant that Geoffrey could be diverted from his instructing duties to perform the role of PTP. In 1935 this was formalised and he joined the flight test department under CTP 'Bob' Waight*. While preparing for a speed record attempt Bob was killed in the one-off DH Aeronautical Technical School's TK.4 G-AETK on 1st October 1937 and aged 27, Geoffrey became the company CTP.

Bob had been engaged in testing the prototype Albatross, G-AEVV, and Geoffrey took on this four-engined airliner. Among its innovations was retractable main gear and on 31st March 1938 Geoffrey was in command when G-AEVV belly-

Geoffrey de Havilland JR in front of the DH Aeronautical Technical School's TK.2 G-ADNO at Hatfield in 1938. Geoffrey raced the TK.2 at events in 1937-1938. *Peter Green Collection*

The prototype Flamingo under test early in 1939. *Rolls-Royce*

The flight deck of a Flamingo, Geoffrey de Havilland JR is in the left hand seat. In the P2 position is *possibly* George Gibbins – see under John de Havilland. *KEC*

landed at Hatfield – it was soon repaired. After landing the second example, G-AEVW, on 27th August 1938, the fuselage – made of laminated wood to create a stressed skin – failed and broke behind the trailing edge. A 'fix' was soon devised and applied to the first two machines and the five that followed. Later in 1938 Geoffrey and George Gibbins* were in charge of another airliner prototype at Hatfield, the twin-engined, all-metal, Flamingo. This was a huge leap forward for both DH and the British aircraft industry. Sixteen Flamingos were eventually built, but the onset of World War Two eradicated its commercial prospects. See under John Cunningham* for an incident in April 1939 when he and Geoffrey baled out of a Moth Minor.

Hatfield's industrial prospects changed completely on 25th November 1940 when an all-yellow twin-engined type was given its maiden flight by Geoffrey with John E Walker, the head of the Engine Installation Department, assisting. This was the first Mosquito wearing the B Condition ('trade plate') marking E-0234, but soon to take up its serial W4050. This revolutionary private venture machine capitalised on the moulded laminate construction pioneered by the company and was to be followed by 7,780 others. The prototypes had been designed and built in great secrecy at nearby Salisbury Hall, London Colney, in a staggering eleven months from being given the go-ahead. The first night-fighter-version, Mk.II W4052, was ready at Salisbury Hall in May 1941. W4050 had been carefully dismantled and taken by road to Hatfield, just over three miles to the north. The one-piece wing was particularly difficult to transport and the entire operation was time-consuming. Geoffrey took a look at the fields that surrounded Salisbury Hall and decided to turn the first flight into a delivery sortie to Hatfield. With Fred Plumb, who had supervised the construction of both prototypes, sitting alongside Geoffrey took W4052 skyward on 15th May 1941 from an improvised airstrip. Geoffrey spent his time exploring the Mosquito's flight envelope and showed this off brilliantly

during a demonstration to still sceptical Air Ministry officials at Hatfield; he performed a spirited aerobatic routine and then repeated most of the sequence, on just one Merlin engine! Prototype W4050 today is preserved at the place of its birth, Salisbury Hall, as the 'star' exhibit in the exceptional de Havilland Aircraft Museum.

As the Mosquito entered mass production, Hatfield's design office was already at work on another world-beater. Gloster had pioneered jet-propelled flight in the UK and the first Meteor twin-jet fighter took to the air in March 1943. De Havilland's response to Specification E6/41 was the single-engined, twin-boom Vampire jet fighter. The wings and tail were all-metal, but the fuselage 'pod' used the same wooden laminate structure as the Mosquito. Geoffrey took the prototype, LZ548, into the air for the first time on 29th September 1943 at Hatfield. In Martin Sharp's superb *DH – A History of de Havilland*, Geoffrey's assessment of the prototype Vampire is quoted: "So smooth, it was like driving a quiet car off into the sky. I found myself tapping the instruments to make sure the needles weren't sticking." Like the Mosquito, the Vampire was destined for a long production run, including many variants. With Hatfield dominated by construction of the 'Wooden Wonder', Vampire manufacture was entrusted to English Electric (EE) at Samlesbury, setting the Lancashire company on the way to becoming a centre of jet excellence. Geoffrey was at the helm of the first EE-built Vampire F.1, TG274, for its maiden flight from Samlesbury on 20th April 1945.

The next de Havilland fighter was not a jet, but a mixed-construction single-seat twin-engined fighter capitalising on the experience gained by the Mosquito. This was the Hornet, a beautiful-looking creation clearly showing its Mosquito lineage, destined for post-war use with the RAF and the Fleet Air Arm. The prototype Hornet, RR915, flew from Hatfield with Geoffrey at the controls in July 1944.

Shrouded in tarpaulins, the Mosquito prototype at Hatfield, December 1940. *British Aerospace*

The prototype Mosquito, W4050, in its Robin hangar at Salisbury Hall, 1982. *Stuart Howe*

A stoic-looking Geoffrey de Havilland JR leaning on the leading edge of the Vampire prototype, Hatfield, September 1943. *British Aerospace*

The second prototype Hornet, RR919, with underwing pylons for bombs or drop tanks, 1944. *Rolls-Royce*

Geoffrey's next prototype was a swept-wing, tail-less derivative of the Vampire that was initially conceived as a flying test-bed for a jet airliner concept. This layout was abandoned for what was to become the Comet in March 1946 but development of three DH.108 prototypes continued. The first, TG283, was moved to Woodbridge where the long runway and lack of prying eyes facilitated test flying the new jet. Geoffrey carried out the maiden flight on 15th May 1946 and continued to explore its characteristics. The second DH.108, TG306, was more refined, with slightly increased sweep-back and was fitted with powered flying controls. As such it had the potential to achieve supersonic speeds and could path-find for the Comet, which also would have powered controls. Geoffrey flew TG306 from Hatfield on 23rd August 1946 and was soon achieving speeds that could set a world record. On 7th September 1946 Gp Capt E M Donaldson flew Meteor F.4 EE549 of the RAF High Speed Flight around a calibrated course centred on Tangmere to achieve a world speed record of 616mph. (Today EE549 is displayed at the Tangmere Military Aviation Museum.) Geoffrey began to practise flying a similar flight profile, along the Thames Estuary and it was

Geoffrey de Havilland JR in the cockpit of DH.108 TG306 at Hatfield on 27th September 1946. *Peter Green Collection*

beginning to look as though the Meteor would not hold the laurels for long. On 27th September 1946 Geoffrey took off from Hatfield for a final trial run before taking TG306 to Tangmere for a crack at the record. As the evening drew on it was clear that Geoffrey was overdue and after extensive searching wreckage of the DH.108 was found off Gravesend and the 36-year-old's body was washed ashore at Whitstable. The DH.108 had reached Mach 0.875 in a dive from 10,000ft and suffered structural failure. John Cunningham succeeded Geoffrey as CTP and flew the third and much-modified DH.108 in July 1947. Geoffrey Raoul de Havilland OBE was buried alongside his brother, John, at Tewin, west of Hertford – see under John's section for more.

John de Havilland

John de Havilland born 1918, the third son of Louie and Geoffrey de Havilland. Apprenticed to the de Havilland Aeronautical Technical School at Hatfield February 1937 to September 1939 and learned to fly at the London Aeroplane Club, Hatfield.

JOHN followed in the footsteps of his elder brother, Geoffrey, and by 1943 was involved in production testing Mosquitos at Hatfield. On 23rd August 1943 John was flying FB.VI HJ734 with John H F Scorpe alongside as FTO. Up at the same time was George V Gibbins* in Mk.VI HX897 accompanied by the flight test foreman G J 'Nick' Carter. The two aircraft collided at about 500ft, the shattered wreckage falling to the ground near St Albans; all four were killed.

John de Havilland, aged 24, was buried in the churchyard of St Peter's at Tewin, west of Hertford. In September 1946 his brother, Geoffrey, was laid to rest beside him. Close by, their mother Lady Louie de Havilland was buried in July 1949; she took the deaths of her sons badly and never recovered her health. The headstone of the de Havilland brothers carries the following: "They gave their lives in advancing the science of flight. To strive, to seek, to find and not to yield."

'Jimmy' Dell

29 Mar 1962	EE Lightning T.5 XM967
	2 x 13,200lbst RR Avon 301
12 Oct 1969	SEPECAT Jaguar S.06 XW560
	2 x 4,620lbst RR/Turboméca Adour

Notes: Lightning T.5 was first flown at Filton; the Jaguar at Warton.

James 'Jimmy' Leonard Dell, born 1924. Joined the RAF in 1942, becoming an instructor and later served at the Central Gunnery School, Leconfield. Operational flying with 43 Squadron at Tangmere on Gloster Meteor F.4s. Exchange posting with the USAF's 60th Fighter Interceptor Squadron at Westover, Massachusetts, USA, initially with North American F-86E Sabres. On 5th August 1952, flying F-86E 50-611, Jimmy lost contact with his flight leader and in increasingly bad weather, the fuel state became critical and the engine flamed out. Jimmy successful ejected at low level. After this he converted to radar-equipped F-86Ds. He returned to the UK and in 1955 instructed at the Fighter Weapons School, Leconfield, becoming a Squadron Leader. In January 1957 he was posted to Warton as Fighter Command Liaison Officer and RAF Project Officer for the nascent Lightning programme.

'JIMMY' DELL'S exchange with the USAF gave him great experience of single-pilot operation of a radar-equipped interceptor, the North American F-86D 'Sabre-Dog'. When the RAF decided on the innovative creation of a liaison officer for the English Electric P.1B (named Lightning in October 1958) development programme Jimmy was easily the best choice and in February 1957 he flew a P.1A, WG763, for the first time. On 8th May 1958 he was flying P.1B XA853 when there was an explosion in the engine bay and he encountered control problems. He elected to attempt to bring the badly damaged prototype back to Warton, making a successful emergency landing. It nearly a year before the rebuilt XA853 was flying again. Jimmy displayed P.1B XA847 at the SBAC airshow at Farnborough in September. On the last day of the show, he accidently engaged the afterburners at 100ft, shattering windows all over the airfield and beyond! He could well have been disciplined, but long afterwards said that he believed the project was at such a critical phase and he would have been difficult to replace. All must have been forgiven; he was promoted to Wing Commander in 1959 and put in charge of the Central Fighter Establishment's Air Fighting Development Squadron, newly-established at Coltishall.

Jimmy's RAF career came to an end in 1960 when the 'pull' of Warton proved too much and he took the post of Deputy CTP. In January 1961 he became CTP at Warton, still under Beamont but in Bea's new role as Deputy CTP to 'Jock' Bryce, who was CTP for the *whole* of the newly-established British Aircraft Corporation. (Bea's title soon settled on Manager Flight Operations, Warton.) Jimmy's first 'first' was the T.5 two-seat version of the F.3 which had been converted at Filton; he took XM967 into the air on 29th March 1962. Jimmy promoted Don Knight* to Deputy CTP January 1964.

Jimmy Dell wearing state-of-the-air g-suit, Warton, 1960. *English Electric via Graham Pitchfork*

Jimmy was flying Lightning T.4 XM968 on 27th September 1964 at Boscombe Down, with a photographer as passenger, providing the 'chase-plane' for Bea's maiden flight of TSR.2 XR219. The sixth test flight was Jimmy's debut on TSR.2, with Don Bowen as systems operator. Jimmy became XR219's highest time pilot, with 7 hours 52 minutes over 12 flights; he piloted the 24th flight, which turned out to be the last sortie, with Brian McCann, on 31st March 1965.

Along with flight test engineer Graham 'Elk' Elkington, Jimmy was assessing Lightning T.5 XM966 in rapid roll with the rocket pack extended under the forward fuselage on 22nd

...

July 1965. They were at 35,000ft over the coast of Cumberland, travelling at Mach 1.82 and 'pulling' about 3g. There was a catastrophic failure – it was later determined that the fin detached. At first the pair blacked out, but quickly ejected and sat it out in their dinghies. (See Johnny Squier for a very similar incident.) A Westland Whirlwind HAR.10 from Valley plucked them from the Irish Sea an hour later. Jimmy suffered cracked and crushed vertebrae and was out of action until November 1965. While checking out Peter Williams, a pilot for Airwork Ltd (a major sub-contractor on the Royal Saudi Air Force programme), on Lightning T.55 55-710 on 7th March 1967, the crosswind component at Warton increased considerably. Jimmy was faced with no alternative than to land over the accepted limits. On touch down the aircraft started to slew, the drag chute was deployed and was whipped away instantly and the landing continued to go pear-shaped. Colliding the with runway arrester system the starboard undercarriage collapsed, the nose gear followed suit and the entire nose broke away as the wreck came to a halt. Peter smashed a thigh, Jimmy fractured an ankle and was again laid-up, until August 1967.

Collaboration with France was not limited to the BAC/Sud Concorde supersonic airliner project, Warton was hard at work with Breguet on the Jaguar attack and advanced trainer project. The organisation established to oversee the co-operative venture basked in the name Société Européenne de Production de l'Avion d'Ecole de Combat et d'Appui Tactique, unsurprisingly, most people adopted the abbreviation SEPECAT when referring to it! Jimmy was heavily involved in the development of Jaguar. Breguet CTP Bernard Witt flew the first prototype, E.01, from Istres, France, on 8th September 1968 with Jimmy monitoring from the Dassault Mirage IIIB chase-plane. Jimmy had soon gone solo on E.01 and in October 1969 flew the first Warton-built single-seater, XW560, taking it supersonic during the 50-minute sortie. (The cockpit of XW560 is preserved by the Boscombe Down Aviation Collection at Old Sarum.)

A medical issue brought Jimmy's test flying days to an end in December 1970 and Paul Millett* took over as CTP. Jimmy's fighter experience and his firm grasp of international collaboration were not going to be wasted; he was appointed as Manager Panavia Flight Operations (PFO) as the Tornado programme gathered momentum. This was upgraded to Deputy Director PFO and in 1979, upon Bea's retirement; Jimmy became Director PFO, working hard shuttling between Warton, Germany and Italy until retiring in 1989. Wg Cdr James 'Jimmy' Leonard Dell OBE died on 25th March 2008. Frank Barnett-Jones's biography, *Tarnish 6*, named after Jimmy's call-sign, was published in 2008.

Jimmy Dell flying the Lightning T.5 prototype, XM967, 1962. *BAC*

The UK-assembled Jaguar prototype, S0.6 XW560, fully armed up at Warton for a publicity photograph, 1970. *BAC*

Jet Gyrodyne XJ389 during its first transition flights at White Waltham, March 1955. For early sorties the access door was not installed, to allow John Dennis ease of escape. *Fairey Aviation*

John Dennis

| 1 Mar 1955 | Fairey Jet Gyrodyne XJ389 |
| | 1 x 520hp Alvis Leonides |

Flt Lt John N Dennis was serving with RAE Farnborough in 1948. On 19th August 1948 he was delivering Sikorsky Hoverfly I KL109 to AFEE Beaulieu when it encountered difficulties and was written off in a crash. Dennis and RAE FTO A Bishop were unhurt.

JOHN DENNIS joined the nascent helicopter department of Fairey Aviation in June 1949. The second Gyrodyne was converted into a machine that could trial the flight regime and control rules for the projected Rotodyne transport; this was the Jet Gyrodyne. The Leonides nine-cylinder buried within the fuselage was intended to work hard for its living. It drove two pusher propellers mounted on stub wings and, via a clutch, a pair of modified centrifugal compressors from Rolls-Royce Merlin engines that pumped kerosene into pressure jets at the tips of the 60ft diameter rotor blades. The latter were the 'jet' element of the Jet Gyrodyne. The tip-jets allowed the rotorcraft to take-off and land vertically, but the main rotor could also 'coast' unpowered, allowing for auto-rotation for a controlled, rolling landing if needs be. John Dennis started tethered hovers in January 1954 at White Waltham but it was another year before free hovers were achieved. The first transition, vertical take-off, forward flight, vertical landing was performed on 1st March 1955. As the Rotodyne project progressed, Ron Gellatly* and John Morton* used XJ389 to build experience.

Keith Dennison

Keith Dennison gained his glider rating at 16 and, via an RAF flying scholarship, his private pilot's licence a year later. He joined the RAF in 1975 and graduated with a degree in aeronautical engineering in 1978. Operational flying on McDD Phantom FGR.2s with 23 and 56 Squadrons at Wattisham and 19 Squadron at Wildenrath, West Germany. In 1988 he attended the US Navy Test Pilot School at Patuxent River, Maryland, USA. Returning from this, he started a long association with A&AEE Boscombe Down, becoming the CO of the Fast Jet Testing Squadron and later CTP.

AIR CDRE KEITH DENNISON took up the post of CTP Combat and Training Aircraft at BAE Systems, Warton, in September 2005. He was involved in a variety of Typhoon development programmes and also in the introduction of the Hawk T.2 for the RAF and Mk.132s for India. Keith left BAE Systems in 2008, establishing himself as an independent pilot and aviation consultant. He is an active display pilot, flying for the Shuttleworth Collection, among others. He followed in the footsteps of 'Bea' Beamont* by test flying light aircraft, taking the prototype E-Go Aeroplanes E-Go canard pusher, G-EFUN, on its maiden flight on 17th October 2013 at Conington, near Cambridge. Keith is also assisting Electroflight as the company develops a prototype all-electric powered light aircraft.

John Derry

2 Sep 1949   DH Venom VV612
                    1 x 4,850lbst DH Ghost 103

John Douglas Derry, born 1921. Tried to enlist as a pilot in the RAF but frustrated at the delay, joined and trained as a wireless operator/air gunner, serving with 269 Squadron on Lockheed Hudsons, including detachments to Kaldadarnes in Iceland. This was followed by 172 Squadron on Wellington VIIIs at Chivenor, a colleague on the unit being 'Jock' Bryce*. Trained as a pilot in Canada in 1943, then was attached to the Air Transport Auxiliary ferrying a wide variety of types. In October 1944 he joined 182 Squadron, based at Eindhoven, Netherlands, but rapidly advancing westwards, flying Hawker Typhoons. From Flight Commander, he became Officer Commanding, and was awarded a DFC and the Netherlands decoration, the Bronze Lion. In September 1945 John became CO of the Day Fighter Leaders School at West Raynham, on Hawker Tempest Vs.

BRITAIN'S worst-ever airshow accident, a test pilot and an experimental jet – these are the bald facts that come forth whenever the events of 6th September 1952 are written about, or discussed. It was of course a tragedy of massive proportions, with lessons learned in several disciplines, but within is another misfortune: the careers, skills, achievements and courage of a pilot and an observer are overlooked.

Jeffery Quill* recruited Sqn Ldr John Derry as a test pilot for Supermarine in 1946 and at the SBAC airshow at Radlett in early September he got his first taste of display flying, demonstrating a Seafire FR.47. As well as Seafires John tested Attackers, but his time at 'Supers' was short; he joined de Havilland, under John Cunningham*, in October 1947. He took over testing of the third DH.108 swept-wing, tail-less research aircraft, VW120, from John Cunningham in January 1948. Geoffrey de Havilland JR* had been readying the second DH.108 for an attempt at the world speed record and, as John gained experience on the much-improved VW120, the

John Derry (left) with Tony Richards ready for a newsreel interview in front of DH.110 WG240. *via Don Middleton*

decision was taken to have a go at the 100km closed-circuit category. On 12th April 1948 John took VW120 around a pentagonal course near Hatfield averaging 605.23mph, becoming the first pilot to cross into the '600s' in level flight.

Another 'magic' number was looming. From September 1948 John started exploring the DH.108's behaviour at high Mach numbers, in a series of dives from over 40,000ft. The aircraft was packed with pressure gauges and instrumentation to provide a plethora of data to be chewed over by the design department and by aerodynamics 'boffins' at Farnborough. On an early trial, VW120 started to pitch violently and John closed the throttle; he was probably only moments from the airframe tearing itself apart in a glimpse of what Geoffrey de Havilland jr had experienced. On 6th September the dive was entered with a reading of Mach 0.85 with a pronounced pitch-down, which developed into what John called "wallowing" then repeated pitching up and down. VW120 was becoming very nose heavy; he opened the throttle wide but to no avail. The Mach-meter clocked 1.0 and, feeling that all control was being lost, John closed the throttle and – more in desperation than in determination – deployed the trim flaps and began to regain control. Post-flight analysis revealed that he had reached Mach 1.02; he was the first 'Brit' to 'go' supersonic over his homeland (see 'Bea' Beamont).

Amid all of this there was Vampire marketing to be done and John was preparing for the ultimate development of de Havilland's bread-and-butter jet, the Venom. In November 1948 John flew a Vampire FB.5 from Hatfield to Rome in a sizzling 2 hours, 50 minutes as part of the process of getting the Italians to make a purchase; the following year Italy signed a licence agreement with Fiat and Macchi. (John's Rome 'dash' was up-staged by his friend Neville Duke* in 1949.) On 9th April 1949 he flew English Electric-built Vampire FB.5 VV217 from Le Bourget, Paris, to Cannes on the Mediterranean coast in 44 minutes, 51 seconds. A month later the French Air Force received the first of nearly 100 former RAF FB.5s and the Sud-Est plant at Marignane, along the coast from Cannes, was gearing up to produce the Vampire under licence as the Mistral. The Venom was a 'second generation' Vampire, considerably redesigned, including a thinner wing and swept-back leading edge and the more powerful DH Ghost turbojet. John took the prototype, VV612, a converted Vampire FB.5, for its maiden flight at Hatfield on 2nd September 1949. Tucking the gear up, he carried out a roll-off-the-top of the climb out of Hatfield – this was to become a signature manoeuvre. Four days after the debut, John was demonstrating the Venom to the crowds at Farnborough. John's aerobatic prowess included his very own 'reverse roll', which became known as the 'Derry turn'.

John Cunningham had carried out the early tests on the twin-engined, twin-boom, all-weather fighter DH.110 – soon to be called Sea Vixen – and handed the programme over to John Derry. With FTO Tony Richards alongside and below him in the 'coal hole' radar operator's 'cubicle', John had his first flight in the DH.110 prototype, WG236, on 22nd January 1952. The pair took the big fighter supersonic on 20th February; this was a double achievement, it was the first twin-engined jet to break the 'sound barrier' and Tony was the first supersonic FTO! The second prototype, WG240, was ready by July and

The second DH.110, WG240, which was first flown by John Derry on 25th July 1952. *British Aerospace*

John and Tony carried out its maiden flight on the 25th. WG240 was ferried to Farnborough, where John demonstrated it daily, from the 1st to the 5th at the SBAC airshow. John took WG240 back to Hatfield on the 6th and he and Tony Richards returned in WG236 to start their display 'off slot' at height in the overhead with the 'double-boom' of a sonic bang.

Neville Duke* was to follow John by displaying the second prototype Hawker Hunter, WB195. In Mike Lithgow's compendium *Vapour Trails*, Neville described the scene after John and Tony had returned to conventional display height and: "did their normal flypast; and with this manoeuvre over, began to slow down and turn back over the airfield, getting ready to go through his normal routine before landing. The DH.110 disintegrated while it was in a moderate turn. Like everyone else, I was shocked to see the cockpit and the two engines flying through the air..."

As well as John and Tony, the DH.110 claimed the lives of 29 of the record-breaking crowd as wreckage and the engines ploughed into the public area. Another 60 spectators were injured, ranging from emergency treatment in hospital to cuts and shock. It was the first fatal accident to befall an SBAC airshow since the event re-started in 1946. The decision was taken to carry on and Neville Duke noted in his piece in *Vapour Trails* the instructions he received from air traffic, each followed by a "Roger" from him: "Please keep to the right-hand side of the runway on take-off and mind the wreckage... Are you going to climb and do a bang?... Will you soft-pedal your display over the crowd, please?"

Anthony M Richards was 25, he became a de Havilland trade apprentice at 17 and his four-year course at the Hatfield Aeronautical Technical School mostly dealt with aerodynamics. In December 1948 he joined the flight test department as an observer and his first assignment was the Heron. After this, he and John Derry became a well-integrated team, sharing 76 test sorties in the DH.110 prototypes. Sqn Ldr John Douglas Derry DFC was 30 when he died. Both he and Tony were awarded posthumous Queen's Commendations "for services when testing an experimental aircraft". The Guild of Air Pilots and Navigators established the Derry and Richards Memorial Medal for outstanding flying towards the advancement of the science of aviation in their memory.

In *Flight Test*, published in 1956, 'Sandy' Powell* paid tribute: "No one knew better than John Derry the risks he took in the high speed flying he did in the DH.110. Equally, he was not doing anything at Farnborough, at the moment of the accident, that had not been done at much higher speeds before. This tragic accident proved that even today, we are not yet masters of the art and thus test pilots confront the unknown in their daily routine."

Marcel Desoutter

| 7 Sep 1912 | Grahame-White Type 9 |
| | 1 x 35hp Anzani |

André Marcel Desoutter, born 1894 to French parents, living in Britain. Learned to fly at the Blériot School at Hendon, gaining Aviators' Certificate No.186 on 27th February 1912.

Establishing just *who* presided over the maiden flights of Grahame-White designs will probably never be nailed. Try as he might, the author can only pin down Marcel Desoutter and Louis Noël* to a particular type and Reginald Carr and P R T Chamberlayne as 'probables' – see Volume Two for the last two. Claude Grahame-White, who fills the designer-pilot category, acquired Hendon aerodrome and became the all-round aviation entrepreneur; building aircraft from his company's design office and Airco DH.6s, Avro 504s, Royal Aircraft Factory BE.2s and Sopwith Snipes among others under sub-contract; staging airshows and air races; pioneering 'joy-riding' and so much more.

Having learned to fly, Marcel Desoutter continued to aviate at Hendon, acquiring a 50hp Gnome-powered Blériot, and he became part of the Grahame-White 'circus' of pilots: instructing, displaying, racing and test piloting. He was in command of the Type 9 single-seat monoplane designed by Rowland Ding* (who, conveniently, is the next entry) and built by the Grahame-White company; it remained a one-off. During the Easter meeting at Hendon on 23rd March 1913 Marcel was flying his Blériot when it dived in. He was pulled from the wreckage, but needed a leg amputating. With his brother, Charles, the pair designed a prosthetic leg and then went into business, as the Desoutter Brothers, manufacturing artificial limbs. This required considerable research and investment into specialist machine tools and before too long the company was making power tools, becoming a major contributor of fittings to the aviation industry. With a logo of a horse's head, Desoutter today is a global brand in tools and tooling. Marcel left the business in 1927, establishing the Desoutter Aircraft Company at Croydon to manufacture under licence a version of the Dutch Koolhoven FK.41 three-seat monoplane. About 40 'Desoutters', as the monoplanes were generally called, were built between 1929 and 1931; the Shuttleworth Collection operates a survivor, G-AAPZ. Beyond this venture, Marcel Desoutter went on to invest in the aerodromes at Gatwick and Gravesend; he died in April 1952.

Rowland Ding

19 Feb 1915	Mann & Grimmer M1 1 x 100hp Anzani
26 Oct 1915	Blackburn Type I floatplane 1 x 100hp Anzani
1916	Blackburn White Falcon 1 x 100hp Anzani

William Rowland Ding, born 1885. By 1912 he was working with, or for, the Grahame-White company at Hendon and designed the Type 9 monoplane which was first flown by Marcel Desoutter on 7th September. By 1913 he was a leading light in the Northern Aircraft Company, operating floatplanes from Lake Windermere and planning to 'barnstorm' around towns in northern England. Rowland achieved Aviators' Certificate No.774 on a 'Wright' at the Beatty School, Hendon and acquired the Handley Page G/100 biplane, using it for a charter to Calais in May 1914 and then brought it north for a series of flight demonstrations, eg Harrogate in July.*

"A pilot of happy-go-lucky temperament who had been a well-known exhibition flyer just before the war. He was hardly the type to settle down to instructing in the wilds, and was often away, testing aircraft for Handley Page and Blackburn." This is Constance Babington Smith's assessment of Rowland Ding in her exceptional *Testing Time – A Study of Man and Machine in the Test Flying Era*; he certainly got around! Having learned to fly at Hendon, it was there that he got his first test piloting task. The M1 was a private venture two-seat reconnaissance biplane designed by 17-year-old R F Mann with help from his former schoolmaster, R P Grimmer. Rowland carried out the maiden flight, but later in the year wrote it off in a crash and the project was abandoned.

During 1915 Rowland was working for Blackburn, testing Royal Aircraft Factory BE.2cs being produced in Leeds. Also by this time the Northern Aircraft Company (NAC) had a lucrative contract with the Admiralty training RNAS pilots to fly floatplanes; an instructor at Windermere was John Lankester Parker*. NAC came to an arrangement with Blackburn to acquire the Type I monoplane and this was taken to Windermere, fitted with floats, and test flown by Rowland. In 1915 he was taking the Blackburn L floatplane from Scarborough south down the coast to Killingholme Marshes on the Humber Estuary. The engine failed en route and Rowland was forced to put it down; the biplane was wrecked when it was dashed against cliffs by the sea. Rowland commissioned a two seat monoplane from Blackburn, the White Falcon, and this was up and flying by early 1916, perhaps as a means of Rowland getting about on ferrying tasks. Probably 'loaned' from Blackburn, Rowland tested Farman 'Longhorns' built in Bradford by the Phoenix Dynamo company at Killingholme Marshes in early 1917. While piloting a BE.2c at Leeds on 12th May 1917, Rowland engaged in looping, a strut failed and the 32-year-old was killed. His post was taken up by R W Kenworthy*.

Foster 'Dickie' Dixon

12 Dec 1938	Fairey Albacore L7074 1 x 1,065hp Bristol Taurus II
5 Jul 1945	Fairey Spearfish RA356 1 x 2,600hp Bristol Centaurus
cOct 1948	Fairey Primer G-ALBL 1 x 145hp DH Gipsy Major 10

Foster Hickman Dixon, born 1912. Joined the RAF in 1932 and served with 1 Squadron at Tangmere on Hawker Furies. He left the RAF in 1936 to work for Fairey, transferring to the Reserve list.

FOSTER 'DICKIE' DIXON joined Fairey as a test pilot in 1936 as the company was building up Swordfish production and getting ready to produce the Battle. In December 1938 Foster

Rowland Ding in the rear seat of the one-off Handley Page G/100 biplane. The lady in the front is almost certainly Princess Ludwig of Löwenstein-Wertheim (the former Lady Ann Savile) who chartered Rowland to fly her from Hendon to Paris on 21st May 1914. The weather intervened, but Rowland got his passenger to Calais and from there she elected to complete the adventure by train. *Peter Green Collection*

was at the helm of the prototype Albacore biplane at the Great West Aerodrome, Harmondsworth, long since swallowed into the present-day morass that is Heathrow Airport. The Albacore was envisaged as a replacement for the Swordfish torpedo-attack and shipborne reconnaissance biplane. It featured a fully-enclosed cockpit, better take-off and climb performance, hydraulically-operated flaps yet continued to be eclipsed by its 1933 predecessor. Albacore production amounted to 800 units completed in late 1942, while the Swordfish ran to 2,392 with the last ones being delivered in August 1944. To make way for the Albacore on the Hayes production line, Blackburn took over building the Swordfish. On 1st December 1940 Foster was at Sherburn-in-Elmet where he test flew the first 'Blackfish', as the Yorkshire version was known, Mk.I, V4288.

CTP Chris Staniland* was killed in the second prototype Firefly in June 1942 and Foster took his place. Barracudas and Fireflies occupied most of his time but development of a new type, the 60ft 3in-span Spearfish dive-bomber/torpedo-attack aircraft, intended to replace the Barracuda was initiated in 1943. Foster 'first-flighted' the prototype, RA356, in July 1945 at Heston and it was followed by three more; RN241 at Ringway on 20th June 1946 having been built at Fairey's Heaton Chapel factory, near Stockport, and two more from Heston in 1947, RA360 and RA363, by which time the project was moribund. In 1946 Gordon Slade* became CTP, while Foster took on what hopefully would be a new light aircraft division and the rotorcraft department. Specification 8/48 was looking for a Tiger Moth replacement for the RAF and this was potentially massive market. Fairey's Belgian associate company, Avions Fairey, built the prototype Tipsy M (the 'Tipsy' deriving from its designer, Ernest Oscar Tips) as a trainer for the Belgian Air Force in 1939 and this was flying from the Great West Aerodrome by 1940 as an evacuee. This machine, OO-POM, was rebuilt at Gosselies in Belgium in 1947 with an eye on the Tiger Moth replacement and evaluated at Boscombe Down in 1948. It was then stripped down at

Hayes, so that Fairey engineers could draw plans ready for producing a true prototype; the original plans having been destroyed as the Blitzkrieg swept through Belgium. Two British examples, renamed the Fairey Primer, were made and Foster tested both (G-ALBL and G-ALEW) from Hamble. The RAF opted for the de Havilland Canada-designed Chipmunk and no more Primers emerged.

Fairey invested considerably in a compound helicopter, the Gyrodyne. Basil Arkell* was brought in as project pilot and details can be found in his section. Foster shared the testing with Basil and spent time during the spring of 1949 readying the prototype, G-AIKF, for an attempt on the 100km close-circuit speed record. On a sortie out of White Waltham on 17th April 1949 with Derek Garroway as FTO, G-AIKF suffered structural failure and Foster (aged 37) and Derek were killed.

The second prototype Spearfish, RN241, at the SBAC display, Radlett, September 1946. *Peter Green*

The first Hamble-built Primer, G-ALBL, flying over the Solent, 1948. *Fairey Aviation*

Intended to replace the Swordfish, the Albacore was effectively superseded by the older design. *Rolls-Royce*

N G Donald

F G OFF N G DONALD, a production test pilot at Hucclecote, engaged on testing Armstrong Whitworth Albemarles being built at the Gloster plant under the aegis of A W Hawksley. (Gloster and Armstrong Whitworth were part of the Hawker Siddeley Group and 'A W Hawksley' was an administrative creation to manage the manufacture of Albemarles at Hucclecote.) On 21st October 1943, Fg Off Donald, with T Timms as observer and two Air Training Corps cadets on air experience, J F S Cheriton and L W White, took Mk.I V1741 up for an air test. A turn at about 3,000ft increased into a steepening spiral to port; control was regained but at extreme low level and the aircraft impacted at Purton on the Severn Estuary, 17 miles southwest of the airfield. All four were killed.

Sholto Douglas

W ILLIAM SHOLTO DOUGLAS was a reluctant test pilot and serves as an interesting insight into the nature of the work! Sholto joined the Royal Artillery in August 1914, aged 21, but had transferred to the RFC by 1915, initially as an observer. He was a pilot with 14 Squadron by the end of 1915 and in the following April he was appointed as Officer Commanding 43 Squadron, later going on to command the Royal Aircraft Factory SE.5a-equipped 84 Squadron. In 1919 Major Sholto Douglas was appointed as the chief pilot for Handley Page Transport (HPT).

Handley Page was busy trying to develop a practical airliner both for HPT and the wider marketplace. The Cricklewood factory was working on a hybrid amalgamating O/400 and V/1500 bomber components and sub-assemblies. This prototype was based upon O/400 C9713 and it was referred to as the 'W/400'. Initial tests had been carried out by a Lt Carruthers, but he was no longer available by August 1919 when the next iteration of C9713 was ready to test. Geoffrey Hill* who was serving both as chief pilot for the factory and its aerodynamicist/stressman was a victim of the influenza pandemic that killed millions across the planet during 1918 and 1919. (He recovered and was to make his mark on aeronautics.) Frederick Handley Page wanted to speed things up and turned to Sholto, as chief pilot of HPT, to do the honours. Realising that he was not going to receive the anticipated bonus for a test flight, Sholto protested, but Frederick would not budge. So, he carried out a test on 22nd August 1919 and made his report. The 'W/400' was further morphed into an airliner, becoming practically a new type; it was civilian registered as G-EAPJ in November 1919 with the designation W.8. The following month Robert Bager, also with HPT, carried out what can be determined as the W.8's true maiden flight. Eventually, Arthur Wilcockson*, another HPT pilot, took over, becoming an established – and presumably bonused – test pilot. Sholto Douglas meanwhile resigned his post at HPT rather than continue to fly beyond his remit. He re-joined the RAF in 1920 and commenced a stellar career, becoming Marshal of the Royal Air Force in January 1946. MRAF William Sholto Douglas, 1st Baron of Kirtleside GCB MC DFC died in 1969.

Christopher Draper

| cOct 1919 | BAT FK.28 Crow
1 x 40hp ABC Gnat |
| early 1920 | BAT FK.27 K-143
1 x 200hp ABC Wasp II |

Christopher Draper, born 1892. Learned to fly at the Grahame-White school at Hendon, gaining Aviators' Certificate No.646 on 9th October 1913. Joined the RNAS in January 1914 and while stationed in the UK gained reputation for 'adventurous' aviating, reportedly flying under the Tay bridge at Dundee and under the footbridge crossing the track at Brooklands. He became a Flight Commander with 3 Wing, flying Sopwith 1½ Strutters on the Western Front in 1916, followed by service with 6 and then 8 (Naval) Squadrons, on Sopwith Camels. Between November 1916 and May 1918 he was credited with nine victories, including one observation balloon.

I N May 1919, Peter Legh, chief pilot for British Aerial Transport (BAT) company was killed while attempting an altitude record in the Basilisk, designed by Frederick Koolhoven*. His friend, Christopher 'Mad Major' Draper took over the role. At Hendon's Aerial Derby in June 1919 Christopher raced the clipped down BAT Bantam K-125, averaging 116.78mph and was placed fourth in the speed category. In late 1919, Christopher again earned his 'Mad Major' nickname by testing the diminutive Crow 'flying motorcycle' at Hendon. Performance on the temperamental ABC Gnat was not impressive and it is reported that on one sortie from Hendon Christopher had flown *five miles* before he had climbed

The BAT Crow 'flying motorcycle', tested by Christopher Draper at Hendon in 1919. *Peter Green Collection*

The side-by-side two-seater BAT FK.27 K-143 aimed at a market that did not exist in 1920. *Peter Green Collection*

to 500ft! Koolhoven went back to his native Holland in the last days of 1919. Christopher attempted to resurrect BAT's prospects by flying the previously untested two-seat FK.27 K-143 in early 1920. ('K' being the temporary national identifier used from April to August 1919 before the familiar 'G' was adopted.) Reportedly he only flew this once, perhaps intending to return to it. Demonstrating the single-seat Bantam fighter biplane as a potential sportsplane at Hendon on 23rd March 1920, G-EAFM (the former K-154) spun in at low level. Christopher was badly injured, but did return to flying later in the 1920s. BAT, however, did not recover from his enforced absence, and the company was wound up. Major Christopher Draper DSC, French Croix de Guerre, wrote his autobiography, *The Mad Major* in 1953. He died on 16th January 1979, aged 87.

Rodney Dryland

Rodney Dryland, born 1922. Joined the RAF in 1941 and served with 3 Squadron on Hawker Typhoons in 1943, converting to Hawker Tempest Vs in February 1944. Credited with the destruction of 15 V-1 'doodlebugs'. While flying Tempest V EJ747 on 24th December 1944 flak damage resulted in a forced-landing near Malmedy, Belgium. Rodney evaded capture and re-joined his unit.

RODNEY DRYLAND started work as an experimental and production test pilot for Gloster in 1946 on the steady flow of Meteor twin-jets. With CTP 'Bill' Waterton* in South America, Rodney was Acting CTP and was engaged in the first flight of Meteor FR.5 prototype VT347 at Moreton Valence. The FR.5 was a conversion of the F.4 fighter, featuring cameras in the rear fuselage and the nose. On returning to the airfield, the Meteor went into a high-g pull-over and it broke up and crashed, killing Flt Lt Rodney Dryland DFC, aged 27. It was discovered that the centre section tank had failed and a modification was devised for all F.4s. VT347 remained the only FR.5; Gloster returned to photo-recce Meteors with the FR.9 and PR.10, both based on the F.8 fighter, in 1950.

A page from an album commemorating the 'dash' to Rome while delivering a Sea Fury Mk.60 to Pakistan. *KEC*

LONDON - ROME 2hrs. 31mins 51secs.

Neville Duke

20 Jul 1951	Hawker P.1067 WB188 1 x 7,500lbst RR Avon RA7
30 Nov 1952	Hawker P.1067 WB202 1 x 8,000lbst AS Sapphire 101
8 Jul 1955	Hawker P.1101 XJ615 1 x 7,700lbst RR Avon RA21
1 Sep 1958	Garland-Bianchi Linnet G-APNS 1 x 90hp Continental C90-14F
10 Jun 1977	BN Ducted-Fan Islander G-FANS 2 x 300hp Lycoming IO-540-K185

Notes: P.1067 WB188 prototype Hunter F.1, WB202 prototype Hunter F.2; P.1101 prototype Hunter T.7. WB188 first flew from Boscombe Down; WB202 and XJ615 from Dunsfold; G-APNS from Fairoaks; G-FANS from Shoreham.

Neville Frederick Duke, born 1922. Patiently worked in the office of an auctioneer and estate agent until his 18th birthday, then tried, unsuccessfully, to join the Fleet Air Arm – but RAF snapped him up in June 1940. Operational flying started with 92 Squadron in April 1941, flying Supermarine Spitfire Vs. His next posting was 112 Squadron with Curtiss Tomahawks (Kittyhawks from November 1941), in Libya. On 30th November 1941 he was shot down by Obfw Otto Shultz of II/JG 27 in a Messerschmitt Bf 109 and five days later he was again brought down, by another JG 27 pilot. (He was dishing it out as well, see later.) Following a spell instructing in Egypt, he caught up with 92 Squadron, still on Spitfire Vs (later Mk.IXs), in November 1942 also based in Libya. Promoted to Squadron Leader, he was the CO of 73 OTU in Egypt before joining 145 Squadron, flying Spitfire VIIIs, in Italy from March 1944. Anti-aircraft fire forced him to bale out from his Spitfire, he landed in Lake Bracciano, northwest of Rome.

Sqn Ldr Neville Duke DSO DFC ended his operational tours in September 1944 as the RAF's top-scorer in the Mediterranean with 27 victories, 2 shared, 1 'probable', 6 damaged in the air and 2 shared on the ground and one 'probable' on the ground. His tally included the following German types: Bf 109, Focke-Wulf Fw 190, Junkers Ju 52 and Ju 87; and Italian: Fiat CR.42, Fiat G.50, Macchi MC.200 and '202 and Savoia-Marchetti SM.82. In October 1944 Neville was seconded to Hawker at Langley, flying as a PTP under Philip Lucas and in 1946 he graduated from ETPS Course No.4 at Cranfield and it was here that he flew his first jet, a Gloster Meteor III. In June 1946 Neville served on the High Speed Flight (HSF) with specially-modified Meteor F.4s, based at Tangmere. Also on HSF was Sqn Ldr 'Bill' Waterton*. Gp Capt E M Donaldson of the HSF successfully took the world airspeed record to 616mph on 7th September 1946. After HSF, Neville served at A&AEE Boscombe Down before leaving the RAF in June 1948 to join Hawker.*

NEVILLE DUKE returned to Hawker Aircraft at Langley in June 1948 and was quickly engaged in Tempest and Sea Fury production testing along with Sea Hawk trials, under CTP

Tomtit G-AFTA in Hawker house colours at Old Warden, in August 1964, four years after Hawker Siddeley presented it to the Shuttleworth Collection. *Roy Bonser*

'Wimpy' Wade*. The flight test department were also involved in moving out of Langley and establishing the new facility at Dunsfold. Between 1950 and 1951 Neville was also commanding officer of 615 (County of Surrey) Squadron, Royal Auxiliary Air Force, operating Meteor F.4s, and later F.8s, from Biggin Hill.

To celebrate his new job, in April 1949 Neville bought himself an aeroplane, one that came endorsed by kindred spirits. It *had* to be a Hawker and he discovered that the only surviving Tomtit, G-AFTA, was available for sale at Kidlington; to clinch the deal he'd had to sell his beloved MG sports car. Briefly during 1946 the Tomtit had been flown by 'Pat' Shea-Simmonds, a production test pilot for Supermarine. When Neville took delivery of the 1929-built biplane it was fitted with a distinctive windscreen – from a Spitfire – and streamlined fairing behind the pilot's head. These were modifications instigated by Alex Henshaw, chief pilot of the Castle Bromwich Aircraft Factory, who operated G-AFTA as a personal runabout from 1941 to 1946. (Much more about Alex in Volume Two.) In July 1950 Neville transferred the Tomtit to Hawker and continued to fly it at many air events. By then the company had a small 'circus' of former products: Hart G-ABMR and Hurricane II PZ865 *The Last of the Many*, both of which Neville enjoyed piloting. (The Tomtit is still airworthy with the Shuttleworth Collection, the Hart is at the RAF Museum, Hendon, and the Hurricane flies with the Battle of Britain Memorial Flight. For more on G-ABMR and PZ865, see under 'George' Bulman.) Throughout his life, Neville owned and flew light aircraft, including a Piper Comanche and a Cherokee; the latter he was piloting up to the day he died.

Display flying was part and parcel of Neville's tasks and he piloted the Sea Hawk prototype VP413 at both the 1949 and 1950 SBAC airshows at Farnborough. For the 1951 event, he flew the P.1052 VX272 and provided the debut of the

sensational P.1067 WB188. For tragic reasons it is for the 1952 Farnborough that Neville is most remembered. Again he was flying WB188, but on the final day of the show his friend John Derry was killed in the prototype DH.110 in the worst-ever UK airshow accident. Neville had to follow on and display – turn to John Derry's section for a poignant description. Neville's stoicism solicited the following communication from the Prime Minister, Winston Churchill: "My dear Duke, it was characteristic of you to go up yesterday after the shocking accident. Accept my salute." Such was Neville's test piloting longevity that he was back flying at the 1984 Farnborough SBAC display demonstrating the ducted-fan Egdley Optica.

Delivery flights were another regular feature of Neville's early work for Hawker. The Sea Fury was enjoying considerable export success and a large order from Pakistan for Mk.60 fighters and Mk.61 trainers allowed for a stab at two point-to-point records. John Derry* had flown a de Havilland Vampire FB.5 to Rome in 1948 and Neville decided he could beat his time, even though he would be flying in a piston-engined fighter. Departing from Heathrow on 12th May 1949 Neville was non-plussed by Rome's Ciampino airport being weathered-out and elected to land at nearby Urbe, in a flying time of 2 hours, 30 minutes 58 seconds – slicing an incredible 20 minutes, 18 seconds off John's flight. From Urbe, Neville flew the Sea Fury to Akrotiri, Bahrain and on to Mauripur. When he touched down, he had flown from the UK to Pakistan in 15 hours, 18 minutes and 36 seconds flying time. Not content with this, on 16th February 1950 Neville ferried a Sea Fury to the Egyptian Air Force, routing from Blackbushe to Luqa and then to Heliopolis, a distance of 1,310 miles in 6 hours, 32 minutes, 10 seconds. Record flying and other activities took a back seat when Wimpy Wade was killed in the swept-wing Hawker P.1081 VX279 on 3rd April 1951 and Neville was appointed CTP in the worst possible circumstances. (With no

Neville Duke flying the pale green P.1067 WB188 in 1951. *Hawker*

time to train up a pilot on either the P.1052 and the P.1067 this was why Neville carried out two demonstration flights at the 1951 Farnborough show.)

It is of course the Hunter with which Neville is indelibly linked. With this world-beater, Hawker underlined its predominance in fighter design and the genius of Sydney Camm and his design office. In response to Specification F3/48 Hawker proposed the P.1067 single-seat swept-wing fighter and following the 'belt-and-braces' policy of the day, two powerplants were to be embraced from the beginning: the Rolls-Royce Avon and the Armstrong Siddeley Sapphire. Painted pale green the prototype, WB188, was taken to Boscombe Down for its maiden flight. In his autobiography *Test Pilot*, Neville describes the debut on 20th July 1951 almost as though the reader was in the cockpit. It is an exceptional piece of writing, of which this small element provides the flavour: "It handles beautifully and you get a sudden feeling of exhilaration. You've got it up all right with no hitches and the initial tension is over. Now go through the flight programme." When Neville brought WB188, call-sign *Hawker Baker*, back to Boscombe, it was clear that a thoroughbred had been created. A year later, the Sapphire-powered version was ready, effectively the Hunter F.2 prototype, and Neville was at the controls, this time from Dunsfold. Although produced in far smaller numbers, under sub-contract by Armstrong Whitworth at Bitteswell, the F.2 had a much smoother introduction to service than its Avon-propelled sibling.

The prototype P.1067 was re-engineered as the one-off Hunter Mk.3 to reclaim the world absolute speed record. A USAF North American F-86D Sabre had raised the bar to 698.5mph on 19th November 1952. Changes to WB188 included an Avon RA7R of 7,130lbst 'dry' and 9,600lbst in reheat was installed, petal-style air brakes built in to either side of the rear fuselage, a pointed nose section and a re-profiled windscreen; the most noticeable of all being the overall gloss red colour scheme. The same calibrated 'race track' off the Sussex coast that had been used by the RAF High Speed Flight in 1946, when Neville was part of the team, was to be employed for the new attempt. Operating from Tangmere, on 7th September 1953 Neville took WB188 to 727.6mph to clinch the record and on the 19th took the 100km close-circuit record to 709.2mph for good measure. The Supermarine team were determined to steal Neville's laurels and in Libya on 25th September, Mike Lithgow* piloted Swift F.4 WK198 to 735.7mph to keep the headlines going. Such was the nature of record-breaking in the 1950s that the ink was hardly dry on the Fédération Aéronautique Internationale's certificate when it was announced that *just two days* later a Douglas F4D-1 Skyray had seized the record again for the USA, this time at 752.9mph. (Today, WB188 is on show at the Tangmere Military Aviation Museum, on loan from the RAF Museum and the fuselage of Lithgow's Swift WK198 is at the Brooklands Museum, Weybridge.)

A jubilant Neville Duke in the cockpit of all red Hunter Mk.3 WB188. *via Graham Pitchfork*

Prized possession, a RAF Aerospace Museum Cosford souvenir postcard of WB188, signed by Neville Duke. *KEC*

The Hunter programme had many development problems, some of which Neville painstakingly helped to iron out. Despite these glitches it became an exceptional aircraft; it was *the* RAF mainstay fighter of the 1950s and became a phenomenal export success. In July 1955 Neville took the P.1101 XJ615 on its maiden flight – this was the prototype T.7 two-seater which was 3ft longer than the fighter versions. Establishing the configuration of the side-by-side cockpit and the fairing behind it, took considerable time, eventually settling upon a distinctive 'area-ruled' format. The first T.7 did not enter RAF service until August 1958.

'Spud' Murphy* piloted F.1 WT562 on its maiden flight from Dunsfold on 29th October 1952 and it was destined to remain with the company's Hunter test fleet. Neville took it aloft on 6th August 1955 for gun-firing trials, heading for the south coast. Quickly he realised that the thrust had decayed and his options were running out. He could see the distinctive peninsula, near Chichester, and the airfield at Thorney Island looked achievable. He made it, but it was an overly fast arrival and WT562 bounced and bucked until Neville selected gear 'up' and the Hunter slithered beyond the perimeter and settled in a ditch. Neville extricated himself and, although in a lot of pain, at first thought he'd gotten away with it. The emergency crew disagreed, he'd fractured his spine. The year before this accident, on 22nd January 1954 Neville had 'first-flown' the P.1099, XF833. Fitted with an Avon 200 turbojet, this was the prototype of the F.6 variant, destined to become the most produced and most potent Hunter. After a sortie on 9th May 1956 Neville returned to Dunsfold in XF833 but suffered a very heavy landing. He needed five months off to recuperate but was back on the flight line in October, only to have to come to terms with that while he could fly, he could not take high 'g' loadings. He handed over to his deputy, Bill Bedford* and stood down as CTP.

So began a life of freelancing and variety. Early assignments included testing Royal Canadian Air Force Canadair Sabres and Avro Canada CF-100s fresh from overhaul by Field Aircraft Services at Wymeswold and delivering Percival Provost T.53s to Burma in 1956. From 1958 Neville was engaged by Garland-Bianchi Aircraft at Fairoaks to carry out trials of an Anglicized version of Frenchman Claude Piel's Emeraude two-seater. Neville made the first flight of G-APNS in September 1958 and helped to

clear it for British certification through the following year. One more was completed in 1962 before the Linnet was remodelled by Fairtravel Ltd; three were completed up to 1965.

At its Staverton base, the Dowty Group took delivery of de Havilland Dove 8 G-AVHV on 20th September 1967. It was the last of 542 built since 1945 and it was to be the new 'office' for the personal pilot of Sir George Dowty – Sqn Ldr Neville Duke. This post was held until 1969 when Neville handed over the contract to another operator. In 1970 Neville was back as chief pilot for the Dowty Group, this time with Dove 8 G-ASPA, followed by a Beech King Air 100 and then a 200. During this time Neville was also appointed as nominated test pilot for Miles Dufon at Shoreham. These two positions coalesced on 10th June 1977 when Neville first flew a very different version of the Britten-Norman Islander twin-engined transport. This was G-FANS, powered by a pair of Lycoming engines, each driving a Dowty Rotol-developed 48in diameter 7-bladed propeller within what was termed a ducted propulsor. The project was funded by Dowty and sub-contracted to Miles Dufon, the latter carrying out the installation and overseeing test flying. The conversion was intended to prove the ducted propulsor as a means of considerably quietening piston engines and to showcase the technology for shrouded propeller blades. G-FANS was converted back to standard Islander status in 1983. As mentioned earlier, Neville was involved in flying the radical Edgley Optica – also ducted fan-powered – observation aircraft from 1984 to 1986. Neville was test pilot for FLS Aerospace, later Brooklands Aerospace Group, 1987 to 1992, continuing development of the Optica and also the NDN Fieldmaster.

Neville wrote several books, *Sound Barrier – The Story of High Speed Flight* (1953) with Edward Lanchbery and his autobiography, *Test Pilot*, in collaboration with Alan W Mitchell, first appeared in 1953 and a new edition was published in 1992 by Grub Street. Other titles included: *Neville Duke's Book of Flying – The Saga of Flight* (1954) with Edward Lanchbery, *The Crowded Sky* (1959) and *The War Diaries of Neville Duke*, with Norman Franks (1995). On 7th April 2007 Neville took his wife, Gwen, flying from Popham in his Cherokee. Feeling unwell, he returned to the aerodrome, made a perfect landing but collapsed as he exited the aircraft; he died that evening. Sqn Ldr Neville Frederick Duke DSO OBE DFC** AFC (and Czech MC) flew to his last day.

Above: Superb view (from a Shackleton?) of P.1101 XJ615 in near definitive Hunter T.7 format. Note the large wing tip-mounted pitot tube. *British Aerospace*

Right: Neville Duke at White Waltham in 1991 for a press demonstration of the Fieldmaster 65. *Dave Allport – Key Publishing www.keypublishing.com*

Bottom: G-FANS, the Dowty Rotol ducted propulser test-bed Islander at Shoreham in 1978. *Ken Ellis*

Below: The prototype Garland-Bianchi Linnet, G-APNS, at Coventry in 1961. *Roy Bonser*

Freddy Dunn

26 May 1919	Tarrant Tabor F1765
	6 x 450hp Napier Lion

CAPTAIN FREDERICK 'FREDDY' GEORGE DUNN AFC, a pilot who had cut his teeth at Hendon prior to 1914, and Captain P T Rawlings DSC, who had flown operations with a Handley Page O/100 bomber in 1917, were given a challenging task at the newly-named Royal Aircraft Establishment (RAE) – the re-invented Royal Aircraft Factory. Awaiting them at Farnborough was a massive long-range bomber of triplane configuration: the top and bottom wings being of smaller span than the middle one, which was 131ft 3in from tip to tip. From its main wheels to the top wing was 37ft 3in and to start its engines, each needing to be hand-cranked, a wooden access tower – looking like a medieval siege engine – had been specially built. Between the top and the middle wing a pair of tractor Napier Lions was mounted. Alongside the fuselage, mid-set between the middle and lower wings were four more Lions, in pairs mounted back-to-back, one pushing, one pulling.

In charge of the design of this monster was W H Barling, who had commenced the task while Farnborough was still 'The Factory'. Rawlings had been appointed manager of the RAE's Tarrant Aeroplane Department some time before. As related in the section on Geoffrey de Havilland, during its existence the Royal Aircraft Factory had to adopt elaborate subterfuge to make it seem that no designing, or construction, of aircraft was going on. The Tarrant Tabor, at least four years in gestation, was the final example of this mind-set. Much of the aircraft had been built at Farnborough, but a lot of the woodwork had been sub-contracted to W G Tarrant Ltd at Byfleet; hence its designation – a further attempt to employ smoke and mirrors?

Came the day, 26th May 1919, and Dunn and co-pilot Rawlings were joined by Captain T M Wilson acting as observer, Lt Adams as engineer, Mr Grosert of the RAE and two mechanics. After the laborious process of starting the engines, the Tabor was taxied out and began a series of runs, one of which developed into a 'straight' with the biplane tail off the ground. Then the Tabor lurched forward and nosed over, crushing the forward fuselage. Rawlings died that day in hospital; Dunn succumbed to his injuries by the end of the month. The rest of the 'crew' scrambled clear. The entire project, for several years an irrelevancy, was axed. The consensus was that Dunn and/or Rawlings had gunned the top Lions first, hence the aircraft nosed over.

In its report for 29th May 1919 – the day of a solar eclipse by the way – *Flight* magazine had either been taken in by the RAE's 'camouflage', or knew something other sources didn't, when it sympathised with Walter George Tarrant: "...we also express our sincerest sympathy in the misfortune that has overtaken the machine into which, with rare courage, he had put so much thought and treasure. We understand that so certain is Mr Tarrant that his principle is right that another machine [F1766 was allocated] will be put in hand immediately incorporating, it may be taken, many alterations in design, but utilising the same constructional principle".

David Eagles

27 Oct 1979	Panavia Tornado F.2 ZD254
	2 x 9,000lb st Turbo Union RB.199-34R-04
8 Aug 1986	BAe EAP ZF534
	2 x 9,000lb st Turbo Union RB.199-34R-104D

John David Eagles, born 1936. Joined the Fleet Air Arm in 1953 and trained in the USA with the US Navy, at Pensacola, Florida, and Corpus Christie, Texas, among others. Returned to the UK in 1955, he went on to fly Hawker Sea Hawks with 736 and 738 Squadrons. David began a two-year exchange with Royal Australian Navy (RAN) from 1956, flying Fairey Firefly AS.5s with 851 Squadron. On 27th November 1956, David was piloting Firefly AS.6 VX381 over the bombing range at Jervis Bay, south of the RAN airfield at Nowra, New South Wales. VX381 was hit by AS.5 WD887; despite losing 5ft of wing, David and his observer managed to bale out; the pilot of WD887 was killed. During 1957 David was serving with 805 Squadron on Hawker Sea Fury FB.11s and became a member of unit's aerobatic display team, his first taste of this sort of flying. He was back in the UK in 1958 and flew DH Sea Venom FAW.21s with 893 and then 891 Squadrons. During 1961 he converted to DH Sea Vixen FAW.2s with 766 Squadron and was part of the unit's 'Fred's Five' team at the 1962 Farnborough display. He flew 'Vixens from HMS Hermes during 1962 and 1963.

David graduated from No.22 Course ETPS at Farnborough in 1963 and joined 'C' Squadron, Royal Navy Test, A&AEE at Boscombe Down. Blackburn Buccaneer S.2 XN979 took off from HMS Victorious off the Cornish coast on 9th June 1966 with weapons on the pylons; it immediately pitched up and became uncontrollable: its two crew ejected successfully. David was tasked with replicating the situation that led to this accident and on 26th October 1966 he and RAF Flt Lt Colin Scriven (the later on secondment to 801 Squadron) blasted off the deck of Victorious in S.2 XV153, steaming in Subic Bay, the Philippines. Instantly there was a violent pitch up and a roll to port and David and Colin banged out, being rescued by helicopter. Trim adjustment on the all-moving tailplane was discovered to be the culprit; a finer setting being required with the appropriate weapon load. His tour with A&AEE over, David flew Buccaneers with the Fleet Air Arm from 1967, with 764, 736 and then 809 Squadrons. With the latter, he led the 'Phoenix Five' team at the 1968 Farnborough SBAC airshow.

LT CDR DAVID EAGLES AFC joined BAC at Warton in October 1968 as an experimental test pilot, under CTP Paul Millett*. As with all in the flight test department at Warton, David's work took in all aspects, including Canberras and Lightnings, deliveries and demonstrations. In 1970 David was appointed as MRCA Project Pilot and in 1971 he became Assistant CTP. MRCA stood for Multi-Role Combat Aircraft, called Tornado not long after Paul Millett captained the prototype at Manching, West Germany, on 14th August 1974. Paul also 'first flighted' the first UK-assembled Tornado, P.02 XX946, at Warton on 30th October 1974 and David converted to the type on this aircraft that November. David flew the maiden flight of P.03 XX947 – the first 'twin-stick' (conversion trainer) version – at Warton on 5th August 1975 with BAC DCTP Tim Ferguson* in the rear seat. In February 1977 David was appointed CTP at Warton as the pace of the Tornado programme quickened. With navigator Ray Woollett in the back, David took the first production Tornado GR.1, ZA319, into the air on 10th July 1979, clocking over Mach 1 on the 92-minute sortie.

Along with the IDS version – interdictor strike – which had been ordered by all three participant nations, Britain, Germany and Italy, the UK had gone it alone with the ADV – air defence variant – long-range interceptor. David took the prototype ADV, A.01 ZA254, for its first flight from Warton on 27th October 1979; the rear seat being occupied by the ADV Project Navigator, Roy Kenward. A.01 represented the Tornado F.2 interim interceptor, the more developed F.3 entered RAF service in April 1987.

Upon Paul Millett's retirement on 1st January 1983, David was appointed as Executive Director, Flight Operations. By then David's major responsibility was a project that had been given the go-ahead the previous year. European collaboration projects involving a changing mixture of nations had been examining an advanced interceptor under the Agile Combat Aircraft banner. Led by BAe, with investment from the UK Ministry of Defence and Italy's Aeritalia, and further contributions from partner nations in the UK, Italy and West Germany, a single-seat technology demonstrator was to be built: EAP, the Experimental Aircraft Programme. This one-off was to pave the way for what was called EFA – European Fighter Aircraft – in 1984 and later would be known as Eurofighter 2000 and then Typhoon. David took the world's first full-authority quadruplex fly-by-wire control system, which was at the core of EAP ZF534, into the air at Warton on 8th August 1986 for 67 minutes, including a short spell at Mach 1. EAP was an incredible achievement, playing a major role in making what was to become Typhoon the ground-breaking programme it is. It was an exceptionally bold move and proved to be the last of its kind in UK skies, certainly with a man inside it. While Aeritalia worked on the wing and other elements, EAP was a Warton project heart and soul and as such several sources referred to it at the time as "Britain's last fighter". Withdrawn from use in May 1991 ZF534 is now cherished at the RAF Museum Cosford.

For Lt Cdr John David Eagles AFC, EAP was to be a fitting swansong; with 46 types under his belt and 6,000-plus hours in the logbook, he retired as Executive Director, Flight Operations on the last day of 1986 and was succeeded by Chris Yeo. During 1987 David took up the post of Deputy Managing Director of Panavia, the conglomerate that ran the Tornado programme. Retiring in 1993, David settled in New Zealand, but was tempted back to aviation three years later when he became Director, Flight Test of the German Deutsche Aerospace combine at Manching. By 2001 David had retired for a second time, and he lives in the UK.

David Eagles in 1984, having taken on the role of Executive Director, Flight Operations, Military Aircraft at BAe. *British Aerospace*

Tornado P.03 XX947 was first flown by David Eagles in August 1975. *British Aerospace*

In-flight refuelling probe extended, gear down, wings forward and four Sky Flash missiles under the belly, the prototype Tornado F.2, ZA254. *British Aerospace*

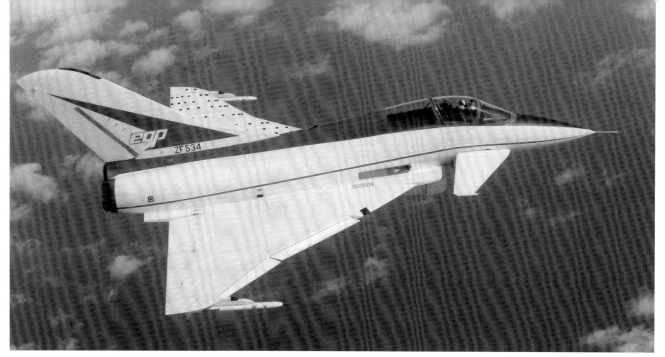

The exceptional, one-off EAP ZF534 with airflow sensors on its port wing. *British Aerospace*

Ronald 'Taffy' Ecclestone

Ronald Vivian Ecclestone, born 1923. Served with Bomber Command on Short Stirlings and then with a Bomber Defence Training Flight, flying Hawker Hurricanes and Supermarine Spitfires, during World War Two. Then followed a spell with the Central Bomber Establishment at Marham, A&AEE Boscombe Down and RAE Farnborough. Graduated from No.8 Course ETPS Farnborough 1949 followed by a posting to the Air Ministry.

SQN LDR 'TAFFY' ECCLESTONE DFC AFC was recruited by Handley Page (HP) CTP Hedley Hazelden* as his deputy on the death of Ken Dalton-Golding* in March 1954. He first flew as pilot-in-command of the prototype Victor, WB771, on 28th June 1954. Early in July 1954, Hedley was involved in low-level airspeed calibration flights with WB771 at Cranfield. The Bedfordshire airfield was home to the College of Aeronautics which possessed the necessary ground-based instruments to allow such tests to be carried out. On 14th July 1954 Hedley was due to resume the calibration flights, which were to be staged at 100ft – the so-called 'sea level' assessment – at increasing speeds. A prospective Japanese customer for the Marathon had arrived at Woodley earlier than scheduled and – as Hedley was checked out on the airliner but his deputy wasn't – Taffy was tasked to fly WB771 that day. After several runs across Cranfield, WB771's tailplane broke away and the V-bomber prototype crashed in a ball of flame on the airfield. Taffy was killed instantly, along with HP's chief FTO Ken Bennett (29) and additional FTOs Bruce Heithersay and Albert Cook (24). John Allam* was appointed in Taffy's place and a major investigation was launched to establish the cause, which was tracked to a fatigue failure of the tailplane attachment bolts.

Maurice Edmond

| 30 Jul 1910 | Bristol Boxkite No.7 |
| | 1 x 50hp Gnome |

HARD on the heels of Cecil Grace*, the man determined as the first-ever test pilot in the UK in Chapter One, came Maurice Edmond, a Frenchman with considerable experience of Farman biplanes. He was hired by Sir George White of the British and Colonial Aeroplane Company (later to be renamed Bristol) to test out the newly-established company's first product, the Zodiac. Sir George's French agent, Émile Stern, had set up a licence agreement to build a version of the Voisin biplane and suggested that Maurice would be a suitable test pilot. Maurice arrived at Brooklands and started coaxing the first Bristol-built Zodiac to fly on 10th May 1910 and gave up on 15th June having only got glimpses of light under the wheels. As the Filton factory scrapped the five other Zodiacs that were under construction, Maurice suggested that the Farman was a far better prospect. Rather than go to the expense of a licence, Sir George decided to copy the design, but to greatly improve its fittings and the standard of construction. The first Boxkite as the Anglicized Farman was named, was flown with ease by Maurice at Larkhill, reaching a dizzy 150ft. The Boxkite proved to be very successful and set Bristol on the way to becoming a major manufacturer. Maurice also acted as an instructor at the Bristol school on Salisbury Plain; his first pupil was 'Joe' Hammond*.

Boxkite No.12A – to avoid using the number 13! – of late 1910 was very smilar to the prototype first flown by Frenchman Maurice Edmond. *Bristol Aeroplane Co*

The one-off and anonymous Auster Type H under test at Rearsby, 1943.
Auster

Trevor Egginton flying specially-marked record-breaker Lynx G-LYNX in 1986.
Westland Helicopters

Geoffrey Edwards

FOR such a productive organisation, pinning down test pilots associated with Auster at Rearsby has proved challenging. The company was founded by Lance Wykes*, who carried out a lot of the flight testing himself. As Auster took on more and more work as part of the Civilian Repair Organisation, DH Tiger Moths initially, followed by Hawker Hurricanes and Typhoons, there was a need for a resident pilot capable of flying the fighters and Geoffrey Edwards was taken on by 1943. Throughout this time Auster IIIs, IVs and Vs were rolling off the production line and Geoffrey would have been heavily involved in this. He is known to have test flown a very unusual Auster type on 6th July 1943, the one-off Model H. This was a glider conversion of the Mk.III with an additional cockpit and forward fuselage in front of the firewall and the 130hp DH Gipsy Major I. It was based on the Taylorcraft TG-6 and was intended as a simple-to-produce trainer for assault glider pilots, but that task remained the domain of the General Aircraft Hotspur. Geoffrey Edwards retired during 1946 and was replaced by George Snarey*.

Trevor Egginton

| 9 Oct 1987 | EHI EH.101 PP1 ZF641 |
| | 3 x 1,279shp General Electric CT7-2A |

John Trevor Egginton, born 1933. Joined the RAF aged 18 and after basic instruction in the UK, completed his training in the USA. Operational flying with the RAF on NAA Sabre F.4s with 67 Squadron at Wildenrath, West Germany, 222 and 43 Squadrons on Hawker Hunter F.1s/F.4s at Leuchars. Converted to helicopters in 1961 and flew Westland Whirlwind HAR.10s with 22 Squadron at Chivenor. During 1964 he and his crew were involved in the rescue of French fishermen from a trawler in distress off the Cornish Coast. Trevor was awarded the Chevalier Order du Merite Maritime and the equivalent of the AFC for his endeavours. In 1965 he graduated from No.3 Rotary Wing Course ETPS Farnborough, moving on to 'D' Squadron A&AEE at Boscombe Down, then in 1969 he returned to ETPS (which by then was at Boscombe) as a Rotary Wing Tutor. Trevor left the RAF in 1973 with the rank of Squadron Leader.

THERE are many speed records mentioned in the two volumes of *Testing to the Limits*, but seldom do they stand as long as the world's fastest helicopter, which was not just clinched but smashed by Trevor Egginton and Derek Clews in Westland Lynx G-LYNX in the skies over Glastonbury in 1986. This combination beat the Soviets by a comfortable 20mph and the USA by a demonstrative 38mph. In June 2013 some of the world's press heralded the Eurocopter X3 as the world's fastest helicopter when it achieved 293mph, but that was a *compound* helicopter, G-LYNX boasted no such augmentation. Trevor died in November 2014, still the holder of the record he achieved 28 years previously – that in itself is surely a record.

Sqn Ldr Trevor Egginton joined Westland at Yeovil as DCTP in 1973 (becoming CTP in 1980) the bulk of his work being involved with Sea Kings, Lynx and WG.30s. Developments on the Lynx were producing very promising performance hikes, utilising technologies from Westland's British Experimental Rotor Programme (BERP), including composite construction and the distinctive 'paddle' tips. Westland decided to fit the company demonstrator, G-LYNX, with 1,200shp Rolls-Royce Gem 60s turboshafts, a BERP III main rotor and other improvements to have a go at the helicopter absolute speed record. Two helicopters held records within the category, a Soviet Mil A-10 (modified Mi-24 *Hind* gunship) at 229.2mph and a US Sikorsky S-76A at 211.5mph. The aim was to break through the 'magic' 400km/h figure.

On 11th August 1986 Trevor and FTO Derek J Clews flew G-LYNX on an out-and-back 15km straight course near Glastonbury to achieve 249.1mph. Four out-and-backs were flown and the speed was averaged over two runs; the last being the fastest as the weight reduced with fuel consumption. Monitoring this on behalf of the Fédération Aéronautique Internationale was the Royal Aero Club chief timekeeper Andrew McClymont, assisted by John Bagley and Ray Kingdon. The speed of 249.1mph converted to 400.87km/h which was a fabulous feather in the cap for Westland. Indeed a special commemorative tie with a '400.87' logo was produced. (Today, G-LYNX takes pride of place at the Helicopter Museum, Weston-super-Mare.)

PP1 ZF641, the Anglo-Italian EH.101 prototype in its original guise, 1987.
EH Industries

During 1986 Trevor was working in readiness for the EH.101 transport and maritime helicopter being developed by Agusta in Italy and Westland under the European Helicopter Industries (EHI) banner. From the spring of 1987, Trevor and DCTP Colin Hague* began the long and complex task of ground testing PP1 ZF641, the prototype EH.101. Trevor and Colin were at the helm for it its maiden flight from Yeovil in October 1987 and, known as the Merlin for the Fleet Air Arm and the RAF, the type is still in production. (ZF641 is still 'on duty', acting as an instructional airframe with the School of Flight Deck Operations at Culdrose.) Trevor stood down as CTP at Yeovil in 1988 but stayed on for another two years of flying duties, before retiring fully in 1990. Sqn Ldr John Trevor Egginton OBE died on 23rd November 2014, aged 81.

'Jock' Elliot

J Elliot, born 1921. Joined the Fleet Air Arm, initially flying Fairey Swordfishes and Albacores (the latter with 786 Squadron) including Arctic convoy duties. He was posted to 778 Squadron, the service trials unit, starting in mid-1944, flying Blackburn Firebrands, Fairey Fireflies, Grumman Avengers, among others. He graduated from No.7 Course ETPS, Farnborough 1948, before joining RAE Farnborough, piloting DH Vampire F.1s and F.3s, including landing trials on HMS Illustrious in November 1949. Lt Jock Elliot made the first-ever landing by a swept-wing jet on 8th November 1950, flying Supermarine 510 VV106 on and off Illustrious.

Lt Cdr J 'Jock' Elliot joined de Havilland in 1954 and became the CTP of the Christchurch division, taking over from George Errington. He played a major part in the development of the Sea Vixen for the Fleet Air Arm. With FTO John Allan, Jock piloted the first navalised Sea Vixen, Mk.20X XF828 on its maiden flight, landing at at Hurn, which was used for flight tests – on 20th June 1955. Jock handed over the role of CTP at Christchurch to Chris Capper* by 1958; he died in 1975.

'Bill' Else

William Henry Else, born 1921. Joined the RAF in 1941, training in the USA. Flew Hawker Typhoons with 182 Squadron. Seconded to A&AEE Boscombe Down in 1944 and involved in extensive rocket projectile trials on Typhoons. 'Bill' was then posted to A&AEE, 'A' Squadron. Graduated No.4/5 Course ETPS Cranfield, returning to duties at A&AEE until June 1947.

Early in 1947 Armstrong Whitworth (AW) senior pilot George Franklin was looking for a new member of the team, working initially from Baginton and, from the early 1950s, Bitteswell. George asked his friend Sqn Ldr Ralph 'Titch' Havercroft, then an instructor at ETPS, for a recommendation. 'Titch' named one of his pupils, Flt Lt 'Bill' Else, who he had also flown with on Typhoon rocket projectile trials while with A&AEE in 1944. (Titch was so named not through the usual irony, he *was* of small stature!) Bill settled into flight testing Hawker Sea Hawks and the AW.52 flying-wing jet. While piloting the second AW.52, TS368, in the spring of 1949 with FTO Arthur Payne during a demonstration to employees at the Baginton plant, Bill encountered violent oscillations during a low-level run. He chopped the throttles and regained control; after landing, it was discovered that TS368 had registered +12g and -4g during the frightening sequence. On 10th April 1949 Bill was co-pilot when George took the prototype Apollo on its maiden flight. From 1950 AW built Gloster Meteors and, commencing in 1953, Hawker Hunters. AW had design and test responsibility for the night-fighter Meteors. On 23rd October 1953 Bill took the ultimate 'long-nose' prototype, NF.14 WM261, for its debut from Bitteswell. Bill was in the right-hand seat on 8th January 1959 when George captained the first Argosy. Bill, having become DCTP at Bitteswell by the late 1950s, moved to another Hawker Siddeley factory, testing Avro Shackletons, Vulcans and later HS.748s and Nimrods from Woodford. He retired in 1976, after 28 years with AW and then HSA. He joined Air Anglia at Norwich, becoming a training captain on Fokker Friendships. Flt Lt William 'Bill' Henry Else died in 1985, aged 64.

Gordon England and Geoffrey England

cDec 1910	Weiss No.2 Monoplane 1 x 40hp ENV 'D' [1]
May 1912	Bristol GE.1 1 x 50hp Clerget
Aug 1912	Bristol GE.2 [2]
cNov 1912	Bristol GE.3 1 x 80hp Gnome
c1913	Radley-England Waterplane 1 3 x 50hp Gnome [3]
Sep 1913	Wight Navyplane No.2 1 x 160hp Gnome [4]
23 Nov 1913	Lee-Richards Annular Monoplane 1 x 80hp Gnome [5]
1914	HRL HL.1 1 x 150hp NAG-Conrad [6]
Mar 1915	W&T 'Bognor Bloater' 1 x 70hp Renault [7]
6 Aug 1915	Wight Twin Landplane 2 x 200hp Canton-Unné [8]

Notes: [1] Tested at Brooklands. [2] GE.2 No.103 had a 100hp Gnome, No.104 a 70hp Daimler-Mercedes; [3] Flown initially at Portholme. [4] Flew from Cowes. [5] Flew at Shoreham. [6] HRL = Hamble River Luke & Co, *believed* tested at Hamble. [7] W&T = White and Thompson, *thought* flown from Middleton-on-Sea. [8] Flew at Eastchurch.

Eric Cecil Gordon England, born 1891 in Argentina; family returned to the UK when he was aged 10. By 1909 he had met French-born José Weiss who had built at single-seat tail-less monoplane glider. Along with Graham Wood and others, Gordon - despite having no previous experience – flew this at Amberley, Sussex. The glider was launched down a slope and on 27th June 1909, Gordon achieved a

The grounds of Roedean School, Brighton, 13th May 1911, during the publicity tour by Gordon England and Graham Gilmour in a Bristol Boxkite. Left to right: Gordon England, Oscar C Morison (also a pilot), Graham Gilmour, Mr Preston. *Peter Green Collection*

height of 40ft – some sources quote 100ft – this was a UK gliding 'first'. By 1910 he was at Brooklands learning to fly Boxkites, also piloting a Hanriot monoplane. Gained Aviators' Certificate No.68 on a 'Bristol' at Brooklands on 25th April 1911 and just before, or around, this time, Gordon joined Bristol at Filton, initially as a pilot.

THREE brothers, Gordon, Geoffrey William – both described here – and the youngest, Thomas Harry, see separate entry. Each had aviation careers that included test piloting: one of the trio's time was tragically short. (Several sources have decided wrongly that Gordon England was a hyphenated gentleman, ie Gordon-England, thus condemning him to exile in the 'G' section of an index.)

Before Gordon took a post with Sir George White's British and Colonial Aeroplane Company (renamed as Bristol Aircraft in 1920) he renewed his association with José Weiss and tested the British-domiciled Frenchman's second powered monoplane at Brooklands. Gordon managed several sustained flights, but on 22nd December 1910 he ended up in the famous sewage farm and trials seem to have drawn to a close. Gordon showed interest in design as well as flying at Filton and Sir George let him develop his thoughts. Sir George boasted three design 'houses': Romanian Henri Coanda was appointed as chief designer in January 1912; Frank Barnwell*, assisted by Harry Busteed*; and Gordon. All were encouraged to beaver away and it seems that Sir George was content to see who showed the greatest potential. From early on, Gordon held reservations about Coanda's methods and concepts.

By May 1911 Gordon and another Bristol pilot, Graham Gilmour, took a Boxkite on a series of tours, giving pleasure flights and demonstrations in Somerset, Dorset, the south coast and across to the Isle of Wight. Gordon and Graham also instructed on Boxkites at Larkhill. Four Type 'T' biplanes were built to enter into the *Daily Mail* 'Circuit of Britain' challenge to be staged in July 1911 with a gigantic £10,000 in prize money on offer. Gordon was allocated one of the four, but it suffered engine trouble and he did not compete. His first design was a reconfiguration of a Type 'T' into a tractor biplane and this was carried out with the assistance of yet another Bristol pilot, George Challenger. Fitted with a 60hp ENV this was known as the Challenger-England Biplane and Gordon *may* well have been its test pilot.

Gordon's first 'blank sheet' design was the GE.1 (Gordon England 1) two-seat general purpose military biplane which had several novel features, including easily detachable wings for ease of ground transportation. An improved version, the GE.2, was aimed at the Military Aeroplane Competition to be staged at Larkhill in August 1912; two were built, differing only in powerplant. Gordon piloted No.103 in the trials and Howard Pixton* flew No.104, but neither was successful. During one sortie from Larkhill, Gordon had been up for about 90 minutes and decided to return to the field. He discovered that the elevator travel was severely restricted; thankfully the double-row 100hp Gnome had an ignition system that allowed one row of cylinders to be cut at a time, giving a degree of controlled descent, although the landing was still at high speed. Gordon's engineer had been carrying out some 'tweaks' and had immobilised the elevator cables to help him with ground runs. Keen to get airborne, Gordon had ignored the pre-flight checks, almost at his peril. The elegant GE.3 was a long-range reconnaissance type aimed at a promising Turkish government order but testing proved the type needed strengthening and only two were built.

Gordon's younger brother, Geoffrey William England, was also a keen aviator. He learned to fly at the Bristol school on Salisbury Plain, gaining his 'ticket', No.301, on 17th September 1912. Gordon was horrified to find that his brother had joined Bristol and was assisting Henri Coanda. Efforts to find Geoffrey other employment failed and relations between Gordon and Henri fractured. Gordon resigned from Bristol in February 1913 and joined James Radley in a new venture. Coanda had secured orders from the Romanian government for his Bristol-Coanda Military Monoplane and on 5th March 1913 Geoffrey volunteered to carry out an endurance test, as specified by the customer. He took No.146 to 3,000ft and had been flying for nearly an hour and began a steep descent, having turned off the 80hp Gnome rotary. At about 600ft the monoplane broke up, the port wing collapsing. Geoffrey was killed in the crash.

Gordon and James Radley jointly designed and built a large pusher seaplane, hopefully to enter the 1913 'Circuit of Britain' race. Built at Radley's Portholme workshop near Huntingdon, Gordon tested the Radley-England Waterplane from a nearby field, with a temporary wheeled undercarriage. The Waterplane was powered by three Gnome rotaries mounted in line, giving the image of a single, three-row, engine. This bulky powerplant took up the space normally devoted to pilot and passengers; these were located in the twin hull-like floats below the lower wing, the starboard example held the pilot, with two passengers

sat behind, the port hull accommodated three passengers. The Waterplane was flown by Gordon from the River Adur near Shoreham, but a collision with a buoy on landing necessitated a rebuild. It was given a more practical 150hp Sunbeam in place of the trio of Gnomes and the capacity for just four people in totally redesigned floats.

Cedric Lee and Tilghman Richards contracted James Radley to build a monoplane fitted with the pair's incredible annular – circular – wing. The round wing was joined to the fuselage at the nose and the tail. Dallas Brett, in his superb compilation *History of British Aviation 1908-1914*, set the scene for the debut by describing Gordon as: "ever ready to take on the wildest propositions". On take-off at Shoreham, Gordon at once realised that the craft was tail heavy, it stalled at about 150ft up, but came down on telegraph wires which cushioned the impact – Gordon was only shaken. Despite its unusual configuration, the repaired Lee-Richards flew well and two others were built. Two more seaplanes types were tested, both two-seat pushers that remained one-offs: the Hamble River Luke and Co HL.1 and the Wight Navyplane. Gordon's last powered test flight was the first of a dozen of the so-called 'Bognor Bloater' two-seat general purpose monoplanes.

From September 1914 until 1919 Gordon was the general manager of the aviation division of the Peterborough-based Frederick Sage Company building Short 184s and Avro 504s among others and several original designs. In 1919 Gordon joined his father, George, in the motor industry and using his aviation experience developed lightweight car bodies. George England Ltd built thousands of Austin Seven body shells, among other work. Gordon entered the 1925 Le Man 24-hour race in a car of his own design, but did not finish. In 1934 he returned to aviation becoming the managing director of General Aircraft Ltd, holding that post until 1942. He retired from industry in 1949. Eric Cecil Gordon England died in February 1976, aged 85.

The 'Bognor Bloater' of 1915 was noted above as Gordon's 'last *powered* test flight', in 1922 he managed to return to gliding. He entered the *Daily Mail's* contest for the longest glide of over 30 minutes duration, to be staged at Itford, near Lewes, over 16th to 21st October. Gordon designed a 28ft span, all-wooden single-seat glider and it was built at the Walton-on-Thames factory of George England Ltd. (Among the competitors at Itford was Frank Courtney* and 'Freddy' Raynham*.) The Gordon England glider flew well but in stormy conditions on the last day of the contest, it crashed, Gordon breaking an ankle.

Bearing the competition number 12, the first GE.2, flown by Gordon England at Larkhill, August 1912. *Peter Green Collection*

Tom Harry England

26 Mar 1927	HP Hinaidi I J7745 2 x 440hp Gnome-Rhône Jupiter
24 Feb 1928	HP Hare J8622 1 x 440hp Gnome-Rhône Jupiter
30 April 1929	HP Gugnunc G-AACN 1 x 135hp AS Mongoose I
14 Nov 1930	HP HP.42 G-AAGX 4 x 500hp Bristol Jupiter XI
25 Oct 1932	HP HP.46 1 x 825hp RR Buzzard III
27 Nov 1933	HP HP.47 K2773 1 x 690hp Bristol Pegasus III

Notes: Hare and Gugnunc first flown from Cricklewood; all others from Radlett.

Thomas Harry England, born 1893 in Argentina, family returned to the UK in 1901. Younger brother to Eric Cecil Gordon England and Geoffrey William England – for both, see above. In 1913 Thomas was working for Howard Flanders Ltd at Brooklands which operated a flying school and built a series of monoplanes and biplanes, tested by 'Ronnie' Kemp* and 'Freddy' Raynham*. By March 1925 he was a Squadron Leader, commanding 22 Squadron, the service test trials unit operating within A&AEE.

Sᵠᴺ Lᴅʀ Tᴏᴍ Hᴀʀʀʏ Eɴɢʟᴀɴᴅ ᴅsᴄ ᴀꜰᴄ joined Handley Page from Martlesham Heath in April 1927. He was mostly known as 'Tom Harry' and that is how he will be noted here. During Easter 1927, Tom Harry was competing in the Bournemouth air races and, in the section known as the 'Pub-Crawl', was flying Westland Widgeon III G-EBPW when its Cirrus engine quit and he executed a forced landing in a field that turned out to be water-logged. The Widgeon turned over, but both he and his passenger were unhurt. One of Tom Harry's duties at A&AEE in March 1927 was the first flight of the prototype Hinaidi night bomber, converted from a Hyderabad by fitting French-built Jupiter radials at Martlesham. Production Hinaidis had metal framed fuselages in place of the all-wood of their predecessors; a transport version, the Clive, was also built.

Tom Harry's appointment at Handley Page was full time, breaking the mould adopted by Frederick Handley Page, who used freelancers as and when required. Previously 'HP' had hired Hubert Broad* and Arthur Wilcockson*, the latter 'seconded' from Imperial Airways whenever the airline could spare him. Always keen to extract the maximum value from any arrangement, 'HP' defined Tom Harry's post as chief technical adviser, but Harald Penrose in *British Aviation – The Adventuring Years* was more precise: "his job in effect combining those of sales manager and test pilot". However he was defined, Tom Harry had a heavy workload which was lessened by the arrival of 'Jim' Cordes* as his assistant in early 1928.

A major income stream for Handley Page in the 1920s and beyond were royalties from patented leading edge slots to improve the slow speed characteristics of almost any type – refer to the section on Jim Cordes for more details. An early task given to Tom Harry was the Harrow shipboard torpedo bomber biplane which had been going through protracted development. The Harrow's leading edge slots required Herculean strength to manually operate them. Tom Harry astounded everyone by *disconnecting* the linkage from the slots to the cockpit. When the biplane slowed close to the stall, the slats came away from the leading edge where they had been forced by the airflow and performed perfectly, automatically and without *any* complex control wires or rods! Bristol F.2B Fighter Mk.III F4967 was issued to Handley Page in October 1927 and fitted with auto-slots; Tom Harry demonstrated this to RAF 'brass' at Cricklewood on 18th November. In April 1928 a brand-new de Havilland Moth, G-EBXG, was acquired and given similar treatment; it became a superb way of showing the light aircraft industry the application of auto-slots. In 1929 Tom Harry made the first flight of the ultimate slot 'technology demonstrator', the Gugnunc – again refer to Jim Cordes for more.

Tom Harry's inaugural first flight for his new employers was the Hare two-seat day bomber, which suffered from engine selection and development problems and was destined to remain a one-off. Although only eight examples were built, Tom Harry's next prototype became an icon of the 1930s, the HP.42 four-

Built as a Hyderabad, J7745 was converted at Martlesham Heath to become the prototype Hinaidi I and was flown by Tom Harry England. It is illustrated with definitive Jupiter VIIIs fitted. *Rolls-Royce*

The one-off Handley Page Hare, J8622, with the leading edge slots extended. *Peter Green Collection*

engined biplane airliner for Imperial Airways. The airline had imposed tough penalty clauses in the contract and the pressure was on to deliver on time; yet there were many changes to the specification. Tom Harry started taxi trials at Radlett on 31st October 1930 and was not to be hurried as he found out as much as he could about the 130ft-span monster. Perhaps mindful of the fate that befell the Tarrant Tabor – see Frederick Dunn – Tom Harry discovered that he *could* open the throttles on the upper engines before the lower ones and *not* nose-over. Nevertheless it was determined that the throttles be fitted with a 'gate' to prevent over-enthusiastic use. He presented a list of things to be done before flight and it was not until 11th November that 'straights' were attempted, this time with Jim Cordes in the right hand seat. Handley Page publicist and chronicler S A H Scuffham (quoted in Penrose *British Aviation – Widening Horizons*) described the first flight at Radlett: "The '42 shaped nicely on ground runs and gave them [England and Cordes] confidence, despite the overpowering sense of great size. They decided to try a low hop. Throttles were opened and the lightly loaded machine began to roll forward. Within a few seconds it was in the air, and before the two men could do much more than look at each other it was at 500ft."

The prototype HP.42 G-AAGX *Hannibal*, flown by Tom Harry England and Jim Cordes on its maiden flight. *Handley Page*

Pressures from within, mostly in the form of Frederick Handley Page relentlessly trying to speed up development and keep costs down, began to take its toll on Tom Harry. The HP.46 two-seat shipboard torpedo bomber was aimed at fulfilling a Japanese Navy requirement *and* an ever-changing Fleet Air Arm specification. Tom Harry started very cautious 'straights' on 25th October 1932 and produced a long 'snag list'. It was not until 6th December that he was confident enough to take the prototype on a brief circuit. The wildly ambitious project was abandoned the following year; the one-off HP.46 having flown for less than six hours.

Equally advanced was the HP.47 general purpose military type; not only a monoplane, it was fully flapped and slotted and represented a major leap forward. Both Tom Harry and Jim Cordes requested an off-the-shelf purchase of a type that would help bridge the gap. To their amazement, the Air Ministry agreed and a Heinkel He 64, registered G-ACBS, was imported from Germany. The pair flew this extensively in the first half of 1933, after which it went to RAE Farnborough. Specification G4/31 was hotly contested and deadlines loomed, and went. Taxi trials of the HP.47 started on 11th November 1933 with mid-January as the target to get a prototype to Martlesham Heath. Tom Harry took K2773 for its debut on the 27th, with Jim Cordes piloting it later in the day. On the 29th Tom Harry refused to fly it again unless its canopy was removed and a wider windscreen be fitted to achieve a classic open cockpit layout. Both pilots requested more changes and modification and the January date came and went. On the last day of August 1934 Tom Harry had had enough, he tendered his resignation and Jim Cordes took over. (It was Vickers that carried the day with G4/31 with what became the Wellesley.)

Tom Harry England became the sales manager for engineering products manufacturer Guest Keen and Nettlefold (GKN, which in 1993 consolidated its aviation sub-contracting business, becoming the giant, multi-national GKN Aerospace.). Later he worked for the Bristol-based Aero Engines Ltd before joining the Austin Motor Company in 1937 as a special adviser for what became the huge Longbridge aircraft 'shadow' factory. He was back with GKN by 1939.

George Errington

11 Jun 1937	Airspeed Queen Wasp K8887 1 x 310hp AS Cheetah IX
18 Oct 1940	Airspeed Night Shadower N1323 4 x 130hp Pobjoy Niagara V
19 Feb 1941	Airspeed Cambridge T2449 1 x 750hp Bristol Mercury VIII
12 Sep 1941	Airspeed Horsa DG597 glider
10 Jul 1947	Airspeed Ambassador G-AGUA 2 x 2,625hp Bristol Centaurus 661

Notes: All took place at Portsmouth, other than the Horsa which flew from the Great West Aerodrome (Harmondsworth) and the Ambassador, from Christchurch.

George Bertram Sainsbury Errington, born 1904. Studied engineering at Sheffield University, then worked for Vickers steel works division. In 1929 he joined Avro at Woodford, taking an aeronautical engineering course, gaining both his 'A' and 'B' licences -the first of many – and learned to fly at the co-located Lancashire Aero Club. At this point he befriended Edgar Hart, who gave George the use of his 1929-built Avro Avian IV G-AAHK, and he 'clocked' many hours in it. George next worked for Comper Aircraft at Hooton Park as an inspector and doing some flying. He moved with the company to Heston in 1933, later transferring to Heston Aircraft, working as an inspector and part-time pilot. He joined Airspeed at Portsmouth, again as an inspector, in late 1934.

George Errington, complete with signature cravat, at the controls of an Ambassador. *Airspeed*

IN *Vapour Trails*, the 1956 compilation of test piloting memories by Mike Lithgow*, by the far the biggest contribution comes from George Errington. At 45 pages, his chapter entitled, 'Riding a Horse with Wings', is easily twice that of the next largest contribution. To read it is to know that neither Mike Lithgow, nor his publisher, dare wield the editorial knife. It remains an engaging narrative that deserves a far wider, 21st century, audience. George joined the expanding Airspeed company at Portsmouth in late 1934 as an inspector, but his flying experience was too good to miss and in 1935 he became a test pilot. In *Vapour Trails* George expressed this in typically under-spoken manner, his job was: "dogsbody pilotage duties". In 1939, George's boss, 'Percy' Colman* re-joined the RAF and George took over as CTP, a role he kept until the last of the Ambassador airliners departed in 1953.

When the time came to hand Avian G-AAHK back to Edgar Hart, George realised that he could not go long without another 'runabout'. Working for Nicholas Comper* provided many contacts and he acquired Comper Swift G-ACTF in damaged state and by August 1934 he'd got it flying again; taking it with him to Portsmouth. George passed the Swift on to Francis Luxmoore* in 1936 and he ran G-ACTF until the end of the war. Post-war, George met *Tango-Fox* again, his assistant Ron Clear* had bought it, cherishing it from 1949 to 1955. (Today, it is a part of the Shuttleworth Collection.) In April 1938 George became the proud owner of another Pobjoy-powered aircraft, two-year-old BA Swallow 2 G-AEZM which he named *Puddlejumper*. He sold this in September 1944.

George's first flight test was an Envoy and he was soon involved in delivery flights, to South Africa and to China. Envoys gave way to Oxford crew trainers and George was heavily engaged in clearing hundreds for service use. George began an unusual task in January 1939 as Airspeed linked up with the Coventry-based Alvis company to help in the development of a promising series of radial engines. Bristol Bulldog Trainer K3183, previously used by Napier as an engine test-bed, was converted at Portsmouth to take an early 9-cylinder 450hp Alvis 9ARS. With John Marlow of Alvis as FTO, George discovered that the 9ARS was: "a winner from the start and in hundreds of hours of flying it gave no trouble." The war got in the way of the project, but beyond 1945 the engine gained fame as the Leonides.

Vapour Trails includes an account of spinning trials in an Oxford in September 1939 that nearly ended in tragedy. To paraphrase George's words is a crime, but a necessary one. Wisely, a spin-recovery parachute had been fitted on the rear fuselage upper decking, activated by controls located above the pilot's head. Doubly wisely, George had rigged a rope from the cockpit to the access door on the port side of the fuselage. He'd carried out hundreds of spins earlier in the week on this

Alvis 9ARS test-bed Bulldog Trainer K3183 at Portsmouth, 1939. *Alvis*

machine, in many different configurations. He noted that in a stabilised spin he could pause to take photographs of the instruments to help with the debrief.

The next test was with the Oxford fully loaded with the centre of gravity set *behind* the aft limit. He went through the procedure: level off at 16,000ft, scan the sky for other aircraft, check the instruments, photograph them, trim and throttle back, drop the wing and count eight full turns. Standard

The second prototype Queen Wasp, K8888, in floatplane configuration. *Airspeed*

N1323, the first of two bizarre Fleet Shadowers, 1940. *Airspeed*

recovery: rudder-stick-throttles, no response, the Oxford deepened its gyrations which: "to say the least, disappointed..." wrote George in 1956. He'd gone through 8,000ft, so pulled the anti-spin 'chute lever. Nothing! George got up, using the rope to get him to the exit. En route, the Oxford's tail lifted, the spin stopped and it went into a steep, turning dive. George returned to the cockpit and gave the emergency parachute lever another tug and then a *very* hefty pull and the entire device came away from its attachments. At 4,000ft the Oxford entered clouds and George again made his way to the door. The Oxford started to flatten out and George returned to the controls. At something like 1,500ft, the aircraft burst out of the clag and George pulled out of the dive and headed for Portsmouth. The emergency parachute *had* streamed, but had fallen under the tailplanes, where it opened. In doing so, it had damaged the tailplane and ruined any chance of a recovery. Eventually the parachute parted company, leaving a thoroughly rattled George to regain command.

The first 'first' that George carried out was the Queen Wasp radio-controlled gunnery drone intended to replace the Tiger Moth-based de Havilland Queen Bee. K8887 was completed with undercarriage, the second, K8888, had twin-floats. A handful of production examples were completed before the contract was axed in 1940. The next prototype was a bizarre four-engined, two-crew, shipborne reconnaissance machine aimed at Specification S23/37. The idea was to create a slow, long endurance, stable and quiet platform to keep tabs on enemy shipping from a distance, Both Airspeed and General Aircraft built prototypes, each choosing four Pobjoy Niagaras as the solution to a tricky requirement. Airspeed initially referred to the type as the Night Shadower, but both machines became known as Fleet Shadowers. The choice of the word 'Night' was more appropriate, as only the cover of darkness and its slow speed – around 40 knots – would afford any form of protection to the unarmed craft. Unsurprisingly, nothing further came of the project.

Specification T4/39 sought an advanced trainer, and George flew the first of two prototypes of the Cambridge in February 1941. In *Vapour Trails*, George wrote of an eventful sortie in a Cambridge, although he declined to name it, describing it as a low-wing monoplane, powered by a Mercury VIII. In the type's first dive to maximum speed the inboard upper surface of the starboard ply-covered stressed-skin wing detached. George's assessment: "This was in no way a catastrophe. I felt some [right hand] drag, some loss of lift, easily counteracted, and that was all". He chose a 'runway in the sky' and tried mock approaches, discovered what extra drag he needed to compensate for and then performed an uneventful landing on terra firma. With Miles Masters in full flow and deliveries of North American Harvards increasing, the requirement for the Cambridge was soon dropped.

While the Oxford trained tens of thousands of aircrew through the war and into the early 1950s, it was the Horsa assault glider that was unquestionably the most important Airspeed design. The company had been acquired by de Havilland in 1940, but still traded under its own name until 1951. Airspeed designer Hessell Tiltman and his team worked at Salisbury Hall, near Hatfield, to develop what became the Horsa and most of the first two prototypes were built there, much in the same manner as the Mosquito – see Geoffrey de Havilland JR. Horsas were designed to be mass manufactured by dispersed woodworking companies and assembled at maintenance units prior to their one-way journey to a battlefield. Towed aloft by an Armstrong Whitworth (AW) Whitley flown by Flt Lt W R H 'Nick' Carter RNZAF from the Great West Aerodrome George piloted the first example. He went on to fly many of those produced at Portsmouth and helped to develop the ideal approach manoeuvre to very restricted landing zones. George praised the all-wood 88ft span glider: "of all of the hundreds of production Horsas we made, we never had an accident of any sort though every landing was 'forced'."

Airspeed had been set up with Sir Alan Cobham* as a director and strong connections were maintained with his Flight Refuelling Ltd (FRL) company. For a couple nights in February 1940 George was at the helm of the one-off AW.23 G-AFRX out of Boscombe Down working in association with Geoffrey Tyson* flying a Handley Page Harrow tanker. George's experience with the Horsa, helped with an FRL scheme to increase the range of single-engined fighters, particularly when being ferried long distances. At Staverton in 1942, George flew a Hawker Hurricane I modified to accept tow ropes in the leading edge of each wing. Attached to a Vickers Wellington, the Hurricane would take off then throttle back and let the bomber do most of the work. Later trials, involving FRL, took the idea further with a Hurricane trailing its V-shaped tow line, ready to be intercepted by another aircraft towing a hook that would 'catch' the fighter and commence a tow – see under Bryan Greensted. During 1943 George was 'loaned' to Jeffrey Quill of Supermarine assessing Spitfires and Seafires from Worthy Down. In *Vapour Trails*, he describes this episode as: "perhaps the happiest years of my test work". Other duties carried out by George during the war years included testing DH Mosquitos from Christchurch.

Post-war, the Oxford provided much reconditioning work for Airspeed and a more refined civilian conversion, the Consul, also helped keep the factory going. But it was the Ambassador airliner upon which the future depended. Arthur Hagg produced a beautiful design but its looks could not overcome the fact that only British European Airways (BEA) wanted it, taking delivery of just 20 beyond the trio of prototypes. With J Pears acting as FTO, George took G-AGUA for its eventful debut at

The first Airspeed Cambridge, T2449. *Airspeed*

A Horsa assault glider under tow; the side access door has been removed. *KEC*

A 1948 Airspeed advert, immediately recognisable as from the brush of Frank Wootton, showing off the Ambassador as a work of art.

AMBASSADOR

AIRSPEED LIMITED · CHRISTCHURCH AND PORTSMOUTH · HAMPSHIRE · ENGLAND

The first Ambassador 2, G-ALFR, with specially marked wings and tailplane, 1950. *Rolls-Royce*

Christchurch in July 1947. During the climb out the spring tab on the middle rudder separated and later, the electrical system failed, only to recover prior to landing. Worse was to follow on 22nd November when bolts securing the port undercarriage jack failed; ripping away hydraulic lines and leaving the port leg down and locked. This rendered the starboard gear locked up and the flaps useless. George carried out a textbook landing, with the starboard propeller chewing up the airfield. Hagg created durable aircraft: *Uniform-Alpha* was back in the air in mid-December. George flight tested all of the Ambassadors; the last one departing in March 1953. His place at Christchurch was taken by 'Jock' Elliot*.

By 1966, George was assisting with the production testing of Hawker Siddeley Tridents. On 3rd June he was co-pilot to Peter Barlow on the maiden flight of G-ARPY, destined for BEA. As related in the section on Peter, *Papa-Yankee* entered a flat spin and George was one of the four on board killed when it crashed in Norfolk. George Bertram Sainsbury Errington OBE was 62 and had amassed about 4,100 hours on 104 types,

'Red' Esler

4 Sep 1949	Avro 707 VX784 1 x 3,500lbst RR Derwent 5
17 Sep 1949	Avro Athena T.1 VM129 1 x 1,400shp RR Dart 1

Samuel Edward Esler, born 1918. RAFVR pre-war, joining up in May 1942. Operational service with 120 Squadron, flying Consolidated Liberators from Northern Ireland. On 14th June 1942 his aircraft attacked and damaged the U-boat U-449 in mid-Atlantic; Esler was awarded a DFC in December. Attached to Avro at Woodford for production test pilot duties on Lancasters, before returning to 120 Squadron. Graduated ETPS No.2 Course at Boscombe Down 1944-1945.

'RICKY to some, 'Red' to most of his colleagues, Ulsterman Sqn Ldr S E Esler DFC became a PTP for Miles Aircraft, testing Messengers at Long Kesh and, from February 1946, at Newtownards, Northern Ireland. He also carried out extensive development work with Airspeed Oxford II X7265 fitted with a Miles-designed autopilot and Alvis Leonides-engined Oxford I LX119 during 1945 until late 1947. In June 1948 he returned to Woodford, becoming DCTP to 'Jimmy' Orrell*. Work involved Lancasters, Yorks, followed by Tudor airliners, including the jet-powered Tudor 8 VX195. During in early August 1949 Jimmy Orrell was seconded to Avro's Canadian division to test fly the C102 Jetliner. So 'Red' took on the Athena trainer and the Avro 707 single-seat delta research test-bed, intended to pave the way for the Vulcan V-bomber, that ordinarily would have been Jimmy's responsibility. The Athena had been conceived as a turboprop from the start, but the contract was altered and a limited run of Rolls-Royce Merlin-powered T.2s was ordered in addition to the turbine prototypes. Jimmy Orrell piloted the first example, Armstrong Siddeley Mamba-powered VM125, in June 1948 and the first Merlin T.2, VW890, on 1st August. Red made a 20-minute maiden sortie in the 707 from Boscombe Down on 4th September and 13 days later he was at Farnborough for the debut of the one-off Rolls-Royce Dart Athena, VM129. Red ferried the 707 to Farnborough where it was shown off in the static during the SBAC airshow 6th-11th September. On the 30th September 1949 VX784 departed Farnborough and it appears to have been unintentionally stalled; it did not recover and crashed near Blackbushe, killing 31-year-old Red Esler. VX784 had flown for just 2 hours, 43 minutes of 27 days. 'Roly' Falk* continued the 707 project, flying the much-modified, and ejection seat-equipped, 707B in September 1950.

The diminutive 707 VX784 had a wingspan of 30ft 6in. To speed construction it used parts from other types; including Athena main undercarriage legs and a modified Gloster Meteor canopy. *Peter Green Collection*

Major Evans

1917	Saunders T.1
	1 x 150hp Sunbeam Nubian

RFC pilot Major Evans presided over the maiden flight of the first design from the East Cowes-based S E Saunders Ltd at Somerton, Isle of Wight, during 1917. The T.1 remained a one-off and no more is known of its pilot.

Colin Evans

FLT LT J COLIN EVANS served as an instructor with 5 Flying Training School at Sealand. By 1940 he was engaged as a production test pilot with Boulton Paul at Pendeford, working mostly on Defiants but also, in May 1942, he was undertaking trials of a ferry tank fit for Supermarine Spitfire Vs. Colin joined Fairey in 1942 under Foster Dixon* and was involved in the intensive trials getting the Firefly into frontline service. Examples of his work included Mk.III aerodynamic testing on the prototype, Z1826, in the spring of 1944; Mk.IV development in mid-1945 using Z2118; the first flight of FR.I MB404 on 13th October 1944. As an interesting aside, Colin flew the debut of Mk.I Z2033 on 28th March 1944: this is now preserved at the Fleet Air Arm Museum, Yeovilton. On 27th November 1945 Colin took FR.I PP463 for its first flight, at about 7,000ft the Firefly's canopy separated and the aircraft crashed near Staines, killing Colin. It was thought that he may have been stunned by the canopy hitting him.

'Tommy' Evans

THOMAS BENJAMIN OSWYN EVANS flew operationally with the RAF in the Far East in 1944, followed by fighter development flying, including jet experience. Flt Lt 'Tommy' Evans DFC joined English Electric as a production test pilot in 1950, initially on DH Vampire FB.5s and FB.9s from Samlesbury. He converted to the Canberra in 1951 and displayed B.5 VX185 at the SBAC airshow at Farnborough in September. On 25th March 1952 he was preparing for the

maiden flight of B.2 WD991 at Samlesbury. An equipment snag delayed the duty FTO and the decision was made to go solo. Not long after take-off, to the west of Preston, WD991 was seen to go into a steep dive, from which it did not recover and 29-year-old Tommy Evans was killed in the crash – he had just under 2,500 flying hours experience. A mangled box spanner was found in the wreckage but no cause could be attributed with certainty from the crash analysis. Tommy was the first English Electric pilot fatality.

'Roly' Falk

14 Jun 1951	Avro 707A WD280
	1 x 3,600lbst RR Derwent 8
30 Aug 1952	Avro Vulcan VX770
	4 x 6,500lbst RR Avon RAE3
3 Sep 1953	Avro Vulcan VX777
	4 x 9,750lbst Bristol Olympus 100

Notes: 707A first flown from Boscombe Down, all Vulcan debuts from Woodford. VX770 flown with Avons as interim prototype. VX777's maiden flight in 1953 as the representative B.1.

Roland John Falk, born 1915. Studied at the de Havilland Technical School, Hatfield, and learned to fly there, 1932. In June 1935 he briefly joined Air Commerce at Croydon, before working on a freelance basis for Air Dispatch, also based at Croydon, and its associate business, Commercial Air Hire (CAH) of Heston. Air Dispatch had contracts to fly newspapers to and from the Continent, including Madrid and Paris, as well as charter work, mostly using Airspeed Envoys. CAH specialised in flying film crews, news reporters, film reels and high-value packages. 'Roly' flew press representatives to Abyssinia (present day Ethiopia) during the Italian invasion in October 1935, returning in early December. In 1936 Roly found himself amid another conflict, the Spanish Civil War. On 21st July 1936 Roly flew three journalists in Envoy G-ADAZ to Barajas, Madrid, then in the hands of Republican forces. Four days later, he had four passengers and two resident Air Dispatch staff to extract, *but was lacking in paperwork. Roly bluffed his way through, but found that he was pursued by fighters as he headed for the French border, thankfully the 170mph Envoy was more than a match for its followers. From February Roly became a test pilot for the Air Registration Board on an 'as and when' basis. He joined the RAF in February 1940 and was posted to the RAE at Farnborough, becoming its CTP in 1943, succeeding Wg Cdr H J Wilson*. He flew a staggering 300 different types and around 2,000 hours during his time at RAE. He piloted a wide range of captured Luftwaffe types, including: Heinkel He 162A, Messerschmitt Bf 109G, Bf 110C, Me 163B as a glider only, Me 262B, Focke-Wulf Fw 190As and a variety of Junkers Ju 88s.*

W G CDR ROLAND FALK AFC* joined Vickers at Brooklands in January 1946, working for CTP 'Mutt' Summers* and initially was engaged in testing Vikings. As part of the programme leading up to the Viscount four-turboprop airliner, Wellington B.X LN817 had been fitted with reversible pitch propellers. These were intended to help shorten the landing run, but there was a belief that they may well be able to decelerate the new airliner on approach. Roly was tasked with trying this out. On 5th July 1946, flying solo, he took LN817 up for a circuit, engaging the reverse pitch about half-a-mile from the threshold. The Wellington's nose dipped violently downwards and Roly

Dapper Roland Falk in the cockpit of Avro 707A WD280. *British Aerospace*

became a passenger; it ploughed through the farmhouse at Cuckoo Farm, near Ockham, and came to rest in a ball of flame on a minor road. Roly had been thrown clear; he had broken both legs, an arm and had a spinal fracture. He faced a long time in hospital and recuperation and his job with Vickers came to an end. In his 1998 autobiography (with Sally Edmondson) *Test Pilot* Brian Trubshaw declared that his good friend Roly: "...would have succeeded Mutt Summers but for an unfortunate accident in a Wellington fitted with reverse pitch propellers." It was determined that the prop pitch control mechanism on LN817 malfunctioned, causing a violent pitch-down on approach.

Against all the odds, by April 1947, Roly was up and flying, reverting to the role of a charter pilot. In September 1949 'Red' Esler was killed in the prototype Avro 707 delta test-bed and in January 1950 Roly joined Avro at Woodford in 1950 under CTP 'Jimmy' Orrell*. Effectively, Roly was project pilot for the 707 and the programme that dominated all others at Woodford, the Avro 698 V-bomber that took the name Vulcan in December 1952. Such was Roy's level of experience that his appointment was rationalised as Superintendent of Flying, instead of DCTP, in the spring of 1954. Apart from the human tragedy, the first 707 had less than three hours 'on the clock' when it was lost, so had not begun to contribute aerodynamic experience or data to the programme. While it appeared that the delta configuration did not contribute to the demise of VX784, no real cause could be attributed. The second mini-delta, the 707B, featured many design changes and an ejection seat; Roly took VX790 into the air for its maiden flight on 6th September 1950. The following year the much refined 707A, which dispensed with the single upper-fuselage intake of the first two examples and adopted wing root intakes to emulate the format of the Vulcan, had its debut in Roy's hands. Two more 707s followed, both beyond that of the prototype Vulcan, in 1953: 'Jimmy' Nelson'* with 707A WZ736 and Jack Wales* in the two-seater 707C WZ744. (WD280 survives in Australia, WZ736 is displayed at the Museum of Science and Industry in Manchester and WZ744 is at the RAF Museum, Cosford.)

Roly flew the prototype Vulcan, VX770, solo from Woodford on 30th August 1952, for 36 minutes. His flying alone was not bravado, nor a reflection of how fearful he and Avro were of the moment: VX770 was in interim condition; its Olympus engines were not ready, so Avon's were fitted and there was no second seat for a co-pilot available. The sortie was a great success, the only 'wobble' occurring on landing back at Woodford when two main undercarriage doors fell off. Operating out of Boscombe Down, Roly and VX770 stunned the airshow audience at Farnborough in the first week of September, flying in formation with 707A WD280 and 707B VX790. In September 1953, Roly was in command of the second prototype, VX777, for its debut. This had Olympus 100 engines and took on the bulk of the development flying. For the 1953 Farnborough, Avro wanted to increase the 'wow factor' still further, especially as the prototype Handley Page Victor was also in attendance. Flying VX777, Roly was 'escorted' by 707As WD280, WZ736, 707B VX790 and 707C WZ744 before he started his solo display which included slow rolling the big delta.

As Chief Test Pilot of the Royal Aircraft Establishment, Roly Falk flew captured Junkers Ju 88R-1 PJ876 during 1943. Today it is on show at the RAF Museum, Hendon. *MAP*

The prototype Vulcan, VX770, powered by Rolls-Royce Avons. *Hawker Siddeley*

Avro 707A WD280, first flown by Roly Falk on 14th June 1951. *AVRO*

The second prototype Vulcan, VX777 lingered at Farnborough until the early 1960s. *Roy Bonser*

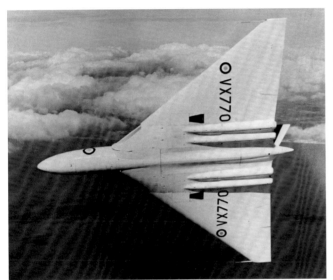

While showing an RAE crew the Vulcan's slow flying characteristics in VX777 at Farnborough on 27th July 1954 a control spring in the rudder jammed and Roly found himself with a full deflection on the rudder while the pedals were centred. He returned to Farnborough, made a fast approach and over-ran; the delta ending up on its belly but with only minor injuries to the crew. VX777 was back in the air during March 1955. Trials proved that the 'pure' delta needed modification and in in July 1955 Roly piloted VX777 with the distinctive 'kink' on the outer leading edge, the so-called Phase 2 wing. With the retirement of Jimmy Orrell in 1955, Roly became CTP and in August 1957.

Wg Cdr Roland John Falk OBE AFC* retired from flying in January 1958, taking up a role as a sales representative for the Americas with Hawker Siddeley, his place at Woodford being taken by 'Jimmy' Harrison*. In 1963 Roly set up Aerospace Associates, working as a freelance consultant. Roly settled in Jersey in 1967 and ran his own charter business there. He died on the island on 23rd February 1985, aged 69. Peter Clegg's biography of Roly was published in 2010.

The 1953 Farnborough show was dominated by Roly Falk in Vulcan VX777, flanked by Avro 707As WD280, WZ736, 707B VX790 and 707C WZ744. In the foreground is Air France DH Comet 1A F-BGNX. *KEC*

John Farley (right) with his DCTP, Andy Jones, and a Hawk in the background. *British Aerospace via Tony Buttler*

John Farley

| 20 Aug 1978 | BAe Sea Harrier FRS.1 XZ450 |
| | 1 x 21,500lbst BSE Pegasus 104/106 |

John Frederick Farley, born 1933. Began a five-year student engineering apprenticeship at RAE Farnborough in 1950 and during this time determined that he wanted to be a test pilot. He joined the RAF in 1955 as the next step to reaching his goal. John gained his 'wings' in June 1957. He was posted to a ground tour at the Royal Radar Establishment, Malvern, before going on to 229 OCU at Chivenor and Hawker Hunters. From 1958 to 1960 he served with 4 Squadron at Jever, West Germany, the unit converting from Hunter F.4s to F.6s. He then trained as an instructor with CFS and taught at RAF College, Cranwell. He graduated from ETPS Course No.22 in 1963 at Farnborough after which he was posted to the Aero Flight at RAE Bedford (Thurleigh). Here he flew extensively, including helicopters and the experimental types of the day; for example: BAC 221, Fairey FD.2, Handley Page HP.115, Hunting 126 and Short SC.1. In November 1964 he had his first flight in Hawker P.1127 XP831 and became Aero Flight Project Pilot for the type – starting an association with the Harrier that would last to 1999.

I N his seminal 1985 book *Test Pilots*, Don Middleton singled out John Farley as follows: "It is, perhaps, quite invidious to compare one test pilot with another, but there can be no possible doubt that John Farley, with his engineering background and analytical, enquiring mind, is one of the finest in the world..." *This* author would like to add that John is also a superb writer, commanding the detail and procedure one would expect from an engineer, but equally superbly capable of creating the most engaging and characterful prose via his many magazine articles and his book *A View from the Hover*. More will be written about John in Volume Two in the chapter dealing with demonstration and airshow flying.

Flt Lt John Farley AFC joined Hawker Siddeley (HS) at Dunsfold in 1967, working initially for Hugh Merewether* and, from 1970, for Duncan Simpson*. Testing centred on getting the HS Harrier ready for its service entry into the RAF, which took place in the spring of 1969. Prior to that USAF pilot Major Chuck Rosburg was killed in Harrier GR.1 XV743 at Dunsfold on 27th January 1969. The Harrier had entered an uncontrollable roll during a turn in transition from vertical take-off. John was involved in many hours of trials to establish how this occurred and how to counter it. The USMC became the first export customer for the Harrier and in the summer of 1969 John demonstrated the type at Norfolk, Virginia, USA. As will be detailed in Volume Two, this was the first of many overseas 'deployments' to potential purchasers by John, a lot of them involving the company two-seat demonstrator, Harrier Mk.52 G-VTOL. As well as weapon trials, for example the Martel anti-ship missile, John was also heavily involved in the development of the ski-jump (or ramp) launch technique, pioneered at RAE Thurleigh during August and September 1977 using GR.1 XV281 and G-VTOL.

In the hands of A&AEE, Sea Harrier FRS.1 prototype XZ450 during trials on HMS *Hermes*, October-November 1979. Behind is the Flight Systems Bedford Harrier T.2 XW175 – see Chapter Five. *Rolls-Royce*

Hawker Siddeley became part of British Aerospace (BAe) in 1977. The following year John succeeded Duncan Simpson as CTP and was at the helm of the last purely British fighter to enter production, the Sea Harrier. (Take a look at the EAP, described in the section on David Eagles, this was also described as the last of the kind, but of course remained a one-off.) To underline that test piloting was never a Monday to Friday job, John first flew FRS.1 XZ450 on Sunday 20th August 1978. In *A View from the Hover*, he described XZ450 as: "...no run of the mill Sea Harrier. It was the first one to fly, the first one displayed in public, the first one up the ski-jump, the first fully equipped to fire Sea Eagle [missiles] and the first one shot down during the Falklands War." On 30th August John took XZ450 into the air via the ski-jump installed at RAE Farnborough and then displayed it at the SBAC airshow the following month, again using the ski-jump. (Assigned to 800 Squadron, XZ450 'went south' on HMS *Hermes* on 5th April 1982. Piloted by Lt Nick Taylor and armed with cluster bombs, XZ450 was hit by anti-aircraft fire on 4th May and he was killed when XZ450 crashed near Goose Green.)

In November 1979 John got his first experience of the second generation Harrier, the McDonnell Douglas-led AV-8B, which led to the RAF Harrier GR.5 and subsequent developments. Two Dunsfold-built AV-8A Harriers were rebuilt at St Louis, Missouri, USA, to interim YAV-8B status, the first of which, 158394, flew on 9th November 1978. John tried out a YAV-8B in November the following year. As the Falklands crisis kicked off in April 1982 John was in the USA carrying out engine trials on the second prototype AV-8B Harrier II, 161397. From 1974 the

Harrier had been joined by another success story at Dunsfold, the Hawk trainer. During John's time as CTP he concentrated on the Harrier, entrusting the Hawk workload to his DCTP Andy Jones* along with Jim Hawkins* and Chris Roberts*.

Having reached 50, the age at which BAe then retired its military test pilots, in 1983 John handed over to Andy Jones. John took on a new role, as manager of Dunsfold airfield, later moving to Kingston-upon-Thames in what was termed the 'special ops office'. He left BAe in April 1990 and for the next decade worked as freelance test pilot, aviation consultant and chartered engineer. He'd flown 60-plus types up to this point and his new venture allowed him to sample another 20. Among these, John was the first western test pilot to fly the Mikoyan MiG-29 *Fulcrum*, others included the McDonnell Douglas T-45 Goshawk, the navalised version of the Hawk and the Israeli Aircraft Industries Lavi fighter prototype. From 1992, John was test pilot for FLS Aerospace, succeeding Neville Duke, continuing development of the Optica. Another interesting task was in Indonesia flying a locally-built Airtech CN.235 twin turboprop transport to gain data for a simulator for Merpati Nusantara Airlines. In 1999 John re-acquainted himself with the Harrier, piloting the VAAC-configured T.2 XW175 – see Chapter Five. Throughout this time, John was writing regularly for the magazine *Flyer*, among other commissions. In 2008 he wrote the fabulously readable *A View from the Hover – My Life in Aviation* which went to a second edition two years later. Now living on the south coast, John Frederick Farley OBE AFC is busy perfecting the third edition.

The Harrier most associated with John Farley, Mk.52 demonstrator G-VTOL, taxying out at the Farnborough display September 1980. *KEC*

Cecil 'Fluffy' Feather

11 Aug 1937	BP Defiant K8310
	1 x 1,030hp RR Merlin I
early 1941	BP P92/2 V3142
	2 x 130hp DH Gipsy Major II

CECIL FEATHER joined the RAF in March 1924, initially serving in the Middle East. By the early 1930s he was a Flight Lieutenant with 15 Squadron at Martlesham Heath; the unit acting as an armament testing flight within A&AEE. In 1936 Boulton Paul (BP) was busy relocating from Mousehold, Norwich, to Pendeford, Wolverhampton. The company's CTP, Cecil Rea*, did not wish to migrate and 'Fluffy' Feather was appointed as the CTP on 1st July 1936. (Although in late 1934 he carried out tests on the P.71A biplane airliner, G-ACOY, probably from Mousehold.) BP built Hawker Demons for the RAF, and Cecil Feather piloted the first example off the Mousehold line, K5683, on 21st August 1936. At Pendeford, the prototype Defiant turret fighter was ready during the summer of 1937, but its four-gun, powered-assisted turret was not. To keep the programme moving, K8310 was fitted with a fairing in place of the turret and flown by Cecil for the first time on 11th August 1937. It was then sent for interim assessment by A&AEE, and the turret was fitted by February 1938. As well as mass production of Defiants, the Pendeford factory was also manufacturing the turreted version of the Blackburn Skua dive-bomber, the Roc. Blackburn had enough

on its plate building Skuas and Bothas and, as the turret supplier, BP was ideally placed. The first Roc, L3057, was flown at Pendeford by Blackburn CTP Hugh Wilson* in December 1938 but after that all testing was carried out under Cecil. Beyond Defiants and Rocs, the factory built Fairey Barracudas, with Cecil's team air testing them.

BP's adherence to the turret fight concept was taken to the ultimate with its P.92 design, aimed at Specification F1/37 for a twin-engined, long-range escort fighter. Buried within the centre section was a cluster of four 20mm cannon, only the barrels of which would protrude from a dome-shaped cupola. Like the Defiant and the Roc, the idea of the P.92 was to provide concentrated firepower from a fast, reasonably manoeuvrable platform. The turret allowed the fighter to approach targets from unconventional angles: indeed the favoured tactic was to fly alongside a bomber stream, broadsiding the enemy. A half-scale test-bed was approved and, with the Pendeford factory at capacity and BP no longer a company skilled in wooden construction, the P92/2 was sub-contracted to Heston Aircraft, under the local designation of JA.8. Cecil squeezed himself into the tiny cockpit of the one-off V3142 and carried out the maiden flight, from Heston, in early 1941. By then the P92/2 was of academic interest only, the P.92 project having been axed in March 1940. Despite some combat successes, particularly at night, the Defiant had also proved to be a flawed fighter. Flt Lt Cecil Feather retired as BP's CTP on 22nd September 1945, his place being taken by Lindsay Neale*.

Cramped in the cockpit, the pilot provides scale in this view of the P92/2 during its time at A&AEE, August 1943. The 'hump' fairing for the turret is evident. *Les Whitehouse-Boulton Paul Association*

The prototype Defiant, K8310, with gun turret, at Pendeford, 1938. *Boulton Paul*

Robert Fenwick

29 Nov 1910	Planes Ltd Biplane 1 x 60hp Green
15 Jul 1911	HP Type D Monoplane 1 x 50hp Isaacson
cAug 1912	Mersey Monoplane 1 x 45hp Isaacson

Robert Cooke Fenwick was very probably the first British test pilot to perish while trialling an aircraft. The Mersey Monoplane, which he had designed, crashed on its third flight: he was the sixteenth British pilot fatality. The second to die in a UK flying accident was Cecil Grace*, the man determined in Chapter One to be the 'founder' British test pilot. Grace was lost over the North Sea on 22nd December 1910 while attempting to cross to the Continent, but that was not a testing sortie.

In 1909 W P Thompson of Freshfield, up the Mersey coast from Liverpool, patented what he called a 'pendulum-stability' biplane with all of the weight as close to the centre of gravity possible. He commissioned Frederick Handley Page to build it, at the latter's Barking workshop. The machine was damaged on its first outing, and was then wrecked when part of the workshop fell on it during a gale. 'HP' seems to have had very little time for it, naming it *The Scrapheap*. Thompson's assistant, Robert Fenwick, was sent south the retrieve it and it was dispatched by rail to Liverpool. Re-thought and rebuilt, the Planes Ltd Biplane, piloted by Robert carried out a 'straight' at Freshfield and later circuits in November 1910. This qualified Robert for Aviators' Certificate No.35.

Robert had caught 'HP's eye and he returned to Barking, becoming the great man's first test pilot. The Handley Page Type D monoplane, powered by a 35hp Green, was ready to fly immediately after its appearance at the Aero Show at Olympia, London, in April 1911. Trials at Fairlop were unsuccessful and a 50hp Isaacson was fitted while 'HP' entered it and Robert for the *Daily Mail* 'Circuit of Britain' contest, to be staged in July 1911. The Type D flew from Fairlop just before the competition was to start, but it crashed on landing and 'HP' sacked Robert on the spot! Frederick's next test pilots were the Petre* brothers, Edward and Henry. Later in 1911 Robert was working for Vickers at Brooklands, involved with Vickers-REP Monoplane testing. While demonstrating the ability of one of these to take a passenger for a potential customer, Robert engaged in a sharp climb out, turned and span in; he and Lt H E Watkins were shaken but otherwise intact.

Along with Sydney T Swaby, Robert founded the Mersey Aeroplane Company and he set about building a monoplane to meet the requirements of the Military Trials to be staged on Salisbury Plain in August 1912. The Mersey Monoplane was a radical design, with a 45hp Isaacson in the nose, driving a *pusher* propeller via an extension shaft. The tailplane was mounted on twin booms projecting from the pod-like fuselage. With the competition number '19' painted on its rudder, Robert successfully flew the Mersey Monoplane on 9th and 10th August 1912 at Salisbury Plain. In his *History of British Aviation 1908-1914*, R Dallas Brett described the flight of the

13th: "The aircraft had reached a point about a mile and a half from the sheds when it was seen to dive, recover for a moment, and then drop into an over-the-vertical dive in which it hit the ground. Mr R C Fenwick was killed instantaneously."

Tim Ferguson

Timothy Maynard Scott Ferguson, born 1932. Electronics apprenticeship at Marconi in Edinburgh, before joining the RAF in 1950. After his RAF service he returned to Marconi and flew within the RAFVR with 603 (City of Edinburgh) Squadron RAuxAF on DH Vampire FB.5s from Turnhouse.

Running from Preston to Blackpool, the M55 motorway carries all sorts of traffic, but on 26th April 1975 it witnessed its fastest-ever 'vehicle': Tim Ferguson was 'driving' a local product, SEPECAT Jaguar GR.1 XX109. The M55 was shortly to open and the opportunity to prove that such an 'improvised' airstrip could be used by the Jaguar was too good to miss. Tim, who had converted to the Jaguar at Warton in October 1969, used the westbound carriageway and landed XX109 amid a phalanx of the press and plenty of public, many of whom had trudged a long way across fields to witness the event. In a 'bombing-up' demonstration, XX109 was fitted with a quartet of dummy bombs and then Tim took off, running under a bridge then over the B5260 at Weeton and took off, returning to Warton.

Tim joined English Electric as a PTP in January 1955, initially on Canberras, then Lightnings. He maintained his RAuxAF links, joining 613 (City of Manchester) Squadron at Ringway on DH Vampire FB.5s and '9s until the 'Auxiliaries' were stood down in March 1957. In 1959 he was appointed as Senior PTP and in 1967 became Chief PTP. With the retirement of Don Knight* in January 1968, Tim was promoted to DCTP. He was the 'back-seater' on the first flight of Panavia Tornado P.03 XX947 on 5th August 1975, with David Eagles* in command. Tim retired from test flying in 1979, taking up a position in the product support organisation. He died in 1997.

Pat Fillingham

22 May 1946	DHC Chipmunk CF-DIO-X 1 x 140hp DH Gipsy Major 1C

William Patrick Ingram Fillingham, born 1914. Studied at the de Havilland Aeronautical Technical School, Hatfield. Learned to fly at 11 RFS, Perth, gaining his 'wings' in November 1938. Graduated as an aeronautical engineer in 1939.

In late 1939 Pat Fillingham joined de Havilland (DH) at Hatfield as a PTP, initially on Tiger Moths. He had been appointed Chief PTP by September 1942 and was heavily engaged on clearing Mosquitos and, from late 1944, Hornets. He travelled to Australia and Canada as part of a team helping set up production with DH associate companies at Bankstown, Sydney, New South Wales and Downsview, Toronto, respectively. Later in his career, Pat was to 'keep his hand in' on the Mosquito, flying T.3 RR299 which was maintained by DH, and from 1963, Hawker Siddeley for heritage flying.

Pat Fillingham carried out the first flight of the prototype DHC Chipmunk, CF-DIO-X, at Downsview, Canada, on 22nd May 1946. *DH*

Pat returned to Downsview in 1946 to take charge of the testing of the first aircraft entirely designed by de Havilland Canada – the DHC.1 Chipmunk – which he first flew in May 1946. Conceived by Polish-born Wsiewołod J Jakimiuk, the Chipmunk was aimed at requirements for both the RCAF and RAF to replace the Tiger Moth. He maintained his connections with the 'Chippy', piloting G-AKDN to victory in the 1953 King's Cup air race, staged out of Southend, at a speed of 142.0mph. Post-war production and testing at Hatfield included Doves, Herons, Vampires, Venoms, Comets and Tridents. By the Trident era, Pat was Hawker Siddeley's DCTP at Hatfield. Pat was one of the pilots that ferried DH Comet 4 G-APDB to Duxford to join the airliner collection of the Duxford Aviation Society, on 12th February 1974. He retired in 1975, having 'clocked' nearly 12,000 flying hours on 120 types. William Patrick Ingram Fillingham died in 2003, aged 89.

Charles Flood

Gp Capt Charles G P Flood joined Blackburn at Brough as CTP in May 1947, taking over from Arthur Thompson*. The bulk of the work was with the Firebrand torpedo-fighter and Charles flew the bulky machine in the air races at Lympne in August 1947, piloting TF.5 EK850 to second place at 310mph. Under development was the B.48 (or YA.1) naval strike fighter, RT651, but it fell to Pete Lawrence*, deputy to Charles, to carry out the maiden flight in April 1947. Charles displayed RT651 at the September 1947 SBAC airshow at Farnborough. He left Blackburn in March 1948 and was succeeded by Pete Lawrence.

Ian Forbes

| 31 Mar 1957 | Miles HDM.105 G-35-3 |
| | 2 x 155hp Blackburn Cirrus Major III |

Ian A Forbes worked for F G Miles Ltd, established at Redhill in 1951, following the collapse of Miles Aircraft at Woodley in 1947. Fred Miles* and George Miles* headed up the company which was involved in design, consultancy and a range of non-aviation activities. Ian was sales manager for the company, but was also involved in test flying. Fred Miles devised a more powerful version of the Gemini, known as the Aries, with a pair 155hp Blackburn Cirrus Major IIIs. Wearing the 'B Condition' ('trade plate') markings G-35-1, the first Aries was flown by Ian in February 1951 from Redhill and later registered as G-AMDJ. Only one other Aries was built, G-AOGA, in 1956.

In 1955 George Miles entered into negotiations with the Hurel-Dubois of Villacoublay, south west of Paris, France, regarding that company's development of ultra-high aspect ratio wings. In a piece of classic Miles thinking, it was decided to build a test-bed to evaluate the wing and acquired 1947-built Miles Aerovan G-AJOF in 1955 for the purpose. An Anglo-French company, H D et M (Aviation) Ltd was set up, with Hurel-Dubois conducting the initial design, while F G Miles Ltd built the wings, carried out the conversion and undertook flight test. The Aerovan had a span of 50ft, but the new machine designated HDM.105, stretched out to 75ft 4in. Ian took the test-bed for its maiden flight, with the trade plate marking G-35-3, from Shoreham in March 1957. (Later the HDM.105 wore the appropriate registration G-AHDM, previously allocated to a Handley Page Halton in 1946.) *Delta-Mike* was written off in a landing accident at Shoreham in June 1958. The rights to the design studies were sold to Shorts and they provided background for the Skyvan project of 1963.

The one-off Miles HDM.105 high aspect ratio wing test-bed, 1957. *F G Miles Ltd*

Ken Forbes

Kenneth Burton Forbes, joined the RAF in January 1941 and trained in the USA. Majority of his operational flying was with photo-reconnaissance Supermarine Spitfires and from 1944 to 1945 he served as a ferry pilot. Post-war he flew for British European Airways and then for Sivewright Airways, the latter based at Ringway.

FLT LT KEN FORBES DFM joined Fairey Aviation at Ringway in April 1951, working for Senior TP David Masters*. Tasks involved testing late marks of Firefly and Fairey-assembled Vampires and Venoms for de Havilland. On 22nd February 1954 Ken was piloting Fairey-built Venom FB.1 WK390 on a sortie out of Ringway. The aircraft is believed to have broken up at low altitude; Ken was killed when the jet impacted at Coclins Farm, near Caverswall, Staffordshire.

Eric 'Frankie' Franklin

13 Nov 1947	AW AW.52 TS363 2 x 5,000lbst RR Nene
10 Apr 1949	AW Apollo VX220 4 x 1,135shp AS Mamba
31 May 1950	Gloster Meteor NF.11 WA546 2 x 3,700lbst RR Derwent 8
10 Feb 1954	Gloster Meteor F.8 prone-pilot WK935 2 x 3,600lbst RR Derwent 8
8 Jan 1959	AW Argosy 100 G-AOZZ 4 x 2,020shp RR Dart 526

Notes: AW.52 flown from Boscombe Down; Apollo and NF.11 from Baginton; prone-pilot F.8 took off from Baginton, landed at Bitteswell; Argosy flew from Bitteswell.

Eric George Franklin, born 1920. Took up an apprenticeship with Armstrong Whitworth (AW) in 1937. Learned to fly at Leamington Aero Club, 1939 and joined RAFVR that year. Trained for bombers and was first posted to 78 Squadron on, appropriately, AW Whitleys. Posted to 35 Squadron on Handley Page Halifax Is and IIs at Linton-on-Ouse. Later became an instructor on Conversion Flights at Linton, Leconfield and Marston Moor. Captaining a training exercise with 35 Squadron's Conversion Flight at Linton on 16th April 1942, Flt Lt Franklin was conducting engine-out circuits in Halifax II R9425 when the undercarriage and flaps failed to tuck up during a go-around. Eric attempted to restart the fourth Merlin, but the sink rate was too much and it force landed. Eric and four others on board were OK; R9425 was a write-off.

IN late 1942 Sqn Ldr Eric 'Frankie' Franklin DFC AFC was 'rested', becoming a PTP on Handley Page (HP) Halifaxes. This *may* have been at Rawcliffe, Yorks, and the HP-operated Yorkshire Aircraft Repair depot (known as 'the YARD'). He was posted to A&AEE at Boscombe Down, joining 'B' Squadron before opting for a second tour of 'ops' and returning to 35 Squadron, by then part of the Pathfinder Force at Graveley. He was back with A&AEE by early 1944 and graduated from No.2 Course ETPS there, 1944-1945. Eric was posted to Armstrong Whitworth (AW) as a PTP in April 1945, working initially under Charles Turner-Hughes* and then Ronald Midgley* at Baginton and Bitteswell. Testing involved Lancasters and then Lincolns built for Avro, followed by a long association with Gloster Meteors.

After Eric Franklin had ferried the AW.52 TS363 from Boscombe Down to Bitteswell in December 1947, the press were allowed a close inspection. *Armstrong Whitworth*

The Apollo prototype first appeared in military guise, as VX220. *Armstrong Siddeley*

The major project at time was the AW.52 flying-wing which could trace its roots back to 1942. Eric was introduced to the programme via the AW.52G glider and, promoted to Senior TP at the age of 27, was responsible for the first flight of the full-scale jet version. Two prototypes were constructed, TS363 with Roll-Royce Nenes and TS368 with RR Derwents. Both were two-seaters, but only the pilots had Martin-Baker ejection seats. The Nene-powered TS363 was taken by road to Boscombe Down and Eric took it for its maiden flight on 13th November 1947 – a very challenging type for the 27-year-old's inaugural 'first'. Eric ferried TS363 to Bitteswell on 1st December to begin exploring its characteristics. The second AW.52, TS368, Eric flew from Bitteswell on 1st September 1948 and both machines appeared at the SBAC airshow at Farnborough that month. Trials of the AW.52 did not meet expectations and in May 1949 TS363 crashed – see 'Jo'

Lancaster – so the programme was quietly shelved, with TS368 joining the RAE at Farnborough.

Eric was promoted to CTP in 1948 and his next prototype was of more traditional layout but for its day still radical, the four-turboprop Apollo airliner. Designed to meet a Brabazon Committee requirement for post-war transports, the Apollo was a 30-passenger medium range airliner. When Eric took the prototype, initially with military serial VX220 (later G-AIYN), into the air at Baginton in April 1949 it was already ten months behind Vickers and its Viscount. The second Apollo, VX224 (later G-AMCH) flew on 12th December 1952 by which time Vickers were building Viscount 701s for British European Airways and attracting orders from all over the world. Funded by the Ministry of Supply, the two Apollos were passed on to test establishments and another AW programme ground to a halt.

Armstrong Whitworth had plenty of work in hand for other concerns within the Hawker Siddeley Group. As noted earlier, Lancasters and Lincolns gave way to Meteor F.4s and then F.8s and from August 1952 all testing was centred at Bitteswell. In June 1951 the specially-modified Reid & Sigrist Bobsleigh (see A G Bullmore) had begun prone-pilot experimentation and AW was given a contract to transform a Meteor F.8 into a high-speed research platform to further such research. Eric flew WK935 out of Baginton on 10th February 1954, completing the sortie at Bitteswell. WK935 – the longest-ever Meteor – was handed on to the RAE at Farnborough in August 1954. (Today it is preserved at the RAF Museum Cosford.) With Gloster deeply involved in the Javelin fighter, AW was given design responsibility for night-fighter versions of the Meteor. The first of these was the NF.11 and Eric piloted the prototype, WA546, from Baginton in May 1950 and the first production example, WD585, having its debut at Bitteswell on 14th November 1950.

Meteor work kept Bitteswell busy through to mid-1954, by which time Hawker Sea Hawks and Hunters were also swelling the production lines and Javelins followed from early

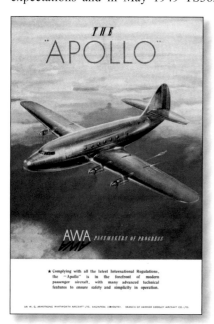

With flying wings and turboprop airliners, Armstrong Whitworth chose the phrase 'Pacemakers of Progress' to sum up the firm's capabilities – a 1947 advert.

The prone-pilot Meteor on flight test from Bitteswell. *Armstrong Whitworth*

With Eric Franklin at the controls, the prototype Argosy, G-AOZZ, trundles off the snow-cleared runway at Bitteswell, on its maiden flight, 8th January 1959. *Armstrong Whitworth*

1956. Eric and his team had plenty to keep them occupied. Meanwhile AW had conceived another four-turboprop transport, the Argosy, aimed at the civilian freighter market and an RAF requirement to replace the venerable Vickers Valetta. At a snow-covered Bitteswell on 8th January 1959 the prototype Argosy, G-AOZZ, was ready to go. Eric captained *Zulu-Zulu*, with his deputy, Bill Else* as co-pilot, Roy Hadley as FTO and Kenneth Oldfield as engineer. The 62-minute maiden flight was uneventful and the Argosy went into production, the last one flying in November 1966 by which time the AW 'brand' had given way to Hawker Siddeley. Eric was Bitteswell's last CTP and by 1967 he was at Woodford instructing on HS.748s. He retired from flying in 1975, at which point Sqn Ldr Eric George Franklin OBE DFC AFC had over 9,000 hours and 100 types in his logbooks and 30 years of test piloting experience.

C F French

9 Jul 1945	R&S Desford G-AGOS
	2 x 130hp DH Gipsy Major 1

UNDER A G Bullmore, the prone-pilot conversion of the Reid & Sigrist Desford, the Bobsleigh, was outlined. The RS.3 Desford was the first, and last, aircraft project to see the light of day at R&S. It was intended to bring the concept of a twin-engined trainer as pioneered by the company's pre-war RS.1 Snargasher (see George Lowdell) up to date. Named after

the airfield where it was built, Desford G-AGOS was first flown by R&S CTP C F French on 9th July 1945. Along with J A Hart, French carried out testing and demonstrations of the type. G-AGOS appeared at the 1947 and 1947 SBAC airshows at Radlett. With plenty of war surplus advanced trainers available and its 'tail-dragger' layout dating the Desford somewhat, it was destined to remain a one-off.

A 1946 Reid & Sigrist advert for the Desford in its original configuration.

Harrier Mk.52 G-VTOL during mock-up Skyhook trials at Dunsfold, April 1985. G-VTOL is preserved at the Brooklands Museum. *British Aerospace*

Heinz Frick

Heinz Erwin Frick, born 1940 in Switzerland, moving to the UK aged 12. Joined the RAF in 1959; his first operational posting was 20 Squadron at Tengah, Singapore, on Hawker Hunter FGA.9s. On 21st April 1964, XG293 suffered asymmetric flap deployment and entered a spin, at 5,000ft Heinz elected to eject; he suffered crushed vertebrae and was hospitalised for a while. Heinz relates that the Straits Times *reported that he was saved because he had "ejaculated into a swamp"! Converting to the EE Lightning, Heinz flew F.6s with 74 Squadron at Leuchars and 5 Squadron at Binbrook. He graduated from Course No.27 ETPS at Boscombe Down in 1968 and was posted to A&AEE. By 1971 Heinz had joined the Rolls-Royce flight test team at Filton and, among others, flew the Avro Vulcan RB.199 and Vickers VC-10 RB.211 test-beds.*

WITH the closure of the Rolls-Royce test facility at Filton in 1978, Flt Lt Heinz Erwin Frick AFC took up the offer of British Aerospace CTP Dunsfold's John Farley* to join him. Work at Dunsfold was varied including: helping to perfect the smoke system on the HS Hawks of the 'Red Arrows', Sea Harrier testing and demonstration; AV-8B Harrier II engine trials at Edwards Air Force Base, California, USA, and Harrier GR.5 weapons trials. In 1986 Heinz was promoted to DCTP and in 1988 he became CTP, taking over from Mike Snelling*. Heinz gained two world time-to-height records on 14th August 1989, flying Harrier GR.5 ZD402 fitted with a Pegasus 11-61. He flew to 6,000m (19,685ft) in 55.38 seconds and to 12,000m in 126.63 seconds.

Heinz is most associated with the Skyhook system, which he invented to increase the number of vessels that could operate the Sea Harrier, increase the number of aircraft a ship could accommodate and improve the fighter's range. The concept was to 'capture' a hovering Harrier using a specially-modified crane with a 'grab' that would secure the fighter from above at the centre section. The aircraft could then be 'parked' on a trolley and manoeuvred into a hangar deck. It was entirely possible, using Skyhook, to have Harriers without undercarriage, saving on complexity and weight and hence increase range. Using the two-seat demonstrator Harrier, Mk.52 G-VTOL, BAe carried out feasibility trials, but nothing further came of the project. Heinz retired from test piloting in 1990, with Chris Roberts* taking on as CTP at Dunsfold. Heinz took up a post with Boeing 737 and 757-equipped Air Europe, but the Gatwick-based airline ceased operations the following year. He moved on to fly corporate jets in Europe and the Middle East and then worked for a fixed-wing air ambulance operation bringing patients long distance to the UK. Dunsfold closed in 1999 and shortly before it did, Heinz carried out the first flight of Isaacs Fury II single-seat homebuilt biplane G-BZAS, which he helped build and part-owned. Heinz claims this as the last test flight at the famous airfield. By 2012 he had a share in a glider.

Frank Furlong

Having previously served in the Army, Frank Furlong worked with his father, horse trainer and owner Noel Furlong, as a jockey. Frank won the 1935 Grand National at Aintree, Liverpool, on Noel's horse Reynoldstown. Frank learned to fly privately and joined the Fleet Air Arm by 1940. Initially, he flew Fairey Fulmars, at first from HMS Illustrious *in the Mediterranean and the Indian Ocean. In May 1941 he transferred to HMS* Victorious *and 800Z Flight and took part in the hunt for the German battleship* Bismarck *in the Atlantic. On 25th May three Fulmars took off from* Victorious *in a sweep to try and find the enemy warship. Only one of the fighters returned. It transpired that two had been forced to ditch after running short of fuel. The crew of one of these Fulmars perished, but Lt Frank Furlong and Sqn Ldr J E M Hoare took to a dinghy and miraculously, after 36 hours, they were rescued by the SS* Braverhill. *With 881 Squadron at Donibristle, Scotland, on 21st December 1942, Frank ditched again, this time in Grumman Martlet II AJ120, but was swiftly back in action. (The Martlet was the original British name for the Wildcat, in January 1944, the latter name was adopted.)*

LT FRANK FURLONG RNVR was recruited by Supermarine CTP Jeffrey Quill* and he became his deputy at the test airfield of Worthy Down, and later High Post. In his magnificent *Spitfire – A Test Pilot's Story*, Jeffrey describes

Frank as: "almost as good a test pilot as he was a steeplechase jockey." An early task for Frank was to take over testing the first production Spitfire XIV, RB140. Frank later shared the work on the Spiteful prototype, NN660, with Jeffrey. A sortie out of High Post in NN660 on 13th September 1944 is described by Jeffrey: "[Frank] was returning to the circuit in NN660 and encountered Philip Wigley in a Spitfire XIV; the two began to 'mix it' in a mock dogfight. When both were at a fairly low height and pulling 'g', Frank flicked the Spiteful over on to its back. Before he could recover, he had hit the ground close to the airfield and was killed instantly." Jeffrey wrote that Frank had become a close friend and that the tragedy hit him badly. He was convinced that the cause of the accident was nothing simple, such as Frank paying more attention to his 'foe' instead of the airspeed. Soon Jeffrey had found what he believed was the cause of Frank's demise. When testing Spiteful NN664 in a high 'g' turn he discovered that the ailerons had jammed; Jeffrey eased off the turn and gave the stick a wallop, clearing the jam. The ailerons were activated by solid rods and it was found they could be prone to sticking and a 'fix' was instigated.

Peter Garner

Peter J Garner flew with the Merchant Ship Fighter Unit, on escort for convoys from catapult-equipped vessels. Launched in a Hurricane, at the end of the intercept sortie the pilot would bale out or ditch and – hopefully – be recovered to his ship. His next posting was with the Admiralty for deck landing trials. In 1943 he joined 603 Squadron flying DH Mosquito VIs on intruder operations. After three tours he moved to Fighter Command HQ as an intruder controller.

Sqn Ldr Peter Garner was recruited by Westland CTP Harald Penrose* as his assistant in 1945 and he was involved in testing Yeovil-built Supermarine Seafires, Welkin development trials and Westland-Sikorsky Dragonfly demonstrations. He graduated from ETPS Course No.4 at Cranfield in 1946 and returned to Yeovil ready for the new Westland programme, the Wyvern shipborne torpedo-fighter. Harald flew the prototype, TS371, powered by a 3,500hp Rolls-Royce Eagle piston engine, on 16th December 1946. This machine was somewhat basic: it carried no arrester hook, the wings did not fold, and it lacked the intended ejection seat.

On 15th October 1947 among the tasks the Yeovil flight test team had for the day was an air-to-air photographic session for *Flight* magazine; its photographer John Yoxall, having arranged for a Fairey Firefly from nearby Yeovilton to act as a camera-ship. In his autobiography *Adventure with Fate*, Harald poignantly noted that he and Peter tossed a coin for it. Peter won, declaring "I'd like to get my name in the papers". After the 'shoot' was complete, Peter reported that the forward propeller of the contra-rotating unit had detached and shortly afterwards announced that he was making a forced landing. TS371 came down near Cerne Abbas in Dorset and caught fire: Sqn Ldr Peter J Garner was killed. Post-accident analysis discovered that a propeller bearing had failed; Peter must have elected to bring the all-important prototype 'home' other than

attempt a bale out. Two days prior to the sortie, the Ministry of Supply had decreed that it no longer wanted the Eagle as a powerplant option for the Wyvern, preferring the Rolls-Royce Clyde turboprop. *Flight's* issue for 23rd October 1947 published the first air-to-air images of the new Wyvern: "as a last tribute to a test pilot of quite exceptional calibre."

Ron Gellatly

14 Aug 1955	Fairey Ultra-Light XJ924 1 x 252shp Turboméca Palouste BnPe2
6 Nov 1957	Fairey Rotodyne XE521 2 x 2,800shp Napier Eland N.El.7
28 Oct 1962	Westland Wasp HAS.1 XS463 1 x 1,050shp BS Nimbus 103
21 Mar 1971	Westland Lynx XW835 2 x 700shp BS Gem 2

Notes: Ultra-Light and Rotodyne flown from White Waltham; Wasp and Lynx from Yeovil.

Wilfred Ronald Gellatly, born 1920 in New Zealand. Joined the RNZAF in 1940 and from 1942 he flew Avro Ansons and Lockheed Hudsons on coastal patrol. Transferring to the RAF, he went on to command 293 Squadron with Vickers Warwicks in Italy. Ron took a permanent commission in the RAF in 1947 and graduated from ETPS Course No.9 at Farnborough in 1950. From 1951 to 1954 Ron was OC 'D' Squadron A&AEE Boscombe Down. In 1954 Ron taught Tom Brooke-Smith* of Shorts to fly helicopters, in readiness for his flying the SC.1 VTOL test-bed.

Sqn Ldr Ron Gellatly afc joined Fairey Aviation in 1954, taking charge of the company's rotorcraft projects, taking on John Morton* as his deputy. The twin-turbine Rotodyne high-capacity compound helicopter (or convertiplane) was the major project on the horizon, but in between was the Ultra-Light Helicopter. With its pioneering for the Gyrodyne (see Basil Arkell) and the Jet Gyrodyne (see John Dennis), Fairey was

Bearded John Morton, Ron Gellatly's deputy flying G-APJJ, the sixth and last Fairey Ultra-Light Helicopter. *Blackburn*

The impressive Fairey Rotodyne, XE521, hovering at White Waltham, 1958.
Fairey

Despite an impressive advertising campaign, the Rotodyne failed to attract purchasers.

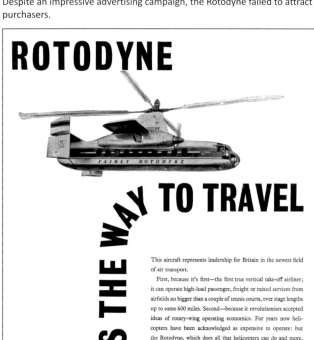

ROTODYNE

THIS IS THE WAY TO TRAVEL

This aircraft represents leadership for Britain in the newest field of air transport.

First, because it's first—the first true vertical take-off airliner; it can operate high-load passenger, freight or mixed services from airfields no bigger than a couple of tennis courts, over stage lengths up to some 600 miles. Second—because it revolutionises accepted ideas of rotary-wing operating economics. For years now helicopters have been acknowledged as expensive to operate: but the Rotodyne, which does all that helicopters can do and more, is not a helicopter—and *is* a sound economic proposition.

Third, the Rotodyne is the world's *fastest* rotary-wing aircraft, and holds a new world record to prove it. The Rotodyne's great superiority in speed—and in safety—is an important factor in its operational effectiveness.

In the Fairey Rotodyne we see the promise of tomorrow's airbus systems. Air travel everyday, everywhere. Look forward to Rotodyne travel!

FAIREY FAIREY AVIATION LTD · HAYES · MIDDLESEX

A Subsidiary of The Fairey Company Limited

act as a compressor driving 'jets' in the rotor tips and provide a degree of thrust. Ron flew the first of six prototypes at White Waltham on 14th August 1955; despite many trials and sustained demonstrations no sales, civil or military, were forthcoming.

The Rotodyne was make-or-break for Fairey's long-standing faith in compound rotorcraft technology. Using Napier Eland turboprops for the prototype, larger production examples would have standardised on the Rolls-Royce Tyne turboprop. Both Elands acted as a conventional propeller turbines mounted on stub wings wih a tip-to-tip span of 46ft 6in that would help generate half of the lift in forward flight. The Elands also created compressed air to drive the enormous 90ft diameter four-bladed rotor. The 58ft 8in long fuselage could seat 30 passengers, or accept freight via twin clam-shell doors in the rear, which also permitted use as a tactical military transport. Both Ron and John used the Jet Gyrodyne to familiarise themselves to fly the 33,000lb monster – the largest rotorcraft ever flown in the UK. After many months of ground runs and tethered 'hops', the pair took XE521 on its first untethered sortie at White Waltham on 6th November 1957. The test programme was always going to be a long process; it was not until April 1958 that the first transition from helicopter (rotor-borne) to compound (rotor-plus-wing lift, rotor plus jet efflux propulsion) flight was achieved. The Rotodyne was demonstrated at the 1958 SBAC airshow at Farnborough and again the following year. XE521 exceeded expectations in its performance and on 5th January 1959 Ron flew it to clinch the 100km close-circuit Class B.2 world airspeed record, at 190.7mph. En route to the Paris Salon at Le Bourget on 16th June 1959 XE521 was flown to the Allée Verte Heliport in Brussels, Belgium, and on to the Paris equivalent at Issy-les-Molineaux; a distance of 165 miles in 58 minutes, including the turn-around at Brussels. Early airline interest waned and the world's military remained unconvinced. Westland acquired Fairey's helicopter assets in February 1960 and two years later the Rotodyne programme was axed. XE521 had made 454 flights, 302 transitions in around 154 hours of flying time. (Major components of the centre section and rotor-head survive at The Helicopter Museum, Weston-super-Mare.)

successful in getting a development contract for a small helicopter capable of carrying out surveillance, training and casualty evacuation *yet* be small enough to be transported on the back of an Army three-tonner truck. A Palouste turbojet was modified to

Record-breaking Lynx AH.1 XX153 is displayed at the Museum of Army Flying, Middle Wallop. *MoAF*

Ron transferred to Westland at Yeovil in the spring of 1962, working for CTP 'Slim' Sear*. He was in command of the first pre-production Wasp HAS.1 shipboard anti-submarine helicopter in October 1962. Along with the Army version, the Scout, this was a development of the Saro-originated P.531 – see Ken Reed. In 1967 Ron became Westland's CTP, 'first flighting' another Westland success story, the prototype Lynx, in March 1971. As with the Scout/Wasp, the Lynx was offered in utility and naval versions and – as the Wildcat – is still in production today. Ron flew the pre-production Lynx AH.1 DB Utility XX153 on 20th June 1972 over a 15-25km closed-circuit course to raise the Class E.1 helicopter speed record to 199.9mph. Two days later, with his deputy Roy Moxam* at the helm, XX153 seized the 100km closed-circuit record. (XX153 is displayed at the Museum of Army Flying at Middle Wallop.) Ron retired as CTP in 1976, taking up a post in sales until retiring from Westland in January 1983. Sqn Ldr Wilfred Ronald Gellatly OBE AFC died later that year, aged 63.

'Wally' Gibb

Walter Frame Gibb, born 1919. Joined the Engine Division of Bristol Aeroplane at Filton as an apprentice in 1937. Enlisted in the RAF in 1940 and became an instructor. Posted to 264 Squadron in 1942, flying DH Mosquito IIs. In July 1943 he transferred to 605 Squadron, with Mosquito VIs on intruder sorties. He was 'rested' from October 1943, first at the Empire Central Flying School at Hullavington where he flew a wide range of types and then at 1692 Bomber Support Training Flight at Great Massingham, from July 1944. Next came 515 Squadron at Little Snoring with Mosquito VIs before joining 239 Squadron, as its CO, on Mosquito VIs and later Mk.30s, in September 1944. His combat career included 5½ victories, one each Focke-Wulf Fw 190, Heinkel He 219, Messerschmitt Bf 110 and 2½ Junkers Ju 88s. From July 1945 he served with the Telecommunications Flying Unit at Defford.

"WELL, my side's airborne – what about yours?" Oft-quoted words attributed to Bristol CTP 'Bill' Pegg* addressing his co-pilot, 'Wally' Gibb, on the maiden voyage of the huge Brabazon airliner on 4th September 1949. Pegg

A press release photo sent out to celebrate the new world height record set by 'Wally' Gibb and F M Piper in May 1953. Olympus-powered Canberra climbing out of Filton with the huge Brabazon hangar behind and a solitary Britannia to the left. *Bristol*

and Gibb were destined to be the only pilots of the abortive project. Wally's first flight as pilot-in-command was Brabazon G-AGPW's 13th sortie and there was a hydraulic failure that prevented the huge area of flaps from coming down. Wally landed back at Filton, engaging the reverse thrust on the eight engines, bringing it to a halt with space to spare.

Wg Cdr 'Wally' Gibb DSO DFC left the RAF in February 1946 and became a test pilot for Bristol at Filton and was appointed as Bill Pegg's deputy in January 1953. As has already been related, the 'airframe' airmen at Filton were often 'seconded' to the Engines Division. On 5th August 1952 English Electric Canberra B.2 WD952 had its maiden flight at Filton, having been converted to take a pair of Bristol Olympus turbojets limited to 8,000lbst each. With Wally piloting and F M Piper as FTO, on 4th May 1953 the pair took WD952 to a record height of 63,668ft. They had beaten the previous record by 4,222ft and that had also been set in an English Electric-built aircraft, a Vampire F.1, flown by John Cunningham* in March 1948.

Filton's last airliner was the Britannia, and Wally was heavily involved in its testing, development and demonstration. He was co-pilot on 22nd December 1953 when Bill Pegg made a two-engine forced-landing in the second prototype, G-ALRX. This episode, which could have ended in tragedy, is fully dealt with in Bill's section. Wally was flying the prototype Britannia, G-ALBO, in May 1954 and was undertaking stall tests, at height. Selecting flaps up, Wally found *Bravo-Oscar* buck and roll over, almost inverted. As the airliner plummeted downwards, control was regained and he made an emergency landing. The Britannia was destined for the hangars again, it had 'pulled' 3g and needed a thorough inspection; it had suffered asymmetric flap retraction. When asked how he had recovered, Wally explained that he reverted to training: "I undid the last action I made." The flaps fully deployed and the aircraft assumed a balanced flight profile.

Promoted to CTP in 1955, Wally retired from Filton's test flight office in 1960 with Godfrey Auty* succeeding him. Wally became BAC Product Support Manager at Filton and in 1978 was appointed as Managing Director and Chairman of British Aerospace Australia. Wg Cdr Walter 'Wally' F Gibb DSO DFC died on 4th October 2006, aged 87.

George Gibbins

GEORGE V GIBBINS illustrates the 'can do' attitude for recruitment at de Havilland: he was also part of one of the family tragedies. George joined de Havilland at Stag Lane in 1925 as an apprentice and became a service engineer, moving with the company to Hatfield. In 1937 he was picked to undertake training as a pilot and joined the flight test department. George flew as co-pilot with Geoffrey de Havilland JR* during development of the Albatross airliner and was with him during the first flight of the Flamingo prototype, G-AFUE, in December 1938 and throughout the type's testing. John de Havilland* was flying Mosquito FB.VI HJ734 with John H F Scorpe as FTO on 23rd August 143. George was up at the same time in Mk.VI HX897 accompanied by the company flight test foreman, G J 'Nick' Carter. The two aircraft collided at about 500ft, the shattered wreckage falling to the ground near St Albans; all four were killed.

Syd Gleave

Sydney Gleave, born 1905. A very keen motorcyclist, he set up his own business – Gleave Engineering – in Macclesfield building to his own design, including the SGS (Syd Gleave Special). Learned to fly and gained his pilot's licence in 1932. He set a new average speed record at the Isle of Man TT races of 71mph in 1933 – he held this until 1936. Syd was seriously injured in a motorcycle accident in 1935. During 1938 he joined the Civil Air Guard and in 1938 started training with the Fleet Air Arm. Aged 33, he was seconded from the FAA to the Air Transport Auxiliary.

IN 1942 Syd became a PTP with Avro at Woodford, mostly on Lancasters. On 11th September 1944 he and FTO Harry Barnes took off in Lancaster III PB579 for a standard dive test to establish terminal velocity figures. The fuel jettison pipes came away during the dive and they hit the tailplane and stripped the elevator skin. The Lancaster crashed near Alderley Edge, south west of Woodford; killing Syd and Harry.

Frank Goodden

Nov 1914	Royal A/c Factory FE.6 1 x 120hp Austro-Daimler
15 Oct 1915	Royal A/c Factory FE.8 7456 1 x 100hp Gnome
23 Jun 1915	Royal A/c Factory SE.4a 5610 1 x 80hp Gnome
14 Aug 1915	Royal A/c Factory BE.9 1700 1 x 90hp RAF 1a
Mar 1916	Royal A/c Factory FE.4 7993 2 x 140hp RAF 5a
17 Jun 1916	Royal A/c Factory RE.8 7996 1 x 140hp RAF 4a
22 Nov 1916	Royal A/c Factory SE.5 A4561 1 x 150hp Hispano-Suiza

Frank Widdenham Goodden, born 1889. During the summer of 1909 he regularly attended Lea Marshes in Essex to watch Alliott Verdon Roe as he attempted to fly his triplane. (Roe succeeded on 29th July 1909.) In 1910 Frank assisted Ernest Thompson Willows with his No.3 airship City of Cardiff and crewed for him on his epic flight from London to Paris – in stages! (At 19, Willows built his first airship, in 1905, and it flew well.) In 1912 Frank built his own monoplane at Wolvercote, Oxford, powered by a 35hp JAP, which he flew until 1913. (Some sources attribute this as a 'bitza' – an amalgamation of one or more wrecked machines.) At some stage during this period (1909-1913) he parachuted from balloons during exhibitions. Learning to fly at the Ewen School, Hendon, Frank qualified for Aviators' Certificate No.506 on 3rd June 1913, in a Caudron. He then worked for Claude Grahame-White at Hendon – sharing lodgings with Frank Courtney and Freddy Dunn*. Frank flew extensively during the events and displays at Hendon, in 1914 perfecting a night-time routine looping a Caudron fitted with lights and landing with the aid of petrol-laden cans acting as flares arranged along the landing ground.*

MERVYN O'GORMAN, Superintendent of the Royal Aircraft Factory, appointed Frank Goodden as a test pilot on 7th August 1914; three days after Britain declared war on Germany. Frank worked initially under CTP Ronald Kemp* before taking over as CTP. Frank's first 'first' was the FE.6 a pusher designed to take a Coventry Ordnance Works' one-pounder' gun in the podded fuselage. The tail surfaces were carried on a boom, which was attached via a bearing to the propeller shaft. On 14th

November 1914 (*possibly* the first flight) Frank landed it heavily, the damage was not repaired and the FE.6 was dismantled.

The FE.8, which Frank first flew in October 1915, was another pusher biplane again attempting to create a gun-toting single-seater fighter – or 'scout' in the vernacular of the day. Ironically, the most successful of this format was the DH.2, designed by former Royal Aircraft Factory test pilot/designer Geoffrey de Havilland for Airco. The first prototype FE.8, 7456, was dispatched to the Central Flying School at Upavon for acceptance trials and in mid-November 1915 was returned to Farnborough by the British pioneer of the loop and one-time test pilot 'Benny' Hucks*. He had the misfortune to write off 7456 on landing, perhaps in Frank's view, whose career had much in common with Benny's. In service, FE.8s gained a reputation to being prone to spinning, from which there was no escape. Knowledge of spinning was rudimentary and it was *the* manoeuvre that brought many pilots out into a cold sweat. On 23rd August 1916 Frank took an FE.8 up to deliberately spin it, and find how to recover. His report of his experiences should have helped to allay irrational fears and his methods are essentially those still taught to this day:

"At a height of 3,500ft I put on gradually all right rudder, and at the same time gradually pulled the control stick over to the left. In this way the aeroplane was turned to the right without any bank. When I had turned the machine in this manner for about 180-degrees the speed had dropped, due to the turn and the resistance of the fully-over rudder, and flaps, to near stalling speed. The nose of the aeroplane then went gradually down, due to the loss of speed. I next pulled back the control stick and this increased the turning speed, and when I had completed 300-degrees of turn the spinning suddenly started." The FE.8 did not have flaps; he was referring to ailerons; which were generous and on both top and bottom wings. He tried three spins to the left and three to the right and issued a life-saving three-point recovery procedure: switch off the engine; centre the stick and push it forward; centre the rudder. This put the aircraft into a dive and after speed built up it was a case of back on the stick and recover. Frank concluded: "I could only succeed in making the aeroplane spin by the misuse of the controls I have described, and from reports I have of the spinning accidents to FE.8 aeroplanes this seems to have been the cause." Despite the clarity of Frank's descriptions and that his report was widely distributed, spinning remained a dreaded killer.

As explained under Geoffrey de Havilland's section, the designation system adopted by the Royal Aircraft Establishment for its designs was intended to throw a curve to the authorities that Farnborough was not in the habit of building aeroplanes. By the war years, this subterfuge was hardly necessary. Yet the SE.4 – as flown by Norman Spratt* – and the SE.4a, which at first would seem to be a merely variant change were completely different single-seat scouts, their main link being their designer, Henry Folland. Frank flew the prototype in June 1915, but it did not go into production. Known as the 'Pulpit', the BE.9 was a radical solution to putting a machine-gun ahead of the propeller. Bristol-built BE.2c 1700 had its forward cockpit faired over and a brand new nacelle suspended *in front* of the propeller by a system of struts from the undercarriage, and was redesignated BE.9. The gunner certainly had an unrivalled field of fire and

The second prototype Royal Aircraft Factory SE.4a, 5611. *Peter Green Collection*

An RE.8 with ground crew and an Avro 504 in the background. *KEC*

the pilot could enjoy the flying characteristics of a 'conventional' tractor biplane although the crew were separated by the propeller and engine. Inevitably perhaps the BE.9 was not accepted for service. The terribly under-powered FE.4 twin-engined bomber, which Frank tested in March 1916, was not greeted with elation: only one other was built.

During 1916 Frank succeeded Ronald Kemp as CTP at Farnborough. Given the nickname 'Harry Tate' after a famous music hall comedian and as a play on the pronunciation of its designation, the RE.8 was one of the 'Factory's' success stories. It was intended as a replacement for the ubiquitous BE.2c, becoming famous as a reliable observation platform for artillery barrage gun-laying. The prototype had its maiden flight at the hands of Frank in June 1916 and the RE.8 was soon in mass production. Henry Folland's wartime experience in designing scouts – by 1916 more and more being referred to as fighters – culminated in the SE.5. When refined into the SE.5a it was arguably the finest British fighter of the Great War. Paul Hare's seminal study *Royal Aircraft Factory* describes the debut of the prototype: "Frank Goodden took it up for its initial flight at about 10am on 22nd November [1916] and, on landing after about 10 minutes, exuberantly announced to the waiting spectators: 'She's a pixie!'. Captain Albert Ball, who was allowed to make a short flight the following day while on a visit to Farnborough, was less enthusiastic, comparing the new machine unfavourably with the lightness of the rotary-powered Nieuport which was then his usual mount. However, he was later to revise his opinion."

Frank took the second example, A4562, up for its debut on 4th December 1916. Flying this machine on 28th January 1917 Major Frank Widdenham Goodden, aged 28, was killed when the aircraft crashed. He was succeed by Roderic Hill* as CTP for the 'Factory'. In a glowing salute to his friend, *Flight* columnist 'Dreamer' described the incident in the 1st February issue: "The accident appears to have been caused by a wing breaking at 12,000ft, and, game to the last, Goodden made valiant efforts to right the machine, but without succeeding."

Mike Goodfellow

22 Jan 1971	HS HS.125-600B G-AYBH 2 x 3,750lbst BS Viper 601
28 Jun 1976	HS HS.125-700B G-BFAN 2 x 3,700lbst Garrett TFE731-3
3 Sep 1981	BAe 146 Srs 100 G-SSSH 4 x 6,700lbst Avco ALF 502R-3

Michael Spencer Goodfellow, born 1930. From 1947 to 1950 he was an apprentice at the de Havilland Aeronautical Technical School, Hatfield. Joined the RAF in 1950 and initially was an instructor, going on to fly Hunters F.2s at Wattisham and F.5s with 208 Squadron. He graduated from No.16 Course ETPS at Farnborough and was posted to RAE Thurleigh before returning to Farnborough as a tutor with ETPS.

S<small>QN</small> L<small>DR</small> M<small>IKE</small> G<small>OODFELLOW</small> took over as 'small aircraft' CTP at Hawker Siddeley, Hatfield, from Geoffrey Pike* in 1969, also carried out testing on HS Tridents. The HS.125 programme at Hawarden, near Chester, was also part of his remit and he was in command of the stretched and revised HS.125 Series 600 prototype, G-AYBH, for a two-hour maiden sortie on 22nd January 1971; the flight ended at Hatfield where the bulk of the testing was carried out. By 1976 Mike was HS Divisional CTP Hatfield-Chester and he was once again at Hawarden at the helm of another 125 variant, the refined and re-engined Series 700, with Garrett AiResearch turbofans, on 28th June. As well as Mike on *Alpha-November* for the 2-hour, 44-minute flight that date were Chris Capper* and FTOs D L Norris and B V Rowe. Hawker Siddeley morphed in British Aerospace in 1977 and three years later Mike became BAe CTP civil projects upon the retirement of John Cunningham*.

Mike was the captain of the maiden flight of the last all-British airliner, the BAe 146, at Hatfield on 3rd September 1981. With its ultra-quiet Avco turbofans, the prototype was registered appropriately G-SSSH! Crew for the 95-minute sortie were: Mike, DCTP Peter Sedgwick*, assistant flight test manager Roger de Mercado and senior instrumentation engineer Ron Hammond. Mike described the 146 as "delightfully stable" and that all went "exactly as expected". In 1987 G-SSSH was converted into the prototype of the stretched Series 300 as G-LUXE. It is still flying, from Cranfield on weather research duties with the Natural Environment Research

Flight crew of the prototype BAe 146-100 G-SSSH at Hatfield after the first flight 3rd September 1981. Left to right: Mike Goodfellow, Peter Sedgwick, Roger de Mercado, Ron Hammond. *British Aerospace*

The third prototype BAe 146, G-OPSA, 1984. *British Aerospace*

Council. The 146 was revised with more powerful engines and all-digital avionics and re-styled as the BAE Systems RJ in 1992. During that year the production line moved to Woodford.

Cecil Grace

As outlined in Chapter One, in the words of Harald Penrose in *British Aviation – The Pioneering Years* Cecil Grace was: "The first test pilot to be employed by a British constructor." Appropriately, he flew for the Short brothers – the world's first series aircraft manufacturer.

Cecil Stanley Grace was born in 1880 in Chile of Irish-American parentage. In 1909, he was one of the original customers for the batch of Short-Wright biplanes. In April 1910, he was granted Aviators' Certificate No.4 on a Short-Wright at Eastchurch. By this time he was lobbying Horace Short that the French Farman layout was far more practical than the Wright. He switched his order to a new biplane that became known as the S.27 and he flew this for the first time in June 1910. It was at this point that the Shorts nominated him as test pilot. Cecil was a man 'of independent means', so it is unlikely he was looking for a wage, more that he was seduced by the new-found flying 'bug'. He began carrying out flight tests, experiments, demonstrations and training.

On 20th June 1910 he took his S.27 over Sheerness where he circled the battleships HMS *Bulwark* and *Victorious* while beginning a climb. R Dallas Brett in his *History of British Aviation 1908-1914* notes that this exploit was: "in a manner which gave the Lords of the Admiralty furiously to think". Before long, Cecil began instructing Royal Navy would-be pilots on the type – at no charge. The flight did more than influence the Admiralty; Cecil reached a height of 1,180ft, setting a new British record. He also gave a full report to Horace Short that the ailerons on the S.27 and its wheeled undercarriage were vastly superior to the wing-warping and skids of the Wright biplane. The fledgling company abandoned the Wright format and never looked back.

The Midland Aero Club staged a 'meet' from 27th June to 2nd July 1910 at Wolverhampton and Cecil demonstrated the S.27 to great effect, flying confidently for 30 minutes before 'dead-sticking' from 150ft. He also took the prize for the greatest altitude, 600ft. The order book was beginning to swell. Cecil's vision went further; he was also advocating the 'tractor' biplane as the ultimate flying machine – both the Wrights and the Farmans were 'pushers'. During this busy time, Cecil acquired a Voisin biplane and, later a Blériot.

Through all of this activity, the clock was ticking. Baron de Forest had offered £4,000 (£440,000 in present-day values) for the first British pilot to fly in an all-British aircraft from any point in England to the farthest point in the Continent during 1910. Cecil took the S.29 biplane to Dover on 5th December, and attempted a crossing on the 18th, only to abort. On the 22nd he flew to Les Baraques, south west of Lille and decided to return to Dover, so that he could have a better crack at the prize in the days beyond. It was foggy over the Channel and 30-year-old Cecil Stanley Grace was never seen again. His cap and flying goggles were washed up on a Belgian beach as sad testament to a very skilful and visionary aviator.

Bob Graham

16 May 1924	Brennan Helicopter
	1 x 230hp Bentley BR.2

Louis Brennan CB was a prodigious inventor; among his successes he had perfected guided weaponry and the torpedo. During World War One he had interested the Ministry of Munitions in his 1916 patent for a helicopter and in June 1919 this led to its adoption as a project by the Royal Aircraft Establishment, with funding from the Air Ministry. Brennan was such a mother-lode of inventions and notoriously insular that he was given his own facilities at Farnborough, including space within the original balloon shed and more or less left to it. Brennan's machine had a Bentley rotary in upright position which drove tiny propellers at the tips of the 60ft diameter twin-blade rotor. Small paddle-like balances were carried at the end of tubes at 90-degrees to the rotor. This whirling mass was encased in a pyramidal tubular structure and hung below that was the control car and an 'undercarriage' of multiple 'feet'. A universal joint carried fuel and the flying controls from the cockpit to the spinning edifice above.

Robert G Graham was attached full-time to the project, acting as assistant engineer to Louis Brennan. As the project progressed in 1921, the elderly inventor (then 69) invited 'Bob' to be the pilot. RAE had other ideas, Flt Lt 'George' Bulman* and Fg Off C A Bouchier were allocated as duty pilots. Bulman certainly tried it out during its first runs inside the balloon shed, but it was clear that the helicopter was so complex that Bob was more than qualified to take command. During the January 1922 sequence of indoor tests, the craft reached a height of 20ft, maximum safe 'altitude' inside the massive shed.

The first time the Brennan was brought outdoors, 16th May 1924, Bob carried out a series of 'hops', and more were staged the following May. During these the Brennan reached no more than 8ft into the air. Further trials were set for 2nd October 1925 and up to that point, 10 hours of flight had been achieved, each sortie averaging 3 minutes. All of this would be considered today to have been in 'ground effect' only. On the third outside trial, 2nd October 1925, Bob succeeded in a more sustained flight, but the Brennan flipped over, wrecking the complex rotor. Ten days later, Frank Courtney* commenced demonstrating the Cierva C.6A Autogiro at Farnborough and this must have helped put the nails in the Brennan's coffin. It is estimated that, since 1919, in excess of £55,000 had been poured into the project. No more money was forthcoming and the machine was not rebuilt. Nevertheless, Bob had entered the history books as Britain's first helicopter pilot. He continued to work for the RAE, becoming Director of Aircraft and Mechanical Engineering Equipment and earning a CBE.

Mike Graves

| 23 Mar 1949 | Westland Wyvern TF.2 VP109 |
| | 1 x 3,560shp AS Python 1 |

In January 1945 the Gloster Meteor Is of 616 (South Yorkshire) Squadron moved into Colerne, prior to deploying to the Continent. No.616 was the first unit to fly the Gloster jet fighter operationally. Westland CTP Harald Penrose* requested jet experience and was sent to Colerne and Sqn Ldr Mike Graves talked him through the Meteor – there being no two-seat trainers at that point. With the death of Peter Garner* in a Wyvern in October 1947, Harald was casting around for someone to replace him. Rolls-Royce at Hucknall suggested Sqn Ldr Michael A Graves DFC, unaware that Harald had met him previously. Mike started work in January 1949 and flew a Rolls-Royce Eagle-engined Wyvern and then the turboprop Rolls-Royce Clyde-engined Mk.2, which Harald had first flown that month. Harald handed the responsibility of the debut of the turboprop Armstrong Siddeley Python prototype, VP109, to Mike. This took place at Boscombe Down on 23rd May 1949 and Mike criticised the throttle response and in subsequent flights declared that the Python had a tendency to surge.

Mike displayed the second Python Wyvern TF.2, VP113, at the September 1949 SBAC airshow at Farnborough and put it through a full aerobatic routine. On 31st October 1949 Mike was detailed to fly VP113 at Yeovil for the benefit of visitors from the Royal Navy and the Air Ministry. He started with a high speed run across the airfield, then a climb, but the propellers were seen to slow and it appeared that the Python had flamed out. Mike came round for a down-wind landing, but elected to put the gear down and not belly-in. He landed long and VP113 ploughed through the perimeter hedge, demolishing a house on Westland Road. Mike was killed instantly. Mrs W Brown, in the house, was also killed and another lady severely burnt. Wreckage shot out on to Westland Road and six-year-old Ann Wilkins, out riding her bike, was also killed.

Richard 'Dick' Green

J Richard Green, born 1942. RAF career started as an instructor at Oakington, followed by serving as a flight commander with 2 Squadron on Supermarine Swift FR.5s at Jever, West Germany. Graduated from ETPS Course No.18 at Farnborough 1959 and went on to fly with the RAE there.

As the SC.1 vertical take-off programme evolved, former Royal Aircraft Establishment test pilot 'Dick' Green was taken on by Shorts in 1963 to assist CTP Denis Tayler* and Alex Roberts* with development flying. On 2nd October 1963 Dick was flying the second SC.1, XG905, at Sydenham to test the auto-stabilisation system. Five minutes into the sortie, at about 40ft high, the system failed and XG905 rolled upside-down and crashed killing the 31-year-old.

Bob Graham flying the Brennan Helicopter at Farnborough on 2nd October 1925, the day it was badly damaged. S F Cody used this turf as the starting point for many of his flights 17 years previously. *Birks-Thorne*

Bryan Greensted

23 May 1944	Martin-Baker MB.5 R2496
	1 x 2,340hp RR Griffon 83

Leslie Bryan Greensted, born 1915. Joined Air Service Training at Hamble as an apprentice and learned to fly there. He spent some time in Rhodesia and South Africa instructing, possibly *under contract to de Havilland. In 1939 he became CTP for Rotol at Staverton. Rotol was a specialist propeller company that got its name from the two businesses that set it up – Rolls-Royce and Bris*tol*.*

Dramatic image of the Martin-Baker MB.5 – no wonder it was once described as "cross between a Mustang and a V-2 rocket". *Martin-Baker*

Bryan Greensted's job at Rotol involved testing a wide range of aircraft and propeller combinations, culminating in contra-rotating and reversible-pitch systems. During 1940 he was seconded briefly to Gloster to work as a PTP at Hucclecote. During 1942 Bryan carried out trials for another Staverton-based operation, Flight Refuelling Ltd (FRL). In order to increase the range of fighters, FRL had developed a system whereby a Hurricane could be attached by a tow line to a Wellington. Both would take off then the fighter would throttle back while the bomber did the work. Airspeed's George Errington* helped with these trials. The scheme evolved so that the Hurricane could take-off independently and then acquire the tow line, trailed behind a Wellington. Bryan took part in this exacting flying.

Rotol was producing the contra-rotating propeller for the Martin-Baker MB.5 fighter, which had been undergoing protracted development at Denham. With Bryan's experience of contra-rotating propellers, he was well qualified to test the new fighter. The MB.5 was roaded to the more generous runways at Harwell and it was first flown by Bryan on 23rd May 1944. Bryan was involved in much of the development flying of the spectacular-looking fighter, accumulating about 40 hours on it. While demonstrating the MB.5 at an event at Farnborough in late October 1944, Bryan pulled the canopy back to improve his view on approach and it disconnected, hitting the tail, but with little damage. Later he was demonstrating R2496 to 'top brass, reportedly including Churchill, when the Griffon failed and the cockpit filled with fumes. Bryan jettisoned the canopy and made an uneventful 'dead stick' landing. While the MB.5 had all the 'looks', it was rapidly overhauled by the advent of jets and was to remain a 'one-off'. Bryan's connections with Martin-Baker extended to ejection seat development; he flew a Boulton Paul Defiant during the first trials with dummies – see Chapter Four.

Bryan left Rotol in 1946 and became chief pilot for Skyways, flying Avro Lancastrians and Douglas Dakotas on the Berlin Airlift 1946-1948. By the end of the operation, Bryan had flown more sorties than any other British civilian pilot that took part. In the late 1950s he was chief pilot for Hunting-Clan Air Services, on Bristol Britannias. In 1960 the airline became part of British United and Bryan left, setting up as a consultant, with much work coming from Saudi Arabia. He gave up commercial flying in 1963, by which time he had over 22,000 hours on 80 types. Leslie Bryan Greensted MBE died on 25th July 1994, aged 79.

Eric Greenwood

17 May 1945	Gloster Meteor III EE360
	2 x 4,000lbst Derwent 5
20 Sep 1945	Gloster Meteor (Trent) EE227
	2 x 800shp RR RB50 Trent

Notes: Meteor EE360 was effectively the F.IV prototype and first flew from Hucclecote. The Trent Meteor had its debut at Church Broughton.

Eric Stanley Greenwood, born 1909. Joined RAF and began training 1928. Operational flying with 3 Squadron at Upavon on Hawker Woodcocks, Gloster Gamecocks and Bristol Bulldogs. Posted to CFS in September 1930 and rest of RAF career as an instructor. In 1932 he flew for Scottish-based British Flying Boats, captaining Saro Cloud G-ABXW Cloud of Iona, *on charters and a service to Belfast. By late 1933 he was an instructor at the Penang Flying Club, on the Malayan peninsula, remaining there until early 1936. Eric returned to the UK in 1936 and instructed at Air Service Training at Hamble.*

Air Service Training (AST) was owned by the giant Armstrong Siddeley Development Company and Eric Greenwood's skills were drawn to the attention of its Armstrong Whitworth (AW) aircraft division CTP Charles Turner-Hughes*. Eric was taken on as DCTP at Whitley Abbey in 1937 where much of the work involved development of the Whitley bomber, but in January 1938 Eric was back at Hamble. The Coventry factory and Whitley Abbey were at full capacity, so assembly and flight test of the largest airliner built in Britain to date, the AW Ensign for Imperial Airways, was sub-contracted to AST. More is made of the Ensign in the section on Charles Turner-Hughes, but as the first flight of the prototype, G-ADSR, proved the worth of deputies we shall deal with it here. With Charles in the left-hand seat and Eric as his co-pilot, the pair carried out a series of 'straights' on the all-grass Hamble aerodrome on 23rd January 1938. Then it was throttle forward and they took off. 'Sandy' Powell's exceptional *Men With Wing*s described the 15-minute, undercarriage down, maiden voyage: "On the very first flight it is usual, except in large aircraft which

The world's first turboprop aircraft: Trent Meteor I EE227 was first flown by Eric Greenwood. *Rolls-Royce*

sometimes require a flight engineer, for the test pilot to fly alone. In the case of the Ensign, Eric Greenwood, No.2 pilot to Turner-Hughes, was so keen to fly that this was agreed – it was an exceptionally large aeroplane. It turned out to be a blessing as the rudder was over-balanced and with all his strength Turner-Hughes could barely hold it and then only for a very short time. The help of another pilot, and a strong one at that, just turned the scales and they landed safely..."

Eric was *again* at Hamble from October 1941, this time having left AW to become CTP for AST which was a major contributor in repair, overhaul and flight test of types for the Fleet Air Arm and RAF. Supermarine Spitfires and Seafires formed the bulk of the work, but HP Hampdens and then DH Mosquitos also required Eric's attention. AST was responsible for the assembly and checking out of Bell Airacobras and early North American Mustangs, both types powered by Allison V-1710s. Eric claimed that he held the world record for V-1710 engine failures in flight!

Since 1935, AW, Avro, Gloster and Hawker had been part of the Hawker Siddeley Group but each continued to trade under its own name. It was common practise for test pilots to help fill 'gaps' and help out and Eric spent time testing Gloster-built Hurricanes at Hucclecote while he was employed by AW. In 1944 Eric was tempted away from AST to become CTP at Gloster, upon the retirement of Michael Daunt* in June 1944. Michael had flown the prototype Meteor twin-jet fighter and it was on this type that Eric was to spend the rest of his time. During the summer of 1944 Meteor F.Is became the RAF's first operational jets and the next major revision of the type was the Rolls-Royce Derwent 5-engined Mk.IV. Eric flew the prototype of this version, converted Mk.III EE360, in May 1945. His second 'first' was of global importance. Through a reduction gear, a jet engine could drive a propeller and initially this was referred to as a propeller-turbine but became known as the turboprop. Rolls-Royce at Derby used the Derwent as the basis of the RB.50 Trent and Meteor I EE227 was converted by the company to become the world's first turboprop aircraft. The Trent – not to be confused with the present-day turbofan – drove two Rotol five-bladed propellers of 7ft 11in diameter, although later smaller examples were installed. From 1944, Rolls-Royce used the Derbyshire airfield of Church Broughton for Meteor testing and it was from there that Eric took EE227 on its maiden flight on 20th September 1945. Directional stability was questionable, but small 'finlets' above and below the tailplane cured this. Development of the RB.50 did not go far, but a new and important type of powerplant had made its debut.

With the war won, it was clear that there was phenomenal development potential in the Meteor. It was decided that a good way to placard the twin-jet's capabilities was to have a go at the world absolute airspeed record. This was to be a joint Gloster and RAF endeavour and two Meteor IIIs were to be upgraded to Mk.IV status and honed for high speed. These were EE454 which kept its camouflage was given the name *Britannia* and EE455 which was painted overall yellow and officially named *Forever Amber*, but more often than not called *Yellow Peril*. Eric would fly for Gloster and Gp Capt H J 'Willie' Wilson, then OC ETPS, would do the honours for the RAF. Eric was involved in most of the flying while Gloster prepared the jets for the record. For the 13th instalment of *Flight* magazine's series on test pilots, the issue dated 15th August 1946, remarked on the leap in performance that Eric experienced: "while testing Meteors for the world's record attempt, that he first flew at 500mph (on a standard Meteor III with Rolls-Royce Derwent V) and then over 600mph in the record-breaker. It was an amazing piece of development flying to raise the clearance from 500mph to 600mph in a fortnight." The magazine published an image of Eric's knee-pad 'scribbler' for a flight in EE454 on 29th October 1945, showing that he had clocked 606mph at 400ft.

When it came to the Fédération Aéronautique Internationale-monitored record, staged over Herne Bay on 7th November 1945 it was Gp Capt Wilson who took the laurels; his average speed in EE454 being 606.25mph. Eric's runs in EE455 came in at 603mph. During the run-up flying Eric could rightly claim to be the first pilot to 500mph and then 600mph but these figures could not be ratified. While this was a disappointment for Eric and Gloster, it was the Meteor that really stole the limelight; the press playing heavily on the 'ten miles a minute' figure. The previous holder of the record had been Germany in April 1939 with the so-called Messerschmitt Me 209 V1, more exactly a Bf 109R – Wilson's Meteor had surpassed that achievement by a staggering 137.03mph!

Eric retired as CTP in 1946, handing on to Bill Waterton*. In late 1945 Eric had just shy of 6,000 hours on 158 types. He took up the post of Technical Sales Manager for Gloster and, from 1966 to 1970, he was sales director for Beagle at Shoreham. Eric Stanley Greenwood OBE died in 1979, aged 70.

John Grierson

John Grierson, born 1909. Gained his pilot's licence at Brooklands, before joining the RAF in 1929. As a Pilot Officer he was posted to India in October 1930 and flew there in his own DH Moth G-AAJP Rouge et Noir – named so because it was half red and half black. Coming home he set a record for Karachi to London, arriving at Lympne on 28th May 1931 having flown 5,000 miles in 4 days, 10 hours, 30 minutes. Not content with this he flew float-equipped DH Fox Moth G-ACRK Robert Bruce from Rochester (where Shorts had made the floats) bound for Canada on 20th July 1934. There were delays and incidents, but he arrived in Ottawa on 30th August 1934 – he was the first to fly the Atlantic east to west via the Northern (or Arctic) Route. In Ottawa, the floats were removed and wheels fitted to G-ACRK, so John could fly to New York, arriving there on 10th September 1934. After this John joined the Air Ministry's Civil Operations Directorate.

By 1938 John Grierson was flying for Armstrong Siddeley Motors and early the following year was testing AW Whitley II K7243 at Baginton, fitted with a 1,500hp AS Deerhound 21-cylinder engine. On 23rd May 1939 he was undertaking a carburation test on the 845hp AS Tiger VIII engines of Whitley III K8966 at 18,000ft. He dipped into the oxygen supply every so often, but by the end of the test, he was suffering from oxygen starvation and was well into a 'happy' state. He put K8966 into a stalled turn and the bomber hurtled downwards; the port Tiger broke up, the nose hatch blew off and fabric was stripped from the starboard wing. John managed to pull out and returned to terra firma. For the remainder of 1939 he was at Langley, working as a PTP for Hawker on Henleys and Hurricanes. By June 1940 John was at Hucclecote engaged in testing AW Albemarles being built at the Gloster plant under the aegis of A W Hawksley and he also handled Gloster-built Hurricanes and Typhoons.

Under Michael Daunt* John was introduced to jet propulsion. On 1st March 1943 he was given the honour of the maiden flight of the second Gloster E28/39, W4046/G, powered by a 1,200lbst Rover W.2B, from Edgehill. By this stage John was described by Gloster as development test pilot. On 17th April 1943 John made the first cross-country jet flight in Britain when he took W4046/G from Edgehill to Hatfield, where he displayed it in front of dignitaries, including Winston Churchill. ('Gerry' Sayer* flew the first E28/39, W4041/G, from Cranwell on 15th May 1941 and while it was based at Edgehill from early 1942, it made that journey by road and via considerable reconfiguration at Bentham, or Hucclecote.) During early 1944 Meteor I EE210 was shipped to the USA in exchange for a Bell XP-59 Airacomet, which had been presented to the UK. A team from Gloster and Rolls-Royce was despatched to Muroc in California's Mojave Desert to assemble and test the Meteor. (Muroc is now a part of the vast Edwards Air Force Base.) John made a successful test flight of EE210 from Muroc on 15th April 1944.

From late 1945 Wg Cdr Grierson was deputy director of civil aviation in the British Zone of Occupation in Germany. In 1946 John was one of the individuals that set up United Whalers Ltd which acquired five civilianised Supermarine Walruses to act as spotters for their quarry. The whale factory ship SS *Balaena* was fitted with a former Royal Navy catapult and the vessel sailed to the Antarctic in 1946/1947 with three of the amphibians on board. Prior to this John won the Folkestone Aero Trophy race at Lympne on 31st August 1946 at 121mph in Walrus G-AHFL *Boojum*. By 1953 John was an executive of the de Havilland engines division. In 1966 he was the UK representative on the Operation deep freeze expedition to the Antarctic. John wrote prolifically, two of his books being *Jet Flight* in 1946 and *Air Whaler* of 1949, both published by Sampson Low. On 21st May 1977 Wg Cdr John Grierson gave a talk at the Smithsonian Institute's Air and Space Museum at Washington DC as part of the 50th anniversary celebrations of Charles Lindbergh's solo transatlantic flight. John was taken ill shortly afterwards and died that evening, aged 68.

'Norrie' Grove

5 Dec 1982	Slingsby T.67 Firefly G-BKAM
	1 x 160hp Lycoming AEIO-320-D1B

Flt Lt Norris 'Norrie' Grove served for much of his RAF career as an instructor, including two seasons (1965 and 1966) as the leader of the Linton-on-Ouse Hunting Jet Provost formation display team, the Gins. He joined Slingsby Aviation at Kirkbymoorside as CTP as the company was embarking upon production of a civilian and military trainer based upon the French Fournier RF-6B. Initially Slingsby produced a small batch of all-wooden T.67s, following closely the French version. At the end of 1982 the company flew its first totally re-engineered version produced in glass fibre re-inforced plastic. Military Firefly versions, with a 260hp Lycoming, sold well to air forces or contractors and when production finished in 2005 over 250 had been built. Norrie was involved in flight test, demonstration and delivery through to 1995.

'Ben' Gunn

6 Aug 1952	BP P.120 VT951
	1 x 5,100lbst RR Nene 3 RN2
1966	DHC Chipmunk (Rover) G-ATTS
	1 x 118shp Rover TP-90

Notes: The P.120 was first flown from Boscombe Down. Chipmunk converted by Hants and Sussex Aviation on behalf of Rover Gas Turbines and flew in turboprop form at Portsmouth.

Alexander Ewen Gunn, born 1923. Joined the Air Defence Cadet Corps (later the Air Training Corps) in 1938. Signed up for the RAF, initially serving with 501 Squadron on Supermarine Spitfire Vs at Hawkinge, from October 1943. He was posted to 274 Squadron at Manston, with Hawker Tempest Vs on anti-diver (V-1 flying-bomb) sorties and on 1st September 1944 he shot one down. No.274 moved to the Continent in late September 1944, staging through Belgium, Holland and, in April 1945, into Germany. As well as the V-1, 'Ben' was credited with a long-nosed Focke-Wulf Fw 190 (either a Fw 190D 'Dora' or a Ta 152) 'probable' and two damaged in air combat plus aircraft, flak posts, locomotives and rolling stock, a large number of vehicles destroyed or damaged in air-to-ground strikes. In June 1945 Ben was posted to A&AEE Boscombe Down, carrying out armament trials on Tempest IIs. Ben graduated from No.7 Course ETPS at Farnborough, 1948 and returned to A&AEE.

UNIVERSALLY known as 'Ben', from the pirate character Ben Gunn in Robert Louis Stevenson's *Treasure Island*, Flt Lt A E Gunn was seconded to Boulton Paul (BP) at Pendeford, Wolverhampton, on 14th February 1949. The company had just lost Lindsay Neale* and Peter Tisshaw* in the crash of a Balliol on the 3rd. A year later, Ben left the RAF and took up the post of CTP. As well as Balliol clearance and production testing, BP specialised in powered flying controls and there was test-bed and trials work to provide variety.

Ben's greatest workload came with what turned out to be the last BP designs to take to the air, the P.111 and P.120 deltas. The P.111 was built to Specification E27/46 for transonic delta wing research. The one-off prototype, VT935, was first flown from Boscombe Down by Sqn Ldr Robert Smythe*, CO of the RAE's Aero Flight on 10th October 1950. Benn got to pilot VT935 the same day, flying it a total of four times over three days. In 1953 VT935 was rebuilt at Pendeford, emerging as the P.111A: Ben flew it extensively up to early 1954.

The short-lived P.120 VT951 in its funereal black scheme. Ben Gunn was its first, and only, pilot. *Boulton Paul*

The more advanced P.120, VT951, with an all-moving 'T-tail' and other improvements, was ready for test at Boscombe Down in August 1952 and Ben was entrusted with the maiden flight on 6th August 1952. Twenty seconds into the take-off run, with three-quarters of Boscombe's long runway consumed, Ben was worried. The P.120 eventually clawed its way into the air with a very poor rate of climb. The 20-minute flight ended without further drama. Twenty-three days later, Ben took off from Boscombe on the P.120's 20th flight. Off the south coast at 5,000ft there was an almighty bang and VT951 rolled rapidly to port several times. After a struggle, Ben managed to stop the rolling, but the airspeed indicator had stopped functioning and the delta entered a dive. The elevons were no help and Ben decided to try the power-controlled tailplane trim adjustment, bit by bit. This worked, pulling the delta out of the dive. Hopes of bringing the aircraft back to Boscombe faded rapidly as what control there was decayed. Ben jettisoned the canopy at about 3,000ft and, as he ejected, VT951 rolled inverted. He deployed the parachute early and hit trees as he landed and survived.

Ejection seat technology in 1952 was such that the Martin-Baker propelled the pilot out, but the moment to deploy the parachute was his call. Ben had survived the first 'bang out' from a delta planform aircraft and the first from the inverted position. The port elevon was found hours later: flutter had forced a fracture and Ben was left with an uncontrollable aircraft. Three days later, Ben was due to have displayed the P.120 at the SBAC airshow at Farnborough; it had been painted gloss black for that occasion. In his excellent book series, Henry Matthews profiled Ben in *Husky One*. Inside Ben noted that the P.120: "was dubbed by the [other] test pilots the 'Black Widow Maker'. I did not realise how near the truth this remark would be."

Les Whitehouse of the Boulton Paul Association provided a fascinating insight into the incident: "During the P.120 flight [Ben] experienced a rapid 'buzz' from the aileron and then a bang and the aircraft immediately rolled. Our technical office manager had a pin from the P.120 and used to explain its significance and the need for accuracy to apprentices, including me. There was an error of 2,000th of an inch in the pin hole/pin fit and hence the 'buzz' of flutter when it occurred was unusually fierce. It alternately sheared and cold welded the pin in segments increasing the amplitude of the 'buzz' until within fractions of a second the aileron sheared off."

The final Balliol was completed in late 1954 and Boulton Paul left the airframe production business. Powered-controlled flying units (PCFUs) and sub-contracting for other manufacturers became the norm. Additionally, there was plenty of flying on refurbishing, conversion contracts and more. Jet testing was carried out at Seighford and Defford with Canberras, Javelins, Lightnings and Meteors predominating. Ben continued the trials of the electric-actuated PCFU Tay Viscount VX217 that had been pioneered by his deputy, 'Dickie' Mancus*. Ben made the first full 'electric link' (today this would be called fly-by-wire) landing in VX217, from Defford, on 2nd January 1958.

Ben retired from Boulton Paul in 1965 and the following year joined Solihull-based Rover Gas Turbines as CTP. The company was attempting to expand upon its range of auxiliary power units and had developed the TP.90 turboprop with hopes to break into

Rover turboprop Chipmunk 22 G-ATTS at Farnborough, September 1966. *Roy Bonser*

Colin Hague first flew EH.101 PP5 ZF649 on 24th October 1989 and he was in charge of deck landing trials in the English Channel on Type 23 frigate HMS *Northumberland* in March and April 1995. *GKN Westland*

light aviation. After Auster J/1 G-AGVI had been fitted with the turboprop in 1965, Ben was given the task of testing DHC Chipmunk 22 G-ATTS with the new powerplant. Ben demonstrated *Tango-Sierra* at the SBAC airshow at Farnborough in September 1966. The following year Ben joined Beagle Aircraft at Shoreham as Marketing Director for Africa and the Middle East. While with Beagle, Ben kept his hand in on production test work; finally retiring from flying in 1971, having flown 175 types. Beagle went out of business in 1970 and a year later Ben became the manager of Shoreham, in no small way helping to transform the prospects of this wonderful aerodrome. Ben retired from this post in June 1990, a much-loved and respected, unassuming aviation icon. Flt Lt Alexander Ewen 'Ben' Gunn MBE died on 22nd September 1999, aged 76.

Colin Hague

| 6 Jul 1993 | EHI EH.101 PP4 ZF644 |
| | 3 x 2,100shp RTM 322-01/08 |

Colin Watt Hague joined the Royal Navy in 1962. First operational posting was to 845 Squadron flying Westland Wessex HAS.1s during the Borneo Confrontation, 1964. From 1965 to 1967 he served with 826 Squadron, attached to HMS Hermes and from 1968 commanded Yarmouth Flight, flying a Westland Wasp HAS.1 from HMS Yarmouth. Graduated from No.31 Course ETPS at Boscombe Down, 1972; moving on to helicopter trials at A&AEE, including Westland Lynx deck landings and icing trials. He was senior pilot on the Lynx HAS.2 Intensive Flying Training Unit, 700L Squadron, at Yeovilton, 1977.

C DR COLIN HAGUE was appointed as test pilot for Westland at Yeovil in 1979 and was involved across the Gazelle, Lynx, Sea King and WG.30 programmes. He was co-pilot to CTP Trevor Egginton* for the first flight of the Anglo-Italian EH.101 Merlin prototype PP1 ZF641 on 9th October 1987. Colin became DCTP in 1986 and two years later took over from Trevor as CTP. The Merlin programme was Colin's main domain for the remainder of his career at Yeovil. PP1 had been fitted with General Electric turboshafts and Colin carried out the maiden flight of the definitive version, with Rolls-Royce/Turboméca RTM 322s, PP4 ZF644 in July 1993. Colin

carried out the first Merlin deck landing trials, in PP5 ZF649 on HMS *Norfolk* in Weymouth Bay on 15th November 1990 and the maiden flight of the first fully-equipped Fleet Air Arm Merlin HM.1, ZH822, on 14th January 1997. Colin retired as CTP in 2003 and was awarded an MBE; he was succeeded by Donald Maclaine*. Colin and Andy Strachan* are part owners in Vans RV-9A G-CCGU based at Henstridge.

Rollo Haig

| 1931 | Monospar ST-3 G-AARP |
| | 2 x 50hp Salmson AD.9 |

Rollo Amyatt Wolseley de Haga Haig, born 1896. Initially a Captain in the Royal Artillery but in 1916 he joined the RFC, serving in France. He was involved in flight testing Westland-built Vickers Vimys at Yeovil, 1918 to 1919. By 1922 Rollo was at A&AEE Martlesham Heath and in 1924 he was Officer in Charge, Experimental Flying, at RAE Farnborough. He flew the Parnall Pixie III in the September 1924 Lympne Light Aeroplane Trials. On 15th October 1925 he was aboard the airship R-33 and determined to leave it before it landed! Suspended from a trapeze below the airship was DH Humming Bird J7325. At 3,800ft, Rollo climbed into its cockpit, the trapeze was swung down and he engaged a lever that released J7325. The engine was started in a dive and then Rollo performed two loops, climbed back to the R-33, engaged the trapeze and made his way back into the airship.

S QN LDR ROLLO HAIG AFC left the RAF in 1926 and became the manager of the aviation department of William Beardmore and Co – see Jack Noakes for the monster Beardmore Inflexible. Swiss-born Helmuth John Stieger had helped with the design of the Inflexible and had come up with a cantilever spar concept. Rollo helped to set up the Monospar Wing Company to develop Stieger's ideas. Monospar commissioned Gloster Aircraft to build a three-seat twin, the ST-3, to act as a demonstrator. This machine, G-AARP, was first flown by Rollo from Hucclecote in 1931. The ST-3 was so promising that a new company, General Aircraft Ltd, was established in 1932 to create a series of twin-engined types, with Rollo as a director. He also set up a consultancy, the International Aviation Agency. Tragically, Rollo was killed in a yachting accident off Plymouth in 1936; he was 40.

Harold Hamersley

30 Apr 1919	Avro Baby
	1 x 35hp Green
29 Aug 1919	Avro 539 G-EALG
	1 x 240hp Siddeley Puma
Feb 1920	Avro 547 G-EAQX
	1 x 160hp Beardmore
26 Apr 1928	Cierva C.10 J9038
	1 x 70hp AS Genet I

Notes: The Avros flew at Hamble, the Type 539 floatplane from the River Hamble. The C.10 was built by Parnall and trials were attempted at Yate.

Harold Alan Hamersley, born 1896 in Australia. By 1915 he was a 2nd Lt with the 16th Infantry Battalion and he fought at Gallipoli. He transferred to the RFC and in September 1916 joined 60 Squadron on Royal Aircraft Factory SE.5as at Savy, France. On 16th September 1917 he shot down an Albatros D.III, the first of 11 victories plus 2 shared, including a Fokker Dr.I on 18th February 1918. Harold was involved in the dogfight in which German 'ace' Werner Voss was killed on 23rd September 1917. The German, who had 48 'kills' engaged with Harold, the latter's SE.5 suffering damage and he retired from the mêlée. Captain Harold Hamersley MC returned to Britain in May 1918, becoming an instructor on Avro 504Ks.

B Y the spring of 1919 Harold Hamersley was at Hamble and testing and joy-riding for Avro, taking over from 'Freddy' Raynham*. Among his duties, Harold taught chief designer Roy Chadwick to fly. During his career as a test pilot, Harold experienced two very brief 'flights', one in 1919, the other in 1928; both ending in the prototype being wrecked. Harold's first recorded testing was the prototype Avro 536 floatplane, K-114, during April 1919. This was an Avro 504K with a 130hp Clerget rotary that had had its mid-fuselage widened so that it could carry five passengers as a more profitable joy-rider. For his first true maiden flight he did not cover himself in glory. Chadwick had come up with the Type 534 Baby, a small sporting biplane and on the last day of April 1919 Harold took it up from Hamble. At about 300ft he accidently knocked off the ignition switches and the little 35hp Green stopped, the Baby entered a spin and splattered into the mud of the River Hamble. Those watching were convinced they were running towards a fatal incident. But while the Baby was wrecked beyond repair, to quote Harald Penrose in *British Aviation – The Adventuring Years*, Harold's state was: "little more than shocked dismay"! The war hero was not sent packing and he successfully flew the second Baby on 10th May.

The Type 539 was a hasty response to the first post-war Schneider Trophy contest. This was staged off the coast of Bournemouth in September 1919, but was abandoned due to thick fog. The Type 547 was a throw-back to Alliot Verdon Roe's pioneering flight of July 1909, adopting a triplane layout coupled with typical Avro pragmatism using as many stock 504K parts and assemblies as possible. Only one other example of the four-passenger transport was completed. Harold left to fly for Martinsyde, with 'Bert' Hinkler* taking on the role of Avro test pilot. Returning to RAF service in 1920, Harold again joined 60 Squadron which was then stationed at Risalpur, India, and equipped with de Havilland Amiens. He was back in Britain in 1923 and flew for Avro at the Lympne Light Aeroplane Trials in October. He piloted the diminutive biplane Type 558 G-EBHW, powered by a Douglas flat-twin giving around 18hp and was awarded £100 for achieving an altitude of 13,850ft.

Harold was granted a permanent commission in 1926. As a Flight Lieutenant, in April 1928 he went to Yate to test fly the Parnall-built Cierva C.10, J9038. The Autogiro overturned during attempts to get it airborne on the 26th; Harold was unhurt, but J9038 needed considerable repair. 'Dizzy'

The very short-lived Avro Baby prototype, April 1919. *Peter Green Collection*

The first of two Type 547s at Hamble in 1928. *Avro*

Rawson* had another go with the C.10 at Andover on 5th November 1928 and it turned over again: it was not rebuilt. Harold was promoted in 1935 to Squadron Leader. In 1938 he was CO of the University of London Air Squadron at Northolt and in 1940 he was OC RAF Hullavington. Gp Capt Harold Alan Hamersley MC died in December 1967, aged 71.

Joseph 'Joe' Hammond

Joseph Joel Hammond, born in New Zealand. He came to Britain by 1909 and became the first pupil of Maurice Edmond* at the Bristol school on Salisbury Plain. 'Joe' was awarded Aviators' Certificate No.32 on 11th November 1910 on a Boxkite.

'JOE' HAMMOND was engaged by Bristol to demonstrate the Boxkite in Australia and he and Boxkite No.10 were shipped to Perth, arriving in December 1910. The tour was a great success, Joe flying the first-ever passengers in Australia. He had returned to Britain by May 1911 and was among the first to join the Royal Flying Corps in 1912. By December 1913 he was in New Zealand, as an RFC Lieutenant, and in the New Year he was placed on the Special Reserve to become the country's first military pilot. In January 1914 he demonstrated the Britannia Monoplane to the New Zealand Army at Auckland. Joe travelled to Britain again in 1916 and on 19th January 1917 was taken on by Bristol as the company's first full-time test pilot; all those before having been freelancers, or 'diverted' from instructing roles. Joe tested the first F.2B Fighter, A7101, on 10th April 1917 at Filton.

By mid-1918 Joe was in the USA, assisting with the planned licence production of the F.2B by Curtiss of Buffalo, New York, as the O-1. The project was blighted by a series of fatal accidents, the Americans wanting the F.2B to be powered by the ubiquitous Liberty 12 of 400hp. Eventually, Bristol persuaded the Dayton-Wright Airplane of Dayton, Ohio, to use a Wright-built Hispano-Suiza, with better results. While with the British Air Mission, Captain Joseph Joel Hammond was flying an F.2B at Indianapolis, Indiana, on 22nd September 1918 when its engine failed at about 600ft. The aircraft entered a spin and crashed, killing Joe and civilian J L Kinder; Lt R W Pickett of the USAAS was seriously injured.

'Jimmy' Harrison

31 Aug 1957	Avro Vulcan VX777 4 x 12,000lbst Bristol Olympus 102
24 Jun 1960	Avro 748 Srs 1 G-APZV 2 x 1,740shp RR Dart 514
21 Dec 1963	Avro 748MF G-ARRV 2 x 2,970shp RR Dart 201C

Notes: All took place from Woodford. Vulcan VX777 first flown by 'Roly' Falk* 3rd September 1952 as representative B.1; flight of 31st August 1957 as representative prototype B.2. Avro 748MF G-ARRV was the prototype Andover C.1 tactical airlifter and was converted from the prototype, G-APZV.

'Jimmy' Harrison, complete with a tie bearing the distinctive Hawker Siddeley 'arrow' logo at his Woodford desk, 1963. *Hawker Siddeley*

James Gordon Harrison, born 1918. Joined the RAF in 1934 as a 'Halton brat' – an apprentice – training as a fitter. He was selected for pilot training and this was carried out in Canada. Served with 605 Squadron in 1944, flying DH Mosquito VIs on night intruder sorties from Manston. Postwar he commanded 4 Squadron, again on Mosquito VIs, in West Germany. He graduated from ETPS Course No.6 at Farnborough, 1948 and joined RAE. While flying Hawker P.1052 VX272 on 30th September 1949 the engine failed but 'Jimmy' just managed to make it back to Farnborough, crashing through a wooden shed before it came to rest on its belly; Jimmy was able to walk away from it. (VX272 is preserved at the Fleet Air Arm Museum, Yeovilton.)

'JIMMY' HARRISON was recruited from the RAE by Sir Roy Dobson of Avro in January 1954. Vulcan testing and development work was considerable and it was with this type that occupied much of Jimmy's time. The second Vulcan, VX777, was re-engineered as the representative B.2 prototype, and Jimmy captained its maiden flight in August 1957. He succeeded 'Roly' Falk* as CTP on 1st January 1958 and by this time production B.1s were rolling off the Woodford production line. On 24th July 1959, Jimmy was at the helm of Vulcan B.1 XA891, which was being used for Bristol Siddeley Olympus 200 trials. On take-off XA891 suffered a total electric failure; Jimmy discounted a return-to Woodford, headed east and climbed, reaching 16,000ft. As with any V-bomber, the two pilots had ejection seats whereas the three 'back-seaters' did not. In the Vulcan, their egress involved dropping the under-fuselage access door and baling out. Jimmy kept the aircraft stable while Ted Hartley, Bob Hodgson and another aircrew member took to the silk. Then XA891 was pointed towards the Humber Estuary and co-pilot 'Dickie' Proudlove and Jimmy activated their Martin-Bakers. All five crew landed safely; XA891 impacted near Beverley.

HS.748MF G-ARRV with its 'beaver' tail lowered as if for a parachute drop during air tests, 1964. *Hawker Siddeley*

The Vulcan was a massive programme and beyond the B.2s, role changes, upgrades and refits made the programme very lucrative for Avro. However, it was clear there would likely be nothing like it afterwards and Avro turned to the civil market – with an eye on military applications – for its next product. This was the Avro 748 (or Hawker Siddeley 748 from 1963) twin-turboprop airliner. With Colin Allen* as co-pilot, Bob Dixon-Stubbs as navigator, Mike Turner as FTO, Jimmy captained the prototype 748, G-APZV, on its debut at Woodford on 24th June 1960. The 'Seven-Four-Eight' went on to be an extremely successful and long-term programme. *Zulu-Victor* was radically rebuilt in 1963 as the Type 748MF – military freighter. This was aimed at an RAF requirement for a tactical airlifter to replace the venerable Vickers Valetta, the design being designated Type 780 and produced as the Andover C.1. Jimmy flew the 748MF, with the new registration G-ARRV, in December 1963 and was responsible for 'soft' field landings, air drops and other trials.

Hawker Siddeley (HS) won the contest to replace the Avro Shackleton with the Nimrod, based upon the DH Comet airliner. As noted under the section of John Cunningham*, ordinarily Jimmy as CTP would command the prototype, but with John's extensive experience of the Comet, he captained

the Nimrod prototype XV148. Jimmy acted as John's No.2 for the flight from Hawarden to Woodford in May 1967. Jimmy was the pilot for the maiden flight of the first Nimrod MR.1, XV226, from Woodford on 28th June 1968.

Jimmy retired as CTP in 1970, and Tony Blackman* took over. Jimmy's long service for Avro/HS was far from over; he took on Product Support and held this for the next 14 years, retiring to live in Derbyshire. Sqn Ldr James Gordon Harrison AFC OBE, died on 16th April 2007, aged 88. He had flown almost 8,000 hours on 93 different types. During his time at Woodford 'Jimmy' was also affectionately known as 'Lucky Jim' and 'Gentleman Jim', for different aspects of his time as a thoroughly professional and gifted plot.

Maurice Hartford

| 7 May 1946 | HP Hastings C.1 TE580 |
| | 4 x 1,675hp Bristol Hercules 102 |

Maurice W Hartford, born 1915. Commissioned as a Pilot Officer in July 1939. By 1940 was with 214 Squadron on Vickers Wellington Is at Stradishall on 'ops'. He was posted to 148 Squadron, also on Wellington Is, and served from Luqa, Malta, in late 1940 and then in Egypt during 1941. Posted to A&AEE at Boscombe Down and tested Avro Lancaster III ED825 with 'Provisioning' mods (in this case a 12,000lb steel ball) prior to the 'Dam Buster' raid, Manston, April 1943. Graduated from ETPS Course No.1 – see Chapter Five – at Boscombe Down, 1943-1944 and afterwards is believed to have been seconded to the USAAF at Wright Field, Dayton, Ohio.

HANDLEY PAGE CTP 'Jamie' Talbot and FTO 'Ginger' Wright were killed on the maiden flight of the Hermes I airliner prototype on 2nd December 1945. Along with the Hermes, HP had developed a military transport version, the Hastings for the RAF. The prototype Hastings, TE580, was ready for flight test in the spring of 1946 and it was decided to take it by road to Wittering, where the long runway would provide a greater safety margin. With no replacement for Talbot finalised – Hedley Hazelden* took the post – Sqn Ldr Maurice Hartford DFC was loaned to HP for the first flight of the Hastings, which took place on 7th May 1946. After an uneventful test sequence, Maurice ferried TE580 to Radlett on 4th September. He flew the second example, TE583 at Radlett on 30th December 1946. He died in 1974, aged 59.

Maurice Hartford flew the second prototype Hastings, TE583, from Radlett on 30th December 1946. *KEC*

Harry Hawker

27 Nov 1913	Sopwith Tabloid 1 x 80hp Gnome
cNov 1915	Sopwith SL.T.B.P 1 x 50hp Gnome
Dec 1915	Sopwith 1½ Strutter 3686 1 x 110hp Clerget
Feb 1916	Sopwith Pup 3691 1 x 80hp Le Rhône
1916	Sopwith L.R.T.Tr 1 x 250hp RR Mk.I
Jun 1916	Sopwith Triplane N500 1 x 130hp Clerget
Dec 1916	Sopwith F.1 Camel N517 1 x 130hp Clerget
1917	Sopwith Bee 1 x 50hp Gnome
May 1917	Sopwith Dolphin 1 x 200hp Hispano-Suiza
Aug 1917	Westland N.1B N16 1 x 150hp Bentley AR.1
Jul 1918	Sopwith Scooter 1 x 130hp Clerget
Feb 1919	Sopwith Atlantic 1 x 375hp RR Eagle VIII
29 May 1919	Sopwith Gnu K-101 1 x 200hp Bentley BR.2
Aug 1919	Sopwith Schneider G-EAKI 1 x 450hp Cosmos Jupiter

Notes: Confirming 'firsts' by Harry Hawker, or specific dates – or even years! – of maiden flights, has been festooned with contradictions or worse. The exceptionally well-written 'Putnam' *Sopwith Aircraft 1912-1920* by H F King has been the shining light throughout, supported by Jack Bruce's trusted *The Aeroplanes of the Royal Flying Corps*. There are more Sopwith types that very likely could be added to this list, but not with certainty. All took place at Brooklands other than N.1B floatplane (which is *believed* to have used 'dolly' wheels for a launch from the grass at Yeovil) and the Schneider which flew from Southampton Water. Sopwith designations can be impenetrable; the T.B.P. bit of SL.T.B.P is Tractor Bi-Plane; L.R.T.Tr is Long Range Tractor Triplane.

Harry George Hawker, born 1889 in Australia. Early employment included a cycle shop, a car dealership and then chauffeuring. By 1911 Harry and friend Harry Busteed* had designed, built and raced motorcycles. Harry and his friends were deeply impressed by the flying demonstrations of Erlich Weiss – the 'Great Houdini' – flying a Voisin biplane at Diggers Rest, Victoria, in 1910. Harry Busteed was already

A pleasing, but uncharacteristic, image of Harry Hawker at a desk.
Peter Green Collection

hell-bent on travelling to Britain to become an aviator and had booked his passage for early 1911. Harry decided to join him, as did Eric Harrison and Harry A Kauper.

BEFORE dealing with the exceptional career of designer-pilot-adventurer Harry George Hawker, it is as well to reflect on the three friends that sailed with him; arriving in Britain in May 1911. Harry Busteed* has a section of his own in this chapter. Eric Harrison gained Aviators' Certificate No.131 on a Bristol at Salisbury Plain, 12th September 1911 and went on to be Chief Instructor for the Bristol school at Brooklands. Harry A Kauper became a mechanic with Sopwith in the spring of 1912, and had an adventure with Harry in the 'Circuit of Britain' of 1913. Harry Kauper exhibited great engineering talent and by 1916 had perfected the Sopwith-Kauper gear, an efficient synchronizing (or 'interrupter') mechanism allowing a machine-gun to fire 'through' the propeller.

On arrival in England, two of the Harrys, Hawker and Kauper, shared lodgings. Harry spent time watching the comings and goings at Brooklands in between looking for work. Harry Hawker secured work with the Commer Company in the summer of 1911 then briefly with the British divisions of Mercedes and the Austro-Daimler Company until Harry Kauper informed him that Sopwith was taking on staff. An interview with Fred Sigrist, General Manager at Sopwith, on 29th June 1912 changed the fortunes of the 23-year-old-Australian, Mr Sigrist and the man whose name the company carried, Thomas Octave Murdoch Sopwith* beyond their wildest dreams. (To avoid any confusion with the company that bore his name, Harry George Hawker will be referred to throughout this entry as HGH.)

All around him were impressed with HGH, he was talented and a 'grafter' with clear ambitions. L K Blackmore's biography of HGH, *Hawker – One of Aviation's Greatest Names* – describes a crucial conversation with the 'boss': "One day Harry asked Tom Sopwith if he would teach him to fly. In reply to Tom Sopwith's question as to what would happen if he broke the aeroplane, Harry took from inside his sock the money he had saved for his fare home and asked if it would cover any damage!" (HGH's 'war chest' was £50, in present day values £5,500. In terms of Edwardian spending power, in 1910 Bristol had been offering brand-new Boxkites for around £1,400, depending on engine choice – 'Tommy' Sopwith was clearly hoping for minimal breakages!) Flying a Sopwith school Farman, HGH showed that he was a 'natural' and was awarded Aviators' Certificate No.297 on 17th September 1912. During a trip to the USA, Tommy Sopwith had acquired a Burgess-built Wright biplane and brought it back with him. Under the guidance of Fred Sigrist, it was almost totally rebuilt and issued to the Brooklands school. HGH tried this machine out in October 1912 and set his sights on the British Empire Michelin Cup which offered £500 for the first flight lasting more than 5 hours. On HGH's second flight in the 'Burgess' he managed 3 hours, 31 minutes. On 24th October he stayed aloft for an incredible 8 hours, 23 minutes. A magazine report at the time noted that as HGH climbed out of the biplane: "he looked easily capable of undergoing the same trial again". At this time Sopwith was establishing the factory at Kingston-upon-Thames and getting ready to build aircraft from his own drawing office, which was located initially in a former ice skating rink. The story that designs were chalked out in full scale on the rink floor, debated and refined, has been told about several Sopwith designs.

The first wholly-Sopwith design was referred to as the 'Tractor' or the 'Three-Seater' – a biplane that had both of these attributes. On 31st May 1913 HGH took this machine to 11,450ft and a fortnight later reached 12,900ft, this time with a passenger for company – both record-breaking exploits. Tommy Sopwith carried out the maiden flight, but by early February 1913 he was letting HGH test the Three-Seater. This was followed by the Bat Boat, combining Tommy Sopwith's passions for sailing *and* flying, the testing of which the Tommy and HGH shared. In July 1913 HGH won the Mortimer Singer £500 prize for endurance and load-carrying using the amphibian.

During the spring of 1913 the *Daily Mail* offered a huge £5,000 prize for a 'Circuit of Britain' by an all-British 'waterplane' in the last two weeks of August. Powered by a 100hp Green, the Sopwith Circuit Seaplane was hastily conceived, but was very workmanlike. HGH was teamed with good friend Harry Kauper for the attempt, but HGH had to drop out when he was overcome by exhaust fumes during the attempt. Fellow Australian Sydney Pickles* stepped in as substitute, but in heavy seas the seaplane took in water. On 25th August, HGH had recovered and with Harry Kauper they got as far as the coast off Dublin on the 27th when the Circuit Seaplane was damaged during a precautionary landing. The 'Two Harrys' had travelled 1,043 miles in 20 hours flying time. The *Daily Mail* made much of presenting a special award of £1,000 to them. Testing a landplane version of the 'Circuit' biplane at Brooklands on 4th

October 1913, HGH was caught by a down-draught on take-off and it side-slipped and crashed; HGH was only slightly hurt.

The first Sopwith type to enter series production was the Tabloid, which HGH tested on 27th November 1913. A special version was flown to victory in the second Schneider Trophy contest at Monaco in April 1914 by Howard Pixton*. The Schneider version also served the RNAS and was later developed into the more capable Baby. From the Tabloid, a string of Sopwith military biplanes followed, some only prototypes, others built in small numbers, some becoming household names with long production runs. As will be seen from the notes appearing with the 'log' of HGH's 'firsts', confirmation of what was flown when-and-by-whom is lacking. It is safe to say that as chief pilot and often designer HGH was involved in the majority of Sopwith prototypes supported by his deputy, Victor Mahl*, and what must have been a small army of production test pilots.

In January 1914 HGH was back in his homeland, having sailed there along with Harry Kauper. Dismantled in the hold was a Tabloid, ready to be demonstrated to Australian interests. In his absence, 'Picky' Pixton served as a stand-in test pilot for Sopwith. Appearances of the Tabloid and its Australian 'hero' pilot were met by huge crowds. Both Tabloid and pilot were back in Britain in early June 1914. Towards the end of the month HGH was testing during the early evening a Tabloid at Brooklands when a loop at about 1,200ft feet went wrong and the aircraft commenced a dive and a spin. It crashed in trees close to the aerodrome; HGH was found standing nearby, unhurt.

Prior to the 1½ Strutter, so-called because of additional support struts at the centre section, a version referred to as 'Sigrist's Bus' was flown to a new height record of 18,293ft by HGH on 6th June 1915. The 'Strutter' itself appeared in December 1915 and allowed Sopwith to penetrate both the RNAS and RFC as markets. The type also helped to develop what became known as the Sopwith-Kauper synchronizing gears. Here was the start of a family of fighters, the Pup, the Triplane, Camel, Dolphin etc. Along with the Royal Aircraft SE.5a, the Camel was the best British fighter fielded during World War One and as with many Sopwith designs, HGH is thought to have had a considerable degree of input into its creation. Harald Penrose, in *British Aviation – The Great War and Armistice*, quotes engine designer Wilfred Owen Bentley who sheds light on the Australian's role and its effect on the Kingston design office. "I had the highest admiration for Harry Hawker. He knew exactly what the fighting pilots wanted, and saw they got it. He was a delightful person, but found it difficult to get along with [Herbert] Smith [chief designer]. In fact they were often at loggerheads, and seemed to have little time for each other." Penrose added his own thoughts: "Perhaps it irritated Smith that the great Sopwith test pilot could criticize and condemn if need be, the projects which were [Smith's] final responsibility..."

The only 'extra-curricular' type flown by HGH was the Westland N.1B, the first machine designed by the Yeovil-based company. Two examples of this single-seat floatplane fighter were built before the Admiralty pulled the plug on production orders. The management at Westland, having previously built designs perfected by other companies, probably felt the need

for expertise when it came to flight testing the N.1B. The
N.1Bs similarity to the Sopwith Baby *may* have been why
HGH was chosen for the job.

Plans by the Americans to cross the Atlantic by air – albeit
in stages – and the *Daily Mail's* £10,000 prize for the first
British non-stop flight over the ocean were very tempting
reasons for several British manufacturers to have a try at the
venture. Based on its B.1 bomber of 1917 and using as many
Cuckoo torpedo-bomber parts as possible, Sopwith created the
Atlantic biplane in very short time. HGH's attention to detail
could be found all over it; a deeper fuselage to allow more
comfort for the crew and plenty of room for fuel; a jettisonable
main undercarriage to help improve fuel consumption; a wind-
driven generator for the potentially life-saving radio. If all else
failed, a substantial lifeboat was available; placed upside-
down, its bottom formed the rear fuselage fairing and its keel
cleverly blended into the tail. Lt Cdr K Mackenzie Grieve, a
good friend of HGH, was the navigator and radio operator. The
Atlantic was test flown in February 1919 and then dismantled
for the sea voyage to St John's, Newfoundland.

At Qidi Vidi airstrip, 'Freddy' Raynham* and Captain C
Morgan were readying their Martinsyde. 'Jack' Alcock* and
Arthur Whitten Brown were busy trying to find a suitable
launch site for the Vickers entrant, the Vimy. All the while the
weather looked set to clamp in not for a day or two, but for a
month. HGH and Grieve departed on 18th May 1919,
dramatically over-flying Qidi Vidi to drop the undercarriage
in a graphic display of finality. (Raynham and Morgan later
crashed on take-off.) As the hours became days, British
newspapers became full of dread. Then a radio message came
through on the 25th from the *Mary*, a Danish freighter – they
had picked up HGH and Grieve! With the ceiling decaying to
about 1,000ft, the weather far from improving and the Eagle
VIII close to seizing, HGH put his hopes in finding the
maritime equivalent of a needle in a haystack – and there was
the *Mary*! The crew put out a lifeboat – itself a huge risk in
those waters – and brought the pair to safety after a textbook
ditching. Back in Britain the aviators were given a massive
welcome, with receptions and awards. The *Daily Mail* gave
them £5,000 for sheer pluck. Then on 15th June Alcock and

An early F.1 Camel at Brooklands, 1917. *Hawker Siddeley*

Sopwith 5F1 Dolphin C3854, 1918. *KEC*

Brown's Vimy ended up on its nose in an Irish bog and the
world's press had other heroes to write about.

In mid-September 1919 Bournemouth was to be the venue
of the first post-war Schneider Trophy contest. Tommy
Sopwith decided that the investment was worth it, especially
as the company was the present holder of the prestigious
award. The second Sopwith type to be called Schneider was
created at breakneck speed and HGH tested it on Southampton
Water in August. The contest, held on 10th September was a
British test pilot gathering: HDH and Vincent Nicholl* of
Fairey retired due to the fog and Supermarine's Basil Hobbs*
crashed. Italian Guido Jannello mis-interpreted the turning
points in the poor visibility and was disqualified.

The publicity helped a little, but the mighty Sopwith
'empire' was in trouble, like most aircraft manufacturers as
military orders dried up. The civilian market failed to blossom,
Sopwith created a version of the Pup, the Dove, offered as a
'sporting' biplane and in May 1919 HGH first flew the Gnu, a
three-seater 'air taxi', but neither did well. At the end of June
1920 Brooklands was holding a motor race meeting and
Sunbeam had announced that it would compete with a 450hp
car. HGH, a passionate Sunbeam owner, asked if he could take
the new car for a run prior to the main event. Up on the famous
banking, clocking something like 125mph, HGH suffered a
blow out and the car crashed. The Atlantic could not claim him,

Personnel helping to prepare the Sopwith Atlantic at Qidi Vidi, Newfoundland, May 1919. *Peter Green Collection*

Harry Hawker taxying the Sopwith Schneider G-EAKI, near Hythe, 1919. *Peter Green Collection*

nor could the Brooklands circuit; he survived. Not so Sopwith Aviation and Engineering Co Ltd, the liquidators were called in on 11th September 1920 and a great 'name' in British aviation was extinguished. A new company was formed on 15th November with the aims of manufacturing motorcycles, general engineering and, maybe, aircraft. Tommy Sopwith, HGH, Fred Sigrist and V W Eyre were directors of H G Hawker Engineering, named in honour of its designer-pilot-adventurer. (In 1933 the enterprise was renamed Hawker Aircraft.)

On 12th July 1921 HGH was testing the one-off Nieuport Goshawk G-EASK at Hendon prior to racing it. At about 2,500ft the Goshawk made a violent turn to port, began a steep dive and started to burn. It was pulling out but impacted the ground and broke up. HGH was thrown clear, dying minutes later. It was determined that the cover of the bottom carburettor had come unscrewed and that fire had broken out. The autopsy carried out on 32-year-old Harry George Hawker MBE AFC discovered that he had advanced tubercular degeneration of the spine – or 'Potts Disease' – which was very likely to have curtailed his valiant life before long. Harry was succeeded by fellow Atlantic chancer Freddy Raynham, on a freelance basis until 'George' Bulman* was appointed in 1925.

With Lt Cdr K Mackenzie Grieve, Harry wrote *Our Atlantic Attempt*, published by Metheun in 1919. Harry's widow, Muriel, wrote *H G Hawker, Airman: His Life and Work*, for Hutchinson in 1922. L K Blackmore wrote a biography of Harry, *Hawker – One of Aviation's Greatest Names*, in New Zealand published by David Bateman Ltd in 1990. For a eulogy, there can be none better than Sir Thomas Sopwith, quoted in H F King's magnificent *Sopwith Aircraft 1912-1920*: "Harry Hawker I got on with very well indeed. He was a beautiful pilot. He used his head."

Jim Hawkins

John Searle Hawkins, born 1939. Joined the RAF in 1961, becoming a flying instructor. Converting to the Hawker Hunter, he was posted to fly FGA.9s at Tengah, Singapore. In 1970 he attended the French test pilot school, École du Personnel Navigant d'Essais et de Réception (EPNER) at Istres before joining 'A' Squadron at A&AEE, Boscombe Down.

AT the top of a vertical zoom climb during a display at Dunsfold on 2nd July 1986 the prototype British Aerospace (BAe) Hawk 200 ZH200 made a quarter vertical roll, exactly following its painstakingly rehearsed routine. It then pitched slowly over, inverted, and made two small bank angle changes to port and starboard. Travelling south, it entered a steepening dive, still inverted. The aircraft impacted about 1½ miles south of the airfield, upright, wings level, at about 25-degrees nose down and 300 knots; its pilot, 47-year-old Dunsfold DCTP James 'Jim' Searle Hawkins, was killed instantly.

Jim joined Hawker Siddeley at Dunsfold in July 1973, under CTP Duncan Simpson* and became part of the Hawk development team working under Project Pilot Andy Jones*. Jim was in command of the second prototype Hawk T.1, XX156, which first flew at Dunsfold on 19th May 1975 with Mike Snelling* as co-pilot. Jim was part of the team that brought the Hawk through to its release for RAF service in November 1976, a remarkably short and smooth development period.

On 19th May 1986 CTP Mike Snelling* took ZH200, the prototype single-seat strike version of the Hawk, for its maiden flight. By this time Jim was DCTP and as well as development flying on ZH200, he worked up a display routine leady for the SBAC display at Farnborough that September. The display that Jim gave at Dunsfold on 2nd July 1986 was ZH200's 43rd sortie. It is believed that Jim suffered g-induced loss of consciousness – G-loc – and he was in the process of a recovery when the Hawk crashed. With some types of G-loc there are no warning symptoms, such as 'grey out', before consciousness is lost – perhaps for as much as 30 seconds. Jim was the first 'Hawker' test pilot to be killed since 'Wimpy' Wade* perished in April 1951 in the P.1081 – 35 years before.

Hedley 'Hazel' Hazelden

5 Sep 1948	HP Hermes 4 G-AKFP
	4 x 2,100hp Bristol Hercules 763
23 Aug 1949	HP Hermes 5 G-ALEU
	4 x 2,490shp Bristol Theseus 502
24 Dec 1952	HP Victor WB771
	4 x 9,000lbst AS Sapphire Sa.7
25 Aug 1955	HP Herald G-AODE
	4 x 870hp Alvis Leonides Major 701/1
11 Mar 1958	HP Herald G-AODE
	2 x 1,910shp RR Dart 527

Note: The Hermes first flew from Radlett, the Victor from Boscombe Down, the Heralds from Woodley.

Gathering in front of Hermes 4, G-AKFP, at Radlett, September 1948. Left to right: Noel Brailsford FTO, Hedley Hazelden, Reg Stafford chief designer, and a Bristol Engines Division flight engineer. *Handley Page*

Headley George Hazelden, born 1915. Started RAF flying training in the spring of 1939 and was posted to 44 Squadron at Waddington, on HP Hampdens. Returning from a raid on Leipzig on 16th October 1940, 'Hazel' was second pilot – in the single-place cockpit Hampden – and Jimmy Kneil was captain. In poor weather, after 9 hours and 15 minutes airborne, the Hampden – serial untraced – ran out of fuel and crash landed at Ramsey St Mary's, near Ramsey in Essex. All of the crew walked away with only minor injuries. As 'skipper' on a mine-laying 'op' to St Nazaire, Hazel had to divert due to fog and crash landed at Boscombe Down – again the crew were unhurt. Awarded a DFC in April 1941, Hazel was 'rested', instructing at 14 Operational Training Unit, Cottesmore (where he had been trained). He next joined 83 Squadron on Avro Manchesters at Scampton in late 1941. On the 12th/13th February 1942 Hazel, flying R5831, took part in mining the mouth of the Elbe, as part of the campaign against the German warships Scharnhorst, Gneisenau *and* Prinz Eugen *– the so-called 'Channel Dash'. On 8th/9th April 1942 the objective was Hamburg and on return his aircraft suffered a fire in the starboard Rolls-Royce Vulture at 9,000ft. Hazel pressed the button to feather the prop, only to find that* both *engines had feathered! After dropping 4,500ft he managed to unfeather the port engine and landed at Horsham St Faith after an over-water flight in a Manchester on one engine – no mean feat! In May 1942 the unit re-equipped with Avro Lancaster Is and 83's first 'op'*

on the new type was Cologne on 30th/31st May as one of the 1,047 aircraft dispatched on the first 'Thousand Bomber' raid. Hazel's last 'op' was 25th/26th June 1942 to Bremen, the third 'Thousand' attack. With his second 'tour' behind him, Hazel again instructed at an OTU before graduated from Course No.1 ETPS at Boscombe Down 1943-1944 – see Chapter Five – and was posted in 1944 to A&AEE. Among his tasks was testing a Lancaster carrying the 22,000lb 'Grand Slam' bomb and by 1945 he was CO of the newly-established Civil Aircraft Test Squadron within A&AEE.

Sqn Ldr Maurice Hartford* held the fort for Handley Page (HP) after CTP 'Jamie' Talbot* died in the crash of the prototype Hermes airliner, near Radlett on 3rd December 1945. He flew the first and second prototype Hastings transports in May and December 1946. Sqn Ldr Hedley 'Hazel' Hazelden DFC* was at Radlett by April 1947, although it was the following July that he officially took up the post of CTP for Handley Page. On 25th April 1947 he piloted the first production Hastings C.1, TG499, while readying for the resumption of the Hermes project. The stretched and somewhat refined Hermes 2, G-AGUB, was first flown by Hazel from Radlett on 2nd September 1947. The decision had already been taken that to put life into the Hermes programme, it needed much further revision and that production would standardise on the Hermes 4 with tricycle undercarriage and Hercules 763 two-row 14-cylinder radial piston engines. A further development, the Hermes 5 with turboprops was also initiated. Hazel flew Hermes 4 G-AKFP for a 75-minute air test

The prototype Hermes 4, G-AKFP, 1948. *Rolls-Royce, Bristol Division*

Sapphire Hastings TE583, first flown by 'Hazel' Hazelden in November 1950 to help pave the way for the Victor. *Peter Green Collection*

Vulcan fans may not like the 'flies fastest, farthest, highest' of this mid-1950s Handley Page advert, but its claims were spot on!

on 5th September 1948 just in time to appear at the SBAC airshow at Farnborough. During testing on 22nd October 1947 an elevator trim tab caused violent flutter, Hazel throttled back and made a hasty return where it was found that the tailplane was close to parting company with the rear fuselage. The first of two Hermes 5s, G-ALEU, had its maiden flight in the hands of Hazel on 23rd August 1949 at which point it was the world's most powerful turboprop.

With a total production run of 29 Hermes of all variants, the programme was a great disappointment, but work was gearing up on what could well be a mother lode of income – the Victor V-bomber. As part of the run up to the new, crescent-winged bomber, the second Hastings prototype, TE583, was modified by HP to flight test the Armstrong Siddeley (AS) Sapphire turbojets that would power the V-bomber. Engine development was such that it actually flew with early F.9s that had been built by Metropolitan-Vickers, before the project was handed on to AS, becoming the Sapphire. Hazel flew the half-jet, half-piston TE583 – with the turbojets in place of the outer Hercules pistons – from Radlett on 13th November 1950 on a 20-minute test and it helped provide experience of the new powerplant. This knowledge increased still further when from late 1951 he sampled the Sapphire Sa.3, later Sa.6, powered English Electric Canberra B.2 test-bed WD933. The final element of preparing the way for the Victor was the HP.88 wing test-bed, VX330, which was first flown by Blackburn's 'Sailor' Parker* on 21st June 1951. This machine crashed on 23rd August 1951, killing 'Duggie' Broomfield*, before it could contribute data to the Victor, or give the CTP a 'feel' for the crescent wing's characteristics.

"Smoothly, effortlessly, the Victor slid into its natural element. By doing so it had become an aeroplane instead of just the expression in metal of so many drawings and hieroglyphics on paper. Whatever happened now we all knew it could fly." Eloquent words from Hazel describing the maiden flight of the Victor, as quoted in 'Sandy' Powell's *Men with Wings*. The prototype Victor, WB771, was taken to Boscombe Down and assembled, ready for the 17-minute maiden flight on Christmas Eve 1952, as described above; Ken Bennett was the FTO. The V-bomber prototype carried out early trials from Boscombe, whereas it would have been more convenient to have it back at Radlett, ready to be worked on if needed. This was a temporary 'detachment' while a runway extension was completed. On landing at Boscombe on 9th February 1953 WB771 gave off a series of bangs, much vibrating and a burning smell – all 16 wheels on both the main gear bogies had burst. When the undercarriage was retracted, the still-spinning wheels were stopped by the parking brake; the huge jet had landed with that brake still on! A method of de-conflicting this was soon introduced. The section on 'Taffy' Ecclestone* charts the demise of WB771, Taffy and three others, including Ken Bennett who had accompanied Hazel on its first-ever flight. It was a sad and salutary day for Hazel, especially as he may well have been captaining the fateful sortie.

Handley Page's acquisition of most of the Miles aviation assets at Woodley in July 1948 provided the company with an in-place airliner programme, the forlorn four-engined Marathon, and several design studies. From this came the

Herald, intended as a Douglas DC-3 replacement, while *doubling* the number of engines that needed looking after! Hazel flew the prototype, G-AODE, powered by four Alvis Leonides, from the turf at Woodley on 25th August 1955 for 30 minutes with the company's chief aerodynamicist, R J Davies, alongside him. *Delta-Echo* appeared at the SBAC airshow at Farnborough the following month. As testing continued in 1957, the belated decision was taken to re-engine the Herald with the highly-successful Rolls-Royce Dart turboprop. The prototype Herald, *Delta-Echo* was substantially re-engineered and emerged as the first Dart Herald at Woodley and was first flown by Hazel on 11th March 1958.

En route from Woodley to Farnborough, ready for the SBAC airshow, on 30th August 1958 a straightforward air-to-air photo-session and a 'commute' turned horrifically wrong. Next to Hazel was Ray Wood, less acting as FTO, more an extra set of eyes as G-AODE and 'Johnny' Allam* in Victor B.1 XA930 formed up at 6,000ft in loose formation – the Herald leading, the V-bomber behind and to port – for air-to-air publicity photos. In *Delta-Echo's* cabin were seven passengers; including Hazel's wife Esma. Near Guildford the low pressure turbine wheel in the starboard Dart turboprop shattered, shards from it cutting and severing the engine bearers and fuel line. As Hazel called-off the 'photo shoot' and peeled away to take stock, an intense fire broke out. Unbeknown to him the starboard tailplane was taking the brunt of the flames leaping backwards and was breaking up. The damaged Dart then fell away and all of Hazel's options were centred on the countryside dead ahead. Hazel took the Herald *under* power lines and belly landed in a field. The airliner slid onwards, across a ditch and collided with the stump of a tree which fractured the fuselage behind the cockpit. It was from this impromptu escape hatch that all nine occupants of *Delta-Echo* made their exit. It had been an exceptional piece of flying. The second Dart Herald prototype, the rebuilt G-AODF, took to the air at Woodley on 17th December 1958.

Hazel retired from test flying in 1965 and was succeeded by Johnny Allam. He flew as a commercial pilot for a number of airlines and from 1978 Hazel was president of the Handley Page Association. Sqn Ldr Hedley George Hazelden DFC* died on 27th August 2001, aged 86.

The first prototype Herald, G-AODE, in the colours of Queensland Air Lines. *Handley Page*

The second prototype Dart Herald, in the colours of BEA, getting airborne from Woodley, 1958. *Handley Page*

Superb lines of the second Victor, WB775. Hazel 'first flighted' this on 11th September 1954. *Handley Page*

Jack Henderson

17 Aug 1961	HP HP.115 XP841
	1 x 1,900lbst AS Viper 9

Jack Morton Henderson, born 1931 in New Zealand. Joined the RAF in 1950 and attended RAF College Cranwell in 1953, becoming an instructor. He graduated from ETPS Course No.18 at Farnborough in 1959 and was posted to the Aero Flight, RAE Thurleigh. On 8th November 1961 he became the first RAF pilot to fly the Hawker P.1127, XP831, and the following year became OC, Aero Flight.

SPECIFICATION ER.197D was issued in December 1959 for a simple jet-powered low-speed test-bed to explore the aerodynamic characteristics of a slender delta wing. Handley Page (HP) won the contract and its HP.115 had fixed undercarriage, a 'podded' cockpit – complete with ejection seat – and, for those days, the engine innovatively placed above the rear fuselage, with the fin and rudder mounted above it. Built at Radlett, XP841 was roaded to what was to be its base for its entire flying career, Aero Flight at RAE Thurleigh. As the OC of Aero Flight and therefore the 'customer', Jack Henderson carried out the 32-minute maiden flight on 17th August 1961. (See also Chapter Five.) RAE therefore carried out the 'contractor flying programme' that ordinarily would have been undertaken by HP before hand-over to operator. Jack signed off XP841 on 29th September 1961 and it started a long career in research flying, including investigating the slow speed characteristics of the upcoming Concorde programme. Today, the HP.115 is displayed within the 'Leading Edge' Hall of the Fleet Air Arm Museum, Yeovilton, alongside Concorde 002. During his time at Thurleigh Jack became a specialist in V/STOL flight testing, before becoming RAF project officer on the Jaguar programme. Wg Cdr Jack Morton Henderson OBE AFC* died in September 1990, aged 59.

The HP.115 displaying at the SBAC airshow, Farnborough, 8th September 1962. *Roy Bonser*

Peter Henley

PETER HENLEY joined the RAF in 1957, completing three tours on HP Hastings at Changi, Singapore in the late 1960s before converting to Lockheed Hercules, first with 30 Squadron and then as the CO of 70 Squadron. He joined British Aerospace at Woodford as a test pilot in 1977 and was appointed as DCTP to 'Robbie' Robinson* in 1982. He succeeded Robby as CTP in 1987 and his post became Vice President, Flight Operations in 1991. During his tenure at Woodford, Peter flew HS Andovers, HS.748s, Nimrods, BAe ATPs and BAe 146s. He also delighted in displaying the company owned DH Mosquito T.3 RR299 (G-ASKH). He retired in 1993, with 'Al' McDicken* taking over. Maintaining RAFVR status, he flew Air Experience Flight sorties in SAL Bulldogs. From 1990 to 1997 he co-owned DH Tiger Moth G-ACDJ, owning it outright from 1997 to 2001 and a series of classic cars, including a 1933 Rolls-Royce. Wg Cdr Peter Henley died on 2nd March 2015, aged 76. He had accumulated about 9,000 flying hours on over 80 types.

'Jim' Heyworth

6 Jul 1953	RR Thrust Measuring Rig XJ314
	2 x 4,900lbst RR Nene 101 IV

Alexander James Heyworth, born 1922. Was reading medicine at Cambridge, but volunteered for the RAF in May 1940. By July 1941 he had been posted to 12 Squadron at Binbrook on Rolls-Royce Merlin X-powered Vickers Wellington IIs. Returning from a raid on Nuremburg on 14th/15th October 1941 the starboard Merlin failed, but 'Jim' elected to try and get back. The strain of applying full port rudder was telling on him and to give him a rest, the rudder pedals were lashed with rope. Jim managed to force-land in Kent and all of his crew were unhurt, although they suffered 'arrest' by a shotgun-armed farmer! Jim received an immediate DFC for his determination. After a 'rest' posting, Jim returned to 12 Squadron in late 1942, by then the unit was flying Avro Lancasters from Wickenby. With 60 'ops' behind him, Jim was given a staff appointment.

SQN LDR 'JIM' HEYWORTH DFC was seconded to Rolls-Royce (RR) at Hucknall in 1944 as a test pilot. One of his first tasks was flying Fairey Battle I K9222 which had been fitted with the 1,200hp 24-cylinder Exe piston engine. The bulk of his early work was devoted to development of the Whittle W2B jet engine and he was re-united with the Wellington II; Z8570 having been adapted to take a turbojet in the rear fuselage, in place of the turret. As outlined in Chapter Four, the incredible work of powerplant testing is beyond the remit of this book, but Jim was destined to be a rare exception, by 'first flighting' a prototype. On leaving the RAF in 1946, Jim signed on full-time with RR, continuing the varied test work which in the early 1950s was to take him in a new 'direction'.

Co-operation between RR and the RAE starting in 1952 led to a jet-powered test-bed to produce data for a dedicated lift engine and a control and stabilisation system for hovering

The incredible Rolls-Royce Thrust Measuring Rig, understandably called the 'Flying Bedstead' by the press. *Rolls-Royce via Peter Green*

flight. RAE provided the control systems while RR created what was known as the Thrust Measuring Rig (TMR) but which the press readily called the 'Flying Bedstead'. Two horizontally-mounted Nene turbojets were coupled together via T-shaped ducting that provided downward thrust. A small amount of thrust was bled away into four 'puffer' jets to provide stability, projecting starboard and port and fore and aft. The latter two could swivel to provide a limited amount of directional control; it could fly sideways, or in circles.

The TMR was rolled out at Hucknall on 3rd July 1953, carrying its serial number on one of its legs as there was nowhere 'formal' to paint it! It was mounted within a complex gantry arrangement that provided a degree of tethered flight, limited by cables on pullies. Sitting atop the pair of turbojets in an open cockpit protected by a crash-cage, Jim Heyworth piloted the first successful tethered hop three days after the roll-out. 'Shep' Shepherd* carried out the first free excursion on 3rd August 1954. Tests at Hucknall were completed on 15th December 1954 by which time it had clocked up 224 tethered and 16 free flights, the latter amounting to 105 minutes airborne. XJ314 was transferred to the RAE in January 1955 and is today displayed in the 'Making of the Modern World' gallery in the Science Museum, London. A second TMR, XK426, was built but crashed on 27th November 1957, killing Wg Cdr H G F Larson.

Before continuing with Jim's test piloting career, his elder brother, Harvey, cannot be ignored. Born in 1910 Harvey joined the RAF in 1931, becoming an instructor. Leaving the service in 1936 Harvey joined RR at Hucknall as a test pilot. He was recalled to the RAF in 1940, joining 222 Squadron at Hornchurch, flying Supermarine Spitfire Is. In July 1940 he became the CO of 79 Squadron, initially at Acklington then from August 1940 in the thick of it at Biggin Hill. During this time his 'tally' came to 1½ Heinkel He 111s. In March 1942 Harvey returned to RR at Hucknall flying, like his brother, a wide range of types. Harvey became the first pilot in the world to 'clock' 1,000 hours on jets. Sqn Ldr J Harvey Heyworth AFC died in 1959, aged 49.

In 1955 Jim was promoted, becoming CTP and in June he flew Gloster Meteor FR.9 VZ608 modified to test the RB.108 lift-jet for the Short SC.1 – see Tom Brooke-Smith. (VZ608 is today on show at the Newark Air Museum, Winthorpe.) Jim flew 82 types, including Avro Ashton, Avro 707, RR Dart-powered Douglas Dakota and Saab Lansen, among a glittering list. Chapter Four includes details of Jim's involvement in the RR Spey-powered Vulcan test-bed in 1961. Retiring from test flying in 1962, Jim stayed with RR taking on a number of tasks, finally leaving the company in 1981. Sqn Ldr Alexander James Heyworth DFC* died on 10th June 2010, aged 88. The exploits of the two brothers are charted in Robert Jackson's excellent *Men of Power – The Lives of Rolls-Royce Test Pilots Harvey and Jim Heyworth*, published by Pen & Sword in 2006.

Geoffrey Hill

2 Nov 1925	Hill Pterodactyl I
	1 x 32hp Bristol Cherub III

Notes: First flown at Farnborough, later given the serial number J8067.

Geoffrey Terence Roland Hill, born 1895. Built a glider of his own design with his brother, Roderic Hill* (see below), in 1914. Served with the RFC/RAF, flying Royal Aircraft Factory SE.5as with 29 Squadron. Also flew as a test pilot with the Royal Aircraft Factory at Farnborough.

AFTER the Heyworths (above) two more brothers: Geoffrey and Roderic (below). Captain Geoffrey Hill MC was engaged by Handley Page (HP) as a test pilot from November 1918. His time at Farnborough and interest in aircraft structures meant that he increasingly spent time in the design office and carrying out trials. Soon he was helping to create the leading edge slots that became a cash-cow for HP as they were licenced around the world. Most of the test flying centred on civilian versions of the O/400 bomber, for example O/7s for China; Geoffrey testing the first of these in early July 1919. For much of the latter half of 1919 Geoffrey was unable to work, having been struck with the deadly influenza virus that was sweeping across much of Europe. During this time the company relied upon pilots from sister company Handley Page Transport for testing – see Robert Bager and Sholto Douglas. Recovered, Geoffrey set a British record in HP W.8 G-EAPJ on 4th May 1920 by climbing to 14,000ft with a useful load of 3,690lb.

Geoffrey left HP in 1923 to follow up his own ideas. Like Juan de la Cierva* Geoffrey became fascinated in creating an aircraft that could not stall. He came up with a tail-less configuration with rotating 'controllers' at the wing tips that acted as both elevators and ailerons. Small rudders mid-set underneath the wings provided additional directional control. Hill built a glider to prove his point and on the last day of 1924 he flew it at the wonderfully-named Devil's Rest Bottom on the Sussex Downs. This got the RAE at Farnborough interested and eventually, the Air Ministry. Along with his wife, Hill built a powered version, the Pterodactyl I which he flew the first time, for five minutes, at Farnborough on 2nd November 1925. Hill used the name Pterodactyl – a winged dinosaur – as the generic term for all of his tail-less designs. Trials at RAE showed that the concept had prospects and the Mk.I was given the serial number J8067. With official interest increasing, Hill joined the staff of Westland at Yeovil in 1926, taking charge of a department established to exploit the concept. The Pterodactyl II and III remained on the drawing board but the Mk.IV two-seat pusher first flew in March 1931 leading to the tractor-configured Mk.V two-seat fighter in May 1934. (For more see Westland test pilots: Laurence Openshaw, Louis Paget and Harald Penrose.)

Geoffrey accepted a professorship at the London University College in 1935 and work on the Pterodactyls ceased. Professor Hill was not done with 'controller'-like wings; in 1950 he moved to Belfast to create the SB.1 and Sherpa – see Tom Brooke-Smith. Geoffrey donated J8067 to the Science Museum in 1951 and it is displayed at South Kensington, London. Professor Geoffrey Terence Roland Hill MC died on 26th December 1955, aged 60.

A gathering a Yeovil in mid-1929 with a Westland IV behind. Left to right: Captain Claude Petter, Geoffrey Hill, R J Norton. *KEC*

Pterodactyl J8067 coming into land at the 1926 Hendon show over the prototype Armstrong Whitworth Argosy I, G-EBLF. (See Frank Barnard for the Argosy). *KEC*

Roderic Hill

Jan 1917	Royal A/c Factory SE.5a A4563 1 x 200hp Hispano-Suiza V8
Apr 1917	Royal A/c Factory FE.9 A4818 1 x 200hp Hispano-Suiza V8

Roderic Maxwell Hill, born 1894. Elder brother of Geoffrey Hill* (see above). Studied architecture then volunteered for the Royal Fusiliers, 1914; transferring to the RFC in 1916.

Captain Roderic Hill was posted to the Royal Aircraft Factory at Farnborough in 1916. On the death of Frank Goodden* in the second prototype SE.5 on 4th December 1916, Roderic became CTP for the 'Factory' and from 1918 to 1923 was OC Experimental Flying with the RAE. The SE.5 single-seat fighter was rethought and refined, given a lower-set cockpit, a streamlined fairing behind the pilot's head, shorter span wings and a much-needed 200hp 'Hisso' with four-bladed propeller. Roderic flew the first SE.5a – as the new version was designated – in January 1917. He ferried it to Martlesham Heath on 29th May 1917 and it was greeted with much enthusiasm. This could not be said for his second 'first', the two-seat FE.9 pusher, intended as a replacement for the FE.2b. The 'pod' containing observer/gunner, pilot and engine was attached to the top wing via struts and was separate from the bottom wing; being joined by a small forest of struts. After its maiden flight, Roderic ferried it to St Omer in France for operational trials, where it was met with dismay. In 1918, Roderic was involved in very risky flying to perfect methods of aircraft surviving impact with observation balloon cables. One of these trials involved flying a FE.2b with a wire connected at the front of the 'pod' to each wing tip at a balloon's cable. While the wire was deflected 'down' the bracing wire, it snagged on the wing tip of the FE.2, causing serious

Wolseley Motors-built SE.5a D6940 *Parish of Inch No.2* of 29 Squadron at Hooq Huis, France, 1918. *KEC*

damage; Roderic was lucky to make a forced landing. While with the RAE, Roderic met 'George' Bulman* and recommended him for a posting to RAE in 1919; both pilots contributed considerable to the knowledge of spinning and recovery.

Roderic left Farnborough in 1924 to become OC of 45 Squadron, flying Vickers Vernons in Iraq. Beyond this, he had a glittering promotion path which included: Director-General Research and Development at the Air Ministry 1941, AOC 12 Group 1943 and C-in-C Fighter Command 1943-1945. ACM Sir Roderic Maxwell Hill KCB MC AFC* retired from the RAF in 1948 and died on 6th October 1954, aged 60.

Peter Hillwood

19 Mar 1951	EE Canberra PR.3 VX181 2 x 6.500lbst RR Avon 101
27 Jul 1958	EE Canberra PR.9 XH129 2 x 11,250lbst RR Avon 206

Notes: PR.3 first flown from Samlesbury; XH129 was the first from-new PR.9 and flew from Sydenham.

Peter D Hillwood, born 1920. Gained his pilot's licence at Cambridge Aero Club May 1938 and enrolled in RAFVR July 1938. Called up for RAF service 1st September 1939 and joined 3 Squadron on Hawker Hurricane Is, deploying to Merville, France, in May 1940. During combat on 17th May 1940, flying L1899, Peter was shot down by return fire from a Dornier Do 17 and he force-landed at Vitry-en-Artois. The Hurricane caught fire on landing and Peter was burnt on the hands and face. He was back in action in June 1940, at North Weald with 56 Squadron, also equipped with Hurricane Is. In June he claimed a Messerschmitt Bf 109 and on 13th July 1940 a Junkers Ju 87 'Stuka'. On 13th August 1940, flying R4093, Peter was in combat with Bf 110s and was shot down off Sheerness. He baled out and swam 2 miles to the shore.

After a period as an instructor in Canada, he returned to Britain and served with 127 Squadron with Supermarine Spitfire XVIs from bases within the Netherlands – his personal aircraft being SM179 Lady Jane *until April 1945.*

FLT LT PETER HILLWOOD DFC was seconded to the Ministry of Supply in 1945 as a test pilot for Supermarine, under Jeffrey Quill* and for Cunliffe-Owen, working on Supermarine Spitfires and Seafires. He left the RAF in October 1946 and joined English Electric as an assistant test pilot to Roland Beamont* in March 1949. Initially he tested DH Vampires from Samlesbury before joining the Canberra programme. Having owned or operated a Miles Gemini twin, Peter had access to Percival Proctor I G-AIEY and used it to travel up from his farm in Hampshire to Warton. He was at the helm of Canberra PR.3 prototype VX181

on 19th March 1951 and seven years later renewed the photo-recce role when he flew the first from-new Canberra PR.9 XH129 from the Shorts production line at Sydenham. (PR.7 WH793 was converted into the interim PR.9 and was first flown on 8th July 1955 – see Michael Randrup.) As related in Roland Beamont's section, Peter was co-pilot during the Canberra transatlantic out-and-back on 26th August 1952. As well as Canberras, Peter went on to fly EE P.1s and Lightnings, becoming Senior Experimental Test Pilot. He also got to try out an English Electric product of a very different era – the Wren ultralight of 1923. The Preston workshops rebuilt G-EBNV for the Shuttleworth Trust under the guidance of Peter and he carried out the post-restoration test flight on 25th September 1956 at Warton. The Wren was handed over to Shuttleworth on 15th September 1957 and it is airworthy today at Old Warden.

The first true prototype Canberra PR.9, XH129, on its maiden flight at Sydenham 27th July 1958, flown by Peter Hillwood. *Shorts*

Peter Hillwood flying the restored English Electric Wren II at Warton, late 1956. This machine is still flown at Old Warden. *English Electric*

Peter left BAC in March 1963 to concentrate on his poultry farm, but was quickly immersed in historic aviation projects. As a member of the Eastleigh-based Hampshire Aero Club, he was appointed project leader on the creation of two flying and one static replica Avro Type IV Triplanes for the 1965 film *Those Magnificent Men in their Flying Machines.* Peter carried out the research, including tracking down 'Ronnie' Kemp* who had trained on the Type IV in 1911. During the film Peter flew the Hants and Sussex Aviation-built Antoinette Monoplane and the Best Devereux and Co Eardley-Billing replicas. Peter also piloted some of the World War One replicas during the filming of *The Blue Max,* released in 1966. Desmond Norman* flew the prototype Britten-Norman Islander, G-ATCT, on 13th June 1965 and by the following year Peter was on the payroll as a test and demonstration pilot. Returning from a demonstration in West Germany on 9th November 1966 Peter was flying *Charlie-Tango* over the Netherlands. The aircraft crashed, killing the 46-year-old Battle of Britain veteran. Investigation attributed the accident to overstressing in a fast descent that may have been brought on by icing; it is believed that Peter was climbing to fly over deteriorating weather.

'Johnny' Hindmarsh

John Stuart Hindmarsh, born 1907. Enlisted in the Army, trained at Sandhurst and entered the Royal Tank Corps. He was seconded to the RAF in 1930, and joined 16 Squadron at Old Sarum flying Armstrong Whitworth Atlases and then 4 Squadron and Hawker Audaxes, by which time he had transferred to the RAF.

WHEN Flt Lt 'Johnny' Hindmarsh arrived at Brooklands to take up production flight testing Hawker Hurricanes, under Philip Lucas*, his surroundings were very familiar to him. It was the race track, not the aerodrome that he knew well. He was an experienced racing driver and had competed at Brooklands many times. His wife, Violette Cordery, was a record-breaking long-distance competition driver. Settling in to the task of getting Hurricanes out to operational units, Johnny had a prior commitment that his new employer was

happy for him to carry out. Driving a Lagonda Rapide at an average of 125mph, Johnny won the 1935 Le Mans 24-hour race. At Debden, personnel of 85 Squadron were busy converting from Gloster Gladiators to Hurricane Is in the first days of September and Johnny climbed into L1652 which would join the Essex-based unit when he signed it off. Shortly after take-off the fighter was seen to enter a dive and it crashed in a ball of flame, killing the 31-year-old instantly.

'Bert' Hinkler

1921	Avro Bison N153 1 x 480hp Napier Lion II
1922	Avro Aldershot J6852 1 x 650hp RR Condor III
1923	Avro 558 1 x 16hp Grigg B & H
1923	Avro 560 1 x 18hp Blackburne Tomtit
1924	Avro Avis 1 x 35hp Blackburne Thrush
1926	Avro Buffalo G-EBNW 1 x 450hp Napier Lion VA
1926	Avro Avian G-EBOV 1 x 70hp AS Genet
26 Jun 1926	Avro Avenger G-EBND 1 x 525hp Napier Lion VIII
1927	Cierva C.8L J8930 1 x 180hp AS Lynx
4 May 1927	Short-Bristow Crusader N226 1 x 650hp Bristol Mercury I
Sep 1927	Cierva C.9 J8931 1 x 70hp AS Genet
May 1930	Ibis Aircraft Ibis G-AAIS 2 x 40hp Salmson AD.9

Notes: All flown from Hamble other than Short Crusader, which used the waters off Felixstowe. The Cierva C.8L and C.9 were built by Avro and based upon an Avro 504N and Avian fuselage, respectively.

Herbert John Louis Hinkler, born 1892 in Australia. 'Bert' joined Brisbane Aero Club in 1910 and during the next two years designed and built a glider, which he flew with some success. He travelled to Britain in late 1913 and worked as a mechanic for Sopwith. In September 1914 he enlisted in the RNAS and flew as an observer/gunner in France and Belgium – he was awarded the DSM in December 1917. He re-trained as a pilot and flew operationally with 28 Squadron on Sopwith Camels in Northern Italy against Austro-Hungarian forces. Post-war Bert persuaded Tommy Sopwith to loan him a Dove – a civilianised version of the Pup – for a flight to Australia during 1919, but it did not go ahead. Bert worked for Avro as a mechanic during 1919 and in April the following year bought the second Avro Baby, G-EACQ, from the company. On 21st May 1920 Bert took it on a 650-mile non-stop flight from Croydon to Turin, Italy, in just over 9½ hours. After this he had G-EACQ shipped to Sydney, Australia. On 11th April 1921 Bert flew the Baby non-stop 800 miles to his birth place of Bundaberg, Queensland. With great panache, he landed in the main street and taxied up to the gate of the family house! Later registered as VH-UCQ, the Baby now graces the Queensland Museum in Brisbane.

HAVING returned from Australia, 'Bert' Hinkler went back to Avro, but this time as its CTP, based most of the time at Hamble. The diminutive Baby had caught its test pilot, Bert's predecessor Harold Hamersley*, out on its first flight in April 1919 and one was to 'bite' Mr. Hinkler. Testing the short-span G-EAXL at Hamble on 6th September 1922 the engine cut and both pilot and machine were dunked into Southampton Water; the pilot recovered, the Baby was written off.

Two large military biplanes were the first 'clean sheet' Avro designs of the post-war era. First to fly was the Bison shipborne general reconnaissance type, which Bert flew from Hamble in 1921. The second was the massive, 68ft-span Aldershot bomber debuted by Bert at Hamble in 1922 with a 650hp Rolls-Royce Condor. The prototype, J6852, was re-engined with the 16-cylinder X-format Napier Cub of 1,000hp as the Aldershot II. Bert piloted this powerful beast at Hamble on 15th December 1922 and gave a semi-aerobatic routine upon his return from assessing it, followed by a high-speed run of around 140mph in front an august audience, including Napier chairman H T Vane and Alliot Verdon Roe. Beyond the two prototypes, 15 served the RAF up to 1926, using the more sedate Condor III. Two types that remained one-offs were the Avenger, single-seat fighter and the Buffalo shipborne torpedo-bomber, both were brave private ventures.

Avro entered two different designs for the *Daily Mail* light aeroplane competition, staged at Lympne in October 1923. Two Type 558 biplanes, from Roy Chadwick's drawing board were flown by Bert and Harold Hamersley, while the Type 560 monoplane was also piloted by Bert and designed by the great pioneer himself, A V Roe. The converted motorcycle engine powering Bert's 558 let him down, but Hamersley had better success in the other example. During the competition Bert flew the Type 560 for just over 1,000 miles and the company's publicity machine lost no time in declaring that the fuel bill came to just £1. The 1924 competition was for two-seaters and for this a pair of shapely Avis biplanes were created, one powered by a Blackburne Thrush, the other by a 32hp Bristol Cherub. The Thrush-powered example proved temperamental, but Bert managed to win the Grosvenor Challenge air race staged within the Lympne trials, netting £100 for an average of 65.8mph.

Avro built a series of Autogiros for Juan de la Cierva and Bert 'first flighted' two of these, the C.8L and C.9. He tested one aircraft from another manufacturer, the Short-Bristow Crusader racing floatplane which was entered for 1927

A proud Bert Hinkler with the prototype Avian G-EBOV which he had just bought from Avro, 1927. *Avro*

Hinkler with Avro designer Roy Chadwick on his right and general manager Reginald Parrott to his left in front of Avian G-EBOV at Hamble, prior to Bert's flight to Australia. *British Aerospace*

Schneider Trophy contest to be staged at Venice in September. Bert had flown the back-up Gloster IIIA G-EBLJ in the October 1925 contest at Baltimore. That machine was dogged with problems and Bert had to retire, leaving Hubert Broad* to fly the other Gloster IIIA into second place. It was possibly this experience which drove the Air Ministry to select Bert to test the Crusader and not Short's own John Lankester Parker*, or a MAEE Felixstowe pilot. In the event the Crusader was relegated to the practice aircraft at Venice.

Bert took off from Woodford in Avro 504R Gosport G-EBPH on 22nd December 1926 and headed north on a publicity flight. He landed close to the summit of Helvellyn, the highest point in the English Lake District at 3,118ft. The biplane Bert is most associated with is the Avian and it was this machine in which he made his incredible flight back to his Australian homeland. Roy Chadwick aimed the Avian at the September 1926 *Daily Mail* light aeroplane competition. Bert flew G-EBOV, the prototype and during the trials, despite a leaking fuel tank, he flew 1,074 miles during the three days of the event; the Avian came second overall in the judging. The prototype went through a series of evolutions, including a modification Bert created to improve upon the wing-folding system. He introduced a wide-track undercarriage with the ability to move backwards as the wings were folded, this greatly improved ground handling and access to the engine.

With a long-range tank fitted to G-EBOV, Bert left Croydon on 27th August 1927 bound for Riga in Latvia on the Baltic Sea. He succeeded in making the longest non-stop flight in a light aircraft at that time, a staggering 1,200 miles in 10¾ hours. With Robert McIntosh, Bert had been planning to fly from Britain to India via the 'Great Circle' route that would

involve crossing much of central Europe. They had acquired Fokker F.VIIA G-EBTS *Princess Xenia* for the attempt. With fuel on board sufficient for 50 hours, they departed Upavon on 15th November 1927 but after over 20 hours in the air were forced down in present-day Ukraine. An attempt to set off again ended when the Fokker's undercarriage was damaged in a forced landing. The exploit was abandoned.

The Latvian trip had convinced Bert that the Avian was *the* vehicle for his long-held ambition to fly solo to Australia and for this he bought G-EBOV from Avro. Again it was 'tweaked', this time with larger wings and a robust undercarriage and Croydon was again the point of departure. He set of on 7th February 1928 and 15½ days, 128 flying hours and 11,005 miles later, he arrived in triumph in Darwin, Northern Territories. Not content with this Bert took G-EBOV on a punishing 200 hour tour of Australia, drumming up sales and waving the flag for Avro, before arriving in Bundaberg and a tumultuous welcome. The Avian is now the star exhibit at the Queensland Museum in Brisbane.

On his return to Britain, Bert resigned as Avro CTP in February 1928 with 'Sam' Brown* taking up the post. In 1929 Bert formed the Ibis Aircraft Company and set about the construction of a twin-engined amphibian of his own design, Ibis G-AAIS. The two Salmson AD.9 radials were mounted in a pod suspended above the fuselage; one pulling, one pushing. As the project continued, Bert ran out of funds and the Ibis was finished as a landplane, with fixed undercarriage; but it was clear that with further investment a full-blown amphibian version was easily achievable. Bert began test flying G-AAIS in May 1930 from Hamble.

The second prototype Bison, N154, at Martlesham Heath, 1923. *Peter Green Collection*

The prototype Aldershot, in Mk.II guise with the huge Napier Cub at Hamble just prior to its first flight with the 1,000hp powerplant, December 1922. *Peter Green Collection*

The first production Avian, G-EBQN, showing Bert Hinkler's patented wide-track undercarriage and wing folding, 1927. *KEC*

The one-off Avenger fighter, 1926. *Peter Green Collection*

Superb image of Basil Hobbs at the helm of Sea Lion I G-EALP on Southampton Water, very likely 5th September 1919. *Supermarine Aviation Works*

Basil Hobbs

5 Sep 1919	Supermarine Sea Lion I G-EALP
	1 x 450hp Napier Lion IA

SQN CDR BASIL D HOBBS was employed early in 1919 by Supermarine Aviation Works initially to fly charter and joy-riding flights using a small fleet of Supermarine Channel biplane flying-boats in the hope of establishing regular airline operations. The company had also decided to compete in the first post-war Schneider Trophy competition to be staged off Bournemouth on 10th September 1919. For this, designer F J Hargreaves created the Sea Lion I single-seat biplane flying boat. The Sea Lion was ready to test on 5th September, just five days before the competition. Basil took it for its first air test from Southampton Water that day and then ferried the flying-boat westwards along the coast ready for the main event. His time in the competion was fraught with difficulty, there was fog near Swanage and he nearly collided with Vincent Nicholl* in the Fairey III G-EALQ. After this he was unsure of his location and made a precautionary landing but he could get no better 'fix' on his whereabouts. On take-off there was a loud noise, it was clear he had hit something floating in the water. Returning to the start point, he touched down, but water gushed into the holed hull and the Sea Lion partially sank; Basil was rescued by motor launch. After this inauspicious beginning, Supermarine started its domination of the Schneider Trophy in 1922 – see the section on Henri Biard.

In 1931 Bert acquired de Havilland Puss Moth CF-APK in Canada and spent a lot of time preparing it for another incredible long-range odyssey. On 7th December 1931 he completed the first solo crossing of the South Atlantic when he touched down at Hanworth. The trip included a spectacular non-stop sector from New York to Jamaica, a visit to Venezuela and several 'city pair' records broken. He decided to re-live the solo to Australia and using the Puss Moth he set out from Croydon on 7th January 1933. Nothing was heard of him again and it was not until 27th April 1933 that his body was found amid the wreckage of CF-APK in northern Italy's Apennine mountain range. Herbert John Louis Hinkler DSM, AFC engineer, fighter pilot, test pilot, designer and long-range adventurer was 41 years old. As well as his Avro Baby and Avian on show in the Queensland Museum, the Hinkler House Memorial Museum and Research Association at Bundaberg, Queensland, is a spectacular tribute to a great aviator, including replicas of the Baby, the Ibis and Hinkler's house from Thornhill near Southampton which was dismantled brick-by-brick and rebuilt at his birthplace.

Captain Hooper

Sep 1916	Bristol F.2A A3304
	1 x 190hp RR Falcon I

THE otherwise anonymous Captain Hooper was the CO of 5 Aircraft Acceptance Park at Filton. From time to time the neighbouring Bristol factory asked him to test its products and at least once, he was requested to 'first flight' a prototype. The favoured candidate for this sort of work was 'Freddy'

The Hinkler Ibis at Hamble, 1930 – it never wore its registration. *Peter Green Collection*

Raynham*. Mr Raynham was clearly unavailable wen it came to testing Bristol F.2A A3304, which was to lead to the famous F.2B Fighter. *Bristol Aircraft since 1910* by C H Barnes recounts that Hooper returned from his assessment declaring that he could fly no higher than 6,000ft – a deeply disappointing service ceiling. After a series of tweaks, Hooper went aloft again, with the same conclusion. Frank Barnwell, the F.2A's gifted designer, decided to call in bigger 'guns', summoning his brother, Vickers CTP Harold Barnwell*. C H Barnes takes up the story, noting that Harold: "reported a maximum altitude of 6,000ft, although he felt certain he had climbed very much higher. Then the penny dropped, the altimeter was changed and the fault was found." The impressive prototype had climbed to 10,000ft in just 15 minutes. No more is known of Captain Hooper.

Paul Hopkins

Paul Anthony Hopkins, born 1951. Joined the RAF 1969 and in 1973 was operational on Harrier GR.3s with 1 Squadron at Wittering, and 1976 to 1980 on GR.3s with 3 Squadron at Gütersloh, West Germany. After a period on Harrier weapons instruction, he attended the US Navy Test Pilots School at Patuxent River, Maryland, USA. He was posted to A&AEE Boscombe Down 1983 to 1985.

PAUL HOPKINS joined British Aerospace (BAe) at Dunsfold in 1985, flying Hawks, Harriers and Sea Harriers. He moved to Warton in 1989, becoming Hawk 200 Project Pilot and DCTP in 1996. As well as Tornados he was involved in initial testing of the Saab JAS.39 Gripen in which BAe was initially involved in a co-operative agreement with the Swedish manufacturer. On 28th September 1996 Paul was flying Tornado F.3 ZE759 with Alan 'Al' Reynolds as systems operator on a test flight. During a 'go-round' at Blackpool Airport at 600ft ZE759 began rolling uncontrollably; the pair ejected seconds before the aircraft impacted into the shoreline in front of Blackpool's famous 'Golden Mile'; both were unhurt. It was discovered that the starboard taileron actuator had suffered foreign object damage, hence the rolling. In 1997, Paul was appointed CTP and two years later BAe became BAE

Systems and he had added the Typhoon to his repertoire. With Dave Sully as systems operator, Paul flew Typhoon DA4 ZH590 with a fully-functional Raytheon AMRAAM air-to-air missile on 15th March 2005. Over the Benbecula, Outer Hebrides, range, Paul launched the missile against a Galileo Mirach drone, decidedly despatching it. Paul retired in 2012 and following an illness, died on 31st August 2014, aged 53.

Edmund Hordern

Nov 1933	BK Swallow 1A G-ACMK 1 x 75hp Salmson AD.9
1934	BK Eagle G-ACRG 1 x 130hp DH Gipsy Major
18 Aug 1935	Heston Phoenix G-ADAD 1 x 200hp DH Gipsy Six Srs I
1936	Hordern-Richmond Autoplane G-AEOG 2 x 40hp Continental A40

EDMUND GWYN HORDERN was engaged by the British Klemm (BK) Aeroplane Company of Hanworth as a test pilot. BK had secured a licence to produce the popular German-designed L.25 two-seat monoplane as the Swallow. Edmund flew the prototype and production totalled 135. This was followed up by the Eagle, two-seat cabin monoplane with retractable undercarriage; the prototype flew in 1934 and was followed by another 25 examples. The company changed its name to the British Aircraft Manufacturing Company in 1935 and in that year Edmund joined Heston aircraft as a director and test pilot. He 'first flighted' the Phoenix high-wing single with retractable undercarriage. The Phoenix offered both speed and capacity – it was a five-seater – but only six were built. While Edmund was at Heston, he and the Duke of Richmond commissioned the company to build a three-seater twin to their specification. This was the Hordern-Richmond Autoplane, which he flew in 1936. The pair formed Hordern-Richmond Aircraft in 1938, but G-AEOG remained a one-off.

Several BA Swallows survive, including Pobjoy Niagara III-powered G-AFCL, although at the time of writing it was not airworthy. *KEC*

The second Heston Phoenix, G-AEHJ, in 1938. *KEC*

The one-off Hordern-Richmond Autoplane, at Martlesham Heath, 1936. *Peter Green Collection*

Charles 'Sox' Hosegood

24 Aug 1952	Bristol 173 Mk.1 G-ALBN 2 x 550hp Alvis Leonides
5 Jul 1958	Bristol 192 XG447 2 x 1,465shp Napier Gazelle

Charles Thomas Dennehy Hosegood, born 1921 in St Lucia, in the Caribbean. Enlisted in the Fleet Air Arm in November 1939, and first saw service flying air-sea rescue Supermarine Walrus amphibians with 765 Squadron at Sandbanks, Dorset. In 1942 he was in command of a detached flight of 702 Squadron on the armed merchant cruiser HMS Alcantara *equipped with two Fairey Seafox floatplanes. The flight disbanded at Freetown, Sierra Leone, in early 1943. 'Sox' returned to the UK on the SS* Empire Whale, *but it was torpedoed off Cape Finisterre, on the north western coast of Spain, on 29th March 1943. Picked up by the Royal Navy, he was one of only ten survivors. Sox was posted to another Walrus unit, 751 Squadron at Dundee, as an observer. He was sent to the Sikorsky plant at Bridgeport, Connecticut, to convert to the Hoverfly helicopter.*

Back in Britain in late 1944 Sox flew for a while with the General Aircraft-operated Helicopter Unit at Hanworth before moving to the Airborne Forces Experimental Establishment at Beaulieu as Naval Test Pilot. At Beaulieu on 9th June 1945 Sox was involved in a bizarre and tragic accident. Flying Hoverfly I KK978 with O Fitzwilliams as FTO, Sox was involved in stability tests hovering over the airfield

with a pendulum 'bob' weight suspended from a cable underneath the helicopter. Castle Bromwich-built Spitfire FR.XIV NH840, assigned to Supermarine for a variety of trials, impacted with the cable and the fighter crashed near Lymington, killing Canadian Fg Off D M Eastman. Sox and Fitzwilliams were unhurt. Sox left the Navy in November 1946 and worked for two years with the Trinidad Petroleum Development Company.

THERE are at least two stories about how Lt Hosegood got his nickname 'Sox'. The first comes from a former Filton-based Bristol member of the company's design team. He asserted that it was a play on 'Hosiery Goods', that's *socks*. There was a barb in the tale: 'Sox' being a Royal Navy man would never be able to spell 'socks' correctly! The other is less apocryphal, 'Sox' having flown many, many hours in the Bristol Sycamore Mk.3 demonstrator G-ALSX, which was referred to as 'Sox' by Weston-super-Mare staff. However, the sobriquet 'Sox' appears to pre-date G-ALSX! (Sycamore G-ALSX is today preserved at The Helicopter Museum at Weston-super-Mare.)

Sox Hosegood joined Bristol as a helicopter test pilot, based at Weston-super-Mare, in 1948. He was heavily involved in Sycamore development and demonstration flying, particularly in the civil certification of the type. In the early 1950s Bristol began the design of a twin-rotor helicopter with civilian applications as a 13-seater and military roles as transport or air crane. This was the Type 173 which used as many Sycamore components and systems as possible. Sox began ground runs of the prototype in late 1951. The first hover was achieved on 3rd January 1952 but, as C H Barnes noted in *Bristol Aircraft since 1910* Sox: "found difficulty in moving in any direction but backwards". Developing Britain's first and, as it transpired, only twin-rotor helicopter was a long and involved process. It was not until 24th August 1952 that Sox was able to fly around the airfield, enabling him to transit to Farnborough for the SBAC airshow the following month. Fleet Air Arm interest led to trials on the aircraft carrier HMS *Eagle,* these were flown by Sox in 1953.

The second Type 173, G-AMJI was flown initially with stub wings, fore and aft, for evaluation by British European Airways for potential air services, but reverted to conventional helicopter layout for more naval trials as XH379. During an air display at Filton on 16th September 1956 this machine was involved in a spectacular accident and Sox was very lucky to come away with minor injuries. While flying across the airfield at low level, XH379 was struck by turbulence from a Blackburn Beverley airlifter on a flypast and was blown downwards, the cockpit impacting with the ground and the big helicopter rolling over in a cloud of dust. By this time, the twin-rotor design had evolved to much more powerful turboshafts and Sox flew the first Type 192 on 5th July 1958. As the Belvedere HC.1 the type entered limited production for the RAF in 1961. The Bristol helicopter division became a part of Westland in 1960. Sox became the chief pilot, and later manager, for the South West Electricity Board's pioneering helicopter power line patrol operation in 1963; retiring 20 years later. Lt Charles Thomas Dennehy Hosegood died on 17th April 2014, aged 93.

The hard-working Sycamore Mk.3 G-ALSX was flown considerable by 'Sox' Hosegood. *Bristol*

Ground runs at Weston-super-Mare on the prototype Bristol 173: 'Sox' Hosegood carried out the first hover on 3rd January 1952. *Bristol*

Bristol 173 XH379 at the point of impact at Filton on 16th September 1956; 'Sox' survived the crash. *Peter Green Collection*

The turbine-powered Bristol 192 prototype undergoing early trials – note the pitot tube and 'weather vane' – at Weston-super-Mare, summer 1958. *Bristol*

Len Houston

28 Mar 1980	BAe Jetstream 31 G-JSSD
	2 x 900shp Garrett TPE331-10

Len Houston learned to fly with Edinburgh University Air Squadron in 1950 and entered the RAF in 1952, serving operationally with 222 Squadron at Leuchars initially on Gloster Meteor F.8s and, from late 1954, on Hawker Hunter F.1s. In 1956 Len became a test pilot for Ferranti at Turnhouse on weapons system development. He moved to Warton in 1959, flying P.1Bs and early Lightnings, again for Ferranti. In 1965 he was appointed Ferranti CTP on a wide range of development and trials work until 1973.

LEN HOUSTON became DCTP for Scottish Aviation at Prestwick in 1973, under John Blair*. Scottish Aviation became part of British Aerospace in 1977. Len became CTP in 1979, and he 'first flighted' the new generation Jetstream, the 19-seat Series 31 on 28th March 1980 at Prestwick. Co-pilot for the 82-minute sortie was Angus McVitie* with Andrew Eldred and Garrett's Bob Baker as flight test engineers. Len was involved in certification, delivery and demonstration of the type until 1986 when he was appointed as Flight Safety Manager for BAe Commercial Aircraft. Jetstream 31 prototype G-JSSD is today displayed at the National Museum of Flight Scotland, at East Fortune.

The Jetstream 31 prototype, G-JSSD, as first flown by Len Houston on 28th March 1980. *British Aerospace*

'Benny' Charles Hucks

Nov 1916	Airco DH.5 A5172
	1 x 110hp Le Rhône

Bentfield Charles Hucks, born 1884. Initially an apprentice with commercial vehicle manufacturer Thorneycroft. By 1910 he was working as a mechanic for Hendon-based Claude Grahame-White and travelled with him on his tour of the USA that year. Returning to Hendon, 'Benny' started to get experience by 'rolling' Grahame-White school Farmans.

"At Filey RB [Robert Blackburn] established himself with a hangar and a bungalow, and soon his activities attracted the attention of a young man named B C Hucks, who had previously been with Grahame-White [touring] at Blackpool. Hucks persuaded RB to let him try piloting his second Blackburn aircraft 'try' being the operative word as he was not a qualified pilot! He did, however, take his aviator's certificate in the Blackburn monoplane after teaching himself to fly in the machine, and went on to become one of the country's most skilful pilots in the years preceding the Great War, being in fact the first Englishman to loop the loop. ...the partnership between Blackburn and Hucks proved fruitful for both men, the one expertly demonstrating the products of the other." This is how Blackburn Aircraft's commemorative booklet *The Blackburn Story 1909-1959* described the coming together of two pioneers.

The young 'Benny' Hucks certainly made an impression on Robert Blackburn, even though on the completion of his first 'outing' with Robert's monoplanes, 8th March 1911, he side-slipped, resulting in some damage. Both parties persevered with each other and on 30th May 1911 Benny got his 'ticket': Aviators' Certificate No.91. Benny became an instructor at Blackburn's seashore 'aerodrome' at Filey also undertaking tours and demonstrations.

By 1912 he was back at Hendon, on the staff of Grahame-White as a pilot and he acquired a Blériot. Benny became a regular performer at the constant stream of events staged at the aerodrome. At Buc in France in September 1913 Adolphe Pégoud bestowed a phrase on the world, he sensationally 'looped the loop' in a Blériot and instantly shot to fame. Early in November the Frenchman performed the manoeuvre at Hendon and he galvanised Benny, who could see that his Blériot could propel him to new challenges. It is worth pointing out that while Benny was a performer he was *not* a showman. He was not looking for adulation or perhaps even fortune, but he was passionate about taking aviation to the masses. At the last Hendon meeting of the season, on 29th November 1913, in front of a crowd estimated at 50,000 Benny looped the loop and suddenly this spectacle was much in demand. He set about a tour of Britain, starting the following spring.

With the outbreak of the Great War in August 1914, Benny stopped the 'circus' and signed up for the Royal Flying Corps. He was despatched to France, but his operational flying was curtailed by a bout of pleurisy and he was sent home for lighter duties. Benny was posted to Hendon where Geoffrey de Havilland*, chief designer of the Aircraft Manufacturing Company (Airco), appointed him as chief pilot. As Airco got into stride a huge outflow of aircraft needed shaking down and

Famed showman 'Benny' Hucks and his Bleriot -he was far less well known as a test pilot. *Peter Green Collection*

delivering and Benny was joined by more production test pilots. Only the DH.5 with its distinctive backward stagger to its biplane wings can be attributed to Benny as a 'first' as Geoffrey tended to carry out the debuts of his designs. Still an RFC pilot, Benny was assigned other tasks that occasionally took him away from Hendon – see the section on Frank Goodden for an 'arrival' at Farnborough in November 1915.

Original programme for the Scarborough Aviation and Regatta Week, July 1914. Morning and afternoon demonstrations would include, looping the loop, upside-down flying, vertical banking and side-slipping, cart-wheel recovery, the Dutch roll and the 'whip-top twizzle'. The programme warned that the latter "makes one giddy". *KEC*

As well as looping the loop, Benny is synonymous with an invention of his own that became a boon to operators of larger aircraft, civil and military, until electric ignition systems became the norm. At the end of yet another test flight, as Benny prepared to taxi in at Hendon, the engine died. Perhaps it was a DH.4, either way it was a huge propeller and beyond the reach and ability of its tired pilot to even *think* about hand swinging it. It was a long walk back to the flight office to get help. The germ of an idea was growing. Could a machine be developed to throw the propeller over? It would need its own power source and, for ease of operation, be readily portable. Why not mount it on a vehicle, a self-propelled starter? The ubiquitous Ford Model T was the favoured platform and so the Hucks Starter was born. An axle driven via clutch was suspended above the car with a shaft protruding well forward.

Airco DH.5 A9197 of the Australian-manned 68 Squadron in France, 1917. The backward stagger of the wings was to give the pilot a commanding view. *Peter Green Collection*

A Bristol F.2B Fighter of the Royal Aircraft Establishment demonstrating the Hucks Starter, circa 1924. *KEC*

At the end of this was a simple 'claw' that engaged with a similar fitting mounted permanently on the propeller boss. Slip the clutch, let the axle turn, the prop rotated, the engine fired and a spring-loaded device disengaged the revolving axle. Probably thousands Fords and other vehicles took on a new role and were used well into the 1930s.

A bout of influenza led rapidly to pneumonia and 34-year-old Bentfield Charles Hucks died on 7th November 1918 – four days before the Armistice that brought the Great War to an end. In his autobiography *Sky Fever*, Benny's former 'boss', Sir Geoffrey de Havilland praised him: "As a test and demonstration pilot he was outstanding, and he could put a DH.4 into evolutions never seen before."

Douglas Hughes

DOUGLAS HUGHES was an instructor at the Armstrong Whitworth (AW) flying school at Whitley Abbey in the 1920 and, as so often was the case, was occasionally asked to lend a hand with production testing from the neighbouring factory. Frank Courtney* had been involved in a series of extensive sales tours of the Continent between 1922 and 1924 in an AW Siskin V and the Romanian government had signed up for a substantial number. In 1925 a Romanian pilot had died in one of the early deliveries when the fighter broke up in mid-air. The contract was cancelled and worries about the integrity of the Siskin V lingered. These fears were stoked on 19th July 1926 when Douglas Hughes took Siskin V G-EBLQ up for a test and the aircraft crashed, killing him. (Frank Barnard* had won the 1925 King's Cup race in G-EBLQ.) It was discovered that the leading edge of a wing had collapsed during aerobatics and development of the Siskin V went no further.

The half-scale Hamilcar, GAL.50 T-0227 at Hanworth prior to its first flight, September 1941. *KEC*

Charles Hughesdon

15 Nov 1941	General A/c GAL.50 T-0227 glider
27 Mar 1942	General A/c Hamilcar DP206 glider

Notes: GAL.50 first flew from the Great West Aerodrome (Harmondsworth); the Hamilcar from Snaith.

Charles Frederick Hughesdon, born 1909. Briefly trained for the priesthood at Dublin in 1922, but then worked for the Johnny Walker distillery, construction contractor Balfour Beatty before entering the insurance business in 1927. He learned to fly in 1932 and played a major part in setting up the Insurance Flying Club, gaining an instructor's licence. In September 1936 Charles crewed with David L Llewellyn in Percival Vega Gull G-AEAB in the Schlesinger Race to South Africa. On 30th September they had to force-land on the southern shore of Lake Tanganyika, writing off the Vega Gull – though a bottle of Napoleon brandy survived! Charles and David were rescued the following day. (This was the prototype Vega Gull, it had been first flown by Edgar Percival* during November 1935.) Having signed up for the RAFVR in 1934, Charles was called up and started bashing the circuit at 7 EFTS at Desford as an instructor in 1939.

Charles Hughesdon's autobiography, *Flying Made it Happen*, was published in 2003 and within is charted what can only be described as a glittering love-life which, sadly, has no part in this work! At Desford, Charles made it abundantly obvious his skills were wasted and this may have had some bearing on his being seconded to General Aircraft Ltd (GAL) at Hanworth and Heston. There he mostly tested Supermarine Spitfires on modification to photo-reconnaissance status or off overhaul.

Under the design leadership of Hollis Williams* GAL was involved in creating a mammoth assault glider to Specification X27/40. This was to take 60 fully-equipped troops or a 7-ton light tank into battle and emerged as the 110ft wingspan Hamilcar. To prepare the way, the half-scale GAL.50 was created and Charles flew this under tow at Fairey's Great West Aerodrome in November 1941. The prototype Hamilcar was taken to Snaith, near Pontefract, for assembly and its maiden flight, towed behind a Handley Page Halifax, was made by Charles on 27th March 1942. This went well, but a later sortie proved to be full of self-inflicted hazard! On take-off the main undercarriage of the Hamilcar was designed to be jettisoned as the next landing would not require wheels and would use the substantial skid structures under its belly. For the tests, there was only one undercarriage set and retrieving it each time was

A D-Day striped Hamilcar and Halifax over the Army camp at Blandford, Dorset. The glider's 110ft wingspan was 6ft greater than that of the bomber.

proving irksome. Charles was asked to pull the appropriate lever as early as possible, so that the units fell on the runway. With the big glider only 10ft off the runway an over-enthusiastic Charles jettisoned the gear, only to have one of the units bounce violently, hitting the side of the fuselage and crushing part of the inboard trailing edge of the wing. Meanwhile, inside a startled FTO pulled his parachute which blossomed inside the fuselage because of the massive in-rush of air from the gash in the side. The tug pilot was alerted, aborted the climb and brought the combination around for a quick circuit. Once on finals, Charles detached the tow rope, the Halifax carried out a go-around and the Hamilcar slid to a halt, safely.

In 1943 Charles was sent to the British Air Commission at Washington dc, USA. Returning late in 1943 he became an early member of 511 Squadron, flying Avro Yorks from Lyneham. Charles returned to insurance broking post-war, increasingly specialising in aviation-related coverage, retiring from the business as chairman of Stewart Wrightson in 1976. Charles became majority shareholder in the Gatwick-based Tradewinds Airways in April 1969; the airline operating a fleet of Canadair CL-44D-4s on freight charters. He sold his stock in the company in 1977. Charles Frederick Hughesdon AFC died on 11th April 2014, aged 104.

'Bill' Humble

2 Sep 1947	Hawker P.1040 VP401
	1 x 4,500lbst RR Nene I

William Humble, born 1911. Apprenticed as a mining engineer, 'Bill' went on to work in the coal industry. He learned to fly in 1929 and from mid-1935 to December 1936 owned Miles Hawk Speed Six G-ACTE, which he entered for several racing events and based it at Firbeck. He joined the RAFVR and served with 504 (County of Nottingham) Squadron, operating Westland Wallaces and Hawker Hinds from Hucknall. With the outbreak of World War Two, Bill was posted to 11 FTS at Shawbury, but after just ten weeks he was called back to the strategically vital mines. It was nearly a year before the RAF won through and got him back!

'BILL' HUMBLE was posted in 1941 as an instructor to Scotland but never got there; he was seconded to Hawker at Langley as a PTP on Hurricanes and Typhoons. Working under the veteran Philip Lucas*, Bill worked on the development of the Tempest and Fury series. Included in the former was the first flight of the Tempest VI on 9th May 1944 which differed from the Mk.V mostly by fitting a 2,340hp Napier Sabre V and a larger radiator. He also carried out trials in October 1944 with Tempest V SN354 with a 40mm cannon in a fairing under each wing. Philip Lucas retired in 1945 and Bill took over as CTP at Langley. While Tempests and Sea Furies provided a lot of production flying, the big programme looming was the P.1040 single-seat jet fighter for the Fleet Air

Bill Humble flying the well-worn first production Tempest V JN729 which he 'first flighted' on 21st June 1943. *Hawker Aircraft*

The beautiful lines of the Hawker P.1040 VP401 being flown by Bill Humble in early 1948. *Hawker Aircraft – Cyril Peckham*

Arm to Specification N7/46 and eventually named Sea Hawk. The prototype, VP401, was taken to Boscombe Down for its debut and Bill was at the controls on 2nd September 1947. Bill retired the following year, with 'Wimpy' Wade succeeding him. Bill took on a sales management task and by 1953 was the Middle East sales representative for Hawker. William 'Bill' Humble MBE died in 1992, aged 81.

Raymond Huxley

RAYMOND R HUXLEY was a production test pilot for Fairey at Ringway, checking out Stockport-built Handley Page Halifaxes. On 18th March 1944 he and Geoffrey A Leadbetter, acting as flight engineer took brand new Mk.III LK836 for a pre-sign off test. (This machine is confused with Radlett-built Mk.III LV836 in two sources.) The Halifax crashed in flames at Northwich and both men were killed.

Appendix A

UK Aviation Manufacturers – A Brief Genealogy

To help keep track of changing names, below is a *brief* look at who-became-who in the main players of the UK aircraft industry.

Airspeed: Acquired by de Havilland in 1940, still trading under its own name; absorbed into **de Havilland** in 1951.

Armstrong Whitworth: Part of the Hawker Siddeley Group from 1935 – along with Avro, Gloster and Hawker – but trading under its own name. With the setting up of **Hawker Siddeley Aviation** in 1963, the use of its original name stopped by 1965.

Blackburn: Renamed **Blackburn and General Aircraft** in 1949. Became part of **Hawker Siddeley Aviation** in 1963 and use of its original name stopped by 1965.

Auster: Taken over by **Beagle** in 1960.

Avro: Part of the Hawker Siddeley Group from 1935 – along with Armstrong Whitworth, Gloster and Hawker – but trading under its own name. With the setting up of **Hawker Siddeley Aviation** in 1963, the use of its original name stopped by 1965.

Bristol Aeroplane Co: Became part of **British Aircraft Corporation** in 1960. The helicopter division was acquired by **Westland** at the same time.

British Aerospace: Merged with Marconi in 1999, becoming **BAE Systems**.

British Aircraft Corporation: Merged into **British Aerospace** in 1977.

British and Colonial Aeroplane Co: Renamed as Bristol Aeroplane Co in 1920.

Britten-Norman: Has had several owners in its time with changes of name/title, but essentially keeping the original 'BN' identity.

Cierva Autogiro: Merged its organisation with **G & J Weir** in 1943, but used Cierva as trade name. Absorbed into **Saunders-Roe** in 1951. Cierva Autogiro remained a separate legal entity post-1951 and it acquired Rotorcraft Ltd in 1966, becoming **Cierva Rotorcraft Ltd**.

Comper Aircraft: Re-organised as **Heston Aircraft**, 1934.

Coventry Ordnance Works: Became part of the combine that formed **English Electric** in 1918.

De Havilland Aircraft: Became part of **Hawker Siddeley Aviation** in 1963 and use of its original name stopped by 1965.

Dick, Kerr and Co: Became part of the combine that formed **English Electric** in 1918.

Edgar Percival Aviation: Independently established by the founder of Percival Aircraft in 1954; acquired by **Lancashire Aircraft** (Samlesbury Engineering) in 1960.

English Electric: Closed its aviation element in 1926. Re-entered aircraft manufacture in 1938 and became part of **British Aircraft Corporation** in 1960.

Fairey: Acquired by **Westland** in 1960.

Folland: Became part of **Hawker Siddeley Aviation** in 1963 and use of its original name stopped by 1965.

General Aircraft: Merged with Blackburn as **Blackburn and General Aircraft**, in 1949.

Gloucestershire Aircraft: Known as **Gloster** from 1926. For convenience, throughout this book, the company is referred to as 'Gloster'. Part of the Hawker Siddeley Group from 1935 – along with Armstrong Whitworth, Avro and Hawker – but trading under its own name. With the setting up of **Hawker Siddeley Aviation** in 1963, the use of its original name stopped by 1965.

Hawker Aircraft: Officially H G Hawker Engineering until 1933, part of the Hawker Siddeley Group from 1935 – along with Armstrong Whitworth, Avro and Hawker – but trading under its own name. With the setting up of **Hawker Siddeley Aviation** in 1963, the use of its original name stopped by 1965.

Hawker Siddeley Aviation: Merged into **British Aerospace** in 1977.

Hendy Aircraft: Amalgamated into **Parnall Aircraft** in 1935.

Hunting Aircraft: Acquired by **British Aircraft Corporation** in 1960.

Martin & Handasyde: Became **Martinsyde** in 1913.

Miles: Trading from 1933 through **Phillips & Powis Aircraft**, then **Miles Aircraft** formed in 1943, but collapsed 1947. Marathon and other design rights, plus Woodley airfield acquired by **Handley Page (Reading) Ltd** in June 1948. **F G Miles Ltd** formed in 1951; aviation activities to **Beagle** in 1960.

NDN Aircraft: Established independently by Desmond Norman (see Britten-Norman) in 1976; re-named **Norman Aeroplane** in 1985.

Pemberton-Billing: Renamed **Supermarine Aviation Works** in 1916.

Percival Aircraft: Acquired by Hunting Group 1944, but traded under its own name. Renamed **Hunting Percival Aircraft** in 1954 and **Hunting Aircraft** in 1957.

Petters Ltd: building aircraft at the Westland Aircraft Works, Yeovil, from 1915. Universally referred to as 'Westland'; taking the name **Westland Aircraft** in 1935.

Phoenix Dynamo: Became part of the combine that formed **English Electric** in 1918.

Saunders-Roe: Also known as Saro. Acquired by **Westland** in 1959.

Scottish Aviation: Became part of **British Aerospace** in 1977.

S E Saunders Ltd: Became **Saunders-Roe** in 1928.

Short Brothers: To avoid confusion with the word 'short', throughout this book the company is referred to as 'Shorts' where it is used singly. (From late 1947, the company announced it was to be known as Shorts. This was explained as not being plural, or possessive, but as a contraction of Short Brothers.) Formed 1908 and in 1938 **Short & Harland** was established in Belfast. Both companies were nationalised in 1943 and merged, becoming **Short Brothers and Harland** in 1947. Renamed **Short Brothers** in 1977. Acquired by the Canadian Bombardier Group in 1989, becoming known as **Bombardier Aerospace Belfast**.

Sopwith Aviation: went into liquidation in 1920, re-emerging as **H G Hawker Engineering**, renamed as **Hawker Aircraft** 1933

Supermarine Aviation Works: Acquired by Vickers in 1928, but continued to trade under its own name. Restructured as **Vickers-Armstrongs (Supermarine Division)** in 1938 but universally referred to as Supermarine all the way up to the Scimitar. Vickers aviation assets became part of **British Aircraft Corporation** in 1960.

Taylorcraft Aeroplanes (England): Renamed as **Auster** in 1946.

Vickers: Via Vickers Ltd (Aviation Dept) and Vickers (Aviation) Ltd re-organised as **Vickers-Armstrongs (Aircraft) Ltd** in 1955, but continued to be universally referred to as Vickers. Aviation assets became part of **British Aircraft Corporation** in 1960.

Westland Aircraft: Re-organised as **Westland Helicopters** in 1966 and renamed **GKN Westland** in 1994. Merged into Italian-British **AgustaWestland** in 2000.

Appendix B

Abbreviations and Acronyms

These have been kept to a minimum, but those mostly used are as follows:

AAP	Aircraft Acceptance Park	DCTP	Deputy Chief Test Pilot
ABC	ABC Motors – or All British Engine Co	DH	De Havilland
ADC	Aircraft Disposal Company – or Airdisco	DHC	De Havilland Canada
AEE	Aeroplane Experimental Establishment, Martlesham Heath, became A&AEE 1924	DSC	Distinguished Service Cross – DSC* with Bar
		DSO	Distinguished Service Order – DSO* with Bar
A&AEE	Aircraft and Armament Experimental Establishment, Martlesham Heath then, from 1939, Boscombe Down	EE	English Electric
		EFTS	Elementary Flying Training School – Elementary & Reserve Flying Training School (E&RFTS) prior to 1919
AES	Aeroplane Experimental Station, Martlesham Heath, 1917 to 1920: became AEE	ENV	English designed, French-built engine; acronym derived from the French for V-configuration – 'En V'
AFC	Air Force Cross	
AFS	Advanced Flying School	EoN	Elliotts of Newbury
AFDU	Air Fighting Development Unit	ETPS	Empire Test Pilots' School
AFEE	Airborne Forces Experimental Establishment	FAA	Fleet Air Arm
Air Cdre	Air Commodore	FAI	Fédération Aéronautique Internationale
ANEC	Air Navigation and Engineering Company	Fg Off	Flying Officer
AS	Armstrong Siddeley	Flt Lt	Flight Lieutenant
ATP	Assistant Test Pilot	FTE	Flight Test Engineer
AVM	Air Vice-Marshal	FTO	Flight Test Observer
AW	Armstrong Whitworth	FTS	Flying Training School
AuxAF	Auxiliary Air Force (RAuxAF from 1947)	GCB	Knight Grand Cross of the Order of the Bath
BAC	British Aircraft Corporation	Gp Capt	Group Captain
BAe	British Aerospace	hp	horse power, relating to the power rating of a piston engine
BAT	British Aerial Transport	
BEA	British European Airways	HP	Handley Page
B&GS	Bombing and Gunnery School	HS(A)	Hawker Siddeley (Aviation)
BHP	Beardmore-Halford-Pullinger aero engines	ITS	Initial Training School
BOAC	British Overseas Airways Corporation	JAP	J A Prestwich – engine manufacturer
B&P	Boulton & Paul (Boulton Paul from 1934)	lbst	pounds of static thrust, relating to the power rating – without reheat/afterburner – of a jet engine
BP	Boulton Paul	
BS	Bristol Siddeley	Lt	Lieutenant
BSE	Bristol Siddeley Engines	Lt Cdr	Lieutenant Commander
CAA	Civil Aviation Authority	KBE	Knight Commander of the Order of the British Empire
CAACU	Civilian Anti-Aircraft Co-operation Unit	
CB	Companion of the Order of the Bath	MAEE	Marine Aircraft Experimental Establishment, Grain until 1924, then Felixstowe, Helensburgh 1939-1945, Felixstowe 1945-1956. Formed out of the MAES at Grain, 1920
CBE	Commander of the Order of the British Empire	
CDG	Croix de Guerre	
CFI	Chief Flying Instructor	
CFS	Central Flying School	
CO	Commanding Officer	M&AEE	Marine & Armament Experimental Establishment (MAEE from 1924)
CTP	Chief Test Pilot	
DFC	Distinguished Flying Cross – DFC* with Bar	MAES	Marine Aircraft Experimental Station – see MAEE

MAP	Ministry of Aircraft Production		RR	Rolls-Royce
MBE	Member of the Order of the British Empire		RTM	Rolls-Royce/Turboméca
McDD	McDonnell Douglas		RAuxAF	Royal Auxiliary Air Force
MOS	Ministry of Supply		RFC	Royal Flying Corps
MP	Member of Parliament		RNAS	Royal Naval Air Service
MRAF	Marshal of the Royal Air Force		SAL	Scottish Aviation Ltd
NAG	Nationale Automobil Gessellschaft		Saro	Saunders-Roe
NATO	North Atlantic Treaty Organisation		SBAC	Society of British Aircraft (Aerospace from 1964) Companies
OBE	Civil: Order of the British Empire; military Officer of the Order of the British Empire		shp	shaft horse power, relating to the power rating of a turboprop or turboshaft
OCU	Operational Conversion Unit		Sqn	Squadron
OM	Order of Merit		Sqn Ldr	Squadron Leader
OTU	Operational Training Unit		st	Static thrust, power measurement for jets
(P)AFU	(Pilots) Advanced Flying Unit		STOL	Short take-off and landing
P&W	Pratt & Whitney		Sub Lt	Sub Lieutenant
PPL	Private Pilot's Licence		UAS	University Air Squadron
PRU	Photographic Reconnaissance Unit		USAF	United States Air Force – from 1947
PTP	Production Test Pilot		USAAC	United States Army Air Corps, 1926-1941
P1	Pilot-in-command, or captain		USAAF	United States Army Air Force, 1941-1947
P2	2nd pilot		USAAS	United States Army Air Service – to 1926
QFI	Qualified Flying Instructor		V/STOL	Vertical/Short take-off and landing
RAE	Royal Aircraft Establishment		Wg Cdr	Wing Commander
RAF	Royal Air Force			
RAFVR	Royal Air Force Volunteer Reserve			

Appendix C

Bibliography

Amos, Peter, *Miles Aircraft – The Early Years*, Air-Britain, Tonbridge, 2009

Miles Aircraft – The Wartime Years, Air Britain, Tonbridge, 2012

Andrews, C F and Morgan, E B, *Supermarine Aircraft since 1914*, Putnam, London, 1981

Vickers Aircraft since 1908, Putnam, London, 1988

Armstrong Whitworth Aircraft, *Pioneers of Progress – A Brief Illustrated History of Sir W G Armstrong Whitworth Aircraft Ltd, Coventry*, company brochure, 1982

Ashworth, Chris, *Avro's Maritime Heavyweight: The Shackleton*, Aston, Bourne End, 1990

Balfour, Christopher, *Spithead Express – The Pre-War Island Air Ferry and Post-War Plans*, Magna Press, Leatherhead, 1999

Barnes, C H, *Bristol Aircraft since 1910*, Putnam, London, 3rd Ed, 1988

Handley Page Aircraft since 1907, Putnam, London, 1976

Shorts Aircraft since 1900, Putnam, London, 1967

Barnett-Jones, Frank, *Tarnish 6 – Biography of Test Pilot James L Dell obe*, Old Forge, Cowbit, 2008

Beamont, Roland, *Fighter Test Pilot – From Hurricane to Tornado*, Patrick Stephens, Wellingborough, 1986

Bingham, Victor F, *Folland Gnat – Sabre-Slayer and Red Arrow*, J&KH Publishing, Hailsham, 2000

Blackburn Aircraft Co, *Blackburn Story 1909-1959*, Brough, 1960

Blackman, Tony, *Nimrod – Rise and Fall*, Grub Street, London, 2011

Test Pilot – My Extraordinary Life in Flight, Grub Street, London, 2009

Vulcan Boys – From the Cold War to the Falklands, Grub Street, 2014

Vulcan Test Pilot, Grub Street, London, 2007

Blackmore, L K, *Hawker – One of Aviation's Greatest Names*, David Bateman Ltd, Auckland, New Zealand, 1990

Blake, John and Hooks, Mike, *40 Years at Farnborough – SBAC's International Showcase*, Haynes, Sparkford, 1990

Bonser, Roy, *Aviation in Leicestershire and Rutland*, Midland, Hinckley, 2001

Boughton, Terence, *The Story of the British Light Aeroplane*, John Murray, London, 1963

Bowyer, Chaz, *The Short Sunderland*, Aston, Bourne End, 1989

Brett, Dallas, R, *History of British Aviation 1908-1914*, Air Research, Surbiton, 1987

Brew, Alec, *Boulton Paul Aircraft since 1915*, Putnam, London, 1993

Brooks, Peter W, *Cierva Autogiros – The Development of Rotary-Wing Flight*, Smithsonian, USA, 1988

Brooks, Roger R, *Handley Page Victor – History and Development of a Classic Jet*, Pen & Sword, Barnsley, Vols 1 and 2, 2007

Brown, Don L, *Miles Aircraft since 1925*, Putnam, London, 1970

Bruce, J M, *Aeroplanes of the Royal Flying Corps (Military Wing)*, Putnam, London, 1982

Butler, Phil and Buttler, Tony, *Avro Vulcan – Britain's Famous Delta-Wing B-Bomber*, Midland, Hinckley, 2007

Butler, P H and Buttler, Tony, *Handley Page Victor – Crescent-Winged V-Bomber*, Midland, Hinckley, 2009

Buttler, Tony, *British Experimental Combat Aircraft of World War Two Prototypes, Research Aircraft and Failed Production Designs*, Hikoki, Manchester, 2012

Carter, Graham, *ML Aviation Ltd – A Secret World*, Keyham Books, Chippenham, 2006

Chacksfield, J E, *Sir Sydney Camm – From Biplanes and Hurricanes to Harriers*, Oakwood, Usk, 2010

Chartres, John, *BAe Nimrod*, Ian Allan, Shepperton, 1986

Church, Richard J, *The One-Eleven Story*, Air-Britain, Tonbridge, 1994

Clarke, Bob, *Jet Provost – The Little Plane with the Big History*, Amerberley, Stroud, 2008

Clegg, Peter V, *Test Pilots of A V Roe – R J 'Roly' Falk*, GMS Enterprises, Peterborough, 2010

The Quiet Test Pilot – The Story of Jimmy Orrell, Greater Manchester Museum of Science and Industry, Manchester, 1989

Cobham, Sir Alan, *A Time to Fly*, Shepheard-Walwyn, London, 1978

Cooper, Peter J, *Farnborough – 100 Years of British Aviation*, Midland, Hinckley, 2006

Courtney, Frank T, *Flight Path – My Fifty Years of Aviation*, Kimber, London, 1972

Cowell, G, *Handley Page Herald*, Jane's, London, 1980

Cruddas, Colin, *In Cobham's Company*, Cobham plc, Wimborne, 1994

Cummings, Colin, *Category Five – A Catalogue of RAF Aircraft Losses 1954 to 2009*, Nimbus, Yelvertoft, 2009

Final Landings – A Summary of RAF Aircraft and Combat Losses 1946-1949, Nimbus, Yelvertoft, 2001

Last Take-off – A record of RAF Aircraft Losses 1950 to 1953, Nimbus, Yelvertoft, 2000

Curtis, Howard, *Sabre – The Canadair Sabre in RAF Service*, Sutton, Stroud, 2005

de Havilland, Sir Geoffrey, *Sky Fever*, Hamish Hamilton, London, 1961

Delve, Ken, Green, Peter and Clemons, John, *English Electric Canberra*, Midland Counties, Earl Shilton, 1992

Donne, Michael, *Pioneers of the Sky – A History of Short Brothers*, Nicholson and Bass, Belfast, 1987

Dorman, Geoffrey, *British Test Pilots*, Forbes Robertson, London, 1950

Dudley, Roger and Johnson, Ted, *Weston-super-Mare and the Aeroplane 1910-2010*, Amberley, Stroud, 2010

Duke, Neville, *Test Pilot*, Grub Street, London, 2nd ed 1992

Ellison, Norman, *British Gliders and Sailplanes 1922-1970*, Adam and Charles Black, London,1971

Farley, John, *A View from the Hover – My Life in Aviation*, Seager Publishing, 2nd ed, 2010

Floyd, Jim, *Avro Canada C102 Jetliner*, Boston Mills Press, Erin, Ontario, Canada, 1986

Gardner, Charles, *British Aircraft Corporation – A History*, Book Club Associates, London, 1981

Gardner, Robert, *From Bouncing Bombs to Concorde – The Biography of Sir George Edwards*, Sutton, Stroud, 2006

Gearing, David W, *On the Wings of a Gull – Percival and Hunting Aircraft*, Air-Britain, Staplefield, 2012

Gibbings, David, *Fairey Rotodyne*, History Press, Stroud, 2009

Gibson, Michael L, *Aviation in Northamptonshire – An Illustrated History*, Northamptonshire Libraries, Northampton, 1982

Gunston, Bill, *British Aerospace EAP*, Linewrights, Chipping Ongar, 1986

Nimrod – The Centenarian Aircraft, Spellmount, Stroud, 2009

World Encyclopaedia of Aircraft Manufacturers – From Pioneers to the Present Day, Patrick Stephens, Sparkford, 1993

Hamilton-Paterson, James, *Empire of the Clouds – When Britain's Aircraft Ruled the World*, Faber and Faber, London, 2010

Hancock, Ian, *The Lives of Ken Wallis – Engineer and Aviator Extraordinaire*, self-published, Flixton, 2001

Hare, Paul R, *Royal Aircraft Factory*, Putnam, 1990

Harkins, Hugh, *Eurofighter 2000 – Europe's Fighter for the New Millennium*, Midland, Earl Shilton, 1997

Harrison, William, *Fairey Firefly – The Operational Record*, Airlife, Shrewsbury, 1992

Hayward, Keith, *British Aircraft Industry*, Manchester University Press, Manchester, 1989

Hayes, Paul and King, Bernard, *De Havilland Biplane Transports*, Gatwick Aviation Society, Coulsdon, 2003

Henshaw, Alex, *Sigh for a Merlin – Testing the Spitfire*, Crécy Publishing, Manchester, 1996 edition

Hitchman, Ambrose and Preston, Mike, *History of the Auster Aeroplane*, International Auster Club Heritage Group, Ratcliffe on the Wreake, 3rd Ed, 1989

Holmes, Harry, *Avro Lancaster – The Definitive Record*, Airlife, Shrewsbury, 2nd Ed, 2001

Avro – The History of an Aircraft Company, Airlife, Shrewsbury, 1994

Hudson, R K, *A Sound in the Sky – Reminiscences of Geoffrey Alington*, self-published, London, 1994

Hygate, Barrie, *British Experimental Jet Aircraft*, Argus, Hemel Hempstead, 1990

Jackson, A J, *Avro Aircraft since 1908*, Putnam, London, 2nd Ed, 1990

Blackburn Aircraft since 1909, Putnam, London, 2nd Ed, 1989

British Civil Aircraft since 1919, Putnam, London, Vol 1 and Vol 2nd Eds 1973, Vol 3 2nd Ed 1974

De Havilland Aircraft since 1909, Putnam, London, revised ed, 1978

Jackson, Robert, *Avro Vulcan*, Patrick Stephens, Cambridge, 1984

Hawker Tempest and Sea Fury, Blandford, London, 1989

James, Derek N, *Gloster Aircraft since 1917*, Putnam, London, 2nd Ed 1987

Schneider Trophy Aircraft 1913-1931, Putnam, London, 1981

Spirit of Hamble – Folland Aircraft, Tempus, Stroud, 2000

Westland Aircraft since 1915, Putnam, London, 1991

Kay, Derek R, *The Last Grand Adventure in British Aviation?* (A personal history of Britten-Norman), Anthony Rowe Publishing, Croydon, 2008

King, Derek A, *The Bristol 170 Freighter, Wayfarer and Superfreighter*, Air-Britain, Staplefield, 2011

King, H F, *Sopwith Aircraft 1912-1920*, Putnam, London, 1980

Kingsley-Jones, Max, *Hawker Siddeley Trident*, Ian Allan, Shepperton, 1993

Kinsey, Gordon, *Boulton & Paul Aircraft – History of the Companies at Norwich and Wolverhampton*, Terrence Dalton, Lavenham, 1992

Kirby, Robert, *Avro Manchester – The Legend Behind the Lancaster*, Midland, Earl Shilton, 1995

Lake, Jon, and Crutch, Mike, *Tornado – Multi-Role Combat Aircraft*, Midland, Earl Shilton, 2000

Lewis, Peter, *British Aircraft 1809-1914*, Putnam, London, 1962

British Racing and Record-Breaking Aircraft, Putnam, London, 1970

Lithgow, Mike, *Mach One*, Allan Wingate, London, 1954

(ed), *Vapour Trails – Thrilling Exploits of Men Who Fly at Supersonic Speeds*, Allan Wingate, London, 1956

London, Peter, *Saunders and Saro Aircraft since 1917*, Putnam, London, 1988

Longworth, James, H, *Test Flying in Lancashire from Samlesbury and Warton Aerodromes – Military Aviation at the Leading Edge*, Vol 1 *World War One to the 1960s*, Vol 2 *From the 1960s to 1980s*, Vol 3 *From the 1980s into the New Millennium*, BAE Systems, Warton, 2012, 2013 and 2014

Triplane to Typhoon – Aircraft Produced by Factories in Lancashire and the North West from 1910, Lancashire County Developments, Preston, 2005

Lumsden, Alec S C, *British Piston Aero-Engines and Their Aircraft*, Airlife, Shrewsbury, 1994

Masefield, Sir Peter, with Gunston, Bill, *Flight Path*, Airlife, Shrewsbury, 2002

Mason, Francis K, *Harrier*, Patrick Stephens, Cambridge, 2nd Ed, 1983

Hawker Aircraft since 1920, Putnam, London, 1961

Hawker Hunter, Biography of a Thoroughbred, Patrick Stephens, Cambridge, 1981

Hawker Hurricane, Aston, Bourne End, 1987

Tornado, Patrick Stephens, Wellingborough, 1986

Mason, Tim, *British Flight Testing Martlesham Heath 1920-1939*, Putnam, London, 1993

Cold War Years – Flight Testing at Boscombe Down, 1945-1975, Hikoki Publications, Ottringham, 2001

Seaplane Years – M&AEE and MAEE 1920-1956, Hikoki, Manchester, 2010

Secret Years – Flight Testing at Boscombe Down, 1939-1945, Hikoki, Manchester, 2010

Matthews, Henry, *Husky One – A E 'Ben' Gunn Boulton Paul Chief Test Pilot*, HPM Publications, Beirut, Lebanon, 1999, 2nd ed

Prelude to Eurofighter – EAP, HPM Publications, Beirut, Lebanon, 2001

Prelude to the Sea Vixen: DH.110, HPM Publications, Beirut, Lebanon, 2001

and Peter Davison, *Prelude to Concorde – HP.115 Slender Wing Research Aircraft*, HPM Publications, Beirut, Lebanon, 2004

and Allan Wood, *The Saga of SR.53 – A Pictorial Tribute*, HPM Publications, Beirut, Lebanon, 2004

McIntyre, Dougal, *Prestwick's Pioneer – A Portrait of David F McIntyre*, Woodfield, Bognor Regis, 2004

McKay, Stuart, *De Havilland Tiger Moth – Legendary Biplane Trainer*, Midland, Earl Shilton, 1999

Merewether, H C H, *Prelude to the Harrier: P.1127 Prototype Flight Testing at Kestrel Evaluation*, X-Planes Vol.3, HPM Publications, Beirut, Lebanon, 2003

Merrick, K A, *Handley Page Halifax – From Hell to Victory and Beyond*, Classic, 2009

Middleton, Donald H, *Airspeed – The Company and its Aeroplanes*, Terence Dalton, Lavenham, 1982

Tests of Character – Epic Flights by Legendary Test Pilots, Donald Middleton, Airlife, Shrewsbury, 1995

Test Pilots – The Story of British Test Flying 1903-1984, Willow Books, London, 1985

Midland Counties Aviation Research Group, *Beagle Aircraft – A Production History*, Hinckley, 1974

Molson, K M and Taylor, H A, *Canadian Aircraft since 1909*, Putnam, London, 1982

Morgan, Eric B, and Shacklady, Edward, *Spitfire the History*, Key Publishing, Stamford, 1987

Neil, William T, *Just One of the Pioneers – My Days With Scottish Aviation and de Havillands*, Cirrus, Gillingham, 2002

Nicholl, Lt Cdr G W R, *Supermarine Walrus – The Story of a Unique Aircraft*, G T Foulis, London, 1966

Odr-Hume, Arthur W J G, *British Light Aeroplanes – Their Evolution, Development and Perfection, 1920-1940*, GMS, Peterborough, 2000

Oliver, David, *Hendon Aerodrome – A History*, Airlife, Shrewsbury, 1994

Painter, Martin, *DH.106 Comet – An Illustrated History*, Air-Britain, Tunbridge Wells, 2002

Pardoe, Alan J, *Jetstream – A Production History*, Central Scotland Aviation Group, Bearsden, 1979

Pasco, Dennis, *Tested – Marshall Test Pilots and Their Aircraft in War and Peace 1919-1999*, Grub Street, London, 1999

Penrose, Harald, *Adventure with Fate*, Airlife, Shrewsbury, 1984

Architect of Wings – A Biography of Roy Chadwick, Airlife, Shrewsbury, 1985

British Aviation – The Pioneer Years 1903-1914, Putnam, London, 1967

British Aviation – The Great War and Armistice 1915-1919, Putnam, London, 1969

British Aviation – The Adventuring Years 1920-1929, Putnam, London, 1973

British Aviation – Widening Horizons 1930-1934, HMSO, London, 1979

British Aviation – The Ominous Skies 1935-1939, HMSO, London, 1980

Philpott, Bryan, *Lightning*, Patrick Stephens, Wellingborough, 1984

Meteor, Patrick Stephens, Wellingborough, 1986

Powell, H P 'Sandy', *Men With Wings*, Allan Wingate, London, 1957

Test Flight, Allan Wingate, London, 1956

Quill, Jeffrey, *Spitfire – A Test Pilot's Story*, Crécy Publishing, Manchester, 1996 edition, reprinted 2008

Ransom, Stephen and Fairclough, Robert, *English Electric Aircraft and their Predecessors*, Putnam, London, 1987

Rawlings, John and Sedgwick, Hilary, *Learn to Test, Test to Learn – The History of the Empire Test Pilots' School*, Airlife, Shrewsbury, 1991

Reed, Arthur, *BAe Hawk*, Ian Allan, Shepperton, 1985

SEPECAT Jaguar, Ian Allan, Shepperton, 1982

Riding, Richard, *Ultralights – The Early British Classics*, Patrick Stephens, Wellingborough, 1987

Robertson, Alan, *Lion Rampant and Winged, A Commemorative History of Scottish Aviation Ltd*, self-published, Brarassie, 1986

Robinson, Wg Cdr J A 'Robby', *Avro One – Autobiography of a Chief Test Pilot*, Old Forge, Cowbit, 2005

Tester Zero One – The Making of a Test Pilot, Old Forge, Cowbit, 2007

Scott, J D, *Vickers – A History*, Weidenfeld and Nicolson, London, 1962

Scott, Stewart A, *English Electric Lightning – Volume One, Birth of a Legend*, GMS Enterprises, Peterborough, 2000

Sharp, C Martin, *DH A History of De Havilland*, Airlife, Shrewsbury, 1982

Shores, Christopher and Williams, Clive, *Aces High*, and *Aces High Volume 2*, Christopher Shores, Grub Street, London, 1994 and 1999

Shores, Christopher and Franks, Norman, and Guest, Russell, *Above the Trenches*, Grub Street, London 1990

Silvester, R John, *Percival and Hunting Aircraft*, self-published, Luton, 1987

Skinner, Stephen, *Marshall of Cambridge*, Tempus, Stroud, 2003

Smith, Constance Babington, *Testing Time – A Study of Man and Machine in the Test Flying Era*, Cassell, London, 1961

Sturtivant, Ray, *British Research and Development Aircraft – 70 Years at the Leading Edge*, Foulis, Sparkford, 1990

Sturtivant, Ray, with Hamlin, John, *Flying Training and Support Units since 1912*, Air-Britain, Staplefield, 2007

Tapper, Oliver, *Armstrong Whitworth Aircraft since 1913*, Putnam, London, 1988

Taylor, H A, *Airspeed Aircraft since 1931*, Putnam, London, 1970

Fairey Aircraft since 1915, Putnam, London, 1988

Test Pilot at War, Ian Allan, Shepperton, 1970

Temple, Julian C, *Wings over Woodley – The Story of Miles Aircraft and the Adwest Group*, Aston, Bourne End, Bucks, 1987

Thetford, Owen, *Aircraft of the Royal Air Force since 1918*, Putnam, London, 9th Ed, 1995

British Naval Aircraft since 1912, Putnam, London, 1971

Trevor, Hugh, *Lightnings Live On!*, Lightning Preservation Group, Bruntingthorpe, 1996

Trubshaw, Brian and Edmondson, Sally, *Brian Trubshaw – Test Pilot*, Sutton, Stroud, 1998

Turnill, Reginald, and Reed, Arthur, *Farnborough – The Story of the Royal Aircraft Establishment*, Robert Hale, London, 1980

Twiss, Peter, *Faster than the Sun – The Compelling Story of a Record-Breaking Test Pilot*, Peter Grub Street, London, 2nd ed 2000

Unwin, N H F, *Geoffrey de Havilland – Log Book of Test Flying and Some Design Notes*, Royal Aircraft Establishment Museum, Farnborough, 1971

Wallace, Graham, *Claude-Grahame-White – A Biography*, Putnam, London, 1960

Walpole, Nigel, *Swift Justice – The Full Story of the Supermarine Swift*, Astonbridge, Ruardean, 2000

Warner, Guy, *The Last Canberra – PR.9 XH131*, Ulster Aviation Society, Belfast, 2011

Warner, Guy, and Cromie, Ernie, *Aircraft and Aerospace Manufacturing in Northern Ireland*, Colourpoint Books, Newtownards, 2014

Waterton, William Arthur, *The Quick and the Dead – The Perils of Post-War Test Flying*, Grub Street, 2012 edition

Watkins, David, *De Havilland Vampire – The Complete History*, Sutton, Stroud, 1996

Venom – de Havilland Venom and Sea Venom, The Complete History, Sutton, Thrupp, 2003

Webb, Derek Collier, *UK Flight Testing Accidents 1940-1971*, Air-Britain, Tunbridge Wells, 2002

Williams, Paul, *The James Brothers – Pembrokeshire's Aviation Pioneers,* Pembrokeshire Aviation Group, Kilgetty, Wales, 1992

Winkler, Eduard F, *Civilian Affair – A Brief History of the Civilian Aircraft Company of Hedon*, Flight Recorder Publications, Ottringham, 2003

Wittridge, Flt Lt A H 'Witt', *An Evil Boy*, Wunjo Press, Loftus, 2004

Wixey, Kenneth E, *Parnall Aircraft since 1914*, Putnam, London, 1990

Zuk, Bill, with Zurakowski, Janusz, *Janusz Zurakowski – Legend in the Skies*, Crécy Publishing, Manchester, 2007

In his poem *The Rock* of 1934 Thomas Stearns Eliot predicted the minefield that is the 'web', long before pixels became all-dominant:

Where is the wisdom we have lost in knowledge?

Where is the knowledge we have lost in information?

So, bearing in mind that only a *fraction* of things beginning-with-www are helpful – let alone reliable, and that the rest ranges from the well-meaning but ill-informed, to fantasists shrouded in anonymity, to the outright malicious; the following occupy the 'real' world:

afleetingpeace.org – 'Golden Age Aviation' in the British Empire, Terry Mace's study of the inter-war years

agustawestland.com – Europe's innovative rotorcraft combine

airbus.com – Comprehensive site on a global triumph

airsciences.org – Superbly informative site from FAST, the Farnborough Air Sciences Trust

auster.org – Incredibly detailed site of the International Auster Club

baesystems.com – BAE Systems vast and informative site

eurofighter.com – 'Home' of Europe's world-beater

flightglobal.com – *Every* page of every *Flight* and *Flight International*

hatfieldaviationheritage.co.uk – Dedicated to the aviation heritage of the town and airfield

martin-baker.co.uk – Excellent material on the history of the company

theaerodrome.com – 'Aces' and aircraft of World War One

thetartanterror.blogspot.co.uk – Neil Corbett's affectionate tribute to worldwide test pilots

thunder-and-lightnings.co.uk/memorial – Damien Burke's testament to UK test flight fatalities

Index I

Test Pilots by Manufacturer

Listed alphabetically initials only, no honours, decorations or rank by manufacturer.

Airbus: P Chandler

Aircraft Manufacturing Co (Airco): F T Courtney, G de Havilland, B C Hucks

Airspeed: R E Clear, C H A Colman, G B S Errington

Armstrong Whitworth: F L Barnard, A C Campbell-Orde, F T Courtney, W H Else, E G Franklin, E S Greenwood, D Hughes

Auster: G Edwards

Aviation Traders: D B Cartlidge

Avro: C Allen, J D Baker, A L Blackman, H A Brown, S E Esler, R J Falk, H A Hamersley, J G Harrison, H J L Hinkler

Beardmore: R A W H Haig

Blackburn: H Bailey, H Blackburn, A M Blake, W R Ding, C G P Flood, B C Hucks

Boulton (and) Paul: F T Courtney, C Feather, A E Gunn

Brennan/RAE: R G Graham

Bristol (also British and Colonial): G L Auty, A C Capper, H R Busteed, E C G England, G W England, W F Gibb, J J Hammond, Capt Hooper, C T D Hosegood

British Aerial Transport: C Draper

British Aerospace/BAE Systems: T N Allen, P Baker, R P Beamont, A L Blackman, J Blair, J W A Bolton, M N Bowman, J Cochrane, J J Cockburn, J D Eagles, J F Farley, H E Frick, M S Goodfellow, J S Hawkins, P Henley, L Houston

British Aircraft Corporation: D G Addicott, G L Auty, P Baker, G R Bryce, J Cochrane, J J Cockburn, J L Dell, J D Eagles, T M S Ferguson, P D Hillwood

British Klemm/British Aircraft: E G Hordern

Britten-Norman: P D Hillwood

Carden-Baynes: H S Broad

Central Aircraft: F T Courtney

Cierva Autogiro: R A C Brie, F J Cable, J de Cierva, H A Hamersley

Comper: N Comper

Cranwell Light Aeroplane Club: N Comper

Cunliffe-Owen: A G Corbin, P D Hillwood

De Havilland: G Aird, P Barlow, R P Beamont, H S Broad, A C Capper, A J Cobham, J Cunningham, G de Havilland, G R de Havilland, J de Havilland, J D Derry, J Elliot, W P I Fillingham, G V Gibbins

English Electric: R P Beamont, H G Brackley, J L Dell, T B O Evans, T M S Ferguson, P D Hillwood

FLS Aerospace: N F Duke, J F Farley

Fairey: B H Arkell, J N Dennis, F H Dixon, J C Evans, K B Forbes, W R Gellatly, R R Huxley

General Aircraft inc CW Aircraft and Monospar: H S Broad, R A W H Haig, C F Hughesdon

Gloster (Gloucestershire): R P Beamont, H S Broad, L L Carter, J R Cooksey, J A Crosby-Warren, N M Daunt, R Dryland, L B Greensted, E S Greenwood, J Grierson

Grahame-White: A M Desoutter

Handasyde: F T Courtney

Handley Page: J W Allam, J Babington, R Bager, P Baker, R G

Bell, H S Broad, D J P Broomfield, W R Burton, V E G Busby, J L B H Cordes, H P Douglas, R V Eccleston, T H England, R C Fenwick, M W Hartford, H G Hazelden. G T R Hill

Hawker: R P Beamont, A W Bedford, P W S Bulman, N M Daunt, N F Duke, J Grierson, W Humble

Hawker Siddeley: G Aird, C Allen, P Barlow, A W Bedford, A L Blackman, A C Capper, J Cunningham, W H Else, G B S Errington, J F Farley, W P I Fillingham, E G Franklin, M S Goodfellow, J G Harrison, J S Hawkins

Heston Aircraft: E G Hordern

Hunting: D G Addicott, J F Arnold

Ibis Aircraft: H J L Hinkler

Kennedy: F T Courtney

Martin-Baker: V H Baker, L B Greensted

Martin and Handasyde/Martinsyde: R H Barnwell, R G Bell, H A Hamersley

Mersey Aeroplane: R C Fenwick

Miles: S E Esler, I A Forbes

Monospar – see General Aircraft

NDN Aircraft/Norman Aeroplane Co: N D Norman

Panavia: See BAC and BAe

Parnall: H S Broad, F T Courtney, J A Crosby-Warren

Pemberton-Billing – see Supermarine

Percival: L T Carruthers, J F Arnold

Planes Ltd: R C Fenwick

Reid and Sigrist: A G Bullmore

Rolls-Royce: A J Hayworth

Royal Aircraft Factory: E T Busk, G de Havilland, F W Goodden, R M Hill

Saunders/Saro: L Ash, J S Booth, H S Broad, C E Chilton, F T Courtney, Evans

Scottish Aviation: J Blair, N J Capper, L Houston

Short: R G Bell, J S Booth, T W Brooke-Smith, L L Cumming, J R Green, H J L Hinkler

Siddeley Deasy – see Armstrong Whitworth

Sopwith: H G Hawker

Supermarine: H C Biard, L R Colquhoun, J D Derry, F C Furlong, P D Hillwood, B D Hobbs

Tarrant: F G Dunn

Trago Mills: G Cairns

Vickers: D G Addicott, J W Alcock, C Allen, R H Barnwell, R G Bell, F C Broome, G R Bryce, S F Cockerell, R C Fenwick

G & J Weir – see Cierva

Westland/AgustaWestland: F Alexander, A E Bristow, D A S Colvin, F T Courtney, J T Egginton, P J Garner, W R Gellatly, M A Graves, C W Hague, H G Hawker

White and Thompson: E C G England

Wight (J Samuel White and Co): E C G England

Index II

Aircraft Types and 'First Flighting' Pilots

All listed by manufacturer/design house and are British-built unless noted in *round* brackets (). To further aid reference, pilots listed in Chapter Seven who made the first flight are given in *square* brackets [].

Levelling out at 1,800mph.

Everything going to plan.

Fine plane, tell the designer chappie

Tony Hancock in the test pilot sketch

Hancock's Half Hour

BBC Radio, 1959

To complete the set

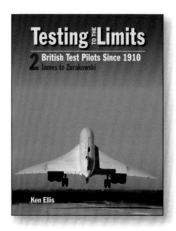

Testing to the Limits Volume 2

Ken Ellis

Continuing the tribute to British production test pilots, including Alex Henshaw at Castle Bromwich and Geoffrey Alington at Longbridge, Ken Ellis charts the careers of men such as 'Mutt' Summers, who flew the prototype Spitfire, and Brian Trubshaw who was at the helm of the British prototype Concorde; culminating with Jan Zurakowski, a master of demonstration flying.

Immortal names from Britain's aircraft industry including the Miles brothers, Desmond Norman and Edgar Percival and, among others, the first man to use a Martin-Baker ejector seat 'in anger', Britain's jet pioneer, world record breakers and 007's involvement in test piloting are also all revealed.

The work of the civilian authorities in making sure that aircraft meet airworthiness requirements is examined and the skills and disciplines of display and customer demonstration flying are highlighted. Alan Cobham's vision of in-flight refuelling and the struggles to perfect the system make a fascinating study and Harrier test pilot John Farley provides the foreword and comments on the future of the profession.

Lavishly illustrated with over 300 photos, Volume Two of *Testing to the Limits* charts the lives of over 170 test pilots from 1910 to the present day to complete the most comprehensive study of the men who risked all to spearhead a world-renowned industry.

ISBN 978 085979 1854
256 pages, hardback
290mm x 216mm
300 photographs
£24.95
Publication Date: October 2015

Also by Ken Ellis

A special tribute to the UK's aviation museums and collections

Britain's diverse aviation heritage owes much to the pioneer museums and collections that still contain our national treasures. Some remain today and others have fallen by the wayside. Ensuring that none are not forgotten, Ken Ellis commemorates our bygone glories by examining, in two volumes those special institutions.

Warbird pioneers such as Richard Nash, Spencer Flack and Charles Church are put into context in *Lost Aviation Collections of Britain* and combine with important institutions such as Cranfield and Loughborough that helped kick-start the aircraft preservation 'booms' of the 1960s and 1970s.

Great Aviation Collections of Britain tells the story of the national icons – Science Museum, Imperial War Museum, RAF Museum, Fleet Air Arm Museum, Museum of Army Aviation and the Shuttleworth Collection including how they developed and their exhibits, past and present. It also pays tribute to provincial, regional and local collections, large and small, revealing the story of the UK's diverse aviation achievements and providing details of nearly 100 venues open to the public.

Lavishly illustrated, each with over 200 period images, these books provide a wonderful trip down memory lane for those who witnessed an incredible era and a fantastic reference to for those who wished they had!

Great Aviation Collections of Britain
ISBN 978 085979 1748
272 pages, hardback
234mm x 156mm
Over 200 photographs
£17.95

Lost Aviation Collections of Britain
ISBN 978 085979 1595
224pages, hardback
234mm x 156mm
Over 200 photographs
£16.95